Automate Everything with Ansible

A hands-on guide to DevOps, cloud, and security automation using Ansible

Ashutosh Chauhan

bpb

www.bpbonline.com

First Edition 2026

Copyright © BPB Publications, India

ISBN: 978-93-65894-509

LIMITS OF LIABILITY AND DISCLAIMER OF WARRANTY

To View Complete
BPB Publications Catalogue
Scan the QR Code:

Dedicated to

My late father, Mr. Surendra Chauhan

and

My mother, Mrs. Shakuntala Chauhan

About the Author

Ashutosh Chauhan has been working as a network developer engineer for more than 14 years, playing central roles in numerous projects as a technical leader and network developer engineer, delivering projects using Ansible and Python for big companies, including successful projects in Europe and the United States. Currently, he is the lead of engineering at Genpact. He is also the founder of a successful company. Ashutosh is also an accomplished graduate completing a degree in electronics and communication engineering. In the meantime, he successfully got many Cisco certifications and Silver peak certifications in network security engineering. Furthermore, he participates in online training programs and teaches many students. He also writes technical articles on Ansible and related topics.

About the Reviewer

Nikhil Kumar is a senior software engineer at HPE with a broad and versatile skill set encompassing development, architecture, and consultancy. Nikhil has made significant contributions across diverse domains for various clients and employers. His areas of expertise include DevOps, Python, cloud, Kubernetes and MLOps. He holds multiple prestigious certifications from Red Hat, including Red Hat Certified Engineer (EX294) and Red Hat Certified OpenShift Administrator (EX280). As a prolific technical blogger, Nikhil shares his extensive knowledge with the broader software engineering community and serves as a technical reviewer for various books on DevOps, cloud, MLOps, and Kubernetes.

Acknowledgement

I want to express my deepest gratitude to my family for their unwavering support and encouragement throughout this book's writing, especially my wife Bela and my daughters Anvesh and Charvi.

I am also grateful to BPB Publications for their guidance and expertise in bringing this book to fruition. It was a long journey of revising this book with valuable participation and collaboration of technical reviewers, and editors.

I would also like to acknowledge the valuable contributions of my colleagues and coworkers during many years working in the tech industry, who have taught me so much and provided valuable feedback on my work.

Finally, I would like to thank all the readers who have taken an interest in my book and for their support in making it a reality. Your encouragement has been invaluable

Preface

Innovation and continuous improvement have always been at the heart of human evolution. From hunting and farming to manufacturing, humans have constantly adapted and advanced. The manufacturing industry, for example, began with handcrafted goods before automation revolutionized the way products were made. For many years, automation was disconnected from the IT industry, but once it arrived, it fundamentally transformed how we work, and its impact is still felt today.

This book is designed to provide you with hands-on experience in automation within your specific field. Whether you are a software developer or an infrastructure engineer, automation can help you streamline your work. We will explore how to apply automation to your role, using tools and programming languages available in the market. While automation is a broad field, this book focuses specifically on the use of Ansible and its capabilities.

Throughout this book, we will begin with the basics of Ansible, gradually progressing to deeper concepts and real-world applications. We will focus on IT technologies and demonstrate how Ansible can be leveraged to automate common tasks in this domain.

This book is ideal for IT professionals looking to work smarter by automating repetitive tasks and improving productivity. Whether you are a seasoned engineer or just starting out, you will find valuable insights that will expand your skill set and improve your efficiency. For beginners, this book serves as a comprehensive introduction to automation, while experienced engineers will benefit from learning advanced techniques to further refine their automation skills.

By the end of this book, you will have the knowledge and skills to automate repetitive tasks, saving valuable time and focusing more on high-value work, such as developing new solutions. Through automation, you will become more proficient in your role and be able to achieve more in less time.

Chapter 1: Getting started with Ansible- Manually logging into the device and configuring them individually is no longer a viable option in today's fast-paced IT industry. Today, the IT industry wants an engineer who can work on hundreds of servers himself using automation and save the cost of 5 more engineers. The IT automation engines are a solution to this requirement. One of the leading IT automation engine in the market is called Ansible. In this book, we will learn about Ansible and how we can use it to perform your daily tasks.

Chapter 2: Introducing Ansible and Ansible Tower- Ansible is an open source configuration management tool that runs best on Linux environments. It is an agent-less configuration management tool, which means it does not need any additional configuration or installation of an agent on the client machine. It uses the SSH or WinRM to connect with remote hosts and manage them.

Chapter 3: Working with Ansible- There are many key components of Ansible which we will learn and explore in this chapter. We will start with tasks, roles, plays, and playbooks. Then we will explore a few additional components of ansible in this chapter.

Chapter 4: Creation and Execution of Ansible Playbooks- In this chapter, we will focus on the roles creation and playbook builds. Ansible has multiple ways of creating roles and tasks, and we will explore all of those options in this chapter. After creating roles, we will learn how we can put all oftheir components in playbooks, and lastly, we will execute them.

Chapter 5: Automating AWS Cloud Provisioning with Ansible- In this chapter, we will learn the working of Ansible with cloud. We will begin our journey with one of the major players in the market, AWS. Ansible works good with cloud platforms too. We will perform some hands-on lab in this chapter.

Chapter 6: Ansible for Cloud Provisioning Microsoft Azure- In this chapter, we will continue from where we left off. We started our cloud journey with AWS, and this chapter will be dedicated to the Azure.

Chapter 7: Configuration Management- As we have learned in chapter 1 that Ansible is a configuration management tool, we are finally at that stage where we will use it for performing continuation changes to the target hosts. In this chapter, we will configure a few servers. We will try to focus on our day-to-day activities and how we can achieve them using Ansible.

Chapter 8: App Deployment- In this chapter, we will focus on the process of deploying an application on Windows and Linux hosts. We will start by deploying various required packages on the target hosts. Then, we will create playbooks to deploy the application and restart the services.

Chapter 9: Routine Use of Ansible- In this chapter, we will focus on a few daily tasks performed in the IT industry. For example, the configuration backup. This chapter will have tasks that range from starting a VM to deleting it.

Chapter 10: Ansible for DevOps- In this chapter, we will try to focus in-depth on roles and playbooks, how Ansible Vault is used, and lastly, we will look at things that are recommended and things that we should never do in production.

Chapter 11: Ansible with Network Automation- Manually logging into the Cisco router and configuring devices is part of history. Today is the age of automation. Whether you have a Cisco IOS router or a Juniper SRX device, whether you want to manage your firewall or wish to automate the load balancer, all of them can be managed using Ansible. Ansible works differently for networking equipment. For all normal Linux-managed nodes, the execution happens on the target host. However, that is not the case with the networking gear; the task execution happens on the control machine. So we will focus and learn how we can use Ansible with networking gear.

Chapter 12: Ansible for Security- Security is not an optional thing anymore. Security is an essential part of any organization. As they say, data is new gold, and the one who has it is considered rich. A data breach hurts every company badly, and financial loss is only a small part of that damage. Losing confidential data of the customers may result in loss of faith from customers, investors, and stakeholders, and regaining that faith can take years and years of hard work. So, security should be the number one priority of any company. In this chapter, we will have a look at a few different things we can do to secure our infrastructure.

Chapter 13: Installation of Kubernetes- Kubernetes is an essential thing for any DevOps engineer so you need to spend some time in understanding and learning K8. Once you have grabbed a good hold on it, we can start automating it. In this chapter, we learn the process of installing Kubernetes on the target host first and then we can go ahead with the other tasks we can perform using Ansible.

Chapter 14: Migration to Ansible Tower- As we have seen so far, Ansible is a powerful tool, and there is a wide range of things we can do with it. Red Hat has not limited itself to simply being an open-source project, and if you are a big fan of paid products, then Ansible Tower is for you. In case you are not comfortable with the command line interface, Red Hat also offers you Ansible Tower. Now, there are a few things that are very useful in Ansible Tower. The first and the most important is a great looking GUI, good dashboard, easy templates, and the list continues. These things will attract you towards the Ansible Tower, and we will explore it in our book.

Chapter 15: Finding and Landing a Job- Once we know the concept of Ansible, we are ready to work in the real production environment. Now, our priority should be finding a job and gaining some production experience. As people say, there is no better instructor than the production environment. Every day you get a new challenge and a few ways of fixing them. In this chapter, we will learn how we can find a job and start our day one journey.

Code Bundle and Coloured Images

Please follow the link to download the
Code Bundle and the *Coloured Images* of the book:

https://rebrand.ly/624c70

The code bundle for the book is also hosted on GitHub at
https://github.com/bpbpublications/Automate-Everything-with-Ansible.
In case there's an update to the code, it will be updated on the existing GitHub repository.
We have code bundles from our rich catalogue of books and videos available at
https://github.com/bpbpublications. Check them out!

Errata

We take immense pride in our work at BPB Publications and follow best practices to ensure the accuracy of our content to provide with an indulging reading experience to our subscribers. Our readers are our mirrors, and we use their inputs to reflect and improve upon human errors, if any, that may have occurred during the publishing processes involved. To let us maintain the quality and help us reach out to any readers who might be having difficulties due to any unforeseen errors, please write to us at :

errata@bpbonline.com

Your support, suggestions and feedbacks are highly appreciated by the BPB Publications' Family.

Piracy

If you come across any illegal copies of our works in any form on the internet, we would be grateful if you would provide us with the location address or website name. Please contact us at business@bpbonline.com with a link to the material.

If you are interested in becoming an author

If there is a topic that you have expertise in, and you are interested in either writing or contributing to a book, please visit www.bpbonline.com. We have worked with thousands of developers and tech professionals, just like you, to help them share their insights with the global tech community. You can make a general application, apply for a specific hot topic that we are recruiting an author for, or submit your own idea.

Reviews

Please leave a review. Once you have read and used this book, why not leave a review on the site that you purchased it from? Potential readers can then see and use your unbiased opinion to make purchase decisions. We at BPB can understand what you think about our products, and our authors can see your feedback on their book. Thank you!

For more information about BPB, please visit www.bpbonline.com.

Join our Discord space

Join our Discord workspace for latest updates, offers, tech happenings around the world, new releases, and sessions with the authors:

https://discord.bpbonline.com

Table of Contents

CHAPTER 1
Getting Started with Ansible

Introduction

Since the evolution of the human race, we have been trying to make human life simpler. We have created many inventions to make our lives better, simpler, and convenient. We are trying to reduce human efforts in all sorts of work. Whether it is cleaning your house or travelling thousands of miles, we are making innovations in each field. In this book, we are going to take the example of manufacturing industries and how they changed over the period.

If we recall the time before industrialization, then everything was handmade, or handcrafted in those old days. That process was much more time-consuming, and human errors were much more common. Now, just to expedite the process of manufacturing the robots, automation has come into the manufacturing industry. That has not only expedited the process but also saved costs. So, in other words, finally, automation started in the manufacturing industry, and changed the entire industry forever.

Similarly, our IT industry started all work manually. If you need to configure the date and time on a server, then we log in to the server, perform the changes, and save them. This was working fine for years, until automation took over and changed the IT industry forever. Today everything is moved to the automation, and manual changes are things of the past.

Structure

In this chapter, we will cover the following topics:

- Defining IT automation engine

- Need for an automation engine
- Benefits of Ansible as an IT automation engine
- Use case of Ansible
- Current requirements of IT automation engine
- Future of Ansible and other automation engines
- Platforms where we use IT automation engine
- Managed nodes
- Control machine
- Uninstall Ansible

Objectives

After reading this chapter, the reader will be able to understand the need for an automation engine. Also, you will understand why Ansible is the best solution for you. By the end, you will understand what an Ansible control machine is and how to install Ansible in our environment.

Defining IT automation engine

For an exceptionally long time, the IT industry was not automated. Let us take a simple example of server implementation and management. It was a manual process, and each time, the engineers needed to manually log in to the server and perform their daily operations. Now, if you have ten thousand servers to manage, then it becomes a tedious task. You will need a bunch of engineers to manage that many servers. For each configuration, the engineer will log into the server and perform the changes. This will take a lot of time and energy, and this was the reason that people realized the urgent need for an IT automation engine.

IT automation engine is a software system that contains a pre-defined set of instructions that perform repetitive tasks, routine configuration, and much more in an efficient way. It reduces human efforts, and saves cost and time; which can be used in towards a more productive work.

Need for an automation engine

An IT automation tool can not only reduce human efforts and speed up the work, but it also helps industries to cut costs. It has made the management of ten thousand servers possible with minimal human resources, which is a huge saving for any industry. So, IT automation tools not only save time, but they also save cost. There is one more benefit of the automation engine, and that is reducing human errors. The chances of machines or software making any error are zero and which makes the infrastructure risk-free.

Benefits of Ansible as an IT automation engine

There are many automation tools in the market, like Ansible, Puppet, Chef, and many more, but there are some reasons why Ansible is one of the leading automotive engines in the market. If we focus on the customer requirements and assume you are looking for something which is free of cost, then you have few options in the market. If you need something that gives a good graphical view, then you have a bunch of options for that. If you are a big fan of Linux and want something Linux-based, then we have something nice on the table for you.

Refer to *Figure 1.1*, where we have covered a few key features of Ansible. We have used Ansible as an automation engine, and it can push the configuration to the entire list of hosts. Now, we are just showing two hosts in the inventory file, but it can be 20/100 and even more. Whether it is a normal physical server in the office or a server hosted in the cloud, Ansible can configure and manage that. Even you can manage the entire cloud using Ansible.

The following figure might be confusing right now. Try thinking of it as your code. This is partially true, but assume this is what the playbook does to understand Ansible. In the next section, we will cover the playbook in detail. So, for now, think of it as a YAML file that contains your code. The Ansible automation engine can be seen illustrated in the following figure:

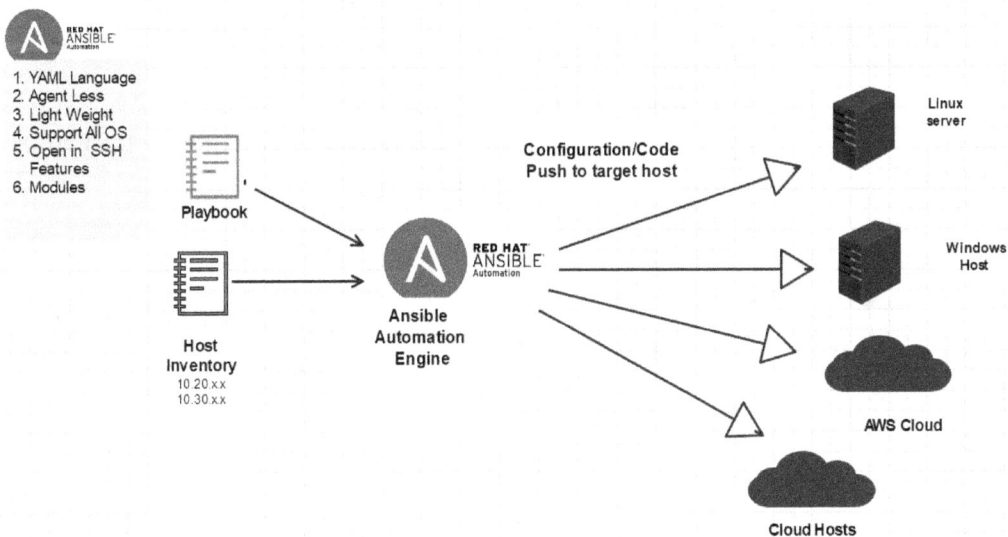

Figure 1.1: Working of Ansible

Even though you have a wide range of IT automation tools in the market, Ansible is the one leading the market. Now, there are various reasons why it is a giant in the market. Let us cover those reasons in the following points:

- Ansible is an open-source configuration management tool.

- Ansible is free of cost. This means that you do not need to pay for using it (Except Ansible Tower).

- Ansible is managed by Red Hat Enterprise, and enterprise support is available from Red Hat Enterprise.

- Ansible is an agentless configuration management tool, which means you do not need to install any software on the client machine.

- Ansible does not need any additional configuration on the client host, and due to this feature, it supports a wide range of platforms like Linux, Windows, cloud networks, containers, etc.

- It uses the **Secure Shell (SSH)**, **Windows Remote Management (WinRM)**, or **PowerShell Remoting Protocol (PSRP)** communication to configure and manage the client machines.

- AWX is another open-sourced version of Ansible. It has many features like Ansible Tower, however, it does not offer support.

Use case of Ansible

If you remember from the last topic, then Ansible is an agent-less automation tool, which requires no additional configuration on the client (target) host, and that makes Ansible the most versatile automation tool. There is no technology in the IT industry where we cannot use Ansible. Whether it is Linux, Windows, or macOS, you can use it in all kinds of platforms.

It is not limited only to the home PC or servers; Ansible can be used in complicated devices like networking equipment, too. We always have the option of installing clients in the home PC or servers, but there is no way we can install any client on the networking equipment. So, if your automation tools need some software installation on the client host or some customized configuration on the client host, then you are in big trouble with this kind of equipment. Since Ansible requires no changes in the client host and it uses SSH to work with the client host, it can easily manage the client like network equipment (router, switch, firewall, etc.).

Ansible is not limited only to the various kinds of operating systems and networking equipment, but it can also be used theoretically on all kinds of IT technologies. Here is the list of a few popular technologies where we can use Ansible:

- **Linux**: Whether it is CentOS, Fedora, RHEL, Debian, or any other flavor of Linux, Ansible can be used on all of them.

- **Windows**: Ansible can be used on Windows servers and home PC as well.

- **macOS**: This might be surprising for a few of you, but we can easily work on the macOS machines using Ansible. It is compatible with macOS just like any other OS.

- **Cloud provisioning**: Whether you want to manage AWS, Microsoft Azure, Google Cloud, Alibaba, or any other cloud, Ansible works fine with them.

- **Docker**: Ansible works great with containers. So, if you want to manage Docker with Ansible, then do not worry, as that can be achieved easily.

- **Kubernetes**: Like Docker, Kubernetes also works great with Ansible.

- **DevOps**: No one can think of becoming a DevOps specialist without learning Ansible. It offers you great modules to become a successful DevOps engineer.

Note: **Now you might be wondering what a module is. Do not worry, we are going to cover it in detail later in this book. For now, think of it as a pre-written reusable script which makes your life easy and works as an intermediate between you and your target host (the device we want to configure using Ansible).**

Daily routine tasks? Now you might be thinking, can it perform my daily repeated tasks so we can relax for five minutes? Well, the answer is yes. It can perform your daily repeated tasks like backing up some configuration, taking database backups, and the rest of the things can be achieved using Ansible.

So, let us have a look at few routine tasks which can be performed using ansible in our daily operations:

- **App deployment**: Application deployment can be done using Ansible.

- **Configuration management**: Ansible was created for configuration management, and it has a wide range of options that can be used to perform configuration changes in an easier manner. It has various configuration management modules which can help us achieve the configuration changes in all sorts of devices/OS.

- **Networking devices**: The beauty of Ansible is that it works great with network equipment. If you try any other configuration management tool for networking, it will make your life potentially worse, as it needs a lot of configuration and changes so your network device can work with that tool. Since Ansible uses SSH, it works great with networking equipment.

- **Security compliance**: Making your infrastructure secure and compliant is not a tedious task anymore. For example, if you want your Linux host to be security compliant, then that can be achieved in a few minutes. We have readymade

Ansible modules that will make your host compliant in a few minutes and push all the required policies and changes to the host.

Ansible can be used to control and manage storage devices through a set of instructions that are written in playbooks. These instructions can perform tasks like setting up storage configurations, checking storage performance, and installing storage software.

Current requirements of the IT automation engine

Today, we are in an era that has extremely high competition in the market. The organizations that are not able to match the current technology and trends are being left behind. At the same time, every organization wants to save costs and time; automation is an effective way of achieving this.

So, we can say the days of manual configurations are over. Whether it is application deployment or cloud provisioning, everything is moving towards automation.

If you remember the example of manufacturing industries, they moved from the handcrafting of products to machines, robots, and automation. This is the right and efficient way of manufacturing any product. Similarly, IT automation engines or tools are those machines/robots that can transform the industry from manual configuration of devices to automated configuration of devices.

IT automation tools play a key role in transforming the IT industry from manual configuration to the automated management of devices. Now, whether it is the IT industry or any other industry, all of them want to move to automation. Whether it is a server team, network team, Load balancer provisioning team, app deployment team, or **site reliability engineering** (**SRE**) team, everyone wants to move to automation, and why not? There is brilliant potential for automation in all these technologies.

So, we can conclude that there is a huge requirement for an IT automation engine in the market for making the transition from manual management of the devices to an automated way. Each department of the industry wants to optimize its resources and work efficiently using automation tools. The demand for IT automation tools is going to stay high for the next few years until all industries and all fields of industry move to automation completely.

High demand for Ansible in the market

There are many IT automation engines in the market, all of which have their own features and drawbacks. Even though we have lots of automation engines in the market, Ansible is one of the leading in the market. There are many reasons for Ansible to lead the market. Whether it is the IT industry or any other industry, all of them have accepted the fact that we need an IT automation engine to make deployment, configuration, and management of infrastructure. The world has moved on from the concept where new applications or new features of the app used to be released in six months. The industry has adhered to the market demand and started using the **continuous integration/continuous delivery (CI/CD)** pipeline. Now, new features are getting added to the application without any delay or any downtime, and IT automation has a big role to play in there. Whether it was the deployment of an app or the configuration of your infrastructure devices, Ansible has modules for all of them. These pre-written modules have made the engineers' lives very easy. In just a few minutes, you can read the documents of that module and start using it, which saves a lot of your time and money.

Another big reason for Ansible being very high in demand is that it is free of cost. All of its features are free of cost, and you can start using Ansible without paying a single penny. There are a few industries that do not prefer the tools that are unmanaged, but the beauty of Ansible is that it is a Red Hat-managed tool. This means they will fix the bugs if there are any.

There is another category of the industry which do not use the tools that do not have enterprise support, but the advantage of Ansible is that you get the enterprise support from Red Hat. Even though this tool is free of cost, you can get enterprise support, but remember, you need to pay for enterprise support.

There is another elite club of industry which do not use the free stuff, or in other words, they do not have faith in free stuff. However, Ansible has something to offer them, and that is Ansible Tower. You need to buy the annual subscription/license to use the Ansible Tower.

Few industries prefer not to take ten different tools for ten different things. For example, one tool for cloud provisioning and another for configuration management. So, in this kind of situation, you may need to pay for two tools and may need to manage more than one IT automation tool. If we choose Ansible, it can do both cloud provisioning and configuration management.

As we discussed earlier in this chapter, whether you prefer a black screen, CLI, or GUI, Ansible has something to offer you. So, whatever the industry type is or whatever their requirement is, Ansible can fulfill all of them. Whether you need an open-sourced free tool or want a paid automation tool, whether you want a Linux-based automation tool or want a good graphical view-based tool, Ansible offers all of this.

We can conclude that Ansible has a wide range of options and it can meet all the requirements of customer. That is what makes it one of the most demanding automation tools of the market.

Future of Ansible and other automation engines

The days of manual configuration are over. The days of manual cloud provisioning and application deployments are over. Just like in the manufacturing industry, we moved from handcrafting of stuff to automation-based manufacturing, the IT industry will continue to move to these automation tools until all enterprise in the industry moves to it. Just like we never switched back to the handcrafting of things in the manufacturing industry, we will never roll back to the old manual configuration or deployments. So, these IT automation engines and Ansible is going to stay in the market for a long.

New technologies are being discovered every day, and the IT industry is growing every hour, so one might think, what will happen to these IT automation engines? Well answer is very simple, we are going to get the new modules for all these new technologies. For example, we can consider the networking devices like switches and firewalls. Initially, Ansible had no support for many network gear, but now we have many modules that support various network gear vendors.

Another question that may come to our mind is, what if my device/technology is not supported in Ansible? Well, the answer is very simple, we can write our own module of Ansible and reuse it again and again as we need it.

Platforms where we use IT automation engine

As we discussed earlier in this chapter, Ansible is agentless IT automation engine. The machine/host where we install Ansible is known as the **control machine**. Not all devices can become control machines. Ansible is supported in almost all distributions of Linux. A few supported platforms are as follows:

- **Red Hat Enterprise Linux (RHEL)**
- CentOS or Fedora
- Debian
- MacOS
- Gentoo Linux
- Solaris (Package is available from OpenCSW)
- All **Berkeley Software Distribution (BSD)**
- Arch Linux
- Slackware Linux
- Clear Linux

The list continues to grow. Right now, Windows is not supported as a control machine (this does not mean that you cannot manage the Windows machines using Ansible; you can configure and manage the Windows host just like any other host). Now, there is a way of installing Ansible on Windows, however, it is not recommended to use Ansible on Windows. We will still cover the process of installing it on Windows.

Note: **We have covered most of the supported platforms at time of writing the books. For the latest data, you may use the official website.**

Managed nodes

As its name suggests, the machine that you manage using Ansible is called a **managed node**. In simple language, the machine/host you configure or upgrade using Ansible is called a managed node. There is no need to install any agent on the managed nodes or client host, but you still need a way for the Ansible IT automation engine to communicate with the managed nodes. Ansible uses SSH communication by default to communicate with managed nodes. It uses the **Secure File Transfer Protocol (SFTP)** as a transfer module by default, but for some reason, if SSH is working and SFTP is not supported or not working on the Managed host, then we can change it to **Secure Copy Protocol (SCP)** from SFTP. We need to modify the Ansible configuration file (**Ansible.cfg** file) to change this default parameter.

Windows hosts only support the connection using WinRM or PowerShell Remoting Protocol. At the time of writing this book, OpenSSH on Windows hosts is just an experimental feature, but in the future it might be supported.

If we state something exaggeratedly for a second about the Ansible, then we will say virtually we can manage all kinds of client host/target hosts and all clouds platforms using Ansible, but this is a more practical world, and we have some limitations when we use it on the client host/managed notes. Here is the list of a few popular platforms or technologies where we can use Ansible.

Operating systems

There are many operating systems in the market. We all use different OS as per our requirement. However, Ansible has support for almost all OS available in the market.

Linux distribution

Here is the list of a few well-known Linux distributions supported in Ansible:

- RHEL
- CentOS
- Fedora
- Ubuntu

Windows

Here is the list of a few well-known Windows distributions supported in Ansible:

- Windows Server 2008
- Windows Server 2008 R2
- Windows Server 2012
- Windows Server 2012 R2
- Windows Server 2016
- Windows Server 2019
- Windows 7
- Windows 8.1
- Windows 10
- Windows 11

Note: Server 2008, 2008 R2, and Windows 7 are deprecated in the Ansible 2.10 release.

- Unix
- IBM Z
- NGINX
- IBM Power System

Virtualization technologies

We are in an era where everything is moving towards virtualization. There are many giants in the market that have made this transition from physical infrastructure to the virtual, but Ansible is not only good with physical appliances, but it is also good with virtualization technologies:

- VMware
- Red Hat Virtualization
- Vagrant

Storage

Now, many of our readers might be from the storage background and might be wondering, whether Ansible has anything on plate? Well, the answer is yes. It does support all giant storage vendors.

- NetApp,
- Pure Storage,

- Dell EMC,
- IBM Storage and so on.

Network and security devices

The journey of other automation tools was not simple with networking devices. As said, many other IT automation tools install their agent in the target host. If we take the example of Cisco routers, then they are not going to allow you to install any plugins into their router, but that is not the limitation with Ansible. Ansible uses port 22 or SSH to connect to the networking devices, and it works with the networking gear without any hassle. Now we could have discussed how other vendors manage this limitation, but that is out of the scope of this book. So let us focus on supported devices, which are not limited to the vendors. They are as follows:

- Arista
- Aruba
- Cisco
- Juniper
- Cumulus networks
- Mellanox
- Dell Switches
- F5 BIGIP
- HP Open Switches
- Palo Alto firewall
- Checkpoint firewall
- IBM Security
- Splunk
- FortiGate firewall and so on.

Cloud technologies

Now, many of you might be working on the top five giants of the market. Still, there are a few people who are working in not well-known clouds. For them, we will say, do not worry, Ansible has modules for your requirements too, and you will be good with them. The list of a few clouds that are supported by Ansible is as follows:

- Amazon Web Services
- Microsoft Azure
- Google Cloud Platform
- CloudScale

- Digital Ocean
- CloudStack
- Oracle Cloud
- VMWare
- Lumen

DevOps tools

Ansible has the capability of integrating with a bunch of DevOps tools. Please find the list of a few popular DevOps tools which can be integrated with Ansible:

- GitHub
- Jenkins
- GitLabs
- Vagrant
- ServiceNow
- Splunk
- InfluxDB
- Containers
- Logic Monitor
- AppDynamics

Now, the support of Ansible is not limited to these listed technologies or platforms. There are tens of supported platforms and technologies that we have not listed in the preceding lists. We tried to cover only a few popular platforms up here, but Ansible has a lot more to offer. So, whatever your use case is, Ansible has a module for your help and your devices/technology, and the best part is that if there is no module for your platform or your technology, then you can always write a new module and start using it repeatedly.

Now you might be feeling this is a lot of theory and concepts, so let us shift our focus from the concept and try some hands-on on the Linux host. Our first work will be preparing the control machine. Before we create the control machine, let us talk more about the control machine.

Control machine

Control machine is a host where you install Ansible. You can run the Ansible commands and Ansible-playbooks from this control node. Ideally, in an enterprise environment, you configure a server as a control machine however, you can also use your home PC, laptop, or shared PC to create the control machine. Any machine with Linux and Python installed can act as a control machine. From the control machine, Ansible manages the remote hosts.

As we learned, by default, it uses SSH communication to manage the remote devices. WinRM and PSRP are used for managing the Windows remote host.

If we focus on the enterprise environment, then high availability is also important, and Ansible also supports multiple control nodes to avoid a single point of failure. Like any other automation tool in the market, Ansible also has some limitations. The Windows host cannot act as control machine.

There are some work-arounds which can be used to install Ansible on the Windows host but in general it is not supported. Neither Red Hat recommends, nor does the author. So, always use the Linux host as a control machine.

Now, there are a few prerequisites we need to take care of before installing Ansible on the control machine. Those prerequisites are different for every version and are given as follows:

- **Ansible version 2.9**: Ansible version 2.9 can run from any Linux machine with Python 2.7 or Python 3.5 and higher installed.
- **Ansible version 3.0 and higher**: Ansible version 3.0 can run from any Linux machine with Python 3.8 or higher installed.

There are two kinds of Ansible packages in the market. They used to call it an **artifact**. So, artifacts are nothing more than a package. So, in other words, there are two artifacts in the market. The end user can choose any of them based on their requirements. The following are the Ansible artifacts:

- Ansible
- Ansible Core (Ansible-base few times)

Ansible package

This is the old package, which was being managed by the Ansible community from the day Ansible was launched. In version 2.10, the same version is expanded with new features and functionality, just like our Windows Host or Mac host used to get. Till version 2.9, this was the only package in the market, and from version 2.10, the same package was updated. We can choose the following method to install Ansible on our host:

1. Install the Ansible package using Python **pip**.
2. Install Ansible using package managers like YUM, **dnf** or **apt-get**.

Installing Ansible using package managers

Based on different OS, we have different package managers and commands. We cannot cover all the Linux platforms here. However, we will try to cover the commands for the most popular Linux platforms:

- For CentOS:

```
yum install epel-release
yum install Ansible
```

- For Fedora:

```
dnf install Ansible
```

- For RHEL:

```
yum install Ansible
```

- For Debian:

```
apt install Ansible
```

We personally prefer using a package manager to install Ansible, as it takes care of all dependencies and is a hassle-free installation. We recommend all readers to install it using **yum**/**dnf** or **apt-get**, as this takes care of everything required in the backend.

Installing Ansible using Python-pip or pip

The first thing we need to do is install **pip** on our host. Once **pip** is there, we can start the installation of Ansible on the host.

Let us also guide you through the process of installing **pip** on the host. Now, just to inform, we are using CentOS Linux release 7.5 in all the examples. So, most of the commands we are going to use in the example will be CentOS or RHEL commands. Now, we will download the Python **pip** package on our host, and then we will install it.

```
wget https://bootstrap.pypa.io/get-pip.py -o get-pip.py
```

This is going to download the Python **pip** package.

Note: **If you do not find wget then you can install the wget using command yum install wget. Alternatively, you can use the curl to download this package.**

If everything is good, then you can proceed further to *page number 15*. The following errors are only for those who ignore the prerequisites of Ansible:

```
pythonget-pip.py
```

Pip is finally installed in our system. We can run the following command to install Ansible:

```
pip install Ansible
```

So, if you have followed the guidelines properly, then you should be good with the installation of Ansible now. However, not all people follow the guidelines as they like the shortcuts. Now those people will get some errors, and we have tried to cover them in the next section. If you are not one of them, then you should jump to the Ansible Core concept and ignore the next error section.

In pip we need to create our **Ansible.cfg** file manually, but when we install Ansible using **yum** or any package manager, it will already be created, so we do not need to do the general configuration of Ansible in case of **yum** or package installer.

Expected error

If you have ignored the prerequisites, then you may get the following error. This error asks for installing 2.7/ (whatever unsupported version you have installed) **get-pip.py** script. However, that is not what we wish to do here. We want to install the latest version of Ansible, hence we will need to upgrade the Python version to Python 3.7 or later.

Sample error: **This script does not work on Python 2.7. The minimum supported Python version is 3.7. Please use https://bootstrap.pypa.io/pip/2.7/get-pip. py instead.**

Now, how do we upgrade the Python version? Well, follow our steps, we will guide you on the same.

Navigate to the website **https://www.python.org/ftp/python/** and choose the Python version you want to install.

In this example, we have chosen version 3.7.4.

Note: Assuming the development tools are already in place for the compilation. If not, then please install it using the command yum groupinstall -y "Development Tools".

Use the following command to install version 3.7.4. Make sure you modify the version details in the command if you wish to install the other version of Python:

```
wget https://www.python.org/ftp/python/3.7.4/Python-3.7.4.tar.xz
```

Now we need to unzip the file using the following commands:

```
tar -xJf Python-3.7.4.tar.xz
```

Let us navigate to the folder and use the configure command to install the package:

```
cd Python-3.7.4
./configure
```

Let us compile the program using the make command and then install Python:

```
make
make install
```

Note: Assuming the development tools is already in the place for the compilation. If not then please install it using the command yum groupinstall -y "Development Tools".

If you find any module error while executing the install execution, then please install the dependency package **libffi-dev**. The command for installing it will be:

```
yum install libffi-dev
```

We are done with the installation of Python version 3.7.4 or whatever version you decide to install on your system. So, if you are done installing the prerequisites now, then you can re-run the command **python get-pip.py**.

Since now Python **pip** in installed and prerequisites are matched, we can install Ansible without any hassle. Please find the following command to install Ansible using **pip**:

```
pip install Ansible
```

Ansible Core

In Ansible release 2.10, Ansible Core was first introduced. It was called Ansible-base in release 2.10. It was built with a few very basic Ansible Core modules and plugins. As a user, you can install your additional required modules using Ansible Galaxy. Now, if your requirements are limited to a few very basic modules, then Ansible Core works great for you. It works great in other situations, too, where you need to get the modules installed using Ansible Galaxy.

How to install the Ansible Core

There are two ways of installing the Ansible Core.

1. The first method is using **pip** just like we used for the installation of Ansible:

   ```
   pip install ansible-core
   ```

2. Installing Ansible from their Git repo. We can access their under-development version, but this is highly unstable and we do not recommend using it in a production environment. However, if you like to explore the new stuffs then this is right place to do so.

Uninstall Ansible

Please find the following commands to uninstall Ansible using **pip**:

For uninstalling **ansible**:

```
pip uninstall ansible
```

For uninstalling **ansible-base**:

```
pip uninstall ansible-base
```

For uninstalling **ansible-core**:

```
pip uninstall ansible-core
```

So now we are done with the installation of Ansible on our control machine. In other words, our control machine is ready for use, and we can play around with it. The first thing we should do is check our Ansible version. As many features and plugins are feature-specific. So here is our first ever Ansible command:

```
ansible --version
```

Conclusion

Just to summarize what we learned so far. We have seen what the needs of an IT automation engine are and why it is a must now for IT industries. Ansible is one of the most popular IT automation engines in the market. It works with most of the technologies and vendors in the market. At last, we installed Ansible on our control machine, which is a machine where Ansible is installed. In our next chapter, we will deep dive into the concepts of Ansible and get a basic understanding of Ansible Tower.

References

- **https://www.ansible.com/**
- **https://www.ansible.com/blog/red-hat-ansible-automation-engine-vs-tower**
- **https://www.ansible.com/integrations/infrastructure**

Multiple choice questions

1. **What is a control machine?**
    a. Physical or virtual machine where we install the Ansible
    b. A machine that will be configured by Ansible
    c. Backup server
    d. None of the Above

2. **How does Ansible communicate with the target host?**
    a. Using an Agent installed on the target host?
    b. Using SSH
    c. Using WinRM
    d. WinRM and SSH are both used based on the type of target host

Answers

1	a
2	d

Questions

1. Ansible is written in which programming language?

2. How does another IT automation engine connect to the target host, like networking devices, which do not allow any modification in them?

Join our Discord space

Join our Discord workspace for latest updates, offers, tech happenings around the world, new releases, and sessions with the authors:

https://discord.bpbonline.com

CHAPTER 2
Introducing Ansible and Ansible Tower

Introduction

In this chapter, we will learn the basics of Ansible, how it works, and where it can be used. By the end of the chapter, we will also explore Ansible Tower, the **graphical user interface (GUI)** version of Ansible.

Structure

In this chapter, we are going to cover the following topics:

- Defining Ansible
- Exploring possible solutions
- Working of Ansible
- Functions of Ansible
- Learning Ansible
- Ansible automation controller
- Ansible AWX

Objectives

This chapter is very important in creating the strong foundation. We will learn some very important basics of Ansible and Ansible Tower. In the end, we will also see how we can install the Ansible Tower.

Defining Ansible

Ansible is an open-source configuration management tool that runs on Linux environments. It is an agent-less configuration management tool which means it does not need any additional configuration or installation of agent on the client machine. It uses the SSH or WinRM to connect with remote host and manage them.

Ansible can be configured only on a Linux environment, but we can manage both Linux and Windows environments using it. Ansible was built for server management, but over time, it started supporting more technologies. Today, whether it is Server management or your personal computer, Ansible can manage it. Whether it is a cloud platform or virtualization technology, a storage technology or network infrastructure, macOS or Unix, Ansible supports all of them and can manage them efficiently.

The Ansible tool was developed by *Michael DeHaan*. The initial version of Ansible was launched in February 2012. Now, if you are thinking that you have heard this name somewhere, then you are right about it. He is the author of *Cobbler (Linux Provisioning server)* too. He started his own company, *Ansible Works Inc.,* in 2013. *SaïdZiouani* and *Timothy Gerlawas* are the co-founders of *Ansible Works*. In October 2015, Red Hat acquired Ansible, and since then, it is known as *Ansible, Inc.* In 2021, Red Hat was acquired by *IBM*, and now it is part of IBM's portfolio of open-source technology.

Red Hat offers enterprise support if needed, but the most important part is that all of its modules are free of cost, and we do not need to pay even a single penny to install or use Ansible.

Exploring possible solutions

As we learnt, Ansible is an agent-less tool and requires no additional configuration on the client hosts. If we talk about the other tools like Puppet and Chef they need the installation of agent on the client host. This is where Ansible is superior to its competitors; it requires zero configurations on the client hosts.

Now, one may wonder what the issue is with the installation of an agent on the client host. Well, what if your client hosts run on a custom OS and you have zero control over the underlying demons/kernel/OS of the host? Let us consider the example of the network equipment, Cisco is the biggest giant in the market that runs its custom OS on its routers, switches, and all networking equipment. The end user has no access to the underlying kernel, and we cannot install any software on their router and many other network equipment. This is where Ansible is very flexible. It works on SSH and does not need the installation of any agent on the Cisco routers/switches. Hence, it is easy to manage those devices without any additional configuration/installation on them. The only thing we need to manage the target/client host is SSH communication between the Ansible host and the target/client host. The second obvious thing will be the credentials, as we know, we cannot SSH to devices without credentials.

Ansible uses the existing OS credentials of the remote machine to gain access to the remote machine. Now, you might think that we have moved on from old username-password methods, and do not use them in our company or workplace. Well, do not worry, Ansible supports key-based authentication too; even by default, Ansible assumes we are using keys to authenticate the remote hosts. So, in simple words, we can use both password authentication and key- based authentication to access the target/client host.

Working of Ansible

Now, a few of you readers might have some idea about Ansible and how it works, but if you do not, we will learn it in this section. Since we are learning how Ansible works, we need to learn about a few basic components of Ansible. They are as follows:

- The first and most important is **control machine.** Control machine is basically a Linux host where we install Ansible.

- The second important part is **managed host/target host**. The managed nodes or target hosts are those hosts/machines that we want to manage using Ansible. In simple words, the hosts that we want to configure using Ansible are known as target hosts/managed nodes. These are stored in the hosts file. There is a wide range of client hosts that are supported in Ansible.

- The third and most important is **engineers** like us who know how to write the playbooks and manage the target hosts using Ansible.

Let us have a look at the following figure to understand how Ansible works better:

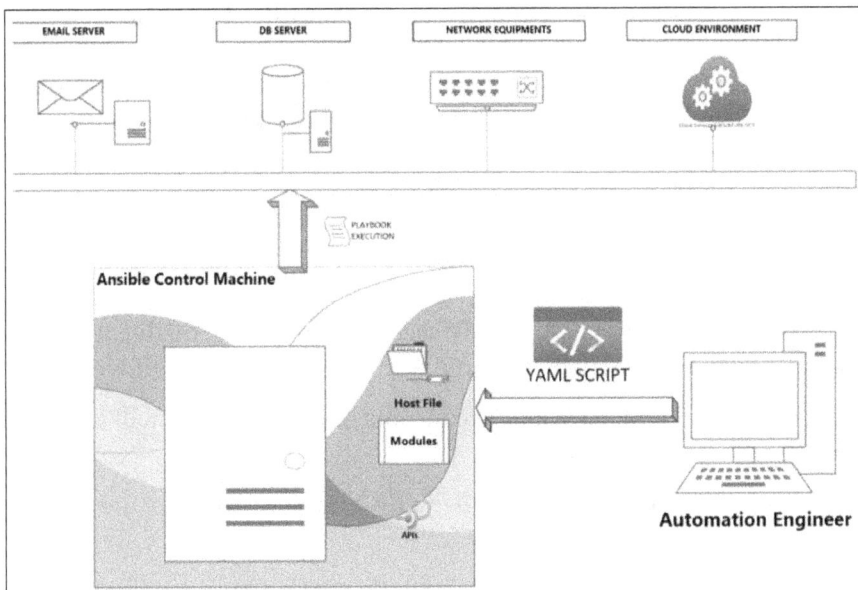

Figure 2.1: The three basic components of Ansible

The control machine is the real brain of Ansible. This is the place where we write our code. The target host information is also defined here, and this is the place where we start the execution of our playbooks.

Functions of Ansible

Let us go back to the figure and try to understand what Ansible does. We will carry out the first step by connecting to the Ansible control machine. We will start with writing the Ansible code in YAML (In reality, we will write the Ansible roles and playbooks that we will explain soon). Once the code or commands are ready, we will go ahead and define the inventory/host file. The inventory/host file is nothing more than a list of the target hosts where we want to perform the changes.

Once our code is ready and we have defined the target host information, we will run the code (run the Ansible playbooks). Everything else will be done by the Ansible control machine. Let us focus on what the Ansible control machine does:

- The Ansible control machine will establish the connection to the target host using SSH/WinRM.

- Once the connection is established, the control machine will push a unique code (known as a module) to the target host. Ansible executes these modules and completes the task/tasks we wrote in our code.

- Once execution is performed, it will collect the output and print it on the terminal. In the end, Ansible modules will be removed.

Think of modules as an intermediate between you and the target hosts. Without these modules, we will need to write hundreds of lines of code to push a single command to the target hosts. Ansible developers have already written that code for us, and that pre-written set of code is called **Ansible modules**. We will discuss the modules in detail later in this book.

Learning Ansible

Whether you have some prior experience or no experience in Ansible, we are going to learn Ansible from scratch. We have already seen how to install Ansible. We will continue from there and pick one component at a time. We will focus on it until we master it.

We will start from theory and learn all the concepts of one topic. We will jump into the lab and try hands-on what we learned.

There will be some demo codes that will guide you step by step until the execution completes successfully.

We will also focus on reading the output of the playbook. Once we master that, the final task will be running the debug and understanding the logs and errors.

Ansible for DevOps

Ansible can be your go-to automation tool for any sort of automation. Whether you want to achieve configuration management or you want to go ahead with the project deployment, Ansible has the solution for all of them. This is the reason why Ansible is the first preference for many DevOps engineers. Mastering Ansible will help you succeed in your career and achieve your goals. Ansible in good hands can completely change how the organization works, develops, and deploys its infrastructure, application, database, network, and other critical components. We will try to cover most of the topics in detail in this book. We will focus on one topic at a time and learn it using an example. That way, we will have much more hands-on experience with Ansible.

Ansible Tower

The first thing that might come to your mind is, why use Ansible Tower if Ansible is already there? Well, we are going to find that answer soon.

You might have heard many people complaining about the black screen, scripting, or programming language. If you are one of those people who love GUI, then Ansible Tower is designed for you. It gives a good graphical representation of almost all Ansible features. Ansible Tower makes Ansible even simpler. You do not need any prior scripting or any programming language experience. It is designed in such a way that any IT professional can use it to configure and monitor their infrastructure.

The best way of learning anything is by trying it ourselves.

Let us create a **virtual machine** (**VM**) in AWS and try to install Ansible Tower in it. We are going to install RHEL 8, because it works great with Ansible Tower, and we will face fewer issues with it.

There are some minimum hardware requirements when creating the Ansible Tower machine. That is not going to run on the t2.micro free tier eligible VM. Ensure you assign good resources to your VM in the cloud.

Ansible Tower has the following requirements:

- **Supported operating systems:**
    - Red Hat Enterprise Linux 6 64-bit
    - Red Hat Enterprise Linux 7 64-bit
    - CentOS 6 64-bit
    - CentOS 7 64-bit
    - Ubuntu 12.04 LTS 64-bit
    - Ubuntu 14.04 LTS 64-bit

- The latest stable release of Ansible
- 64-bit support required (kernel and runtime)
- 2 GB RAM minimum (4+ GB RAM recommended):
  - 2 GB RAM (minimum and recommended for Vagrant trial installations)
  - 4 GB RAM is recommended per 100 forks
- 20 GB hard disk
- **For Amazon EC2:**
  - Instance size of m3.medium or larger
  - An instance size of m3.xlarge or larger if there are more than 100 hosts

Now, the documents say it is supported for CentOS 6/7 and RHEL 6/7, but it creates a lot of issues while making it work. For a beginner's journey, the author recommends going ahead with RHEL8. In production, you can try what works best for you and what your company policies are, but for learning purposes, we can use RHEL8.

For demo purposes, we have created this VM in AWS.

The following figure depicts the control machine running in the AWS Cloud:

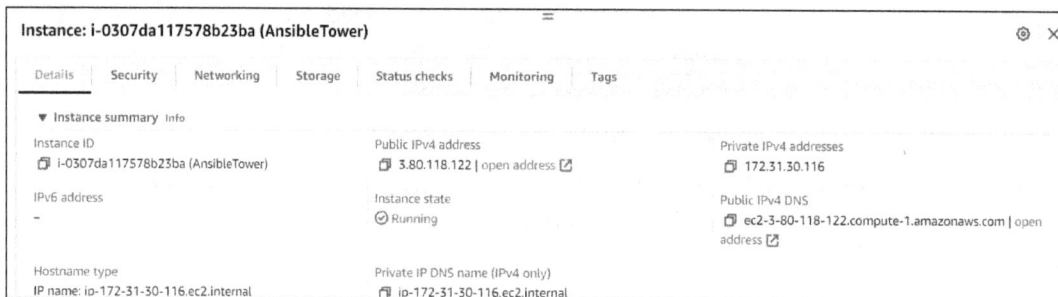

Figure 2.2: Control machine instance running in AWS Cloud

The instance used here is not a t2.micro. You should also not use the t2.micro for sure as it will not be able to handle the load of production. Red Hat suggests m3.medium but t2.xlarge works best for the author, hence their choice. Make sure you increase the size of storage, the default 10 GB is not helpful. We can choose 50 or more for the test use case. In production, you need to analyze your usage and decide on the basis of that.

The following figure shows t2.xlarge instance:

Figure 2.3: We have used t2.xlarge instance type

Once the VM was up, we logged into it using SSH and started running the **yum update** on my RHEL8 host. You can use the Dandified YUM too.

In case you face any issue with your image, we have attached the one we have used in AWS.

AMI ID: ami-002b3a442fc114c66

yum -y update

Since we used the latest VM, it did not have much to update.

The next thing we need to do is update the EPEL repository:

[root@ip-172-31-30-116 ansible-tower-setup-3.8.6-2]#sudodnf install https://dl.fedoraproject.org/pub/epel/epel-release-latest-8.noarch.rpm

```
[root@ip-          ~]# sudo dnf install https://dl.fedoraproject.org/pub/epel/epel-release-latest-8.noarch.rpm
Updating Subscription Management repositories.
Unable to read consumer identity

This system is not registered with an entitlement server. You can use subscription-manager to register.

Last metadata expiration check: 0:01:11 ago on Sun 10 Sep 2023 10:02:06 AM UTC.
epel-release-latest-8.noarch.rpm
Dependencies resolved.
================================================================================
 Package                    Architecture              Version
================================================================================
Installing:
 epel-release               noarch                    8-19.el8

Transaction Summary
================================================================================
Install  1 Package

Total size: 25 k
Installed size: 35 k
Is this ok [y/N]: y
Downloading Packages:
Running transaction check
Transaction check succeeded.
Running transaction test
Transaction test succeeded.
Running transaction
  Preparing        :
  Installing       : epel-release-8-19.el8.noarch
  Running scriptlet: epel-release-8-19.el8.noarch
Many EPEL packages require the CodeReady Builder (CRB) repository.
It is recommended that you run /usr/bin/crb enable to enable the CRB repository.

  Verifying        : epel-release-8-19.el8.noarch
Installed products updated.

Installed:
  epel-release-8-19.el8.noarch
```

Figure 2.4: Updating the EPEL release and showing its result

As we can see, the EPEL updates are done here.

Now we need to install Ansible on the host:

sudo yum -y install ansible

The following figure shows the command execution:

```
[root@ip-172-31-31-157 ~]# sudo yum -y install ansible
Updating Subscription Management repositories.
Unable to read consumer identity

This system is not registered with an entitlement server. You can use subscription-manager to register.

Last metadata expiration check: 0:02:55 ago on Sun 10 Sep 2023 10:03:46 AM UTC.
Dependencies resolved.
================================================================================
 Package                         Architecture        Version
================================================================================
Installing:
 ansible                         noarch              7.2.0-1.el8
Installing dependencies:
 ansible-core                    x86_64              2.14.2-4.el8_8
 git-core                        x86_64              2.39.3-1.el8_8
 mpdecimal                       x86_64              2.5.1-3.el8
 python3.11                      x86_64              3.11.2-2.el8_8.1
 python3.11-cffi                 x86_64              1.15.1-1.el8
 python3.11-cryptography         x86_64              37.0.2-5.el8
 python3.11-libs                 x86_64              3.11.2-2.el8_8.1
 python3.11-pip-wheel            noarch              22.3.1-2.el8
 python3.11-ply                  noarch              3.11-1.el8
 python3.11-pycparser            noarch              2.20-1.el8
 python3.11-pyyaml               x86_64              6.0-1.el8
 python3.11-setuptools-wheel     noarch              65.5.1-2.el8
 python3.11-six                  noarch              1.16.0-1.el8
 sshpass                         x86_64              1.09-4.el8
Installing weak dependencies:
 python3-jmespath                noarch              0.9.0-11.el8

Transaction Summary
================================================================================
Install  16 Packages
```

Figure 2.5: Installation of Ansible packages

The output suppressed, showing the results is as follows:

```
Installed:
  ansible-7.2.0-1.el8.noarch              ansible-core-2.14.2-4.el8_8.x86_64             git-
  python3-jmespath-0.9.0-11.el8.noarch    python3.11-3.11.2-2.el8_8.1.x86_64            pyth
  python3.11-libs-3.11.2-2.el8_8.1.x86_64 python3.11-pip-wheel-22.3.1-2.el8.noarch      pyth
  python3.11-pyyaml-6.0-1.el8.x86_64      python3.11-setuptools-wheel-65.5.1-2.el8.noarch pyth

Complete!
[root@ip-172-31-31-157 ~]#
```

Figure 2.6: Installation output

If **yum** is not completing your installation, you can use the Dandified YUM:

Sudo dnf install ansible -y

If **yum** is helpful in your RHEL8 hosts too you can keep it the same, else, we need to switch to the Dandified YUM and install Ansible using it. Even if you want another way of installing Ansible in your host then go ahead with **pip** and install Ansible using it.

If you have python3 installed, then please use the **pip3 install Ansible** command to install Ansible.

If you are still running the older version of Ansible, then choose Python **pip** and install Ansible using the following command:

```
pip2 install Ansible
```

It might be **pip install Ansible** in your system so use that command and install the Ansible in your host.

We also need **curl** or **wget** in our hosts, so install it if it is not there already.

Now we need to create a directory to keep things clean for us. You can use your home directory for installation, too. It is our choice.

```
mkdir /tmp/AshuDemoTower
```

Now we need to navigate to it. Refer to the following code and *Figure 2.7:*

```
cd /tmp/AshuDemoTower
```

```
[root@ip-172-31-31-157 ~]# mkdir /tmp/AshuDemoTower
[root@ip-172-31-31-157 ~]#
[root@ip-172-31-31-157 ~]# cd /tmp/AshuDemoTower/
[root@ip-172-31-31-157 AshuDemoTower]#
```

Figure 2.7: Navigate to the directory

Now we need to download the Ansible Tower file to our host using **curl** or **wget**. Use the following link:

```
wget https://releases.ansible.com/ansible-tower/setup/ansible-tower-setup-latest.tar.gz
```

Now, you might not have **wget** installed in your host. The simplest command to install the **wget** will be **dnf install wget -y.**

The next thing we have on the table is to extract the files from the **.zip** folder.

```
tar vxf ansible-tower-setup-latest.tar.gz
```

Now, navigate to the directory:

```
cd ansible-tower-setup-3.8.6-2/
```

When you put the list command there, you will find the following files and directories over there:

```
[root@ip-172-31-30-116 ansible-tower-setup-3.8.6-2]# ls -ltr
```

total 60

```
-rwxr-xr-x.  1 root root 11357 May  3 17:12 setup.sh
drwxr-xr-x. 21 root root  4096 May  3 17:12 roles
-rw-r--r--.  1 root root  3492 May  3 17:12 restore.yml
-rw-r--r--.  1 root root  1439 May  3 17:12 rekey.yml
-rw-r--r--.  1 root root  2506 May  3 17:12 README.md
-rw-r--r--.  1 root root  3185 May  3 17:12 inventory
-rw-r--r--.  1 root root  8524 May  3 17:12 install.yml
```

```
-rw-r--r--.  1 root root    626 May  3 17:12 backup.yml
drwxr-xr-x.  3 root root   8192 May  3 17:15 licenses
drwxr-xr-x.  3 root root     33 May  3 17:15 collections
drwxr-xr-x.  2 root root     17 May  3 17:15 group_vars
```

Now we need to modify the inventory file. You can use any editor you like most. We need to set up the following things in the inventory. You can remove all the old content and copy and paste the following inventory file. We need to define the passwords for a few users. Remember, the same password will be used to log in to the Ansible Tower when things are working well. The username for the same is admin:

```
[tower]
localhost ansible_connection=local

[database]

[all:vars]
admin_password='WriteYour password here'

pg_host=''
pg_port=''

pg_database='awx'
pg_username='awx'
pg_password='WriteYour password here'

rabbitmq_username=tower
rabbitmq_password='WriteYour password here'
rabbitmq_cookie=cookiemonster
```

Once the modification is done, you can save the file.

Now we need to run the shell script **setup.sh**. Use the following command to execute the same:

shsetup.sh

This will start the execution Ansible playbook in the backend, and at the end, you will see the output as successful.

In the middle of the execution, you will see the following message on the terminal:

```
################################################################################
#######TASK [packages_el : Install the Tower RPM.] *************************
******************************************************************************
*******************************************

################################################################################
#############
```

At the end of the script, you will find the following output:

```
, "Wants": "redis.servicepostgresql.servicenginx.servicesupervisord.
```

```
service", "WatchdogTimestampMonotonic": "0", "WatchdogUSec": "0"}}

PLAY [Install Automation Hub node] **************************************
**********************************************************************
**************************************

skipping: no hosts matched

PLAY [Install Tower isolated node(s)] ***********************************
**********************************************************************
**************************************

skipping: no hosts matched

PLAY RECAP **********************************************************
**********************************************************************
**************************************

localhost                     : ok=xx changed=xxx   unreachable=0     failed=0
skipped=xx   rescued=0    ignored=2

The setup process completed successfully.

Setup log saved to /var/log/tower/setup-2022-07-10-20:48:34.log.
```

Refer to the following figure:

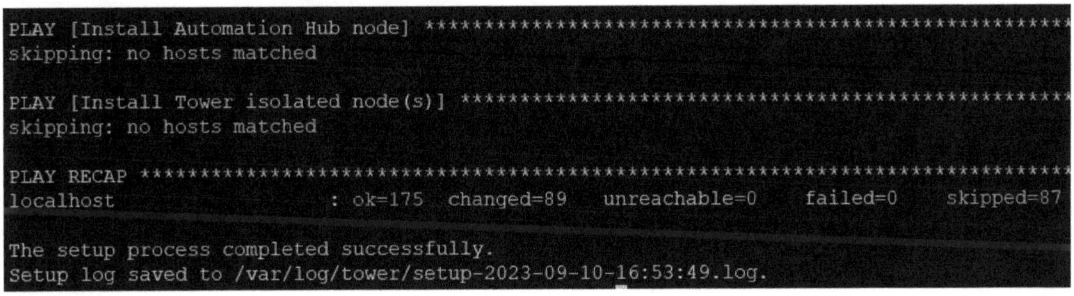

Figure 2.8: Ansible Tower installation playbook results

As soon as we get the successful message, we need to go to the AWS security group of the device and enable the port 80 for the source IP address of US.

When we hit the URL on port 80, we will see the certificate error. Proceed with the self signed certificate and we will find the login window.

The login window can be seen in the following figure:

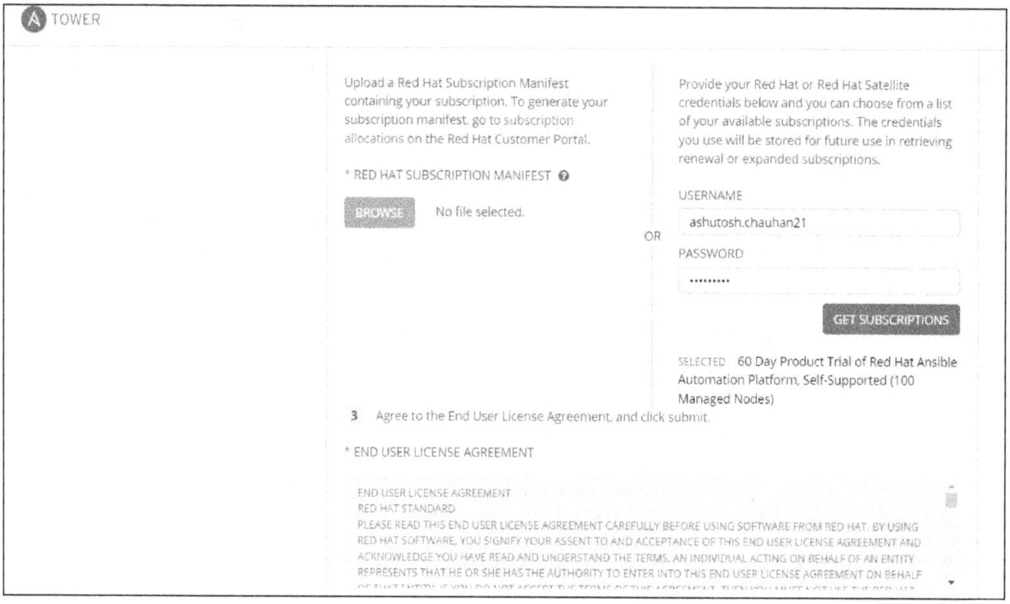

Figure 2.9: Step 1 for activation

The author has used their account to log in and registered the host on Red Hat. Once we click on that, we get a subscription that will pop up a window and give us the information about the license details and its validity. Since we used the 60-day free license, we are getting the same on the terminal.

The license information pop-up window can be seen in the following figure. This is where we will select our license. Since we are using a trial license, we see 60-day product trial:

Figure 2.10: Step 2 for the activation

If you have a paid license, then you need to select and proceed further with the following steps:

1. Select the license and click on **OK**. Now you might have a production license, or a trail license. You can use the license as per your requirement.

2. Once you click on **OK,** it will redirect to the login dashboard.

3. Please look at the following figure to understand what the Ansible Tower login page will look like during the first time login:

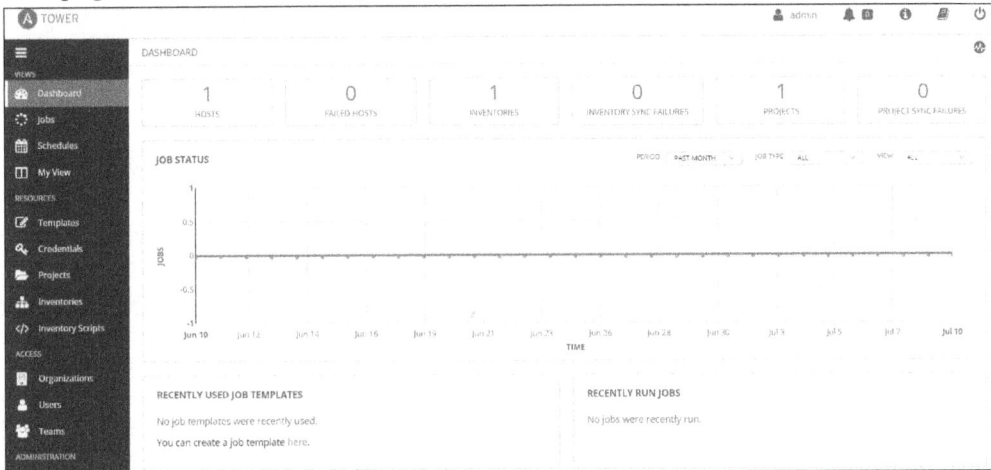

Figure 2.11: View of Ansible Tower on first time login

Ansible automation controller

The first thing that might come to your mind is whether this is the third variant of Ansible. In reality, it is just Ansible Tower with many new features and improvements. You can also say Ansible Tower is renamed as Ansible automation controller. Just like Ansible Tower, it supports the GUI, and you will find almost all the features of Ansible in here too.

Now, you may also hear about the automation controller 4.0, but that is not something different. That is just the new name of the Ansible Tower with new modifications and new features.

THERE are few modifications in the architecture of automation controller 4.0, which we will learn and discuss now in this chapter.

Ansible automation controller is evolving with time. Red Hat is working on the process of making it better every day. They are removing non-required functionality of Ansible Tower.

For example, previously we had the GUI and API, and the execution plane (CLI Ansible) on every single node. Now that is used to create the problems while scaling up. Just to explain how that was problematic, let us assume you want to create a cluster of four servers. We are assuming that we know we need a cluster for redundancy purposes. So, if we are using 4 servers in a cluster, then we have four GUIs on four different servers. However, that was not our requirement. What did we want? Well, we wanted more resources and scalability, but for no reason we were getting multiple numbers of GUIs which were eating up our resources and cost too.

What is different in Ansible automation controller?

We have different execution plane and control plane in Ansible automation controller and this way we can have multiple nodes for the GUI or execution on the basis of our requirement. If we want more servers for execution, we can achieve it.

Ansible AWX

As we have discussed many times, Ansible is an open-sourced project, and we do not need the license to use it. However, if we want to use Ansible Tower, then it is a paid product. However, if you are not a big fan of CLI and do not have the budget, then do not worry, Ansible AWX is there for you. Ansible AWX is an open-source community project that is available to us and as expected, it is sponsored by Red Hat, but remember, there is no paid support for the Ansible AWX.

Basically, AWX is a project where all new development happens. Updates are released more frequently, and that is where it is different from the Ansible automation controller. Only the best and stable releases of Ansible AWX are chosen for the Ansible automation controller.

In simple words, you can think of Ansible AWX as a lab environment where all development and testing are happening. Once they get the final stable product, it is released in the Ansible automation controller. So, it is just an upstream for Ansible automation controller from which we select the stable releases for the Automation controller. Now, we are using the term fast release and one might wonder how often we release the updates? Well, the number is two weeks at the time of writing this chapter. This might change with time, but this is how it is right now.

Conclusion

We have now gone through the basics of Ansible and how it works. We have also seen what Ansible Tower is and how we can install it. You can try installing Ansible Tower on your own and see if everything works correctly for you.

In the next chapter, we will deep dive into more concepts of Ansible. We will have a look at the basic components offered by Ansible.

References

- https://access.redhat.com/articles/6184841
- https://docs.ansible.com/ansible-tower/2.2.2/html/quickinstall/prepare.html
- https://docs.ansible.com/ansible-tower/2.2.2/html/quickinstall/prepare. html#installation-and-reference-guide
- https://www.redhat.com/en/technologies/management/ansible/automation-controller

## CHAPTER 3

Working with Ansible

Introduction

In this chapter, we will learn about the basic components of Ansible. We will start from the very basic and then try to look further into them. We will be using many of these components in our first-ever playbook and role, so it is very important to get familiar with them before we use them.

Structure

In this chapter, we are going to cover the following topics:

- Ansible components
- Ansible ad-hoc commands
- Ansible hosts file
- Ansible playbooks
- Desired configuration state and idempotency
- Ansible pull
- Running Ansible playbooks
- Ansible collections
- Ansible Galaxy
- Ansible loops
- Ansible conditions
- Frequently used Ansible modules

Objectives

Ansible is very easy to work with if you understand the basics of it. After reading this chapter, you will be able to understand the basic components of Ansible and their usage. This chapter will create a strong foundation for your career.

Ansible components

Ansible has many key components that we will list and learn one by one:

- **Inventory**: If we create a list of all the nodes we want to configure using Ansible, the list would be called **inventory**. In simple words, a list of managed nodes is called an inventory. We can define the IP address or fully qualified domain name of the managed node (target host) in the inventory. That is not the only thing inventory can help us with, but we can also create multiple groups in inventory and define the variables for our target hosts.

- **Tasks**: Basically, a task is an action we want to perform on the managed host. Tasks are basically defined as a list inside a play. The playbook contains a series of tasks. Ansible executes tasks in top-to-bottom order. It will always be executed in the order we define it.

- **Plays**: Ansible plays are basically an Ansible playbook object, which is responsible for Ansible execution. The Ansible play contains various things like variables and roles. Based on the mapping defined in the Ansible plays, it decides which task will be executed on which target host.

Ansible roles

An Ansible role is a standardized folder structure that organizes automation content-such as tasks, handlers, variables, templates, files, and plugins—so it is easy to reuse and share.

Instead of writing all commands directly in a playbook, you group related automation steps into a role. Roles help us keep playbooks clean, consistent, and easier to manage. So in simple words Ansible roles is the place where we list our commands we want to execute on the target hosts. The best way to understand the role is to think of it as a YAML file, where we list down all our commands. However, roles offer a lot more than the list of commands. If we want to execute the commands, if only certain conditions succeed, then we can define that logic in the roles. It supports the loops, handlers, plugins, templates, and variables too. We can define the variables in a different file and call them in the roles. We will talk about the plugins, templates, handlers, and variables later in this chapter.

Ansible playbook

Ansible playbook is a configuration management and multi-machine deployment system. Ansible playbooks contain the object names as plays, which are the basic units of Ansible execution. We will talk about the Ansible playbooks soon in this chapter. For now, just to understand it, playbooks are YAML files that contain plays/Ansible execution. The beauty of the Ansible playbook is that it can be reused for repetitive tasks.

Handlers

Ansible handlers are nothing more than a special kind of task. Basically, it is a conditional task only which is executed only when it is notified by the previous task. For example, if you have two tasks to perform. The first one is to install Apache on the Linux host, and the second is to start the services. If you write the tasks for both, chances are that Ansible will try to start the Apache services, even before Apache is installed in the Linux host and that is not what we want.

We want Ansible to wait until Apache is installed, and only then, we want Ansible to start the Apache services. For this kind of special use case, only the handlers were designed. We can define the normal task for installing the Apache service and write a handler to start the service.

Templates

In Ansible templates, files are defined in the **.j2** extension. If you know Python very well, you must be thinking if it is the same as Python's jinja2 template. Well, then you are right. Ansible basically uses Python's jinja2 template to define the Ansible templates. If you have too many variables in your code, then you will find the jinja2 template very handy. We can call almost all possible variables of Ansible in Jinja2 template files.

Variables

Ansible is no different from any other language, it also supports variables. We cannot only use Ansible facts, but can also custom define the variables as well. There are multiple ways of defining the variables in Ansible. We will go through them one by one at the time of the lab.

Plugins

As the name suggests, plugins are nothing more than some small code that extends Ansible's ability to support more and more platforms, add support for more filters, and even control the displays on the console. For example, we can use filter plugins for data manipulation.

Modules

Ansible modules are pre-written code by developers to make our lives easier. They are standalone scripts that can be used by us using Ansible playbooks or Ansible APIs to perform specific tasks on a target host. A module displays the output in the STDOUT format on the terminal.

Modules are written in many different languages. If the modules are not present for your use case, then you can write your own modules. When you run a playbook, Ansible calls for these modules to do the work.

Ansible ad-hoc commands

Ad-hoc command uses the Ansible command line tool to automate a single task on multiple target hosts. If you have a task that you will never repeat or want to perform some diagnostics quickly, then you can run the ad-hoc commands. Ad-hoc commands are handy when you do not have a lot of time to create a well-structured code and want to execute the code quickly on the bulk of the target hosts.

Ansible flags and command options

Ansible has various flags and command options to make our work efficient and convenient. Ansible offers many commands that can modify its configuration at run time. For example, you want to configure the Apache server on the target host. By default, Ansible will log in to the target host using the user details with which you logged in to the control machine. Now that the user might not have enough privileges to perform the change, and if you want to use the root account to log into the target host and perform the installation, then we can use the **become_user** flag to make it root.

Real command will be as follows:

`ansible- -become-userDummyuser`

Now, we can define **root/dummyuser/testuser** or any other user we want the Ansible to become. The following is the list of all the flags and switches we can use in Ansible:

- **Verbosity [x]**: Basically, it enables the debug mode of the execution.

- **Forks [x]**: By default, Ansible will start 5 concurrent sessions. If we want to modify that setting, we can use forks to modify that. `-f <x>` is another way of defining it. Here, *x* is an integer.

- **Become_user[username]**: If you have read only one person as a user and want to become any other user, then this is how we will achieve that. Remember, the default is root.

- **Remote_user[user]**: Well, if you want to define the credentials to log in to the target host, then this is how you will define the username of the target host. You can also put the `user -u[username]` to define a remote user. Let us try it by using an example.

Example: `ansible targethostinventoryname -m ping -u testuser`.

In the preceding example, **targethostinventoryname** is the name of the inventory where we have defined the target host IP address/DNS. –m switch is used to define the Ansible module, and **–u** switch is used to define the user credentials of the target host, so we can log into the host. It is obvious that the username has to be present on the target host, or else, it is not going to work there. **–The k** switch is used last, so we can define the password in hidden characters. When we use the **–k** switch, it will ask us to enter the password on the terminal, and once we enter the password, the execution starts.

Let us have a look on few more option we get with Ansible and what are the usage of them. We will start with become method and then proceed with few more.

- **Become_method [nameofsudomethod]:** This option allows us to define the escalation method. For example, few platforms support **sudo**, while few of them support **dzdo** or **su**, and so on. So, if you want to define or modify the method, we can change it to our allowed method.

- **check [bool]:** As its name suggests, it is used for the syntax check.

- **diff [bool]:** Now, there will be times when you will try to find the difference between the old file and the new file, or the old configuration and the new configuration. You will need to use **--diff** to find out the difference.

- **timeout [x]:** By default, Ansible will wait for 30 seconds before it considers the target host unresponsive and terminates the connection. However, if your task takes more than 30 seconds, then we need to modify the timeout values. Timeout 0 will disable the timeout, but do not use it in production. If you do not know the actual time, then try a few random big values and calculate after that.

- **help[Command]:** It will give us the information about that command. Generally, we do not use it; rather than this command we prefer the official Ansible document. That gives us more information than this help option.

- **!:** Now be careful here, the use of the **!** mark is not the same in Ansible. It will force the shell module in the case of Ansible. If you want to avoid the Ansible module and use the Shell module, then use the **!** mark.

Now there are tons of options in Ansible, and we cannot remember all of them. The following is a list of some of the most frequently used options:

- **--ask-vault-password, --ask-vault-pass:** Keeping the password in clear text is not a good thing; we will save the password in the Ansible Vault. Ansible Vault will keep the password encrypted. Ansible Vaults cannot be accessed by anyone; they need a password for access. When we call the password saved in the Ansible Vault in our code, we need to provide the vault password. There are multiple ways of entering the password of Ansible Vault **–ask-vault-pass** is one of them.

- **--become-pass-file <NameofFILE>:** The **–ask-vault-password** will wait for the user to input the password on the terminal, once the password is entered, and if the password is correct, only then the playbook or ad-hoc command will be successful.

The 'Become password file' option will help you copy the password from a file, and that way, you will not need to manually interfere with the execution.

As we all know, the default authentication in many modern-day clouds is through key-based authentication, and if you want to use key-based authentication, that can also be achieved in Ansible.

- **--private-key <keyfile>:** Now, you might be using key-based authentication for your servers, you need to call that file in your code. This will be your syntax to do so.

- **--scp-extra-args <Arguments>:** Define the arguments to pass to `scp`.

- **--sftp-extra-args <EXTRAValues>:** Defines the arguments to pass to `sftp` only (example, `-f`, `-1`).

- **--ssh-common-args <Values>:** Define common arguments to pass to `sftp/scp/ssh`.

- **--ssh-extra-args <SSHArguments>:** Define extra arguments to pass to `ssh` only.

- **--step:** One-step-at-a-time: confirm each task before running.

- **--task-timeout <TASKTIMEOUTValue>:** This will set the timeout for the task.

- **--vault-id:** We will define the vault ID using this command.

- **--version:** This is the first command we will use after installing Ansible. Ansible `-version` will give us the information about the current version being installed on our control machine.

- **-C, --check:** It is another useful tool of Ansible. It will help us pre-determine what changes will be performed by Ansible and show us that on the terminal.

- **-D, --diff:** Helps us find the differences between the old file and the new file, or even code sometimes. It is totally dependent on us how we use it.

- **-K, --ask-become-pass:** This is how it will ask us for the sudo password on the terminal. Do not get confused between the small k (k) and big K (K). Small k is used for entering the password for the target host whereas uppercase K is used for the privilege escalation password.

- **-M, --module-path:** Prepend colon-separated path(s) to module library: (`default=~/.Ansible/plugins/modules:/usr/share/Ansible/plugins/modules`).

- **-b, --become:** Run operations with become (does not imply password prompting):

- **-c <CONNECTION>, --connection <CONNECTION>:** Connection type to use (default=smart).

- **-e, --extra-vars:** Set additional variables as key=value or YAML/JSON, if the filename prepend with `@`.

- **-i, --inventory, --inventory-file**: Specify inventory host path or comma separated host list. The **-inventory-file** is deprecated.

- **-k, --ask-pass:** As we have discussed, it will prompt you on the terminal to enter the password. Additionally, the password will be hidden so no one can see it.

- **-u <username>, --user <username>:** As we have already seen this option. It is used for entering the username of the target host. **--user<usename>** is another way of using it.

Ansible hosts file

Ansible hosts file is the place where we define the target host information. In simple words, it is the place where we mention the IP address/hostname/DNS of the devices where we want to execute our code. If you want to configure a web server, then mention the IP address of that web server in the host file.

Now, one might think, how do we use that information in our code? We will be covering that later.

Let us consider a situation where you have 100 servers that you manage using automation. However, today you only want to patch the DB servers. Well, Ansible offers the option of creating a group where we can define the information of all DB servers. Once the DB group is created, we can call that group in our code (basically an Ansible playbook).

Ansible playbooks

Well, so far, we have learned where we define all our commands (in roles). We also have learned where we mention the target hosts' information (basically in the hosts file). However, something is still missing. A way to connect everything together. Ansible playbook is the glue that sticks all this information together. It is an Ansible playbook object, namely *PLAY*.

Ansible playbooks offer a simple configuration management and multi-host deployment system. Ansible playbooks are YAML files where we define which roles should be executed on which target host. We can define much more than that in playbooks, that is, what we will learn more when we start hands-on with the lab.

Ansible playbooks can declare the configuration, orchestrate steps of any manual ordered process on multiple sets of target hosts in a defined order. By default, it will launch tasks synchronously; however, we can do it asynchronously too.

A playbook is composed of one or more plays in an ordered list. Each play executes part of the overall goal of the playbook, running one or more tasks. Each task calls for an Ansible module.

Playbook execution

A playbook runs from top to bottom. Tasks also run in top-to-bottom order. If you have multiple tasks defined in the playbook or role. The first task will be chosen first, and the second one will not start until the first is completed. There is one thing we always need to remember. Ansible will complete the first task on all the target hosts and then only move to the second task. We can change this behavior with some configuration. However, we should always remember the default behavior of the execution.

Task execution

Ansible executes one task at a time in a defined order, on all target hosts, once the first task is completed on all hosts. Ansible moves to the second task. So, if you are performing some upgrade activation with any HA pair host, then you need to pay attention to this.

Suppose your steps are like those mentioned in the following figure:

Figure 3.1: Three step process of upgrade

In any of the normal devices, these are the three steps of the upgrade. Now, assume you had a high availability pair. Now you have the task of upgrading them without downtime. You will write the Ansible code for package download, package installation, and reboot at the last. You will write your code in three tasks:

- **TASK1**: Package download
- **TASK2**: Package installation
- **TASK3**: Reboot

In this case, Ansible will download the package on both boxes and then proceed with the package installation. Once installation is completed, Ansible will go ahead with the reboot on both HA pair boxes. Now, if you were assuming Ansible would complete the upgrade (download, installation, and reboot) on one device at a time and proceed to the second device, then it can be a big mistake. Ansible will start the download on both devices together since Ansible performs the execution of one task on all devices and then only goes for the second.

Note: **Ansible does the changes on five devices in parallel. Now we can make that serial, but by default, it is five concurrent executions.**

So, considering this situation, both our HA pair devices will be rebooted at the same time, and we will have the outage; therefore, never assume it will go ahead with the execution of all tasks on one device first and then the second.

Desired configuration state and idempotency

Ansible is a smart configuration management tool. Most of the Ansible modules check whether the desired configuration or state is already present in the device. If it finds the desired configuration or state, it exits without performing any action on the target host. Modules that perform this check are called **idempotent**.

Example: You have a Linux host that you want to manage using Ansible. You have a task of installing the Apache server on that Linux host. Suppose you wrote a playbook that has the task/role of installing the Apache server on a Linux host. Now, Ansible is a smart tool when we have tasks like this. Ansible will check whether the Apache server is already installed on the target host. If the Apache server is already installed, Ansible will skip the installation and give you the output on the console as `all OK Ansible will only install the Apache server in Linux host if it is not already installed on the Linux target host`.

Now, this feature is not limited to the installation of any services on any of the target hosts. This will be applied to the configuration, too. Most of the Ansible modules work like this; however, there are a few exceptions. The best thing to do is test you configuration in the dev or pre-production environment before you use it in the production environment.

Ansible pull

Ansible pull is the total different from of what we have learned so far. It downloads the script from the Git Repo and then runs/applies it immediately on the server. For this use case, you will need to install Ansible on the target machine you want to manage using Ansible. It does not need a centralized server or control machine for this use case.

Running Ansible playbooks

To run the Ansible playbook, we need to use the syntax `ansible-playbook nameoftheplaybook.yaml`.

Example: Suppose we have created a playbook named as `serverupgrade.yaml`, then we can run it using the following syntax:

```
ansible-playbook serverupgrade.yaml
```

In this example, we are assuming you have defined the username and password already in the role or task. If you do not want to do that, then you can use the flags we learned in this chapter. For example, if we want to define the username as **demouser** in the playbook, then the syntax will be similar to the following:

```
ansible-playbook serverupgrade.yaml -u demouser -k
```

At last, we have used the **-k** flag in the playbook syntax. That way, Ansible will ask for the password over the terminal before Ansible starts execution:

```
ansible-playbook serverupgrade.yaml -u demouser -k -b
```

Here, the **–b** flag will help Ansible to execute the script as root user:

```
ansible-playbook serverupgrade.yaml-f 2
```

Similarly, in the preceding example, we have used the **-f** flag. The use of **-f** flag is to define how many parallel sessions will be initiated by Ansible. Since we already discussed Ansible initiate 5 concurrent sessions at a time. **-f** is to modify that option and change it to whatever numbers we want. Sometimes people call it switch as it behaves like switch which flips on/off.

If we do not have become method as root, and we want any other method like **sudo**, **su**, **pbrun**, **pfexec**, **doas**, **dzdo**, then we can define that with **–become-method**:

```
--become-method=BECOME_METHOD
```

For example, if you want the become method to be **su**, then the syntax will be like:

```
--become-method=su
```

Verifying playbooks

Ansible playbook offers the command line options to verify our syntax. It will help us find the errors before we execute anything in the environment. **--check**, **--syntax-check** flags are the few very useful flag offered by Ansible. **--diff** is another one which we will use widely.

Ansible collections

Assume you have a new technology or software that has no Ansible module on the market. Now, you, as a user, would go to Red Hat and ask them to assist you with a module. Suppose they provided you with lightning-fast services and created a module in just 24 hours. However, the next major release is after two months. Which means the module is ready now, but you will get the benefits of this new module after two months. We see this as the major drawback of the traditional way of software release.

Ansible also traditionally uses the concept of releases like any other vendor and software. All new features and bug fixes were published with major/minor releases. This was changed with the introduction of Ansible collection or content collection. Ansible content collections, or collections, represent the new standard of distributing, maintaining, and consuming automation. By combining multiple types of Ansible content (playbooks, roles, modules, and plugins), flexibility and scalability are greatly improved. With the release of Red Hat Ansible Automation Platform, Ansible content collections are now fully supported.

Finding Ansible collections

Ansible collections can be installed and used from the distribution server. Ansible Galaxy is one of them. Please find the following URL to navigate to the same:

https://galaxy.ansible.com/ui/collections/

The following *Figure 3.2* shows the list of available modules of Ansible on Ansible Galaxy:

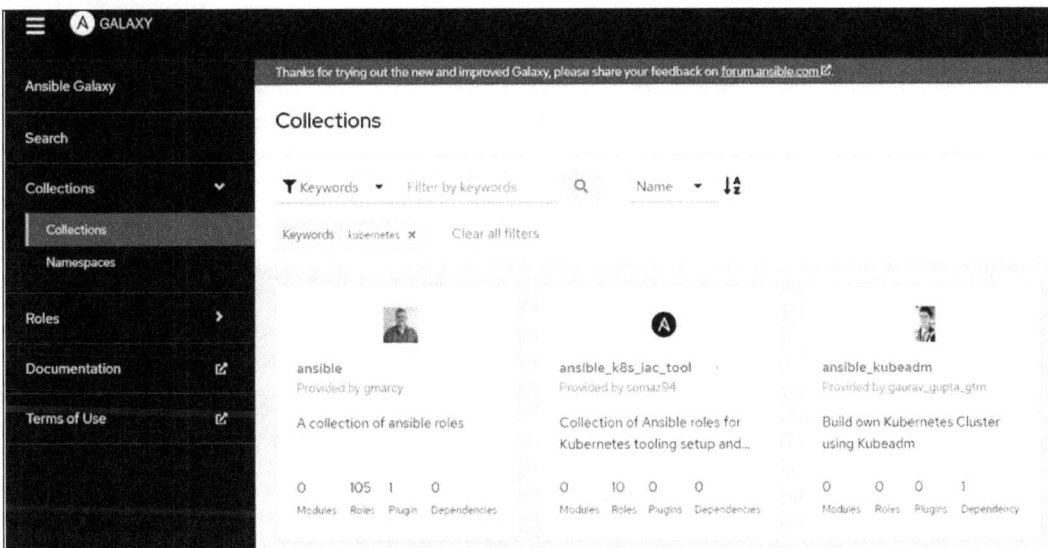

Figure 3.2: List of modules of Ansible on Ansible Galaxy

Now, if we have a requirement to use the cluster module of the Ansible Galaxy collection, then we can easily search the cluster modules in the search window (*Figure 3.3*).

Once the search is complete, you can click on the module, and this is what it will look like. The install page gives you good information about the installation process:

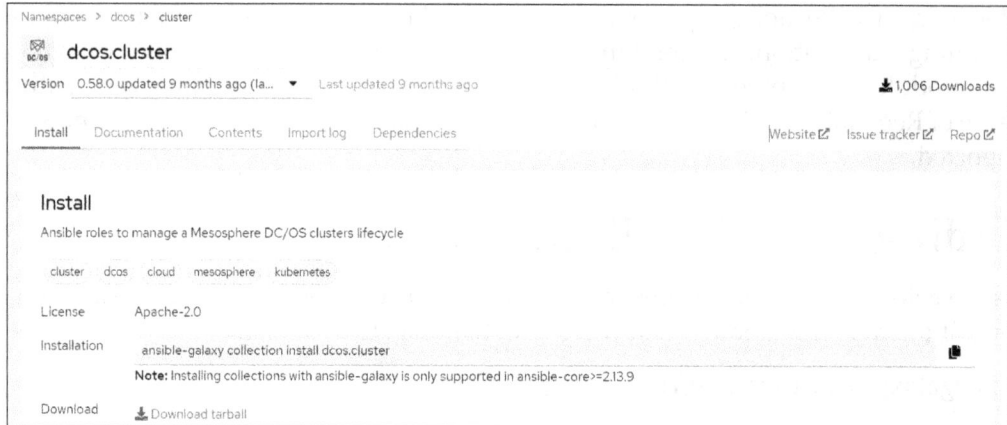

Figure 3.3: Search result for the cluster Ansible modules

Now, we have located the Ansible collection we need to know how to install the Ansible collections.

The best way to install the Ansible collection is using `ansible-galaxy`.

Ansible Galaxy

Ansible Galaxy is basically a public repository of Ansible roles. Any new Ansible collection can be downloaded and installed using Ansible Galaxy. Whenever we use `ansible-galaxy collection install nameofcollection` it will search for the collection on its default Galaxy server. It downloads and installs the collection from the Galaxy server. The default galaxy server is **https://galaxy.ansible.com**. If we want to modify the default server to GitHub, that is achievable as well.

To install the collection hosted in Ansible Galaxy:

`ansible-galaxy collection install nameofcollection`

To upgrade any of the **collection** to the latest, use the following syntax:

`ansible-galaxy collection install nameofcollection–upgrade`

Now, this is going to install the latest version of the **collection**. If you want to install the old version of the **collection**, we need to use the following commands:

`ansible-galaxy collection install nameofcollection:==2.2.1-beta.2`

The preceding example will install the **2.2.1-beta.2** versions of **collection**. This is how we need to define our version in **ansible-galaxy** syntax. If your version is 6.2, then use the 6.2 in the place of **2.2.1-beta.2**.

The collection is not the only thing we can install using Ansible Galaxy. We can also list and install the roles using Ansible Galaxy. Ansible Galaxy can help you auto-create the role structures.

Let us learn how to list down the existing installed roles in the following points:

- To display the list of installed roles:

  `ansible-galaxy list`

- To remove an installed role:

  `ansible-galaxy remove <name of the role>`

- To create the folder structure of the role:

  `ansible-galaxy init <Name of the Role>`

`ansible-galaxy init` is the one command we will be using most frequently. Let us understand what it does. `init` command basically creates the basic skeleton based on the default template included with Ansible.

Ansible loops

Just like any other programming language, Ansible also supports loops. Ansible offers loops to execute the task multiple times. `with_<lookup>` and `until` keywords are also available in our arsenal.

Now we need to understand that the `with_<lookup>` is an old feature; however, it is not yet deprecated. Ansible loop was introduced in Ansible version 2.5. If you are new to Ansible, you should be focusing on the loop rather than `with_<lookup>`.

We will discuss the loop and conditions in depth later in this book. We need to have a look at the syntax to understand it a little more, and we have not started to work on the syntax, hence, we will start having a look at the example later in this book.

Ansible conditions

Just like any other programming language, Ansible also supports conditions. If you do not know them, then let me explain you the same with a very good example.

When we all were kids, our fathers used to tell us they would do something great for us or buy us something great if we get good grades/marks in the school. Else we will be grounded /punished for not studying hard.

This is known as an if-else statement in programming languages:

```
If (we get good marks):
    We get goodies
Else:
    We get yelling from parents
```

Now, we do not have this if else statement named as if statement in Ansible. We have something like it in Ansible, which is known as the `When` statement.

What does the **when** statement do? Well, let us go back to the old example of goodies. In **when** statement, our parents tell us what we will get when we get good marks in exams. They do not give us the else option where we get all the yelling. It is not that great if you only get the good thing and do not worry about what else is going to happen. Let us try to write this in simple code, and then we will write it in the Ansible format:

```
Name: Offer from Parent
We get goodies from parents:
When: If we get good marks
```

Since we have gone through the simple real life example, let us learn how we can do it in Ansible:

```
tasks:
- name:Disable the Firewall Rule
  ansible.builtin.command: /usr/sbin/ufw disable
  when: ansible_facts['os_family'] == "Ubuntu"
```

In this example, please ignore the line tasks; we will cover that later. The second line is **name**, and really that is just the name of the code we are creating. The third line is **ansible.builtin.command:** this is an Ansible module for sending commands to the Linux hosts. The **/usr/sbin/ufwdisable** is a syntax for disabling the firewall in an Ubuntu host. However, there is a catch in the fourth line, which says when you need to do it. Basically, we had written a condition which checks the OS of hosts (**ansible_facts['os_family'] == "Ubuntu"**). If the version is Ubuntu, then the firewall will be disabled. Since we have not learned anything about the Ansible modules' usage, this might look a little cryptic to you. Let us simplify this.

The following lines are just an example created for you to understand it easily. The code is exactly like what we have used previously:

Example:

Note: **Syntax is wrong, it is just created to explain the when condition to you.**

```
Task:
  -name: Disable the firewall Rule
  Ufw disable
  When: If the firewall OS is Ubuntu
```

So, Ansible will check for the server OS, and if that is Ubuntu, it will disable the firewall of that Ubuntu Host. If it is any other OS, then it will skip the task and move to the next host in the inventory/host file.

In the given example, Action is disabled; the firewall and condition are where the OS is Ubuntu.

In our first example, we have taken Ansible facts in the consideration. Now you might be wondering what that is. If we want, Ansible can gather the basic information about the target host like IP address, OS information, BIOS information and even hardware information of the target host. We will talk about that in details further but for now just think of it as your helper who gathers all required information about the target host.

In our case, it helped us by providing the OS information of the target host, and we had configured the action according to the OS information.

However, Ansible fact is not the only thing we can put in the **When** statement, if we want, we can register the output of the last task and save it in a variable. Now we can call that variable in our next task.

What if we have a list of the variables, and we want the **When** statement to match any of those variables?

Do not worry, we can do that too. We can call any of the variables stored in the variable file in the when statement. Now, how do we define a variable in Ansible? Let us learn that.

There are a few main ways of defining the variables in Ansible. We will cover them one by one.

Ansible variables

Ansible variables are values that change based on the condition defined.

Defining variable

The first thing that will come to your mind is, what is a variable? Well, in programming languages, a variable is a value that changes based on some condition.

Suppose you want to perform configuration of some target Linux host. You have the task of installing the Apache server and hostname configuration. Apache server download, and installation process is going to be same, however there will be some changes in system hostname. In this situation variable will be useful. We can use **hostvars** to be specific.

Valid syntax for defining variables

There are some rules which we need to take care of, while defining our variables. A variable should always start with a letter. Variable should be letters, numbers, and underscores only. Anything other than that is not a valid variable.

Example of valid syntax:

```
Demo_variable, Demo_vars, Demo123
```

Example of invalid syntax:

```
123, wrong-demosyntax, demo.syntax, wrong syntax
```

The good news is that YAML supports the dictionaries as well. It means that the key to value is totally valid in Ansible. Let us have a look on the syntax and how can we call that.

Example: The way to define the variables:

```
Demo:
  Example1: one
  Example2: two
```

The way to reference the values in dictionaries:

```
Demo.Example1
```

Alternative way is as follows:

```
Demo['Example2']
```

Variables defined in the playbook

The variables can be directly defined in the playbooks themselves. There are many other options to define the variable, but the easiest one is to define it in the playbook itself, as follows:

```
- hosts: Apachserver
  vars:
    http_port: 443
```

Variables defined in the inventory

If we talk about the industry standards, then Variable defined in the inventory can be considered as best practice. Now, we can define the variable in the inventory in the following two ways:

- Host variable
- Group variables

Host variable

When we create inventory and mention the IP address/DNS of target host; that is not the only thing we can do with the inventory. We can also define the variables very next to it. When we define variable specific to a host, that is known as host variable.

For example:

```
[WEBSERVER]
WEBDEMO1 http_port=80
WEBSERVERhttp_port=403
10.10.10.1 user_name= Demouser
```

As we can see in the preceding example, every host has its own variable defined. For example, 10.10.10.1 has a username defined as a variable.

Group variable

When we apply the variables to an entire group, that is called a group variable. Let us consider another example and understand it.

Example:

```
[WEBSERVER]
WEBDEMO1
WEBSERVER
10.10.10.1
[WEBSERVER:vars]
ansible_user= Demouser
http_port=443
ansible_ssh_pass=youknowmypassword
```

Never store the password in clear text. Always use the Ansible Vault to secure the password. We will learn how to store the password in Ansible Vault and call the password in our playbooks.

In the given example, we have created a group that contains the IP address/DNS of all the target hosts or servers. Then we have defined the variables for that group. Now we can call that variable in our Playbook and task.

Variables defined in the roles

When we create the Ansible role using Ansible Galaxy, we will automatically create a directory under roles/vars. This vars directory will contain the file named as `main.yaml`. Where we will define the variables, this is another way of defining the variables in Ansible.

When we will create our first role, we will have a look on the variable structure too at the same time.

Since we are talking about the variables, we should have a look at some of the important SSH parameters and how to define them. They are as follows:

- **ansible_host**: The name of the host to connect to if different from the alias you wish to give to it.
- **ansible_port**: Communication port if not 22.
- **ansible_user**: The default username to use.
- **ansible_ssh_private_key_file**: Private key file used by SSH.
- **ansible_ssh_common_args**: This setting is always appended to the default command line for **sftp**, **scp**, and **ssh**.
- **ansible_ssh_extra_args**: This setting is always appended to the default SSH command line.

We need to use the preceding names to set up the variables for the few frequently used default settings.

Frequently used Ansible modules

We have many modules in Ansible. We cannot cover all of them here in this single book. However, there are a few very frequently used modules that everyone needs to learn. Let us start with the one which we have used and talked a little about in this chapter only.

Ansible facts

With Ansible, we can gather some useful variables containing the information about the target host or even about the localhost/control machine too. Variable related to the remote hosts are called **facts**. So, let us focus on the target host/managed nodes for now.

Ansible facts are data related to the remote system including the IP address details, OS, BIO, and hardware information. We can access the data in the Ansible facts variable. The best way to learn the Ansible facts is by debugging the facts.

The following is the task to print the Ansible facts on the terminal. You will need the entire playbook to execute this; without playbook, it will not be of any use.

Example:

```
- name: Deubug the variables
  ansible.builtin.debug:
    var: ansible_facts
```

Even **ansible_facts** is a very useful tool for an engineer. However, if you do not want it, you can disable it:

```
- hosts: Webserver
  gather_facts: no
```

This **gather_facts:no** will stop Ansible from gathering information about the target host.

Adding the custom facts is also possible, and we can do that easily.

Magic variables

Variable related to the Ansible are called magic variables. We can access the information about the Ansible operation, the host and groups in the inventory and the directories for playbooks and roles, using magic variables. Magic variable names are reserved, do not set variables with these names. The variable environment is also reserved.

The most used magic variables are **hostvars**, **groups**, **group_names**, and **inventory_hostname**. With **hostvars**, you can access variables defined for any host in the play, at any point in a playbook.

Registering variable and debug modules

Registering the variable and using that in the code later will be your very frequent task, and learning that is important. There will be many occasions when you will try to save the output of any command in a variable and use that later in a condition. Let us assume you want to print the uptime of a device. Now this will be very useful and easy for you to achieve. We all know **uptime** is a command to check the uptime of a Linux host. However, this command will be directly executed in the target host, and you will just receive the successful execution (Message will be different. It is just for explaining the students) message on the terminal. We will need another module to print out the uptime command's output on the terminal.

The first thing we need to do is register the output of the command in a variable named as **demooutput**. Once the output is saved in variable, we will use the **debug** module to print the variable content on the terminal.

In this example, we have used the **shell** module to log in to the target host and run a command **uptime**.

In the third line, we have used the option of debug module to save the output of the **uptime** command.

In the fourth line we have used the **debug** module and in the fifth line we have used its **msg** option of debug module to print out the content of the variable.

Example:
```
- name: Gather the Uptime of device
  shell: uptime
  register: output
- debug:
    msg: "{{output.stdout_lines}}"
```

Copy module

Ansible copy module will be another widely used Ansible module. We will use it to copy the content from local host to a location on the target host.

We need to note one thing here. We can use the copy module to copy the content to the remove host and not from remote host to the local host. If we want the files to be copied from the remote host to the local host, then we need to use the fetch module.

Now, you might be wondering if this is the tool for copy in both Linux and Windows, but that is not right. Copy module is not operational on the Windows host. That is specific to the Linux hosts only. If we want to copy the files to the Windows hosts, then we need to use the win copy module.

The following is the sample code in which the Ansible script will take a backup of the **Ansible.cfg** file.

Example:

```
- copy:
    src: /etc/ansible/ansible.cfg
    dest: ansibleconfigbackup.txt
```

There is a lot more offered by the **copy** module. We will go through them by example soon in our demo.

Conclusion

In this chapter, we have learned the basics of Ansible and its most useful components. If you still have any confusion, we suggest that you go through the concept again as getting strong foundation is very important for learning any new language or automation tool. We have also focused on few very important and widely used modules of Ansible.

In the next chapter, we will begin our hands-on experience. We will begin with very basic stuffs like creation of tasks, roles and playbook and then deep dive into different features of ansible.

References

- **https://docs.Ansible.com/Ansible/latest/network/getting_started/basic_concepts.html**
- **https://docs.Ansible.com/Ansible/latest/cli/Ansible-console.html**
- **https://www.digitalocean.com/community/tutorials/how-to-define-tasks-in-Ansible-playbooks**
- **https://docs.Ansible.com/Ansible/latest/user_guide/playbooks_vars_facts.html#information-about-Ansible-magic-variables**
- **https://www.Ansible.com/blog/getting-started-with-Ansible-collections**

Join our Discord space

Join our Discord workspace for latest updates, offers, tech happenings around the world, new releases, and sessions with the authors:

https://discord.bpbonline.com

CHAPTER 4
Creation and Execution of Ansible Playbooks

Introduction

We are finally in the stage where some real hands-on starts. In this chapter, we will start by creating our roles and playbooks, then we will execute our first ever Ansible code. Once the execution is completed, we will analyze whether it failed or was successful. We will also try to dig into the output.

Structure

The following topics will be covered in this chapter:

- Creating Ansible roles
- Using Ansible Galaxy to create roles
- Defining the target host in Ansible
- Sample host file
- Creating our first playbook
- Output walkthrough
- Troubleshooting and using debug in playbooks
- Defining Ansible.cfg file

Objectives

In this chapter, we will begin by understanding the structure of roles. By the end of this chapter, you will learn how to create the roles and playbook. We will understand how to define the variables in the playbook and parse them in our code. We will begin our journey of executing real Ansible playbooks.

Creating Ansible roles

Ansible has multiple ways of creating roles and tasks. We can either define the tasks directly in the playbook or we can create a role and use the roles option in the playbook. Both of these ways are correct. However, defining a role is the standard industry way of creating Ansible playbooks. A role can be reused with a lot more convenience. However, these are not the major advantages of roles. The biggest advantage of roles is that they automatically load related vars, files, tasks, handlers, and other Ansible artifacts when we use roles. It does so, based on the pre-defined/well-known file structure. Let us define that structure in the next section, so it is easy for us to understand:

Role structure

The following is the role structure for Ansible:

```
roles/
    common/                 # this hierarchy represents a "role"
        tasks/              #
main.yml#  <-- tasks file can include smaller files if warranted
        handlers/           #
main.yml#  <-- handlers file
        templates/          # <-- files for use with the template resource
            ntp.conf.j2   # <------- templates end in .j2
        files/              #
            bar.txt       # <-- files for use with the copy resource
            foo.sh        # <-- script files for use with the script
resource
        vars/               #
main.yml#  <-- variables associated with this role
        defaults/           #
main.yml#  <-- default lower priority variables for this role
        meta/               #
main.yml#  <-- role dependencies
        library/            # roles can also include custom modules
module_utils/      # roles can also include custom module_utils
lookup_plugins/    # or other types of plugins, like lookup in this case
```

Now, one might get confused with the number of directories and files. However, for now, we will just focus on the directory and file from the next section.

Roles/tasks/main.yaml

Roles/tasks/main.yaml is the path where we write our actual commands and code.

In this **main.yaml** file of your role, we will specify what module we want to use. This is the location where we will write all the commands we want to push onto our target host. If we have some conditions, like when (discussed later on in this chapter), then we will define them here.

Let us have a look at the manual way of defining the role in Ansible:

1. Navigate to the **/etc/ansible** directory. This is the home directory of Ansible, which contains the directory named roles. We need to change the directory and navigate to the roles. Once we do that, we will be in the path **/etc/Ansible/roles**.

2. Now we need to decide on a name for our role. We can name it **demorole**. We need to use the simple **mkdir** to create a directory named **demorole**.

3. Navigate to the newly created demorole using the **cd** command and create a directory named tasks. Navigate to the tasks directory.

4. Now your directory should look like **/etc/ansible/roles/demorole/tasks**. Now, here we will create a YAML file named **main.yaml,** and there we will write our code.

5. Use simple **vi main.yaml** to create the file and save it.

Now, our Ansible role is ready to be called on any target host. Let us have a look at some real examples of roles:

Modify the file **/etc/Ansible/roles/demorole/tasks/main.yml**:

```
---

# tasks file for demo role

- name: Run first command to check the uptime of localhost

  ansible.builtin.shell: uptime
```

Figure 4.1: Role to check the uptime of the target host

If we take a look at the preceding code, we have three dashes in the beginning, which is how any YAML code will start. The next thing is a comment that can be anything we want to write, and we can skip that, too. The third line we see there is the name we want to give our code.

The fourth line is very important, **shell** is the name of the module for the Linux hosts. The **uptime** is the command we want to run on our local host or target host. Now, if you have a Linux host, then you can use this shell module without any hassle. We just need to change the command from uptime to something else we want to run on the host. For example, you can run the **ansible --version** command on the target host, and Ansible will give you the output. (Right now, this command will be only executed on the target host output will not be visible unless you use the debug module.) We will need to add some additional configuration to print the output of this command. Let us have a look at that additional configuration:

```
---

# tasks file for demorole

- name: Run first command to check the uptime of localhost

  ansible.builtin.shell: uptime

  register: variabledemo

- debug:

    msg: "{{variabledemo}}"
```

Figure 4.2: Role with register and debug module

The code you see in the bold letters is already written by us to run a code on the target host to print something on the terminal. We need to use two additional modules:

The first module is the **register**, and the second module is the **debug** module.

The work of the **register** is to save the output of the uptime command into the variable. The name of the variable in the preceding example is **variabledemo**. Now, in the next line, we have called our next module, which is named as **debug** module. The next line contains the message we want to print on the terminal. In this case, we want to print the entire output of the variable.

Now, if you are seeing some old configuration in your organization, then you might see the shell module written as shown as follows. It is an old Ansible version that needs to be fixed and upgraded to the new code. However, that is totally supported in all the latest versions we have seen so far.

> Note: **Do not make any changes in the production servers without the change process and approvals or any other standard process being followed at your organization.**

```
---
# tasks file for demorole
- name: Run first command to check the uptime of localhost
  shell: uptime
  register: variabledemo
- debug:
    msg: "{{variabledemo}}"
```

Now, there is a lot more the shell module can offer us. For the latest information and the changes, we can check the following URL:

https://docs.ansible.com/ansible/latest/collections/ansible/builtin/shell_module.html

Similarly, we can also create a directory for the variables and define the variables too. As we learned in the last chapter, if we define the variables in the roles directory structure, then we do not need to define the source details of the variable, and it can be directly parsed in our code.

Just like we had created the task, we need to go ahead and create the variable directories **/etc/ansible/roles/demorole/vars**.

We need to create the file **main.yaml** in the vars directory, and then we can call the variable in the task. This is the file where we can define the credentials and the rest of the variables we want to use in our code.

Create the directories and YAML file. Manually create the entire branch for the Ansible role. However, this is time-consuming. What if there were a single command which could create the entire folder structure for us? One command that could have created the entire directory structure of tasks and variables, and the rest of the useful directories.

Using Ansible Galaxy to create roles

What if all the manual work you did to create the roles is not needed? We need one simple command to create the entire directory structure of the role. With the help of **ansible-galaxy** we can create the entire directory structure in just one simple command. Let us have a look at the following example and learn what it does:

```
ansible-galaxy init Demorole
```

This one simple command creates the entire directory structure for us. All the tasks' vars handlers and all the directory structure will be automatically created for us. What we need to do is just start modifying the **main.yaml** (Actually **/etc/ansible/roles/Demorole/tasks/main.yaml** for creating the tasks in the role) file them.

Let us have a look at how we can do so:

1. First thing we need to do is to navigate to the directory roles.
2. The second command will be using the following command to create the directories:

Example:

```
[root@ip-172-31-18-94 roles]# ansible-galaxy init demorole
- Role demorole was created successfully
[root@ip-172-31-18-94 roles]#
```

Figure 4.3: Industry standard way of creating roles

Now, if you want to see what directory structure it has created, then we can use a simple tree command to see it. It will give us the information about all files, handlers, and tasks it has created on our behalf. We just need to navigate to that directory and start modifying the file. Always remember **ansible-galaxy** is the industry standard way of creating roles in Ansible. You will rarely see the unstructured Ansible role structure in the production environment. It will also create the empty **main.yaml** file for us, we need to modify that file and write our own code there:

```
[root@ip-172-31-18-94 roles]# tree demorole
demorole
├── defaults
│   └── main.yml
├── files
├── handlers
│   └── main.yml
├── meta
│   └── main.yml
├── README.md
├── tasks
│   └── main.yml
├── templates
├── tests
│   ├── inventory
│   └── test.yml
└── vars
    └── main.yml

8 directories, 8 files
[root@ip-172-31-18-94 roles]#
```

So, we have seen both methods of creating the roles. The first one is manual, and the second one is using Ansible Galaxy. Now, if we really want to skip the creation of roles, then we can do that and start writing the task directly in the playbook; however, that is not the industry standard. If we need to learn all things in Ansible, we will teach you how to create the playbook directly without roles later. However, for now, we should focus on mastering the industry standard methods of creating a playbook.

Defining the target host in Ansible

Ansible has multiple ways of defining the target host information. One of the easiest is the host file entry. The second way we can use is to define the host inventory file and call that in the playbook. However, let us focus on the host file for now and learn it.

The host file is a file where we define the target host information. We can define both IP address and **fully qualified domain name** (**FQDN**) in the host file. The beauty of the host file is that we do not need to call the host file in the playbook; it is picked up by default. Also, remember we do not need to define any path information for the host file (unless we modify the hosts file location or create a new one).

The default host file looks like the following sample host file. If we look at the default host file carefully, we can learn a lot about the host file.

Sample host file

In this section, we will look at a sample host file that we can easily get from various locations. It is important to understand the hosts file, as this will end up reducing your troubleshooting hours:

```
# This is the default ansible 'hosts' file.
#
# It should live in /etc/ansible/hosts
#
#    - Comments begin with the '#' character
#    - Blank lines are ignored
#    - Groups of hosts are delimited by [header] elements
#    - You can enter hostnames or ip addresses
#    - A hostname/ip can be a member of multiple groups

# Ex 1: Ungrouped hosts, specify before any group headers.

## green.example.com
## blue.example.com
## 192.168.100.1
## 192.168.100.10

# Ex 2: A collection of hosts belonging to the 'webservers' group

## [webservers]
## alpha.example.org
## beta.example.org
## 192.168.1.100
## 192.168.1.110

# If you have multiple hosts following a pattern you can specify
# them like this:

## www[001:006].example.com

# Ex 3: A collection of database servers in the 'dbservers' group

## [dbservers]
##
## db01.intranet.mydomain.net
## db02.intranet.mydomain.net
## 10.25.1.56
## 10.25.1.57

# Here's another example of host ranges, this time there are no
```

```
# leading 0s:
```

```
## db-[99:101]-node.example.com
```

Example 1: Default host file

The following example has two FQDNs and two IP addresses defined. This is how we can define the target Web and DB servers in our host file. Remember, they are not hashed when we defile them in the hosts file. If we put a hash(#) in front of them, then they are commented and not considered as any IP address or FQDN, or hostname.

```
web011.bpbonline.com
db12server.bpbonline.com
```

It is possible to directly use the IP address information in our host file if we do not have an FQDN. If the target host's IP address is 10.10.20.4, then it can be defined in our host file:

```
10.10.20.4
```

Example 2: Where we have a group of servers

The following example has a group of database servers and application servers. If we want to group the database servers together and call that group in the code (playbook), that is also possible. Just assume that you have some SQL vulnerabilities, and you need to patch the DB servers. Now, if you have a group already created for the DB servers, then you can use that and call that in our patch code. Let us have a look at ways of creating the group:

```
[webservers]
alpha.example.org
beta.example.org
192.168.1.100
192.168.1.110
[dbservers]
10.25.1.56
10.25.1.57
```

As you can see, we have created the first group as web servers and the second group as **dbservers**. Now we can directly call that group (webserver/dbserver) in our playbook. Commands or configurations will be executed in that group only:

```
Playbook Example:

---

- name: Getting Started First Playbook

  connection: local

  gather_facts: false

  hosts: dbservers

  roles:

  -  Demorole
```

Figure 4.4: Playbook with groups used for targeting specific hosts

Now, if we look at the example of playbook, then in the hosts field we see the **dbservers** group as our target host. So, in this situation, the role **Demorole** will be executed on the group **dbservers** only. In other words, it will be executed on the 10.25.1.56 and 10.25.1.57 since they are part of the group **dbservers** in the hosts file.

Example 3: Define the variables for a host specifically

Let us have a look at example 3. In this example, we will learn how we can define the variables for a host specifically. Let us assume you have a situation where the usernames are different for your target hosts. In this situation, the host variable will be a good option, and we can define it directly in the hosts file:

[ApacheServer]

192.168.1.12 ansible_user=demouser
192.168.10.2 ansible_user=newdemouser

Now, you might have different situations on a few occasions where you will have common users for a bunch of machines. For example, assume all SQL users have the username **mysqldemo.** In this situation, you need the variable assignment on the group level. So let us learn how that is done on the group level. Let us create a group named SQLServer for this demo. Now everything will be just like defining the host information. However, there will be a subgroup created for the variables.

Example 4: Common variables for the group of servers

As we said, there will be a subgroup created for the variables:

[SQLserver]

```
192.168.1.12
192.168.10.2
# Everything will be same till this point. Lets define the variable group
now for the SQLserver
[SQLserver:vars]
ansible_user=mysqldemo
```

This is how you can define the variable for the entire group of the target host.

The second option we have on the table is the creation of a custom host inventory. In the custom inventory, we define the same things. However, Ansible does not automatically fetch the data from it. We need to define the right path for Ansible to detect and use variables.

As we discussed earlier, we have two methods of defining the inventories. The first one is **initializing (INI)** file, and the second one is a YAML. As we know, all things in Ansible are written in YAML, so using a YAML file as an inventory is a common procedure. INI is another method of creating the inventory.

So far, we have used INI in our example. The same can be done in YAML as well. However, we need to take care of the right indentation in case of a YAML file.

Let us see an example here of a YAML inventory file:

```
Networks:
  hosts:
    Router01:
      ansible_host: 10.6.20.1
    Router02:
      ansible_host: 10.26.30.2
```

Figure 4.5: Example of YAML inventory file

If you see the preceding example, we have created a group named **Networks** where we have defined a couple of routers. Now, in the preceding example, we have created two aliases, named **Router01** and **Router02**. Inside those aliases, we have defined their IP address details. Alternatively, we could have directly defined the IP address. We can define more parameters like username and password as well here.

We simply need to add another line right below the **ansible_host**. For example, if you want to define the username for the router, then you need to use the keyword **ansible_user: Demousername**, and then mention the value. The example contains the username as **Demousername**.

As we have discussed a few times before, we need to define the right path for the custom inventory. Let us learn how to use the custom inventory at the time of playbook execution. Assume the inventory you created is named **Demoinventory**. If you want to use this inventory at the time of playbook execution, then we need to use the **-i** switch to call our inventory. So **Ansible-playbook** will be the keyword for the playbook execution,**-i Demoinventory** for calling the **demoinventory** in our playbook, and the name of the playbook (which is **demoplaybook.yaml** in our case).

So let us have a look at how we can run our playbook which contains the inventory named as **Demoinventory** and playbook named as **demoplaybook.yaml**:

```
ansible-playbook -i Demoinventory  -k Demoplaybook.yml
```

Figure 4.6: Ansible playbook execution

Remember, if you create the YAML inventory, then it will be **demoinventory.yaml** in the playbook with **-i** switch.

Creating our first playbook

Let us focus on the Ansible playbook and create our first ever playbook. There are multiple ways of creating a playbook, but let us start with the industry standard way of creating it. Since our main motive for learning Ansible is working in the industry and creating production code, we will focus on the production-ready code.

As mentioned before, roles and playbooks are the industry standard way of writing Ansible code. So, we will write our first code using the concept of role in our playbook. We have already learnt how to write the roles in Ansible. It is time to use that role in our playbook.

To create a playbook, we need to create a file named as **FirstDemoplaybook.yaml**.

The contents of the file **FirstDemoplaybook.yaml** are as follows:

```
---|
- name: Demo Playbook
    connection: local
    gather_facts: false
    hosts: all
    roles:
    -   Demorole
```

Figure 4.7: Playbook for execution

Let us try to decode each line one by one.

As we have discussed earlier, any of the YAML code starts with three dashes, and that is why you see the three dashes at the top:

The first line after the three dashes is the name of the playbook. This is optional and is not mandatory but industry standard:

```
-name: Demo Playbook
```

The next line is the connection where we have chosen the connection type as local. Connection is an Ansible plug-in that helps Ansible connect to the target host. As we all know, Ansible uses the **ssh** to connect to the target host in most cases, which makes **ssh** connection plugins obvious. The second option is **paramikossh,** and the third option is a local connection. However, Ansible is not limited to these three options. If we want, we can use custom plugins. For example, if you want to use the SNMP, then we can make that happen by dropping custom plug-ins into the **connection_plugins** dictionary.

The custom plug-in area much more advanced topic and is out of our syllabus. So, we will not deep dive into it. Since we want our first playbook to get executed on our control machine itself, we have used the connection type local. If we do not put the connection type as local, it will try the **ssh** on the target host and execute the thing there:

```
connection: local
```

Let us talk about **gather_facts** now. Gather facts are used for collecting all the information about the target host. It is very helpful once you get familiar with it. It gives us the information about the IP address, memory, host name, disk space, and a lot more, which makes our life much easier:

```
gather_facts: false
```

The next option is hosts. We always need to define where we want to run our code: Since we just have one host in my inventory, we have used all here. If you already have your groups created, you should use that. We have already discussed the hosts in much more detail:

```
hosts: all
```

The next line is roles. This is where we will define which role will be executed on our target host. In our example, **Demorole** will be executed on all the hosts. If we want more than one role to be executed, we can mention that right below **Demorole** with the indentation, as shown:

```
roles:
  - Demorole
```

If you want to execute two roles on all the hosts, then take a look at the following example. First, **Demorole** and then **Role2demo** will be executed:

```
roles:
  - Demorole
  - Role2demo
```

Let us take a look at the compiled code once again:

```
[ansible]# cat roles/Demorole/tasks/main.yml

---

# tasks file for Demorole
- name: Run first command to check the uptime of localhost
  ansible.builtin.shell: uptime

  register: variabledemo
- debug:
    msg: "{{variabledemo}}"
```

Figure 4.8: Role with register and debug module

The output for hostfile is shown as follows:

```
[ansible]# cat hosts
# Ex 1: Ungrouped hosts, specify before any group headers.
172.31.18.94
......
......
```

Output suppressed to keep it simple.

Note: In snapshots, the IP address might be different as we have multiple servers configured in the cloud.

Now, let us learn how to run this first playbook and understand the output after that.

TIP: Before we run the playbook and allow Ansible to connect to the target host, we need to manually perform the SSH connection once to every target. That will save the fingerprint of the target host, and we will not get the fingerprint error while running our playbook.

Execution command:

```
ansible-playbook FirstDemoplaybook.yaml -u ashutoshc -k
```

- **ansible-playbook:** A way of executing the Ansible playbook.
- **FirstDemoplaybook.yaml:** Name of the playbook we want to execute using Ansible playbook.
- **-u ashutoshc:** We use the **–u** switch to define the username.
- **-k:** We need to use the **–k** flags so our playbook will ask us for the password on the terminal. We do not want to put the password in the clear text on the terminal, which is where this option is helpful.

Now, as soon as we enter this command, there will be a prompt for entering password. As soon as the password is entered by the developer, the playbook execution will start, and we will see the output on the terminal.

We get the following output for the code:

```
[root@ip-172-31-18-94 ansible]# ansible-playbook FirstDemoplaybook.yaml -u
ashutoshc -k
SSH password:

PLAY [Network Getting Started First Playbook] *****************************
**************************************************************************
************************************

TASK [Demorole : Run first command to check the uptime of localhost] *******
**************************************************************************
************************************
changed: [172.31.18.94]

TASK [Demorole : debug] ***************************************************
**************************************************************************
************************************
ok: [172.31.18.94] => {
    "msg": {
        "ansible_facts": {
            "discovered_interpreter_python": "/usr/libexec/platform-python"
        },
        "changed": true,
        "cmd": "uptime",
        "delta": "0:00:00.013841",
        "end": "2022-11-06 07:24:34.353240",
        "failed": false,
        "rc": 0,
        "start": "2022-11-06 07:24:34.339399",
        "stderr": "",
        "stderr_lines": [],
"stdout": " 07:24:34 up 34 days, 11:51,  3 users,  load average: 0.05,
0.01, 0.00",
        "stdout_lines": [
" 07:24:34 up 34 days, 11:51,  3 users,  load average: 0.05, 0.01, 0.00"
        ]
    }
}

PLAY RECAP ****************************************************************
**************************************************************************
************************************
172.31.18.94                 : ok=2    changed=1    unreachable=0    failed=0
skipped=0    rescued=0    ignored=0
```

Since we have asked for the debug in our role, we are getting this output, but if we do not choose the debug option, then the output will be smaller. Let us modify the role as follows and see the output.

The code is as follows:

```
---

# tasks file for Demorole
- name: Run first command to check the uptime of localhost

  ansible.builtin.shell: uptime
```

Figure 4.9: *A Simple role that shares the uptime*

Let us run our playbook with this role:

```
[ansible]# ansible-playbook FirstDemoplaybook.yaml -u ashutoshc -k
SSH password:

PLAY [Network Getting Started First Playbook] *****************************
**************************************************************************
**************************************

TASK [Demorole : Run first command to check the uptime of localhost] *******
**************************************************************************
**************************************
changed: [172.31.18.94]

PLAY RECAP ***************************************************************
**************************************************************************
**************************************
172.31.18.94                : ok=1    changed=1    unreachable=0    failed=0
skipped=0    rescued=0    ignored=0
```

Now, if we see this execution output, the script was executed successfully, although the output of the command **uptime** is not visible to us on the terminal. However, the uptime command is still executed on the target host. The only difference is that this time, the output of that command is not captured. To display the content of command execution on the terminal, we need the register module and the debug module. Here, the register module captures the entire execution and saves it to a variable defined in the role. We will have a detailed look at the output of the playbook line by line. For now, we will focus on the **changed=1,** which means one change was performed on the target host, and **ok=1,** which means one task was attempted successfully but no changes were required. If you do not see any message such as failed or unreachable, then we are good so far in this execution.

Output walkthrough

In this section, we will focus on the Ansible playbook execution output and understand it line by line. It is very important for us to master the output so we can understand the real problem and fix it quickly. If we are unable to understand the execution output, then we will have a hard time working with Ansible. So, let us learn it line by line.

Let us start with the small output that came right after we executed our second playbook:

```
[root@ip-172-31-18-94 ansible]# ansible-playbook FirstDemoplaybook.yaml -u ashutoshc -k
SSH password:

PLAY [Network Getting Started First Playbook] ************************************************

TASK [Demorole : Run first command to check the uptime of localhost] ***********************
changed: [172.31.18.94]

PLAY RECAP ***********************************************************************************
172.31.18.94               : ok=1    changed=1    unreachable=0    failed=0    skipped=0
```

Figure 4.10: Ansible play execution summary walkthrough

The first line we see at the execution is **PLAY,** and right after that, we see the name we gave to our **PLAY**. The following screenshot is provided for your reference:

```
[root@ip-172-31-18-94 ansible]# cat FirstDemoplaybook.yaml
---
- name: Network Getting Started First Playbook
  connection: local
  gather_facts: false
  hosts: all
  roles:
  - Demorole
```

Figure 4.11: First playbook to refer the comments

The highlighted section is the name we see in the playbook output. So, if you have multiple **PLAY** created in your playbook, then this helps you understand which output belongs to which task or play.

The second line, shown in *Figure 4.10,* is an important one. This gives us information about the tasks being executed on the target host. Since we are using roles, it will give us the information about the role being executed. Just to make the output simple for everyone, the output has been divided into four different sections and named 1-4. We will discuss all four of these options in detail:

```
1    2                                        3
TASK [Demorole : Run first command to check the uptime of localhost]
changed: [172.31.18.94]
              4
```

Figure 4.12: Close view of execution output with details

Let us start with number 1:

- **Task**: It describes what is happening in a particular line. It starts with **TASK**, which means a task is being executed there.

- **Demorole**: Inside the **TASK**, the chosen role is **Demorole**. If you have multiple roles, then you will see multiple instances of these being executed.

- **Run first**: This is the name of the task/role we have assigned to our role. This helps us understand which task in the role is being executed. If you have multiple tasks in a role, then you will see multiple lines like this.

- **Changed**: Now, this means whatever execution we were trying to perform on the target devices was successful, and the modification has been performed. Sometimes we will see the OK option instead of changed, which means the changes that we were trying to push to the target host were already there. The third option will fail, which means the execution failed for some reason. We will look into it and then fix it later. In the output, just next to changed you will find an IP address too. That will be the IP address of the target host where the changes were performed.

The last line is **PLAY RECAP**. It is the summary of the entire playbook execution. It gives us information about the successful execution and failed tasks, as shown in the following figure:

```
PLAY RECAP **********************************************************************************************
172.31.18.94              : ok=1    changed=1    unreachable=0    failed=0    skipped=0    rescued=0    ignored=0
```

Figure 4.13: PLAY RECAP summary

Let us have a discussion on all the options we see here in the **PLAY RECAP**. The first thing we see here is the IP address of the target host. Next to that, we see seven options. If everything is great and working, then only the **ok** and **changed** fields will contain the numbers next to them. If you have two tasks to be performed on the target host and both were successful in their respective changes, then most of the time you will see **changed=2**.

If you realize any other option is getting into the picture, like unreachable, failed, rescued, or ignored, then that is a sign of a potential problem. We need to dive into the problem and fix it:

- **Skipped**: Skipped will come into the picture as soon as you start putting conditions into the role and tasks. For example, you have created a role that checks the OS information, and if the OS is Linux, it has to reboot the host, else it has to skip the step. Now, if the target host is Linux, then it will reboot the host, and you will see **changed** or **ok = 1**. However, if the host is Windows or any other OS, in that situation, this condition fails. Ansible will skip the task, and you will see the **skipped=1** for that target host.

So, this is how the output will look. Based on the number of hosts and tasks, you will see more tasks and more devices in the PLAY RECAP. However, the concept is going to stay the same.

Troubleshooting and using debug in playbooks

Now, let us go ahead with the alternative methods of creating the playbook. These are much easier but are not the industry standard. However, we will still learn it. We will also try to create some real-life problems we will face in the industry.

Now, most of the things are going to be the same in this example, except role. Rather than calling a role, we will write the tasks directly in the playbook:

```
---

- name: Network Getting Started First Playbook

  gather_facts: false

  hosts: Demoserver

  tasks:
  - name: Demo of Tasks

    ansible.builtin.shell: uptime
```

Figure 4.14: Playbook with a task in place of role

One more thing we want to change here is the host file entry. Now, we have another demo Linux host with me. So, this time, rather than using the local host, we will use the remote host and check the uptime of that. Also, remember that we have created a group of demo servers, which is why we have called the group **Demoserver** in our playbook, and not all hosts.

Remember, we have removed the **connection: local** line from the playbook as we want to run the commands on the target host. If you get confused someday, try running the hostname command using Ansible code; that way, it will be clear where this command is exactly running.

Hosts file:

```
# Ex 1: Ungrouped hosts, specify before any group headers.
[Demoserver]
172.31.27.184
```

Let us run it now. There is an intentional mistake in this case to show you the error. If you remember, according to the previous section, we need to initiate the manual connection to the target hosts before we start using Ansible, otherwise we will get the fingerprint error. So, let us do it without the connection initiation and see how the error looks.

There is another difference we will notice in this case. We will receive the output **failed=1** and not **changed=1**, since our playbook execution is going to fail.

```
[root@ip-172-31-18-94 ansible]# ansible-playbook SecondPlaybook.yaml -u ashutoshc -k
SSH password:

PLAY [Network Getting Started First Playbook] ************************************************

TASK [Demo of Tasks] ************************************************************************
fatal: [172.31.14.62]: FAILED! => {"msg": "Using a SSH password instead of a key is not possible because Host Key checking is enabled and sshpass does not support this. Please add this host's fingerprint to your known_hosts file to manage this host."}

PLAY RECAP ***********************************************************************************
172.31.14.62               : ok=0    changed=0    unreachable=0    failed=1    skipped=0    rescued=0    ignored=0
```

Figure 4.15: Error shown for troubleshooting

Note: The error message: **fatal: [172.31.14.62]: FAILED! => {"msg": "Using a SSH password instead of a key is not possible because Host Key checking is enabled and sshpass does not support this. Please add this host's fingerprint to your known_hosts file to manage this host."}**

If you take a look at the preceding error message, it clearly mentions the fingerprint requirement. The solution for this is an easy one. Add the host to the **known_hosts** file, initiate a manual connection, and add it permanently. That way, next time it will not give you an error. Let us do it together and see how the error message gets fixed:

```
PLAY [Network Getting Started First Playbook] ***************************************************

TASK [Demo of Tasks] ***************************************************************************
fatal: [172.31.27.184]: FAILED! => {"msg": "Using a SSH password instead of a key is not possible because Host
at's fingerprint to your known_hosts file to manage this host."}

PLAY RECAP ***********************************************************************************
172.31.27.184               : ok=0    changed=0    unreachable=0    failed=1    skipped=0    rescued=0    ignore

[root@ip-172-31-18-94 ansible]# ssh ashutoshc@172.31.27.184
The authenticity of host '172.31.27.184 (172.31.27.184)' can't be established.
ECDSA key fingerprint is SHA256:rNtbITPJ/O1OCRf5Y16bnT2VUW0jEBqsWGTUfiviGgY.
Are you sure you want to continue connecting (yes/no/[fingerprint])? yes
Warning: Permanently added '172.31.27.184' (ECDSA) to the list of known hosts.
ashutoshc@172.31.27.184's password:
Last login: Mon Nov  7 05:42:10 2022 from 117.212.229.157

       __|  __|_  )
       _|  (     /   Amazon Linux 2 AMI
      ___|\___|___|

https://aws.amazon.com/amazon-linux-2/
13 package(s) needed for security, out of 16 available
Run "sudo yum update" to apply all updates.
[ashutoshc@ip-172-31-27-184 ~]$
[ashutoshc@ip-172-31-27-184 ~]$ exit
logout
Connection to 172.31.27.184 closed.
[root@ip-172-31-18-94 ansible]#  ansible-playbook SecondPlaybook.yaml -u ashutoshc -k
SSH password:

PLAY [Network Getting Started First Playbook] ***************************************************

TASK [Demo of Tasks] ***************************************************************************
[WARNING]: Platform linux on host 172.31.27.184 is using the discovered Python interpreter at /usr/bin/python,
https://docs.ansible.com/ansible/2.9/reference_appendices/interpreter_discovery.html for more information.
changed: [172.31.27.184]

PLAY RECAP ***********************************************************************************
172.31.27.184               : ok=1    changed=1    unreachable=0    failed=0    skipped=0    rescued=0    ignore
```

Figure 4.16: PLAY execution after fixing the error

Now there are other ways of fixing this error. The solution is available in the error message itself, so consider this as your homework and find out all possible solutions.

Let us look at one more error message that you will get very frequently. Just read the error and try to understand the problem as shown in the following image.

Now, if you see the Play Recap, you will see one newer field getting active. Now it is **unreachable=1**.

```
[root@ip-172-31-18-94 ansible]#  ansible-playbook SecondPlaybook.yaml -u ashutoshc -k
SSH password:

PLAY [Network Getting Started First Playbook] ***************************************************

TASK [Demo of Tasks] ***************************************************************************
fatal: [172.31.27.184]: UNREACHABLE! => {"changed": false, "msg": "Invalid/incorrect password: Permission denied, please try

PLAY RECAP ***********************************************************************************
                            : ok=0    changed=0    unreachable=1    failed=0    skipped=0    rescued=0    ignored=0
```

Figure 4.17: Invalid password error snap for review

The majority of students would have figured out this problem, but if you have not, then it is due to the wrong password. Let us try to put a host in the **hostfile** entry, which is unreachable, and see what error we get.

Now, for this case, we have changed the IP address to 172.31.127.184. There is no host in the inventory that has this IP address. Practically speaking, this IP address is unreachable. Let us see how Ansible finds it out and what error message we get:

```
[root@ip-172-31-18-94 ansible]#
[root@ip-172-31-18-94 ansible]# ansible-playbook SecondPlaybook.yaml -u ashutoshc -k
SSH password:

PLAY [Network Getting Started First Playbook] ********************************************************************************

TASK [Demo of Tasks] ********************************************************************************
fatal: [172.31.127.184]: UNREACHABLE! => {"changed": false, "msg": "Failed to connect to the host via ssh: connect to host 172.31.127.184 port 22: Connection timed out", "unreachable": true}

PLAY RECAP ********************************************************************************
172.31.127.184              : ok=0    changed=0    unreachable=1    failed=0    skipped=0    rescued=0    ignored=0
```

Figure 4.18: Target host unreachable error with connection timed out

If you see the error, it shows connection timed out. Ansible keeps on trying to reach that target host for the next 10 seconds. If it does not find a reachable connection, it will give the error connection timed out and unreachable message. You might get this error message in slow networks, too, if you have a very high latency or lots of packet drops. The easy workaround can be modifying the timeout value from **Ansible.cfg** file. We will learn about it more in this chapter, but it is a fixable problem if you work in a slow environment.

Let us have a look at one more problem, which you will find in your real production environment. We have now modified the IP address back to the original operational IP address. The same can be found in the error message too:

```
root@ip-172-31-7-39:/etc/ansible# ansible-playbook -u ashutmch -k SecondPlaybook.yaml
SSH password:

PLAY [Network Getting Started First Playbook] ********************************************************************************

TASK [Demo of Tasks] ********************************************************************************
fatal: [172.31.14.62]: UNREACHABLE! => {"changed": false, "msg": "Failed to connect to the host via ssh: ashutmch@172.31.14.62: Permission denied (publickey,gssapi-keyex,gssapi-with-mic).", "unreachable": true}

PLAY RECAP ********************************************************************************
172.31.14.62              : ok=0    changed=0    unreachable=1    failed=0    skipped=0    rescued=0    ignored=0
```

Figure 4.19: Error for key based authentication enabled on target host

People working in the cloud environment have a very high chance of getting this error. If you see the error correctly, it is a prompting error of the public key. Yes, you are guessing it right, we have restored the key-based authentication.

Now, you might be seeking the solution too, here. The solution is simple, i.e., a key-based authentication using **Privacy Enhanced Mail (PEM)** file. On another machine, we will run the solution since we do not have PEM file saved for the existing host.

Handling of the private key is as easy as it was for the password method. The playbook execution command will be the same except **–k**. Since we are using a key-based authentication, we will use the key file with relevant options. **-k** option will be replaced with **--private-key** flags. With **-k** flags, we defined our password with a key-based authentication, and we will use a key file. So, let us see how the same is done in Ansible.

Command:

```
ansible-playbook SecondPlaybook.yaml -u ec2-user --private-key MtOWER.pem
```

In simple words, we are just removing **-k** and adding options for the **private-key**. The output of it working in the demo environment is as follows:

```
[root@ip-172-31-18-94 ansible]#  ansible-playbook SecondPlaybook.yaml -u ec2-user --private-key MtOWER.pem

PLAY [Network Getting Started First Playbook] ***********************************************************************

TASK [Demo of Tasks] ************************************************************************************************
[WARNING]: Platform linux on host 172.31.86.86 is using the discovered Python interpreter at /usr/bin/python, but future instal
https://docs.ansible.com/ansible/2.9/reference_appendices/interpreter_discovery.html for more information.
changed: [172.31.86.86]

PLAY RECAP **********************************************************************************************************
172.31.86.86               : ok=1    changed=1    unreachable=0    failed=0    skipped=0    rescued=0    ignored=0
```

Figure 4.20: Playbook summary with private key as authentication method

Let us focus on the debug now. Now, there are a few ways of debugging the code in Ansible. The first one we had already seen in our first ever Ansible playbook, where we saved the execution of the command in a variable and then debugged that variable. However, that is not an efficient way of working. It will not give us all the required details. Hence, let us learn the other ways of debugging code:

```
ansible-playbook SecondPlaybook.yaml -u ec2-user --private-key MtOWER.pem -vvv
```

Figure 4.21: Playbook with verbosity

The simplest way of debugging code is to simply enable the verbose mode while execution. The command is present above. If we want a more detailed level of debugging, we just put more verbose (-v) here to make it the next level of debugging.

The simplest way of debugging code is simply enable the verbose mode. The entire debug output is extremely detailed. The following is an important and relevant snippet from the output.

Command:

```
ansible-playbook SecondPlaybook.yaml -u ec2-user --private-key MtOWER.pem
-vvvv
```

```
[WARNING]: Platform linux on host 172.31.86.86 is using the discovered Python interpreter at /usr/bin/python, but future insta
https://docs.ansible.com/ansible/2.9/reference_appendices/interpreter_discovery.html for more information.
changed: [172.31.86.86] => {
    "ansible_facts": {
        "discovered_interpreter_python": "/usr/bin/python"
    },
    "changed": true,
    "cmd": "uptime",
    "delta": "0:00:00.040208",
    "end": "2022-11-07 08:10:12.142602",
    "invocation": {
        "module_args": {
            "_raw_params": "uptime",
            "_uses_shell": true,
            "argv": null,
            "chdir": null,
            "creates": null,
            "executable": null,
            "removes": null,
            "stdin": null,
            "stdin_add_newline": true,
            "strip_empty_ends": true,
            "warn": true
        }
    },
    "rc": 0,
    "start": "2022-11-07 08:10:12.102394",
    "stderr": "",
    "stderr_lines": [],
    "stdout": " 08:10:12 up 51 min,  1 user,  load average: 0.00, 0.00, 0.00",
    "stdout_lines": [
        " 08:10:12 up 51 min,  1 user,  load average: 0.00, 0.00, 0.00"
    ]
}

PLAY RECAP ***********************************************************************************************************
172.31.86.86               : ok=1    changed=1    unreachable=0    failed=0    skipped=0    rescued=0    ignored=0
```

Figure 4.22: Playbook execution summary with debug

This is how you debug in the case of Ansible.

Defining Ansible.cfg file

If you want to change any parameters of your phone, then you have the settings option for modifying any parameter of your phone. Just like your phone's settings, Ansible has its **own.cfg** file. From this location, you can modify multiple Ansible settings. You can change how Ansible behaves and modify the default behavior of Ansible using **Ansible.cfg** file. Since we started our hands-on, we have been using the hosts file present in our Ansible. As we know, that is the default hosts file. However, what if you do not want that to be your default Ansible host file? What if you want your custom file to be the default host file?

Well, for those kinds of changes, we have **Ansible.cfg**. That is not the only parameter we can modify using **Ansible.cfg**. We can also modify Ansible environment variables, command line options, and keywords too.

However, there are a few problems if we mess with the **Ansible.cfg** file directly. **Ansible.cfg** files are not specific to our playbook or code. Let us suppose you have a centralized control machine that is being used by the server team, the database team, and the application teams. The server team might want ten seconds of command execution time, but the database queries are huge sometimes. They might take forever to execute, which is why they want the longer timeout. Now, if we increase the timeout considering the database team, then it would affect the server team and the application teams too. Your application team might want things to wrap up as quickly as possible with fewer timeouts.

So, now you have one **Ansible.cfg** file and two teams who want different parameters for them. How do you fix it?

We have a fix for this problem. Ansible configuration considers the parameters from both the Ansible config file and environment variables. Now in **Ansible.cfg** file as well we have the precedence rule. Based on where the **Ansible.cfg** file is placed, it takes the precedence.

The highest precedence is given to the environment variables, and then to the **Ansible.cfg** file. (placed on a different location). Let us list it down from higher to lower precedence:

- Ansible configuration (environment variable)
- **Ansible.cfg** file in the current directory from where we are executing our code.
- **Ansible.cfg** file in the home directory. (**~/.ansible.cfg**)
- **/etc/Ansible/Ansible.cfg** file

So, if you are not using environment variables, then for your different teams, you can create different directories and place code along with the **Ansible.cfg** file. For example, the database team can create their own directory named **DBA** and consider that as their home directory. They can write all their playbooks there, create their own **Ansible.cfg** file, which will not affect the other teams. This way, they will be able to modify the timeout and all parameters, and at the same time, they will not affect the rest of the teams' code. Similarly, the server team can also create their own directory and name it whatever they want. Then they can place all their codes and **Ansible.cfg** file in that directory. Now their **config.cfg** file will not disturb the other teams. This is how you handle and manage the **Ansible.cfg** file.

Ansible.cfg has many parameters to modify. However, there are a few important things in **Ansible.cfg** file we need to focus on and have a look at it so we can work efficiently in the production environment.

Let us focus on a few very important things of **Ansible.cfg** file now, such as the important default directories.

Some basic default values are as follows:

```
[defaults]
# some basic default values...

#inventory       = /etc/ansible/hosts
#library         = /usr/share/my_modules/
```

```
#module_utils    = /usr/share/my_module_utils/
#remote_tmp      = ~/.ansible/tmp
#local_tmp       = ~/.ansible/tmp
#plugin_filters_cfg = /etc/ansible/plugin_filters.yml
#forks           = 5
#poll_interval   = 15
#sudo_user       = root
#ask_sudo_pass = True
#ask_pass        = True
#transport       = smart
#remote_port     = 22
#module_lang     = C
```

Now, most of these values and locations are important for the production environment. If you wish to use the custom inventory, you might wish to change the inventory location. You need to uncomment the inventory and give the right path. Similarly rest of the parameters can be modified. One of the important values we wish to highlight here is forks. Ansible initiates five concurrent connections for a single task. So, by default, Ansible targets five hosts together. If we want to modify this default behavior, we can change the forks to any new value we want. Suppose you have a huge environment, and you want Ansible to target 20 hosts at a time. You can change the forks to 20, and you are good to speed up the execution.

If Ansible does not get the SSH response for 10 seconds, then you will get the timeout error. In that situation, we can increase the timeout value:

```
# SSH timeout
#timeout = 10

# This controls the cutoff point (in bytes) on --diff for files
# set to 0 for unlimited (RAM may suffer!).
#max_diff_size = 1048576
```

Suppose you want to verify the current configuration against the old configuration and want to see the differences on the terminal. Generally, you will see the entire difference on the terminal, but if the output is huge, then you might want to adjust the **diff_size** here:

```
[paramiko_connection]

# uncomment this line to cause the paramiko connection plugin to not record
new host

# keys encountered.  Increases performance on new host additions.  Setting
```

```
works independently of the
# host key checking setting above.
#record_host_keys=False

# by default, Ansible requests a pseudo-terminal for commands executed under
sudo. Uncomment this
# line to disable this behaviour.
#pty=False

# paramiko will default to looking for SSH keys initially when trying to
# authenticate to remote devices.  This is a problem for some network devices
# that close the connection after a key failure.  Uncomment this line to
# disable the Paramiko look for keys function
#look_for_keys = False

# When using persistent connections with Paramiko, the connection runs in a
# background process.  If the host doesn't already have a valid SSH key, by
# default Ansible will prompt to add the host key.  This will cause connections
# running in background processes to fail.  Uncomment this line to have
# Paramiko automatically add host keys.
#host_key_auto_add = True
```

Now, if you want Ansible to automatically add the newly added host to the **known_host** file, then this is the location where you will enable that. You will get the answer to your homework here:

```
[persistent_connection]

# Configures the persistent connection timeout value in seconds.  This value
is
# how long the persistent connection will remain idle before it is destroyed.
# If the connection doesn't receive a request before the timeout value
# expires, the connection is shutdown. The default value is 30 seconds.
#connect_timeout = 30

# The command timeout value defines the amount of time to wait for a command
# or RPC call before timing out. The value for the command timeout must
# be less than the value of the persistent connection idle timeout (connect_
timeout)
```

```
# The default value is 30 second.
#command_timeout = 30
```

Sometimes, your command runs longer than you expect. For example, let us take the case of the backup of the device. In that situation, Ansible may need to wait for a longer duration than normal. **Persistent_connection** helps you manage those settings. If your command takes longer than 30 seconds, then modify the **command_timeout** value to a higher value. Similarly, if you want the connection to stay longer at the time of idle connection, then use **connect_timeout**.

You can even modify the color you want for your output. These settings are also available at the bottom of **Ansible.cfg** file.

Remember, if you want to change the parameters for all the users and all codes, then use **/etc/Ansible/ansibl.cfg** file. Else, you can create a custom directory and copy or create a new **Ansible.cfg** file there. Once you are done with the new directory, you can create your code (playbooks and ad-hoc commands) there and run it from there.

Conclusion

We have finally created our first playbook and executed it successfully. Then we had the playbook walkthrough, and towards the end, we looked at the execution result walkthrough. It is important to understand the execution output so we can troubleshoot it better. At last, we have gone through the **Ansible.cfg** file that helps us modify the default behavior of Ansible based on our requirements.

In the next chapter, we will learn more about Ansible and how we can use it to automate any of the cloud environments. We will begin with AWS and move on to Azure.

Join our Discord space

Join our Discord workspace for latest updates, offers, tech happenings around the world, new releases, and sessions with the authors:

https://discord.bpbonline.com

## CHAPTER 5

Automating AWS Cloud Provisioning with Ansible

Introduction

In this chapter, we will learn the working of Ansible with the cloud. We will begin our journey with one of the major players in the market, which is AWS. Ansible works well with the cloud platforms too. We will perform some hands-on labs in this chapter.

Structure

The chapter includes the following topics:

- Beginning cloud journey with AWS
- Defining Boto3
- User creation for our AWS authentication
- Ansible first ever AWS provisioning
- Frequently used modules for AWS cloud
- Playbook for end-to-end deployment

Objectives

By the end of this chapter, you will learn how to work with a cloud environment using Ansible. We will begin our journey from AWS, and then we will cover Microsoft Azure. By the end, you will be able to create a VM from scratch in AWS.

Beginning cloud journey with AWS

For most of the users, Ansible will work fine with AWS, but it might create an issue for some users. This section highlights something for those users. Ansible is written in Python. If you are familiar with Python and have worked with the cloud, then you might be aware of one thing, that is, *Boto3*. If you have not heard of it, we will talk about it right now.

Defining Boto3

Boto3 is the AWS SDK for Python. Boto3 is one thing that makes our life easy by integrating our Python world with AWS services. As mentioned earlier, Ansible is written in Python, and the Python world uses Boto3 to work with AWS. So, if boto3 is not installed in the control machine, with Boto3, then you will get errors, and your code will not run. To correct this, the first thing we need to do is make sure that we are with the Boto3-supported version of Python, and if your box is not running with Python, then you need to install that first. Here is the list of things you need to do to make Ansible work with AWS:

- Install the latest version of Python (Python 3.7 or later. It is suggested that you go with 3.7).
- Install Python **pip** on your control machine.
- Install Boto3 using **pip**.

Use the following command:

```
pip install boto3
```

Note: **If you are using pip2, then upgrade your pip to the latest version and use pip3 to install the latest version of boto3.**

Now that we are done with the minimum requirement of Python code for using our Ansible with AWS, we are good to proceed further in the concept of Ansible.

If you are familiar with AWS, then you might be aware of **identity and access management (IAM)**. IAM is a place where you define your users and the level of access they will have to your infrastructure. For example, if you have a new joiner in your organization, then you can offer them read-only access using IAM. If you want a DB engineer to just have access to their DB servers, then you can limit that using IAM. Now, since we will be interacting with AWS, we need to create an AWS account in IAM. Unlike normal web-based access to AWS, we will use Ansible to communicate with AWS and its services. Since we are using code to configure the AWS resources, we will need to give the programmatic access to our AWS user account.

The user will look like *Figure 5.1*, and it is named **AnsibleAWSDemouser**. Below the username, you will find the option **Select AWS access type**. In this field, we need to **Select AWS credential type**. It can be either password-based authentication or access key-based authentication. In our case, we have chosen **Access key – Programmatic access**. We need to make sure we select the appropriate authentication method based on our requirements while creating the user.

User creation for our AWS authentication

To create a user for our AWS authentication, follow these steps:

1. Let us create the user account for AWS authentication using IAM as shown in the following figure:

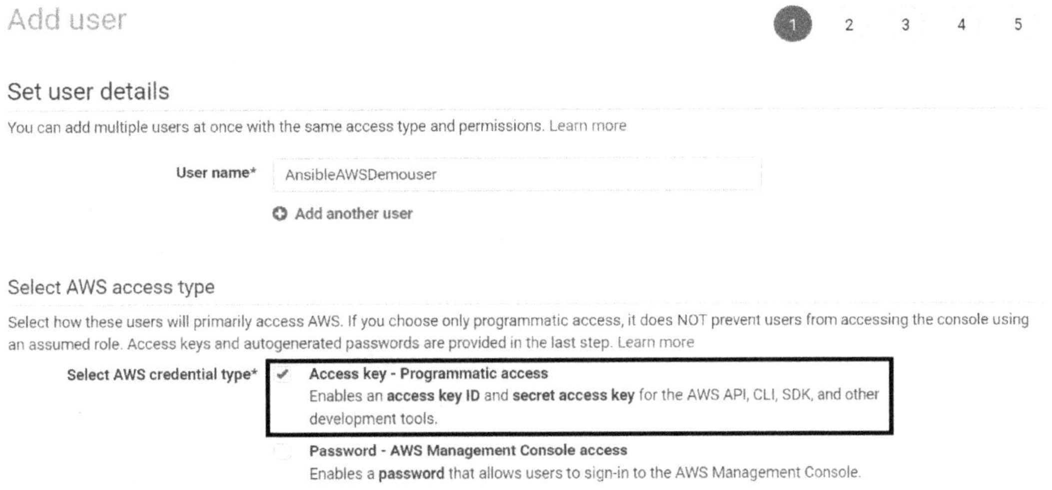

Figure 5.1: User creation process using IAM

2. Allocate some access to the user.

3. Now, we need to create the admin account since we will be managing many of AWS services. However, if you wish to limit the access to just EC2 or any other service, use the appropriate user group. For example, if you will be working on EC2 instances for most of the time, then you can allocate **EC2USERS** group to the user:

Add user

1 **2** 3 4 5

▾ Set permissions

Add user to group	Copy permissions from existing user	Attach existing policies directly

Add user to an existing group or create a new one. Using groups is a best-practice way to manage user's permissions by job functions. Learn more

Add user to group

Create group	⟳ Refresh

Q Search   Showing 4 results

	Group ▾	Attached policies
	abcde	AdministratorAccess
✔	Admin	AdministratorAccess
	EC2USERS	AmazonEC2FullAccess
	Group	AdministratorAccess

Cancel   **Previous**   **Next: Tags**

Figure 5.2: Admin access allocation

4 . We have skipped the TAG allocation process for now and moved to the 4th wizard tab as shown in the following figure:

Add user

1 2 3 **4** 5

Review

Review your choices. After you create the user, you can view and download the autogenerated password and access key.

User details

User name	AnsibleAWSDemouser
AWS access type	Programmatic access - with an access key
Permissions boundary	Permissions boundary is not set

Permissions summary

The user shown above will be added to the following groups.

Type	Name
Group	Admin

Tags

No tags were added.

Cancel   **Previous**   **Create user**

Figure 5.3: Review of user and access levels

5. Click on **Create User**. The following screen will appear:

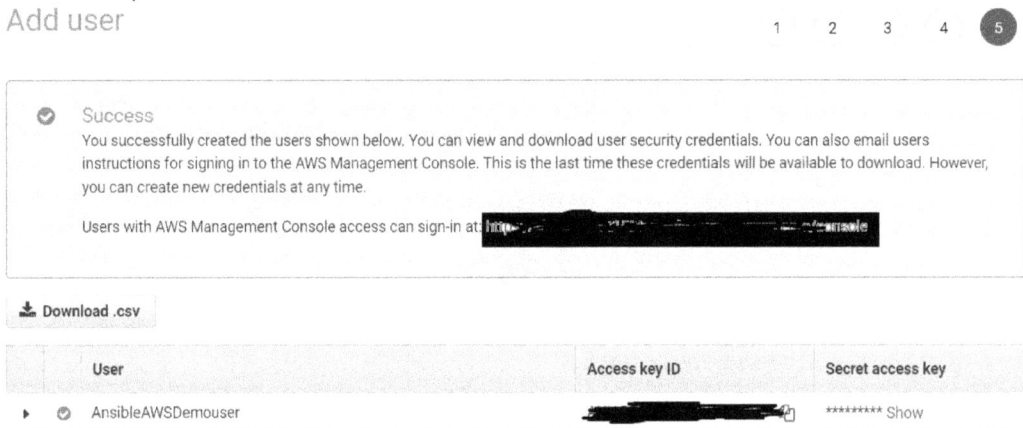

Add user

1　2　3　4　⑤

Success

You successfully created the users shown below. You can view and download user security credentials. You can also email users instructions for signing in to the AWS Management Console. This is the last time these credentials will be available to download. However, you can create new credentials at any time.

Users with AWS Management Console access can sign-in at: http████████████████████████████

⬇ Download .csv

	User	Access key ID	Secret access key
▶ ⊘	AnsibleAWSDemouser	████████████ 🗐	********* Show

Figure 5.4: Successful creation of access key and secret access key

6. Now you need to save this **Access key ID** and **Secret access key**. Alternatively, you can download the `.csv` and save it for later.

Now that you have your Ansible fixed for the AWS and your AWS credentials sorted, we are good to go ahead with the AWS using Ansible. Let us create our first-ever EC2 instance using Ansible.

First ever Ansible AWS provisioning

As we have fixed all the dependencies and created a user for logging into AWS, we can start with our first code. You can start with EC2, S3, VPC, or any other feature you like most. Now, remember the target hosts might change, but our basic concepts are going to be the same. In this situation, the target is a cloud platform, and to be specific, it is AWS. However, we need to stick to our concept of roles, playbooks, and variables.

Just like any other code, we will start by creating the roles where we will define our commands, and then we will create a playbook. So let us begin with our role. Note that Ansible is not limited to the creation of a few EC2 instances, but there is a wide range of things we can do using the Ansible EC2 instance. You can restart the instance, terminate it, reboot it, and do a lot more.

Now, there might be a few people who are still using the old version of Ansible and still want to install an AWS EC2 instance. For those users, please use the module given as follows. It will work for the new version of Ansible, too. However, we will focus more on the new modules. YAML role for the EC2 instance creation is as follows:

```
---
- name: AWS With Ansible EC2 Demo
  ec2:
    key_name: MyATower
    instance_type: t2.micro
    image: ami-0b0dcb5067f052a63
    region: us-east-1
    wait: yes
    group: CentOS 7 (x86_64) - with Updates HVM-CentOS-7.2009-20220825.1-
AutogenByAWSMP--1
    count: 1|
    vpc_subnet_id: subnet-01df03e7847aebce0
    assign_public_ip: yes
    aws_access_key: "{{ aws_access_key }}"
    aws_secret_key: "{{ aws_secret_key }}"


Ansible Variablee:
roles/AWSDemo/vars/main.yml
---
aws_access_key: "AKIARZP2ZHEUWNENDI5B"
aws_secret_key: "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"
```

Figure 5.5: Demo playbook for Ansible with AWS

Let us focus on each line one by one so that we can understand the code better:

- As we can see, we have offered the name to the task defined in the role. You can name it anything based on your task and the motive you want to achieve.

- **EC2** is a module name. We could have used any other module too, like **ec2_instance** or **amazon.aws.ec2_instance**. However, since we want to cover a wide audience, we have used the **ec2** instance here. As this is compatible with the new version of Ansible.

- **Key_name**: This is basically a key pair name we want to use to login into the device. If you do not have any key pair created already, then you need to create a new one and define that, otherwise you will be stuck with no access to the device.

- **Instance_type**: This is the place where we define the size of the instance. We have chosen **t2.micro** since that is free. However, if we have requirement of bigger instance based on your use case then we can select the bigger instance.

- **Image**: Here, we will define the AMI image ID. You should go to the EC2 dashboard and try to find out the AMI ID of the machine you want to run on your AWS.

  To find the various locations of AMI ID, refer to the following figure:

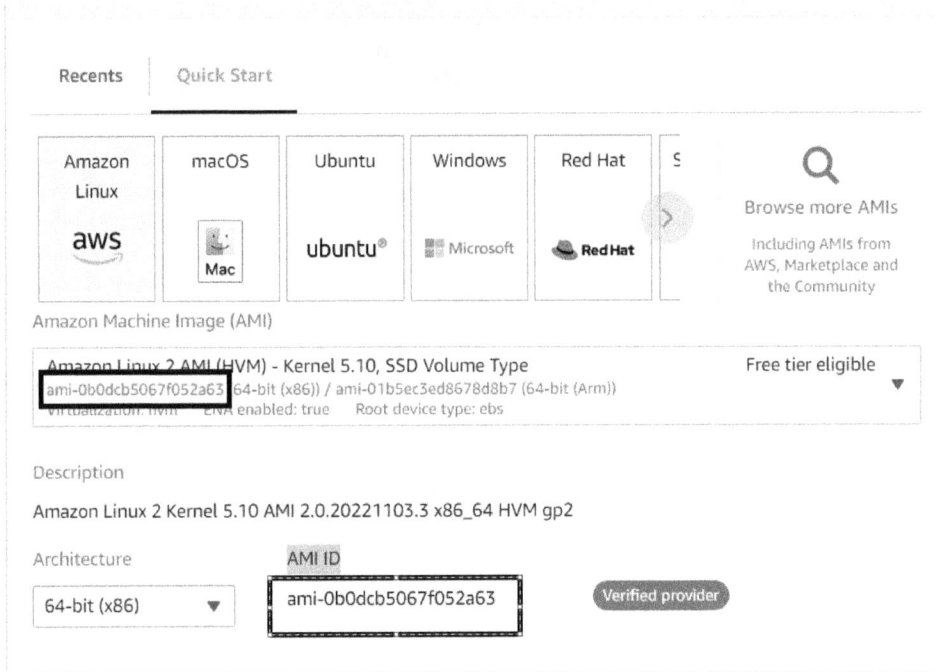

Figure 5.6: Finding the right AMI ID

- **Region**: Defining the region is very important here. We need to make sure we are selecting the right region and spinning the instances in the correct region.

- **Group**: This is where you define the name of the security group. Do not write the group ID here. We need to offer the name of the security group.

- **Count**: This is where we define how many instances we want to spin. If you want to run five instances, then you need to write 5 instances there.

- VPC subnet id is required in this tab. You might have bunch of the subnets in your VPC and you should select the correct subnet id for your instance.

- **assign_public_ip**: It is required at the end as we can see we have the option to assign the public IP address to the instance. If we do not want the public IP address to our instance we can select no.

Note: **The last two lines (11 and 12) would be weird for everyone. You might be wondering why we are defining the variables here in the task inside the Ansible AWS module. Unlike many other modules of Ansible, if you define the variables in the vars file, you still need to refer to them in each AWS module. If you have 10 AWS modules, then you need to do the same in all 10 of them.**

Now, let us go ahead and create our playbook:

```
[root@ip-172-31-91-70 ansible]# cat DemoAWS.yaml
# First ever Code of AWS using Ansible
- name: EC2 Instance Creation
  hosts: localhost
  roles:
   - AWSDemo
[root@ip-172-31-91-70 ansible]#
```

Figure 5.7: Our AWS playbook

Now, let us try to run our code and see the results:

```
[root@ip-172-31-91-70 ansible]# ansible-playbook DemoAWS.yaml

PLAY [Ansible test] ***************************************************************************

TASK [Gathering Facts] ***********************************************************************
ok: [localhost]

TASK [AWSDemo : AWS With Ansible EC2 Demo] *************************************************

changed: [localhost]

PLAY RECAP ***********************************************************************************
localhost                  : ok=2    changed=1    unreachable=0    failed=0    skipped=0    rescued=0

[root@ip-172-31-91-70 ansible]#
```

Figure 5.8: Summary of playbook execution

As we can see, the playbook execution was successful, and a new host has been created in the AWS console. We can also see that the new host is up and running; however, the status check is still in the initializing state. It was successfully created in the US-EAST-1 region, where we asked Ansible to create it. It has the public IP address assigned to it. You can see the proof of the same in the following figure:

	Name	▽	Instance ID	Instance state	▽	Instance type	▽	Status check	Alarm status	Availability Zone	▽	Public IPv4 DNS
☐	ControlMachin...		i-0dd21ff378ce87068	⊘ Running	⊕⊖	t2.micro		⊘ 2/2 checks passed	No alarms +	us-east-1c		ec2-18-212-173-
☐	–		i-0de46daae1089eb4e	⊘ Running	⊕⊖	t2.micro		⊘ Initializing	No alarms +	us-east-1c		ec2-100-26-201-

Figure 5.9: Status of EC2 instance launch

We can log in to the newly initialized host using the same **MyATower** security key that we defined in our code:

```
Using username "ec2-user".
Authenticating with public key "MyATower"

     __|  __|_  )
     _|  (     /   Amazon Linux 2 AMI
    ___|\___|___|

https://aws.amazon.com/amazon-linux-2/
19 package(s) needed for security, out of 31 available
Run "sudo yum update" to apply all updates.
[ec2-user@ip-172-31-93-126 ~]$ []
```

Figure 5.10: Successful login of the target host

So far, we discussed one way of creating our EC2 instance. Now, let us go ahead and jump into the latest modules of Ansible and use them to do something more.

Let us focus on the **ec2_instance** module for now. In our demo, we used this module for the creation of an EC2 instance; however, this module can be used to delete our instances. Let us use this module to delete the instance we created in the preceding demo:

```
[root@ip-172-31-94-253 bin]# cat roles/EC2Restart/tasks/main.yml
---
- name: launching AWS instance using Ansible
  ec2_instance:
    state: terminated
    instance_ids:
    - i-0ff4a97c827f0d0ed
    region: us-east-1
    aws_access_key: "{{ aws_access_key }}"
    aws_secret_key: "{{ aws_secret_key }}"
```

Figure 5.11: Role for terminating the EC2 instance

Since we now have some understanding of roles, we will not define the meaning of names and access/secret key in the code. However, let us focus on a few other things that might be new. Let us begin understanding our code from line three of the role:

- **ec2_instance**: As we have guessed it correctly, this is the name of our Ansible module. This is the latest version of the Ansible module, and this is not going to work on the old version of Ansible. If you have an old version of Python, you will face issues with it.

- **State**: State means what you really want to do with the instance. In this case, we wanted to terminate the instance, so we chose the option: terminated. If we wish to restart the instance, then we can use the restarted option. You might be wondering about the right syntax or keyword for any operation. We will explain all the options and what they are really used for.

  The options are as follows:
  - Present
  - Terminated
  - Running
  - Started
  - Stopped
  - Restarted
  - Rebooted
  - Absent

- **instance_ids**: **Instance ID** is nothing more than an ID of a running instance.

You can easily find it on the EC2 dashboard. Please find the example for your reference. We just need to copy the instance ID, and that instance will be taken into consideration of the action we asked our code to perform.

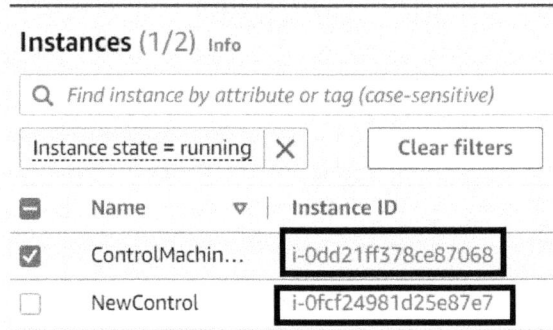

Figure 5.12: Finding the instance id from the EC2 dashboard

Based on our requirement, we can select the right option and proceed further with it. Let us take a look at the playbook and what it looks like:

```
[root@ip-172-31-94-253 bin]# cat Newtest.yaml
# EC2 Instance provisioning Demo
- name: Ansible AWS EC2 Instance Demo
  hosts: localhost
  roles:
  - EC2Restart
```

Figure 5.13: Our playbook for execution

So, as we can see, there is not much difference in the playbook. Remember that the target host is AWS, and it does not have any FIX IP addresses, so avoid putting the IP address of AWS out there. The target host will be localhost, which means that we need to put localhost in our host file or inventory and then refer to it in the playbook. The Ansible will execute the code locally and then use boto3 to communicate and execute the code on AWS.

Let us go ahead and execute our code and see the results:

```
TASK [Gathering Facts] ***********************************************************
ok: [localhost]

TASK [EC2Restart : launching AWS instance using Ansible] *************************
ok: [localhost]

PLAY RECAP ***********************************************************************
localhost                  : ok=2    changed=0    unreachable=0    failed=0    skipped=0    rescued=0
```

Figure 5.14: Playbook execution and play recap

From the execution summary, we can clearly see that the code executed successfully. Remember, when you try to remove the EC2 instance from AWS, it will be **changed=1**, since it will perform the changes and terminate the instance. In our case, we had already removed the instance, which is why it is showing **ok=2** rather than 1. When Ansible realizes that there is no need for any change in the target host, it simply gives us ok signal (**ok=1** for a task, **ok=2** for 2 tasks, and so on) and does not perform the changes once again. In other words, Ansible is much smarter that way.

Most of the Ansible commands behave this way, where they do not perform the changes if they are already present on the target host. For example, you wanted to install the Apache server on the target host. Ansible will first check whether Apache is already installed. If it is present, then Ansible will not perform the installation of Apache and gives us **ok=+1** at the end of the play recap. However, there are a few modules of Ansible that are not smart enough and might do the installation already present on the target host or configure a feature that is already there. The best thing to do is to test it in the lab environment and then run it in production.

Frequently used modules for AWS cloud

There are many Ansible modules in the market, and it would be difficult if we want to sort out a few of the most frequently used modules of Ansible because there are so many cloud profiles or job profiles in the market, and each person will have a different role and task in their job profile. For example, a software developer will use different features of AWS, and hence, they will need different tools and Ansible modules. Whereas, if we talk about a system engineer, they are focused on the EC2 instance. If you hire a security engineer, they will focus more on the DDOS protection and different firewalls in the AWS marketplace or even WAF.

The point is that each profile will have its own frequently used Ansible modules, and it is almost impossible to find and cover all of them in one. So, what we can do here is cover a few very important modules that are necessary to start our AWS journey. Now, that might not contain your daily need or frequently required modules, but the basic concept is going to be the same, just like we had created in our first-ever role and playbook. With the help of this, we can create any of the Ansible playbooks and roles. It will be just the target host that will change; the rest of everything is going to be the same. One more important thing we need to start doing is to understand the Ansible documentation of that module. As soon as you get familiar with them, you can do everything on your own.

So, let us get started. The first thing we need in our AWS cloud is a VPC. By default, you get a default VPC. However, many times that does not help. You might want to create your own VPC, network, and your own subnets. So let us start our work with the VPC creation. We will create a VPC, create a few subnets, create an internet gateway, and associate that IGW with the subnets.

Follow these steps to create an AWS VPC:

1. The name of the module is **ec2_vpc_net** for creating, managing and deleting any of the AWS VPC. It is very simple and easy to use, just like any other Ansible module.

2. Just like any other Ansible role, we will start this role with the **- - -** three dashes.

3. Just like a good developer who always provides a description to their code, we have provided a name to our role, and it is easy to analyze the output of Ansible if you have multiple tasks in your role.

We need to use the credentials for all the AWS Ansible modules, so they will be present here too, just like the last role.

EC2_VPC_NET module

So let us have a look at the code in *Figure 5.15*, where module **ec2_vpc_net** is used which will be used for creating, managing and deleting any of the AWS VPC.

```
---

# tasks file for NewVPC and we will run our first VPC from Zero

- name: Demo VPC

  ec2_vpc_net:

    name: BigNetwork

    cidr_block: 10.20.0.0/16

    region: us-east-2

    tenancy: dedicated

    aws_access_key: "{{ aws_access_key }}"

    aws_secret_key: "{{ aws_secret_key }}"
```

Figure 5.15: Role to create the CIDR block

Now go back to your CCNA days or your basic networking training. What does a network really need? Well, the first thing it needs is a lot of IP addresses. So we will define the CIRD block here in this role. Also, it is important to give names to your newly created VPC because the default is already lying there, and it will create confusion later. We need to define the region and the last tenancy. This is what we have done in this role:

```
[root@ip-172-31-94-253 bin]# cat roles/NewVPC/tasks/main.yml
---
# tasks file for NewVPC and we will run our first VPC from Zero
- name: Demo VPC
  ec2_vpc_net:
    name: BigNetwork
    cidr_block: 10.20.0.0/16
    region: us-east-2
    tenancy: dedicated
    aws_access_key: "{{ aws_access_key }}"
    aws_secret_key: "{{ aws_secret_key }}"
```

Figure 5.16: Roles to create a CIDR in AWS VPC

Now let us go ahead with the creation of a playbook. Basically, the playbook will be same just like the last one except the role name:

```
[root@ip-172-31-94-253 bin]# cat VPCTest.yaml
# EC2 Instance provisioning Demo
- name: Ansible AWS EC2 Instance Demo
  hosts: localhost
  roles:
    - NewVPC
```

Figure 5.17: Playbook with newly created role

Let us execute our code now. Remember you need to put your credentials in the variable files like secret key and access key, as we configured previously.

For your reference:

Ansible variable:

```
roles/NewVPC/vars/main.yml

---

aws_access_key: "AKIARZP2ZHEUWNENDI5B"

aws_secret_key: "gX8PGcY2rzqANo7vUISuj67I8wjdPWJEiwV5tSqg"

ansible_ssh_user: "ashutosh"

ansible_ssh_pass: "Somedummypassword4q234$55"
```

Figure 5.18: Defining the Ansible variables

If you notice the variable file correctly, we have defined the username and password too in the variable file, which means that now we do not need to type the password again and again.

Let us run our code and see the results:

```
[root@ip-172-31-94-253 bin]# ansible-playbook VPCTest.yaml
[DEPRECATION WARNING]: Ansible will require Python 3.8 or newer on the controller starting with Ansible 2.12. Current ver:
(Red Hat 7.3.1-15)]. This feature will be removed from ansible-core in version 2.12. Deprecation warnings can be disabled
[WARNING]: No inventory was parsed, only implicit localhost is available
[WARNING]: provided hosts list is empty, only localhost is available. Note that the implicit localhost does not match 'al

PLAY [Ansible AWS EC2 Instance Demo] ****************************************************************************************

TASK [Gathering Facts] ****************************************************************************************
ok: [localhost]

TASK [NewVPC : Demo VPC] ****************************************************************************************
changed: [localhost]

PLAY RECAP ****************************************************************************************
localhost                  : ok=2    changed=1    unreachable=0    failed=0    skipped=0    rescued=0    ignored=0
```

Figure 5.19: Playbook recap with no username and password options

We can see that the execution was successful and Ansible has successfully created a new VPC in the AWS US-EAST-2 region. Now, let us go back to the AWS console and see the results:

☐ DEMOVPC	vpc-0806cef13e8537715	⊘ Available	10.11.0.0/16
☐ BigNetwork	vpc-0e4b721fa054832e0	⊘ Available	10.20.0.0/16

Figure 5.20: VPC status after playbook execution

We can see the results here. The VPC with CIDR and name **DEMOVPC** is present on the console. However, why should you go to the console now? Should we not check it programmatically and verify it? Let us run another role where we will see the number of VPCs present in this region.

```
[root@ip-172-31-94-253 bin]# cat roles/NewVPC/tasks/main.yml

---

# tasks file for NewVPC and we will run our first VPC from Zero
- name: Demo VPC
  ec2_vpc_net_info:
    region: us-east-2
    aws_access_key: "{{ aws_access_key }}"
    aws_secret_key: "{{ aws_secret_key }}"
```

Figure 5.21: Role to view VPC and CIDR information

Let us run it and see the results. Remember, the code is not complete. We are not using the register and debug module here. You need to register the output of the command execution and debug the variable content on the terminal to see the VPC information. Alternatively, you can also use the verbose mode as follows:

[root@ip-172-31-94-253 bin]# ansible-playbook VPCTest.yaml–vvvv

Output suppressed is shown as follows:

```
},
"vpcs": {
    {
        "cidr_block": "10.11.0.0/16",
        "cidr_block_association_set": [
            {
                "association_id": "vpc-cidr-assoc-0205299cb6e799e4b",
                "cidr_block": "10.11.0.0/16",
                "cidr_block_state": {
                    "state": "associated"
                }
            }
        ],
        "classic_link_dns_supported": false,
        "classic_link_enabled": false,
        "dhcp_options_id": "dopt-e6fd268e",
        "enable_dns_hostnames": false,
        "enable_dns_support": true,
        "id": "vpc-0806cef13e8537715",
        "instance_tenancy": "default",
        "is_default": false,
        "owner_id": "123469379881",
        "state": "available",
        "tags": {
            "Name": "DEMOVPC"
        },
        "vpc_id": "vpc-0806cef13e8537715"
    },
    {
        "cidr_block": "10.20.0.0/16",
        "cidr_block_association_set": [
            {
                "association_id": "vpc-cidr-assoc-09bcd10a5fd5d9a32",
                "cidr_block": "10.20.0.0/16",
                "cidr_block_state": {
                    "state": "associated"
                }
            }
        ],
        "classic_link_dns_supported": false,
        "classic_link_enabled": false,
        "dhcp_options_id": "dopt-e6fd268e",
        "enable_dns_hostnames": true,
```

Figure 5.22: Playbook execution summary with output

As we can see, we are finding the output of two VPC here. The first one is recent, which was created right away, and the second one is the previousone.

Now, we can use the information from the debug output and use that as a variable in our further codes. We can copy the VPC id and use it in further configuration.

Do you want to see it in a real example? We will print the VPC ID on the terminal. We might need to go back and refresh our register and debug modules. If they are still fresh for you, then let us jump in. We will try to create a new VPC and then register the entire output in a variable named **subnetinfo** (it is just a name, you can keep it anything). Now we will use this variable and print out the content stored under this variable using our **debug** module. These are the changes that we have tested a few times already. Here is our code:

```
---
# tasks file for NewVPC and we will run our first VPC from Zero
- name: Demo VPC
  ec2_vpc_net:
    name: TinyNetwork
    cidr_block: 10.45.25.0/24
    region: us-east-2
    tenancy: dedicated
    aws_access_key: "{{ aws_access_key }}"
    aws_secret_key: "{{ aws_secret_key }}"
  register: subnetinfo
- debug:
    msg: "{{ subnetinfo }}"
```

Figure 5.23: Role with register and debug module

Let us run it and understand the output:

```
TASK [NewVPC : debug] ***********************************************************
ok: [localhost] => {
    "msg": {
        "changed": true,
        "debugging": {
            "expected_cidrs": [
                "10.45.25.0/24"
            ],
            "to_add": [],
            "to_remove": []
        },
        "failed": false,
        "vpc": {
            "cidr_block": "10.45.25.0/24",
            "cidr_block_association_set": [
                {
                    "association_id": "vpc-cidr-assoc-0b57f5817f68b1d48",
                    "cidr_block": "10.45.25.0/24",
                    "cidr_block_state": {
                        "state": "associated"
                    }
                }
            ],
            "classic_link_enabled": false,
            "dhcp_options_id": "dopt-e6fd268e",
            "id": "vpc-02031d6f488187le4",
            "instance_tenancy": "dedicated",
            "is_default": false,
            "owner_id": "123469379881",
            "state": "available",
            "tags": {
                "Name": "TinyNetwork"
            }
        }
    }
}
```

Figure 5.24: Playbook execution with debug module

Now, this output is STDOUT, and the beauty of this STDOUT is that we can easily access any of the values from the output. For example, if we want to check whether something was changed on the target host or not, we just need to add the key with a single '.' after the name of the variable.

In this case, my variable name was **subnetinfo**. So "**{{ subnetinfo }}**" was providing us the entire output and if we simply want the change status, then we need to simply use "**{{subnetinfo.changed}}**" and in the response, you will get the value, which can be either true or false.

Let us try to run that code and verify if our theory is correct:

```
TASK [NewVPC : debug] *****
ok: [localhost] => {
    "msg": {
        "changed": true,
```

Figure 5.25: Status information captured successfully

As expected, the entire output is the status of changes on the cloud and that is what we were looking for.

The output is as follows:

```
[root@ip-172-31-94-253 bin]# ansible-playbook  VPCTest.yaml
[DEPRECATION WARNING]: Ansible will require Python 3.8 or newer on
(Red Hat 7.3.1-15)]. This feature will be removed from ansible-co
[WARNING]: No inventory was parsed, only implicit localhost is ava
[WARNING]: provided hosts list is empty, only localhost is availal

PLAY [Ansible AWS EC2 Instance Demo] ****************************

TASK [Gathering Facts] ******************************************
ok: [localhost]

TASK [NewVPC : Demo VPC] ****************************************
changed: [localhost]

TASK [NewVPC : debug] *******************************************
ok: [localhost] => {
    "msg": true
}

PLAY RECAP *****************************************************
localhost                  : ok=3    changed=1    unreachable=0
```

Figure 5.26: Play recap with debug status

However, what we want for our next task is the VPC ID. So, let us navigate down in our entire output and see where the VPC information is in that output:

```
TASK [NewVPC : debug] **********************************************************
ok: [localhost] => {
    "msg": {
        "changed": true,
        "debugging": {
            "expected_cidrs": [
                "10.45.25.0/24"
            ],
            "to_add": [],
            "to_remove": []
        },
        "failed": false,
        "vpc": {
            "cidr_block": "10.45.25.0/24",
            "cidr_block_association_set": [
                {
                    "association_id": "vpc-cidr-assoc-0b57f5817f68b1d48",
                    "cidr_block": "10.45.25.0/24",
                    "cidr_block_state": {
                        "state": "associated"
                    }
                }
            ],
            "classic_link_enabled": false,
            "dhcp_options_id": "dopt-e6fd268e",
            "id": "vpc-02031d6f4881871e4",
            "instance_tenancy": "dedicated",
            "is_default": false,
            "owner_id": "123469379881",
            "state": "available",
            "tags": {
                "Name": "TinyNetwork"
            }
        }
    }
```

Figure 5.27: Summary of VPC information

Now, when we see the values against the key VPC, as shown in *Figure 5.27*, we get a lot of information. So, let us try to grab the entire output first, and then we will fine-tune it later.

The new code will be as follows:

```
[root@ip-172-31-94-253 bin]# cat roles/NewVPC/tasks/main.yml
---
# tasks file for NewVPC and we will run our first VPC from Zero
- name: Demo VPC
  ec2_vpc_net:
    name: TinyNetwork
    cidr_block: 10.45.25.0/24
    region: us-east-2
    tenancy: dedicated
    aws_access_key: "{{ aws_access_key }}"
    aws_secret_key: "{{ aws_secret_key }}"
  register: subnetinfo
- debug:
    msg: "{{ subnetinfo.vpc }}"
```

Figure 5.28: Code with a variable containing VPC information

Let us run the code and see the output. We have just modified the value with variable and this time it is **subnetinfo.vpc** rather than **subnetinfo.changed**.

So here is the output of the key VPC. Now, since VPC has a lot of information, the output is huge, but we can sort the things out here too. Our main goal is to find out the VPC ID here. Let us navigate and try to find out where the VPC **ID** is in the following output:

```
TASK [NewVPC : debug] *************************************************************
ok: [localhost] => {
    "msg": {
        "cidr_block": "10.45.25.0/24",
        "cidr_block_association_set": [
            {
                "association_id": "vpc-cidr-assoc-02c0430a8bc5dfa35",
                "cidr_block": "10.45.25.0/24",
                "cidr_block_state": {
                    "state": "associated"
                }
            }
        ],
        "classic_link_enabled": false,
        "dhcp_options_id": "dopt-e6fd268e",
        "id": "vpc-04f4cea011675b13d",
        "instance_tenancy": "dedicated",
        "is_default": false,
        "owner_id": "123469379881",
        "state": "available",
        "tags": {
            "Name": "TinyNetwork"
        }
    }
}
```

Figure 5.29: Debug with the variable

We can easily see the VPC ID now in To make it more clear to everyone, the author has highlighted block which contains the VPC ID in *Figure 5.30*.

```
TASK [NewVPC : debug] *************************************************************
ok: [localhost] => {
    "msg": {
        "cidr_block": "10.45.25.0/24",
        "cidr_block_association_set": [
            {
                "association_id": "vpc-cidr-assoc-02c0430a8bc5dfa35",
                "cidr_block": "10.45.25.0/24",
                "cidr_block_state": {
                    "state": "associated"
                }
            }
        ],
        "classic_link_enabled": false,
        "dhcp_options_id": "dopt-e6fd268e",
        "id": "vpc-04f4cea011675b13d",
        "instance_tenancy": "dedicated",
        "is_default": false,
        "owner_id": "123469379881",
        "state": "available",
        "tags": {
            "Name": "TinyNetwork"
        }
    }
}
```

Figure 5.30: Finding the VPC id and calling it in the role

Now, just like how **variable.vpc** was used to gather the information about vpv . We can put another '.' with a new variable, and we should get the value of it. So, it should be **subnetinfo.vpc.id,** and we should be able to get the VPC ID.

The new code will be as follows:

Note: Initial code is suppressed.

```
    register: subnetinfo
 -  debug:
       msg: "{{ subnetinfo.vpc.id }}"
```

Figure 5.31: Code to print the VPC ID on terminal using debug module

Let us run it again and see how it works:

```
[root@ip-172-31-94-253 bin]# ansible-playbook  VPCTest.yaml
[DEPRECATION WARNING]: Ansible will require Python 3.8 or newer
(Red Hat 7.3.1-15)]. This feature will be removed from ansible-c
[WARNING]: No inventory was parsed, only implicit localhost is a
[WARNING]: provided hosts list is empty, only localhost is avail

PLAY [Ansible AWS EC2 Instance Demo] ***************************

TASK [Gathering Facts] ****************************************
ok: [localhost]

TASK [NewVPC : Demo VPC] **************************************
ok: [localhost]

TASK [NewVPC : debug] *****************************************
ok: [localhost] => {
    "msg": "vpc-04f4cea011675b13d"
}

PLAY RECAP ****************************************************
localhost                  : ok=3    changed=0    unreachable=0

[root@ip-172-31-94-253 bin]#
```

Figure 5.32: Output sorted with exact VPC id what we wanted to get from the output

From *Figure 5.32*, we know the VPC ID that we wanted to see from the entire STDOUT output of our playbook. If you are new to the VPC, then let me inform you that it is very useful information that we will use in defining our subnets in that VPC.

We need to let AWS know where we want our subnet to land. To achieve this, we will need the VPC ID, and that is what we have figured out from our code. So, our new code will be one that will create the VPC and then create a subnet in that VPC.

ec2_vpc_net module

We need to create a subnet in VPC, but you do not have the VPC ID handy, we are assuming you are about to create the new VPC. The plan is to create the VPC, save the VPC ID in a variable named as **subnetinfo**, and then call that variable in the subnet creation code. This time we will not print the VPC ID but we will call that in our code and use the VPC ID to create our subnets.

Let us decode it line by line. The first task is the same as it was before. The trick is in the second task:

```
---
# tasks file for NewVPC and we will run our first VPC from Zero
- name: Demo VPC
  ec2_vpc_net:
    name: TinyNetwork
    cidr_block: 10.45.25.0/24
    region: us-east-2
    tenancy: dedicated
    aws_access_key: "{{ aws_access_key }}"
    aws_secret_key: "{{ aws_secret_key }}"
  register: subnetinfo

## The code is same till above point.

- name: How to create the Subnet in AWS using Ansible
  ec2_vpc_subnet:
    state: present
    vpc_id: "{{subnetinfo.vpc.id}}"
    cidr: 10.45.25.0/26
    region: us-east-2
    aws_access_key: "{{ aws_access_key }}"
    aws_secret_key: "{{ aws_secret_key }}"
```

Figure 5.33: Creating of subnet using the information gathered in the first task

The second task is used for the creation of the subnet. Just like other tasks, we will provide a name to it. Quickly, we will move to the module **ec2_vpc_subnet**. This is the module we have used for the creation of the subnet. Now this needs a few information like **state**, **vpc_id**, **cidr**, **region,** and the authentications. Let us discuss them one by one:

- **State**: We need to inform Ansible whether we want to create the subnet or delete it. There are only two states present here.
  - o **Present and absent**: Present is for the creation of the subnet, and absent is for deleting the subnet.

- **CIDR**: This is the place where we will define information about our subnet.

- **Region**: Region information is needed as we want to launch our instances in our nearest region. Launching it in other regions might end up in unnecessary latency for our app, websites, and instances.

- **VPC_ID**: It is important to define the VPC information. You might have different VPC and do not want to mess-up with the production VPC. If you have an existing VPC, directly use the VPC ID rather than using the variable like before. Since we were not aware about the VPC ID, we chose the variable and called that here.

VPC internet gateway module

The internet gateway is another important component of the AWS cloud. In this section, we will demonstrate its creation. Let us add something more to it. Let us create an internet gateway and attach it to our VPC:

```
---
# tasks file for NewVPC and we will run our first VPC from Zero
- name: Demo VPC
  ec2_vpc_net:
    name: TinyNetwork
    cidr_block: 10.45.25.0/24
    region: us-east-2
    tenancy: dedicated
    aws_access_key: "{{ aws_access_key }}"
    aws_secret_key: "{{ aws_secret_key }}"
  register: subnetinfo

- name: How to create the Subnet in AWS using Ansible
  ec2_vpc_subnet:
    state: present
    vpc_id: "{{subnetinfo.vpc.id}}"
    cidr: 10.45.25.0/26
    region: us-east-2
    aws_access_key: "{{ aws_access_key }}"
    aws_secret_key: "{{ aws_secret_key }}"

## Same till above point. Below code is to create the Internet gateway.
- name: Create the Internet Gateway
  ec2_vpc_igw:
    vpc_id: "{{subnetinfo.vpc.id}}"
    #The above line is only for attaching it to the VPC.
    state: present
    region: us-east-2
    aws_access_key: "{{ aws_access_key }}"
    aws_secret_key: "{{ aws_secret_key }}"
  register: igw
```

Figure 5.34: Role that creates an internet gateway and its association to the VPC

In the above example as well, we have used the variable to find out the VPC ID. If you are using an existing VPC, your work will be much easier. We can simply remove the variable **"{{subnetinfo.vpc.id}}"** from there and just put the real VPC ID there. Let us run our code.

If we have a look at *Figure 5.35*, then execution is successful and it has created a VPC, a subnet, and then an internet gateway which is associated with a VPC. Let us verify it from the console:

```
[root@ip-172-31-94-253 bin]# ansible-playbook VPCTest.yaml
[DEPRECATION WARNING]: Ansible will require Python 3.8 or newer on the controller starting with Ansible 2.12. Current version
(Red Hat 0.3.1-15)). This feature will be removed from ansible-core in version 2.12. Deprecation warnings can be disabled by
[WARNING]: No inventory was parsed, only implicit localhost is available
[WARNING]: provided hosts list is empty, only localhost is available. Note that the implicit localhost does not match 'all'

PLAY [Ansible AWS EC2 Instance Demo] ***************************************************************************

TASK [Gathering Facts] ****************************************************************************************
ok: [localhost]

TASK [NewVPC : Demo VPC] **************************************************************************************
changed: [localhost]

TASK [NewVPC : How to create the Subnet in AWS using Ansible] *************************************************
changed: [localhost]

TASK [NewVPC : Create the Internet Gateway] ***************************************************************
changed: [localhost]

PLAY RECAP ****************************************************************************************************
localhost                  : ok=4    changed=3    unreachable=0    failed=0    skipped=0    rescued=0    ignored=0
```

Figure 5.35: Play recap with internet gateway creation and association

VPC

Let us verify the VPC status first from the console, and we can see the VPC is present in our console after playbook execution:

	Name		VPC ID		State		IPv4 CIDR
☐	TinyNetwork		vpc-0fb026b820ba90d42		⊘ Available		10.45.25.0/24

Figure 5.36: Playbook has successfully created VPC

Subnet

Let us verify the VPC subnet status now. We can see the subnet is present in our console after playbook execution:

Subnets (3) Info   🔄 Actions ▼

🔍 *Filter subnets*

	Name	▲	Subnet ID		State		VPC		IPv4 CIDR
☐	-		subnet-026b4587fdb759292		⊘ Available		vpc-0fb026b820ba90d42 | TinyNetwork		10.45.25.0/26

Figure 5.37: Successful creation of a subnet

Internet gateway

Let us verify the **internet gateway (IGW)**, and we have found the IGW in the console after playbook execution:

Name	▲	Internet gateway ID	▽	State	▽	VPC ID	▽	Owner
☐ -		igw-0d0562a8587d8ff0d		⊘ Attached		vpc-0fb026b820ba90d42 | TinyNetwork		123469379881

Figure 5.38: Successful creation and association of IGW

Creating an IGW is not enough. We need to associate the IGW with th appropriate VPC. So let us go ahead and verify if VPC is attached to this newly created IGW.

As we can see, the internet gateway is associated with VPC:

igw-0d0562a8587d8ff0d

Actions ▼

Details Info

Internet gateway ID	State	VPC ID	Owner
⎘ igw-0d0562a8587d8ff0d	⊘ Attached	vpc-0fb026b820ba90d42 | TinyNetwork	⎘ 123469379881

Figure 5.39: Successful association of VPC with IGW

Route table

Let us create a route table and then associate it with the internet gateway:

```
[root@ip-172-31-94-253 bin]# cat roles/NewVPC/tasks/main.yml
```

```
---
# tasks file for NewVPC and we will run our first VPC from Zero
- name: Demo VPC
  ec2_vpc_net:
    name: TinyNetwork
    cidr_block: 10.45.25.0/24
    region: us-east-2
    tenancy: dedicated
    aws_access_key: "{{ aws_access_key }}"
    aws_secret_key: "{{ aws_secret_key }}"
  register: subnetinfo

- name: How to create the Subnet in AWS using Ansible
  ec2_vpc_subnet:
    state: present
    vpc_id: "{{subnetinfo.vpc.id}}"
    cidr: 10.45.25.0/26
    region: us-east-2
    aws_access_key: "{{ aws_access_key }}"
    aws_secret_key: "{{ aws_secret_key }}"

- name: Create the Internet Gateway
  ec2_vpc_igw:
    vpc_id: "{{subnetinfo.vpc.id}}"
    state: present
    region: us-east-2
    aws_access_key: "{{ aws_access_key }}"
    aws_secret_key: "{{ aws_secret_key }}"
  register: igw
## Everything is same till above. Below code is new for the creation of Route tabl
- name: Set up public subnet route table
  ec2_vpc_route_table:
    vpc_id:  "{{subnetinfo.vpc.id}}"
    region: us-east-2
    subnets:
      - 10.45.25.0/26
    routes:
      - dest: 0.0.0.0/0
        gateway_id: "{{ igw.gateway_id }}"
    aws_access_key: "{{ aws_access_key }}"
    aws_secret_key: "{{ aws_secret_key }}"
  register: defaultroute
```

Figure 5.40: Role with route table

Now, **ec2_vpc_route_table** is the name of an Ansible module that has a few components that need to be defined by us. Region and authentication keys are obvious so we will not discuss them now.

Now, route table contains the following information:
- Subnet
- The destination address we want to reach
- Next hop to reach that destination network

So, in our example, shown in *Figure 5.40* the subnet was already clear to us, which is 10.45.25.0/26, and since it is a default route, it will be a destination as any or 0.0.0.0/0 and the next hope will be our internet gateway since all traffic to the internet will go through it in our case. If you had multiple subnets, then define them like the following example:

```
subnets:
  - 10.45.25.0/26
  - 10.45.26.0/27
routes:
  - dest: 0.0.0.0/0
```

Figure 5.41: Multiple subnet association using roles

The rest will be the same in code.

Let us run the code and see the results:

```
[root@ip-172-31-94-253 bin]# ansible-playbook VPCTest.yaml
[DEPRECATION WARNING]: Ansible will require Python 3.8 or newer on the contr
[Red Hat 7.3.1-15]]. This feature will be removed from ansible-core in versi
[WARNING]: No inventory was parsed, only implicit localhost is available
[WARNING]: provided hosts list is empty, only localhost is available. Note t

PLAY [Ansible AWS EC2 Instance Demo] ***********************************

TASK [Gathering Facts] ***********************************
ok: [localhost]

TASK [NewVPC : Demo VPC] ***********************************
changed: [localhost]

TASK [NewVPC : How to create the Subnet in AWS using Ansible] ************
changed: [localhost]

TASK [NewVPC : Create the Internet Gateway] ***********************************
changed: [localhost]

TASK [NewVPC : Set up public subnet route table] ***********************************
changed: [localhost]

PLAY RECAP ***********************************
localhost                  : ok=5    changed=4    unreachable=0    failed=0
```

Figure 5.42: Play recap shows successful execution of our code

If we see the results, default route table is created. We just need to go to the console and verify the same. Verification can be done from CLI too using Ansible. However, in this case, we will navigate to the graphical user interface and verify it from there.

We can see that the route table is also created, as shown in the following figure. Let us have a deeper look into the default route we created:

	Name	▽	Route table ID	▽	Explicit subnet associat...	Edge associations	Main	▽	VPC	▽
	-		rtb-06a003066e9965e9f		–	–	Yes		vpc-0fd436abb9accd2aa | TinyNetwork	
	-		rtb-0868bf39275a7bddb		subnet-00e18d7ef323d...	–	No		vpc-0fd436abb9accd2aa | TinyNetwork	

Figure 5.43: Successful creation of route table

The next step is shown as follows:

Destination	▽	Target	▽	Status	▽	Propagated
0.0.0.0/0		igw-00e38ef1afc96aed6		⊘ Active		No
10.45.25.0/24		local		⊘ Active		No

Figure 5.44: Route pointing towards newly created IGW

We can now find out the newly created default route in the table. It is pointing towards the newly created Internet gateway. Remember, we did not use the internet gateway ID. Once again, we used the concept of a variable and called it in our code.

Just for your reference, you can have a look at this line:

gateway_id: "{{ igw.gateway_id }}"

If you already have your Internet gateway, do not worry. You can directly use the gateway ID like the following example:

gateway_id: igw-00e38ef1afc96aed6

Let us go ahead and create our security group. Now, the security group is going to be very easy too. Let us have a look at the code. Now NSG has the rules in two directions, one is outbound and the second is inbound. In simple language, one comes from the internet, and the second goes towards the internet. So, we need to set up two rules here.

The name of the module we will use here is **ec2_group**. The inbound rule is for port 22 from any IP address, and we have allowed ports 22 to 60000 open here. The protocol defined here is TCP. You can do whatever your requirement is.

```
---
# tasks file for NewVPC and we will run our first VPC from Zero
- name: NSG
  ec2_group:
    name: Anyallow
    description: any any allowed
    vpc_id: vpc-0fd436abb9accd2aa
    region: us-east-2
    aws_access_key: "{{ aws_access_key }}"
    aws_secret_key: "{{ aws_secret_key }}"
    rules:
      - proto: tcp
        from_port: 22
        to_port: 22
        cidr_ip: 0.0.0.0/0
    rules_egress:
      - proto: tcp
        from_port: 22
        to_port: 60000
        cidr_ip: 0.0.0.0/0
        group_name: outboundrule
        group_desc: any any instance
```

Figure 5.45: Role with network security group

Let us run our code and see the results:

```
[root@ip-172-31-94-253 bin]#
[root@ip-172-31-94-253 bin]# ansible-playbook  VPCTest.yaml
[DEPRECATION WARNING]: Ansible will require Python 3.8 or newer on the controller
(Red Hat 7.3.1-15)]. This feature will be removed from ansible-core in version 2.1
[WARNING]: No inventory was parsed, only implicit localhost is available
[WARNING]: provided hosts list is empty, only localhost is available. Note that th

PLAY [Ansible AWS EC2 Instance Demo] ************************************

TASK [Gathering Facts] *****************************************************
ok: [localhost]

TASK [keyEC2 : NSG] ********************************************************
changed: [localhost]

PLAY RECAP *****************************************************************
localhost                   : ok=2    changed=1    unreachable=0    failed=0    ski
```

Figure 5.46: Successful execution of playbook

The playbook execution was successful. Let us have a look at the GUI to verify the same:

Figure 5.47: Summary of NSG rule that allows any communication

When we verify that the NSG allowing any source to any destination has been created successfully.

So now we know how to create a VPC, subnet, internet gateway, route table, **network security group (NSG)**, and club them together. We have already shown you the way of creating the EC2 instance. So let us create it now. Create a script that starts from scratch. Create a VPC, then a subnet, an IGW, a route table, a security group, and then launch an EC2 instance. The only thing that is missing here is the key pair. If you are using Windows, we will need PuTTY-compatible **.ppk** file, and if you run Mac, then a **.pem** file. For now, go to the portal and create a keypair and download it to your box. The rest is settled to create your first ever code, which runs from zero to launching an EC2 instance in a fully automated way.

Let us try it on your own and give it a few shots. Remember, if you are running the free tier, you need to make the modifications to the VPC tenancy. Kindly change it from dedicated to the default for the free tier, otherwise, you will not be able to launch an instance in your newly created VPC. The rest will be good. Do not be upset if you are struggling to do it. We are here to guide you. We will create the end-to-end script here only and then we will explain to you all the steps one by one.

Let us have a look at the EC2 instance module and its requirements for a minute. We will also understand how we can use it in a real AWS environment.

Note: **ec2_instance module is used this time, not ec2 module:**

```
- ec2_instance:
    name: FullflowVPC
    key_name: VPCE2E
    vpc_subnet_id: "{{variablesub.subnet.id}}"
    instance_type: t2.micro
    security_group: "{{varnsg.group_id}}"
    network:
      assign_public_ip: true
    image_id: ami-0a606d8395a538502
    region: us-east-2
    aws_access_key: "{{ aws_access_key }}"
    aws_secret_key: "{{ aws_secret_key }}"
```

Figure 5.48: Roles to create an EC2 instance with subnet and NSG information parsed to the task

If we see the requirement correctly, we need the keypair name. As we requested, you all to create the key pair manually and download that. So, you have the name of keypair handy with you.

- **Subnet ID**: Since we are creating the subnet in-line here in the same code. We do not have the subnet ID readily available. In production, it might be available, but you will end up in this situation many times where we will try to provision the Subnet and EC2 instance same time. So, what I have done in this case? Well just like VPC ID information, we have created a variable and then ran the debug on the execution. From there, we were able to get the key subnet.id for gathering the subnet ID of our Subnet.

- **Instance_type**: This in on you how big instance you want and what is your actual requirement.

- **Security group**: Once again we used the same logic created a variable and ran a **debug**. That gives me the information of key which was **group_id** in this case. So this is how we gathered that information and added that variable in our code.

Playbook for end-to-end deployment

So, here is our end-to-end deployment for launching an EC2 instance in AWS. You will start from a very small VPC and move all the way up to launching an EC2 instance. Now, in reality, we cannot cover all the features AWS offers. If we count the services offered by AWS, then they are more than the sum of 3-4 small cloud providers. So, it is impossible to cover all. Still, we have tried a couple of them. Let us paste the entire code here now, so we can have a look at it:

```
# tasks file for NewVPC and we will run our first VPC from Zero
- name: Demo VPC
  ec2_vpc_net:
    name: TinyNetwork
    cidr_block: 10.45.25.0/24
    region: us-east-2
    tenancy: default
    aws_access_key: "{{ aws_access_key }}"
    aws_secret_key: "{{ aws_secret_key }}"
  register: subnetinfo

- name: How to create the Subnet in AWS using Ansible
  ec2_vpc_subnet:
    state: present
    vpc_id: "{{subnetinfo.vpc.id}}"
    cidr: 10.45.25.0/26
    region: us-east-2
    aws_access_key: "{{ aws_access_key }}"
    aws_secret_key: "{{ aws_secret_key }}"
  register: variablesub
- name: Create the Internet Gateway
  ec2_vpc_igw:
    vpc_id: "{{subnetinfo.vpc.id}}"
    state: present
    region: us-east-2
    aws_access_key: "{{ aws_access_key }}"
    aws_secret_key: "{{ aws_secret_key }}"
  register: igw

  - name: Set up public subnet route table
    ec2_vpc_route_table:
      vpc_id:  "{{subnetinfo.vpc.id}}"
      region: us-east-2
      subnets:
        - 10.45.25.0/26
      routes:
        - dest: 0.0.0.0/0
          gateway_id: "{{ igw.gateway_id }}"
      aws_access_key: "{{ aws_access_key }}"
      aws_secret_key: "{{ aws_secret_key }}"
    register: defaultroute

  - name: NSG
    ec2_group:
      name: Anyallow
      description: any any allowed
      vpc_id: "{{subnetinfo.vpc.id}}"
      region: us-east-2
      aws_access_key: "{{ aws_access_key }}"
      aws_secret_key: "{{ aws_secret_key }}"
      rules:
        - proto: tcp
          from_port: 22
          to_port: 22
          cidr_ip: 0.0.0.0/0
      rules_egress:
        - proto: tcp
          from_port: 22
          to_port: 60000
          cidr_ip: 0.0.0.0/0
          group_name: outboundrule
          group_desc: any any instance
    register: varnsg
#New code from next line


- ec2_instance:
    name: FullflowVPC
    key_name: VPCE2E
    vpc_subnet_id: "{{variablesub.subnet.id}}"
    instance_type: t2.micro
    security_group: "{{varnsg.group_id}}"
    network:
      assign_public_ip: true
    image_id: ami-0a606d8395a538502
    region: us-east-2
    aws_access_key: "{{ aws_access_key }}"
    aws_secret_key: "{{ aws_secret_key }}"
```

Figure 5.49: End-to-end deployment

All the modifications in the old code are highlighted in the block so that you can understand the changes required here.

The logic is very simple. Run create a variable using register and run **debug** to understand the output and values. At last, find out the right key from the debug output so you can call the values inside your next line of code.

Let us run and see the results:

```
[root@ip-172-31-94-253 bin]# ansible-playbook  VPCTest.yaml
[DEPRECATION WARNING]: Ansible will require Python 3.8 or newer on the controller startin
(Red Hat 7.3.1-15)]. This feature will be removed from ansible-core in version 2.12. Depr
[WARNING]: No inventory was parsed, only implicit localhost is available
[WARNING]: provided hosts list is empty, only localhost is available. Note that the impli

PLAY [Ansible AWS EC2 Instance Demo] ***************************************************

TASK [Gathering Facts] *****************************************************************
ok: [localhost]

TASK [NewVPC : Demo VPC] ***************************************************************
changed: [localhost]

TASK [NewVPC : How to create the Subnet in AWS using Ansible] **************************
changed: [localhost]

TASK [NewVPC : Create the Internet Gateway] ********************************************
changed: [localhost]

TASK [NewVPC : Set up public subnet route table] ***************************************
changed: [localhost]

TASK [NewVPC : NSG] ********************************************************************
changed: [localhost]

TASK [NewVPC : ec2_instance] ***********************************************************
changed: [localhost]

PLAY RECAP *****************************************************************************
localhost                  : ok=7    changed=6    unreachable=0    failed=0    skipped=0
```

Figure 5.50: Play recap of end-to-end deployment

If we see the output, we can conclude that our code is working fine. We simply need to go to the console and verify if all things are present there.

This is the output of the EC2 dashboard:

Name	Instance ID	Instance state	Instance type	Status check	Alarm status	Availability Zone	Public IPv4 DNS
FullflowVPC	i-0102b8b6b3d5e5b96	Running	t2.micro	Initializing	No alarms +	us-east-2c	ec2-18-188-8-4.

Figure 5.51: Instance launched successfully

Our instance came up. So, we have had a long journey in this chapter. We started from very basic, where we created the VPC from scratch, and reached the point where we launched our EC2 instance in that VPC.

Now you might be thinking, is it really reachable? Well, let us try to connect it and find out.

Here is the proof that it is operational and easily accessible over SSH from the internet.

Figure 5.52: *Successful login to the VM created by our playbook*

Now, everyone will have their own frequently used modules, so go to the Ansible portal. Find out the Ansible cloud modules, and there you will see the ocean of AWS modules

Conclusion

Ansible has done a great job developing AWS modules. We have modules for all your needs. We just need to start finding the modules you need and start practicing them. Since there will be some surprises someday, a few missing pieces that you will need to add before it runs. So, practice many modules of cloud, and you will become better over time. To conclude this chapter, we have learned how to launch any instance in AWS using Ansible from scratch. We have explored few VPC, NSG and EC2 instance modules in our chapter.

In the next chapter, we will focus on the next major cloud in the market. We will cover Azure in our next chapter. We will learn about a few basics of Azure and how it works with Ansible. Then we will create our hands-on lab.

References

- https://docs.ansible.com/ansible/2.9/modules/ec2_instance_module.html#ec2-instance-module

- https://docs.ansible.com/ansible/2.9/modules/ec2_group_module.html#ec2-group-module

- https://docs.ansible.com/ansible/2.9/modules/ec2_vpc_igw_module.html#ec2-vpc-igw-module

- https://docs.ansible.com/ansible/2.9/modules/list_of_cloud_modules.html

- https://docs.ansible.com/ansible/2.9/modules/ec2_instance_info_module.html#ec2-instance-info-module

- https://docs.ansible.com/ansible/2.9/modules/ec2_vpc_route_table_module.html#ec2-vpc-route-table-module

- https://docs.ansible.com/ansible/2.9/modules/ec2_vpc_subnet_module.html#ec2-vpc-subnet-module

- https://docs.ansible.com/ansible/2.9/modules/list_of_cloud_modules.html

Join our Discord space

Join our Discord workspace for latest updates, offers, tech happenings around the world, new releases, and sessions with the authors:

https://discord.bpbonline.com

CHAPTER 6
Ansible for Cloud Provisioning Microsoft Azure

Introduction

We started our cloud journey with AWS, and this chapter will be dedicated to Azure. So far, we have tried to cover even small topics in this book. However, we recommend you go through the basics of Azure for a better understanding of this chapter.

Structure

This chapter includes the following topics:

- Ansible for Microsoft Azure
- User creation for our Azure authentication
- Preparing your VM for Azure
- Creating your role for Microsoft Azure
- Ansible using Microsoft Azure Cloud Shell

Objectives

After reading this chapter, the reader will be able to create the resources in Microsoft Azure. We will understand and learn the use of different Ansible modules designed for Azure. We have also covered some hands-on demonstrations in the chapter where we have created the resources from scratch. We strongly recommend that you follow those labs and practice a few more modules.

Ansible for Microsoft Azure

Just like any other cloud, Ansible works great with Microsoft Azure, too. Now, a few things are going to be different in the case of Microsoft Azure. The logic is going to be the same for the cloud. Just like we had given programmatic access to the user, we will create something similar here. However, that is known differently in the case of Microsoft Azure. In the case of Azure, the programmatic access is given using service principal values. Just like `aws_access_key` and `aws_secret_key` we have the concept of secret and tenant ID. Subscription ID and client ID are two additional fields you will need in case of Azure, and if you are familiar with Azure, then you know it well that we need the subscription ID everywhere in Azure. Just like AWS SDK, we will need to install the Python SDK for Microsoft Azure.

> **Note:** If you delete the VM every time after practice, then there is some good news. Azure offers a very good feature of Azure Shell on its portal, and we can use Ansible from that shell directly. It already has Ansible configured, and it has the entire authentication already in place. So, if you want to skip the authentication process and the Azure SDK installation process, then navigate to the last part of this chapter.

User creation for our Azure authentication

We will talk about Azure authentication in this section. There are multiple ways of enabling the authentication for Azure:

- The first and similar to AWS, uses a service principal
- The second method is using AD credentials
- The last one is the **Azure Data Factory** (**ADF**) username and password

In this section, we will focus on the first two methods and will leave the third as an assignment. Our main focus will be on the primary method only. We will have a closer look at the first, and if we are done with the first method, we will jump to the next topic of the chapter, which is preparing the VM for Azure.

Azure authentication method 1

In case of Microsoft Azure, the credentials have to be defined in the `/root/.azure/credentials` file. The traditional method of defining the credentials using different variables also works fine. However, we will focus on the Azure recommended method of defining credentials in `.azure/credentials` file. Let us see how we can create the director and credentials file:

1. First, we will create a directory:

```
mkdir ~/.azure
cd .azure
create a file named as 'credentials'
touch credentials
```

Figure 6.1: Creation of directory structure for credentials

2. Now, we can modify the file credentials and pass the actual credentials here:

```
[default]

subscription_id=xxxxxxx-xxxx-xxxx-xxxx-xxxxxxxxxxxx
client_id=xxxxxxx-xxxx-xxxx-xxxx-xxxxxxxxxxxx
secret=xxxxxxxxxxxxxxxxx
tenant=xxxxxxx-xxxx-xxxx-xxxx-xxxxxxxxxxxx
```

Figure 6.2: Credentials with dummy credential details

In a real box it will look as shown in *Figure 6.3*:

```
[root@ip-172-31-8-19 ansible]# cat /root/.azure/credentials
[default]
SUBSCRIPTION_ID= 51a23039-7d9b-4900-837f-84d8e83a5591
CLIENT_ID= 39004d74    .. ..95-a333-75ed1f81aebb
SECRET=
TENANT= f12450              21f-34f0275c047a
[root@ip-172-31-8-19 ansible]#
[root@ip-172-31-8-19 ansible]# []
```

Figure 6.3: Azure credentials file

The details, like subscription ID, can be obtained easily from the CLI or the portal. Let us look at how to gather the subscription ID:

1. Navigate to the **Subscriptions** from the search menu and click on it. This will give us the **Subscription name** and ID, as shown in *Figure 6.4*.

2. Copy the **Subscription ID** and paste it in the credentials file, and this will be done. We are ready to go ahead with Azure.

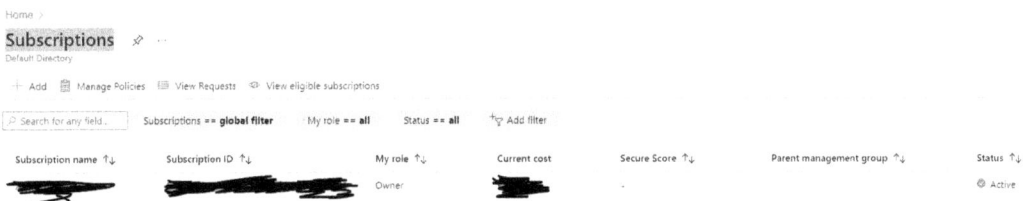

Figure 6.4: Azure subscription with details

3. The next thing is Client ID and secret. That will be created using the service principle in Microsoft Azure.

Let us create the service principle now. There are multiple ways of creating a service principle; we can do it using the CLI or the GUI. Just for simplicity, we will do it using the GUI:

1. The first thing is to navigate to the Azure portal and search for the Active Directory.

2. In **Active Directory (AD)**, we need to navigate to the app registration:

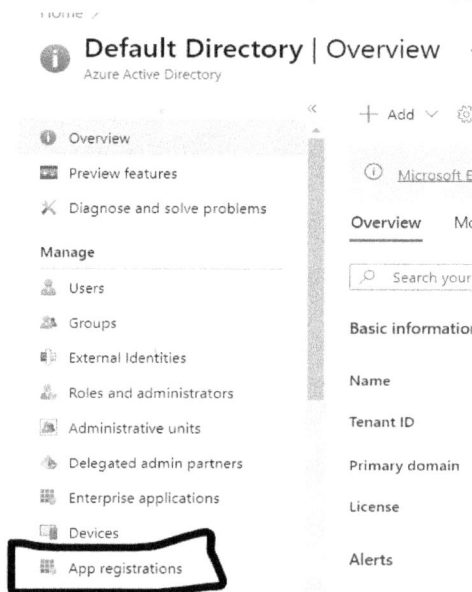

Figure 6.5: App registrations

3. The next thing we need to do is create a new app registration. Click on **New registration** as shown in the following figure:

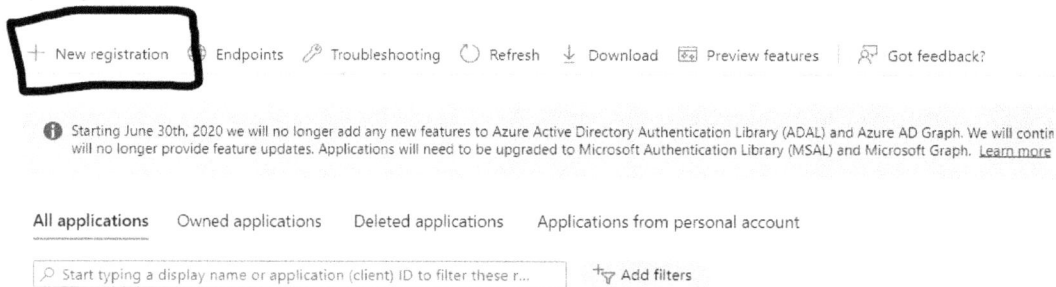

Figure 6.6: New app registration

4. Give it a name and select the supported account type:

Home > Default Directory | App registrations >

Register an application ...

* Name

The user-facing display name for this application (this can be changed later).

DemoAnsible

Supported account types

Who can use this application or access this API?

(●) Accounts in this organizational directory only (Default Directory only - Single tenant)

◯ Accounts in any organizational directory (Any Azure AD directory - Multitenant)

◯ Accounts in any organizational directory (Any Azure AD directory - Multitenant) and personal Microsoft accounts (e.g. Skype, Xbox)

◯ Personal Microsoft accounts only

Help me choose...

Redirect URI (optional)

We'll return the authentication response to this URI after successfully authenticating the user. Providing this now is optional and it can be changed later, but a value is required for most authentication scenarios.

Select a platform ∨	e.g. https://example.com/auth

By proceeding, you agree to the Microsoft Platform Policies ◻

Register

Figure 6.7: Filling in the details for new app registration

5. The next thing we need to do is assign a role to the application. For that, we need to go to the subscription again and click on our subscription:

6. In subscription, we need to select **Access control (IAM)**:

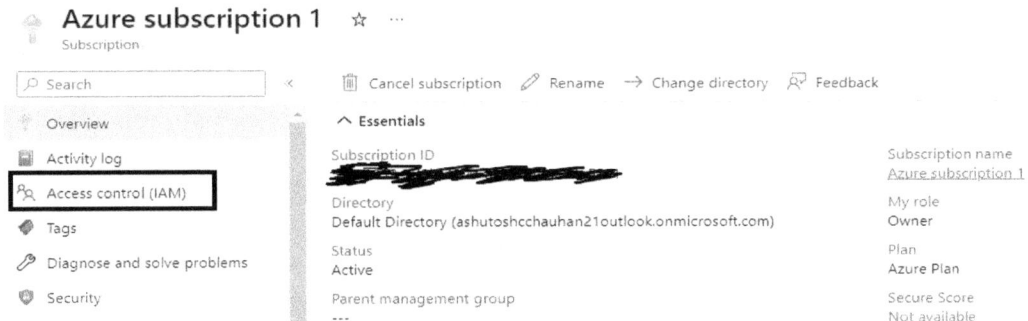

◢ **Azure subscription 1** ☆ ...
Subscription

| 🔎 Search | 🗑 Cancel subscription 🖉 Rename → Change directory 🖓 Feedback |

∧ Essentials

Overview

Activity log | Subscription ID | Subscription name |
| | | Azure subscription 1 |

Access control (IAM) | Directory | My role |
| | Default Directory (ashutoshcchauhan21outlook.onmicrosoft.com) | Owner |

Tags | Status | Plan |
| Active | Azure Plan |

Diagnose and solve problems | | |

Security | Parent management group | Secure Score |
| --- | Not available |

Figure 6.8: Finding Azure Subscription ID

7. We need to navigate to the **Role assignments**. Here we will give enough access to our application, which we registered:

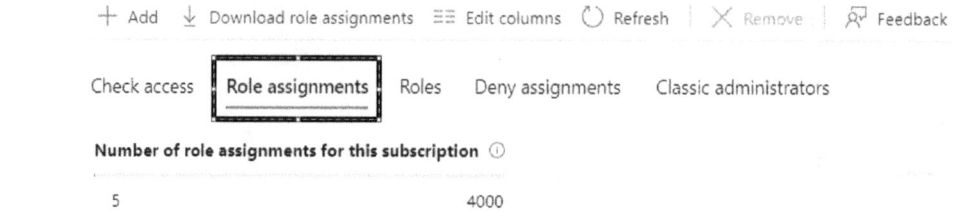

Figure 6.9: Navigate to the role assignments

8. Click on **Add | Select the add role assignment**:

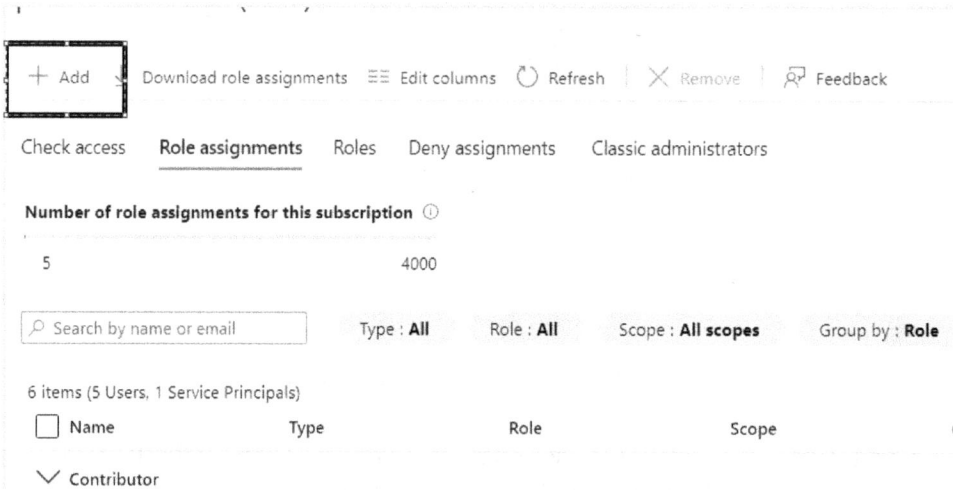

Figure 6.10: New role assignment

9. It is going to look like *Figure 6.11*. We need to provide a few parameters here. First thing is the level of access. We want our application to create the stuffs in Azure, hence we are creating contributor access here for our app.

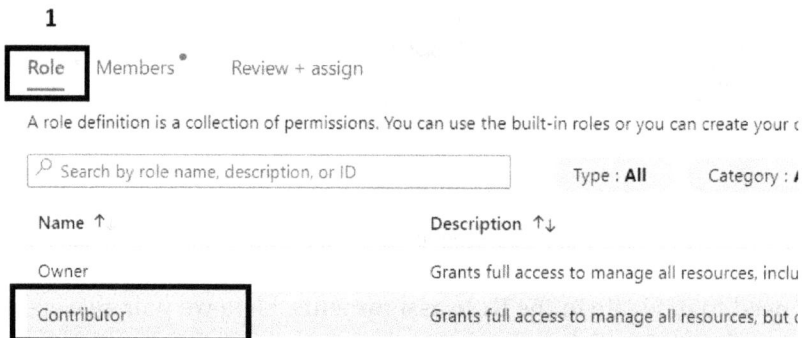

Figure 6.11: Allocating contributor-level access

10. The second thing is **Members**. So, click on that and in members, click on **Select members**:

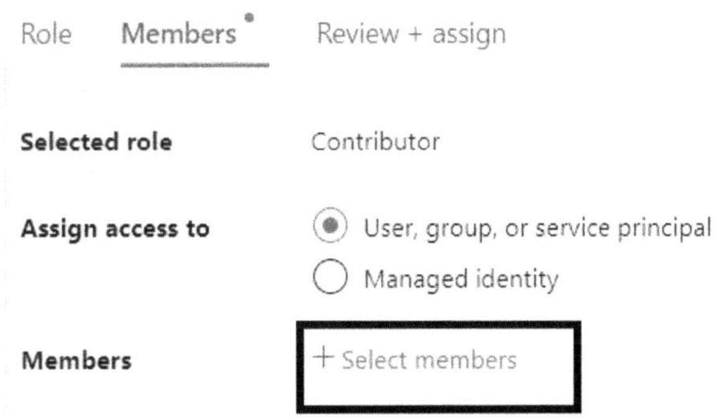

Role   Members   Review + assign

Selected role   Contributor

Assign access to   ◉ User, group, or service principal
                           ○ Managed identity

Members   + Select members

Figure 6.12: Assignment of service principal or group

11. This will give us a few options, but you might not see your recently created app registration. So, type the name of the app registration and enter to search for it. As soon as you enter, you will see your newly created app registration there. Select your registration and you should be good:

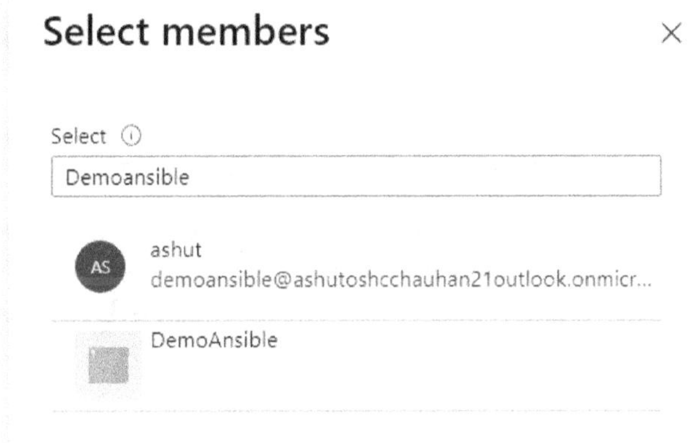

Select members   ✕

Select ⓘ

Demoansible

AS   ashut
         demoansible@ashutoshcchauhan21outlook.onmicr...

         DemoAnsible

Figure 6.13: Selecting the newly created DemoAnsible app registry

This will show us the recently created app registration, like *Figure 6.12*. Select that, and it will look like the following figure once you select that:

Role   Members   Review + assign

Selected role   Contributor

Assign access to   ◉ User, group, or service principal
                         ○ Managed identity

Members   + Select members

	Name	Object ID	Type
	DemoAnsible	afcbdc3d-a464-4147-88ae-3df6a5309517	App

Description   Optional

[Review + assign]   [Previous]   [Next]

Figure 6.14: Summary after selection

12. The last thing you need to do is click on **Review + assign**.

Now we need to generate the secret key. This will be done from Active Directory again. We need to go back to the AD and find our recently created app registration. Select our recently created app registration, which is **DemoAnsible** in our case:

Default Directory | App registrations 📌 ⋯
Azure Active Directory

+ New registration   ⊕ Endpoints   🔧 Troubleshooting   ↻ Refresh   ↓ Download   ▣ Preview features   ⟲ Got feedback?

ⓘ Starting June 30th, 2020 we will no longer add any new features to Azure Active Directory Authentication Library (ADAL) and Azure AD Graph. We will continue to provi
will no longer provide feature updates. Applications will need to be upgraded to Microsoft Authentication Library (MSAL) and Microsoft Graph. Learn more

ⓘ Overview
▦ Preview features
✕ Diagnose and solve problems

Manage
👤 Users
👥 Groups
External Identities
Roles and administrators
Administrative units
Delegated admin partners
Enterprise applications
Devices
App registrations

All applications   Owned applications   Deleted applications   Applications from personal account

🔍 Start typing a display name or application (client) ID to filter these r...   ▽ Add filters

3 applications found

Display name ↑   Application (client) ID

AN AnsibleAuthentication
DE DemoAnsible
MY myrole

Figure 6.15: Finding the newly created App registrations

13. Click on **Certificates & secret**:

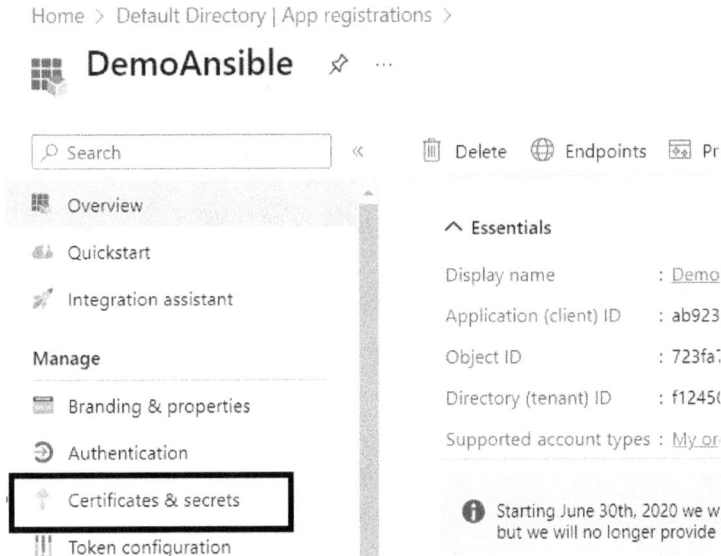

Figure 6.16: Navigating to the Certificates & secrets

14. Click on **New client secret**:

Figure 6.17: Create a New client secret

15. Name it and give it a lifetime as per your company policy. We have kept it at six months here:

Add a client secret   ✕

Description	Demoansible
Expires	Recommended: 180 days (6 months) ⌄

Figure 6.18: Offer it a name and validity

16. The following figure shows the secret key:

Certificates (0)   **Client secrets (1)**   Federated credentials (0)

A secret string that the application uses to prove its identity when requesting a token. Also can be referred to as application password

+ New client secret

Description	Expires	Value ⓘ	Secret ID
Demoansible	10/20/2023	~~━━━━━━━~~ 🗐 ~~a7━~~

SECRET

Figure 6.19: Secret with secret ID

17. Let us go back to the app registration and click on the newly created app registration **DemoAnsible**. This gives us the **client_id**:

Home > Default Directory | App registrations >

▦ DemoAnsible 📌 ⋯

🔍 Search	≪	🗑 Delete ⊕ Endpoints ▦ Preview features

▦ Overview

🕮 Quickstart

✈ Integration assistant

∧ Essentials

Display name   : DemoAnsible

| Application (client) ID | : ~~━━━━━━━~~ |

Figure 6.20: Finding the Client ID

18. At the end, we need to find the tenant ID. That is present in the active directory only. Select the AD again and then go to the properties:

Home > Default Directory

┃┃┃ **Default Directory** | Properties
┃┃┃ Azure Active Directory

« | 🖫 Save ✕ Discard | ⧉ Got feedback?

(A) Identity Governance

▤ Application proxy

▨ Custom security attributes
(Preview)

⚙ Licenses

② Cross-tenant synchronization
(Preview)

◈ Azure AD Connect

▤ Custom domain names

② Mobility (MDM and MAM)

⚷ Password reset

⚙ User settings

┃┃┃ Properties

Tenant properties

Name *

Default Directory

Country or region
Ireland

Location
EU Model Clause compliant datacenters

Notification language

English

Tenant ID

Technical contact

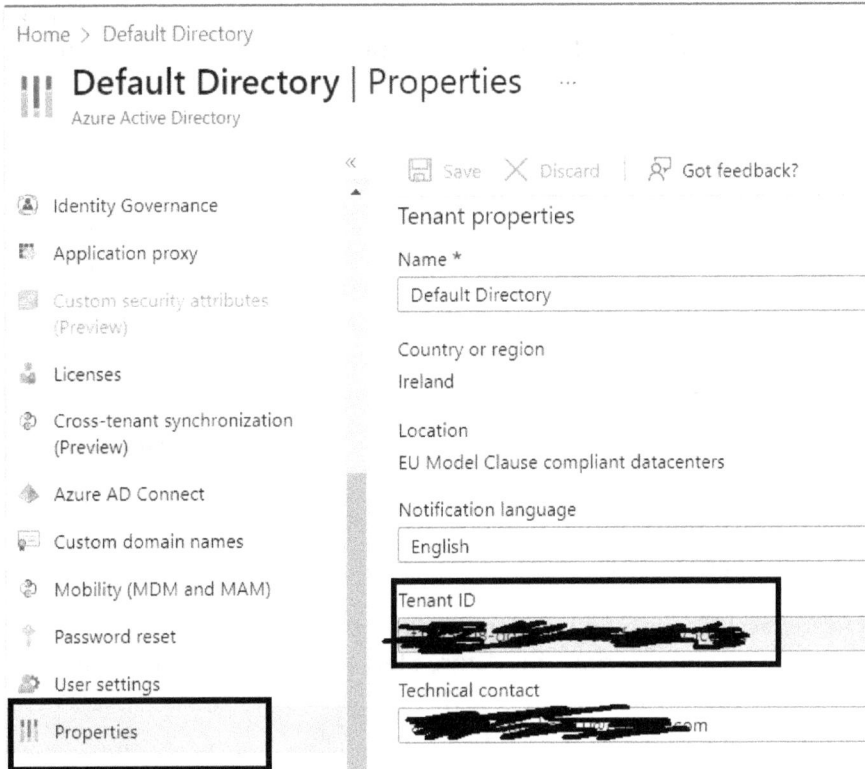

Figure 6.21: Finding the Tenant ID

19. This gives us all four required parameters shown here again:

```
[root@ip-172-31-8-19 ansible]# cat /root/.azure/credentials
[default]
SUBSCRIPTION_ID= 5
CLIENT_ID= 3       HIDDEN CREDENTIALS
SECRET= a
TENANT= f
[root@ip-172-31-8-19 ansible]#
[root@ip-172-31-8-19 ansible]# []
```

Figure 6.22: Credential file with hidden passwords and credentials

So, this means our authentication for Microsoft Azure is sorted. We have listed all the required parameters and saved them in **/root/.azure/credentials**.

Azure authentication method 2

Just for your knowledge, you should know that there is another method available in Microsoft Azure that uses AD authentication parameters. It is not recommended to use your password anywhere on the server. So, we will not discuss this method. However, we should know it for knowledge. This is also an option and can be done with a few tricks and tips.

Preparing your VM for Azure

As we discussed, we will need some additional configuration in our control machine to make it work with Microsoft Azure. We need to install Azure SDK modules on the host running Ansible.

Command:

```
pip3 install 'ansible[azure]'
```

If **pip** is not present in our control machine, then we can simply install it using the following commands:

```
yum install -y python3-pip
pip3 install --upgrade pip
```

Once **pip** is successfully installed, we are good to proceed further. We should re-run the following command, and this time, the Azure SDK should install successfully:

```
pip3 install ansible[azure]
```

Creating your role for Microsoft Azure

In this section, we will go to the control host and create the role. We are using **azure_rm_resourcegroup** module to create a resource group. If we see the *Figure 6.23*, we have used the module **azure_rm_resourcegroup** and created a resource group named as '**testingawerf**' in **eastus** region:

```
[root@ip-172-31-8-19 ansible]# cat roles/testing/tasks/main.yml
---
# tasks file for testing
- name: Creating resource group
  azure_rm_resourcegroup:
    name: "testingawerf"
    location: "eastus"
[root@ip-172-31-8-19 ansible]#
```

Figure 6.23: *Creating resource group*

The work we are doing in this role is creating a resource group using **rm_resourcegroup** module. A few basic required parameters are name and location of **resource group** (RG).

Let us create our first playbook for Azure:

```
[root@ip-172-31-8-19 ansible]# cat firtplay.yaml
---
- name: test
  connection: local
  hosts: all
  roles:
  - testing
[root@ip-172-31-8-19 ansible]#
```

Figure 6.24: Playbook for the resource group

Let us run and see the result:

```
[root@ip-172-31-8-19 ansible]# ansible-playbook firtplay.yaml
/usr/local/lib/python3.6/site-packages/ansible/parsing/vault/__init__.py:44: CryptographyDeprecationWarning: Python
r it is deprecated in cryptography. The next release of cryptography will remove support for Python 3.6.
  from cryptography.exceptions import InvalidSignature

PLAY [test] ************************************************************************************************

TASK [Gathering Facts] ************************************************************************************
ok: [localhost]

TASK [testing : Demo VM] **********************************************************************************
An exception occurred during task execution. To see the full traceback, use -vvv. The error was: ImportError: No mo
fatal: [localhost]: FAILED! => {"changed": false, "msg": "Failed to import the required Python library (packaging) (
make read the                                  it in the appropriate location. If the required library is installed,
cumentation on ansible_python_interpreter"}

PLAY RECAP ************************************************************************************************
localhost                  : ok=1    changed=0    unreachable=0    failed=1    skipped=0    rescued=0    ignored=0
```

Figure 6.25: Play recap with Python interpreter error

So, we have observed an error here in our execution. The error is of Python interpreter. There are multiple ways of forcing Ansible to the required Python interpreter. In this case we will use simple fix which is manually forcing the Ansible to use the Python 3 as Python interpreter. We have used ad-hoc command options to perform this operation. Let us try it again with that:

```
[root@ip-172-31-8-19 ansible]# ansible-playbook firtplay.yaml -e 'ansible_python_interpreter=/usr/bin/python3.6'
/usr/local/lib/python3.6/site-packages/ansible/parsing/vault/__init__.py:44: CryptographyDeprecationWarning: Python 3.6
r it is deprecated in cryptography. The next release of cryptography will remove support for Python 3.6.
  from cryptography.exceptions import InvalidSignature

PLAY [test] ************************************************************************************************

TASK [Gathering Facts] ************************************************************************************
ok: [localhost]

TASK [testing : Demo VM] **********************************************************************************
changed: [localhost]

PLAY RECAP ************************************************************************************************
localhost                  : ok=2    changed=1    unreachable=0    failed=0    skipped=0    rescued=0    ignored=0

[root@ip-172-31-8-19 ansible]#
```

Figure 6.26: Successful playbook execution after fix

After execution if you find all green then that means everything is good and healthy. Let us run the playbook in the debug mode and see the results.

```
ok: [localhost] => {
    "changed": false,
    "contains_resources": false,
    "invocation": {
        "module_args": {
            "ad_user": null,
            "adfs_authority_url": null,
            "api_profile": "latest",
            "append_tags": true,
            "auth_source": "auto",
            "cert_validation_mode": null,
            "client_id": null,
            "cloud_environment": "AzureCloud",
            "force_delete_nonempty": false,
            "location": "eastus",
            "log_mode": null,
            "log_path": null,
            "name": "DummyRG",
            "password": null,
            "profile": null,
            "secret": null,
            "state": "present",
            "subscription_id": null,
            "tags": null,
            "tenant": null,
            "thumbprint": null,
            "x509_certificate_path": null
        }
    },
    "state": {
        "id": "/subscriptions/51a23039-7d9b-4900-837f-84d8e83a5591/resourceGroups/DummyRG",
        "location": "eastus",
        "name": "DummyRG",
        "provisioning_state": "Succeeded",
        "tags": {}
```

Figure 6.27: Result of playbook execution debug

Now that Ansible has lots of modules for Microsoft Azure, it is not possible to cover all of them. However, we will cover a few very important modules here.

Here is the list of a few modules available for Azure in Ansible:

https://docs.ansible.com/ansible/2.9/modules/list_of_cloud_modules.html#azure

- **azure_rm_acs:** Manage an **Azure Container Service** (**ACS**) instance
- **azure_rm_aks:** Manage a managed **Azure Container Service** (**AKS**) instance
- **azure_rm_aks_info:** Get Azure Kubernetes Service facts
- **azure_rm_aksversion_info:** Get available kubernetes versions supported by Azure Kubernetes Service
- **azure_rm_appgateway:** Manage Application Gateway instance

The list is huge and growing every day. Let us start the virtual machine module (**azure_ rm_virtualmachine**). We will provide you with a demo of this module, and then you will need to continue with the rest of the module and practice it.

Let us start with **RM_Virtualmachine** module. This module is used for managing the virtual machines. You can easily create the VM using it. Here is the demo role for your reference:

```
[root@ip-172-31-8-19 ansible]# cat roles/testing/tasks/main.yml
---
- name: Demo VM
  azure_rm_virtualmachine:
     resource_group: testing
     name: DummmyVM
     admin_username: demouser
     admin_password: demouser@1234demo
     image:
        offer: CentOS
        publisher: OpenLogic
        sku: '7.7'
        version: latest
     vm_size: Standard_DS3_v2
[root@ip-172-31-8-19 ansible]#
```

Figure 6.28: Module with sample playbook for creation of instances in Azure

Let us run this with a playbook and see the result:

```
[root@ip-172-31-8-19 ansible]#
[root@ip-172-31-8-19 ansible]# ansible-playbook firtplay.yaml -e 'ansible_python_interpreter=/usr/bin/python3.6'
/usr/local/lib/python3.6/site-packages/ansible/parsing/vault/__init__.py:44: CryptographyDeprecationWarning: Python
r it is deprecated in cryptography. The next release of cryptography will remove support for Python 3.6.
  from cryptography.exceptions import InvalidSignature

PLAY [test] ***********************************************************************************

TASK [Gathering Facts] **********************************************************************
ok: [localhost]

TASK [testing : Demo VM] ********************************************************************
changed: [localhost]

PLAY RECAP ************************************************************************************
localhost                  : ok=2    changed=1    unreachable=0    failed=0    skipped=0    rescued=0    ignored=0
```

Figure 6.29: Playbook execution recap

As expected, the code works fine. Let us go to the console and see if the VM is there:

Figure 6.30: Successful launch of VM after playbook execution

As we can see, **DummyVM** is present in the EAST US with the **Standard_DS3_v2** size we gave it.

Let us create a code to delete the VM here:

```
[root@ip-172-31-8-19 ansible]# cat roles/testing/tasks/main.yml
- name: Demo VM
  azure_rm_virtualmachine:
    resource_group: testing
    name: DummmyVM
    remove_on_absent: all_autocreated
    state: absent
```

Figure 6.31: Roles to delete the newly created VM

Let us run and see the results:

```
            "resource_group": "testing",
            "restarted": false,
            "secret": null,
            "security_profile": null,
            "short_hostname": null,
            "ssh_password_enabled": true,
            "ssh_public_keys": null,
            "started": null,
            "state": "absent",
            "storage_account_name": null,
            "storage_blob_name": null,
            "storage_container_name": "vhds",
            "subnet_name": null,
            "subscription_id": null,
            "tags": null,
            "tenant": null,
            "thumbprint": null,
            "virtual_network_name": null,
            "virtual_network_resource_group": null,
            "vm_identity": null,
            "vm_size": null,
            "windows_config": null,
            "winrm": null,
            "x509_certificate_path": null,
            "zones": null
        }
    },
    "powerstate_change": null
}

PLAY RECAP *******************************************************************************
localhost                   : ok=2    changed=1    unreachable=0    failed=0    skipped=0    rescued=0
```

Figure 6.32: Playbook execution recap after deleting VM

We have successfully deleted the VM.

As we have seen in the last chapter, we need the details like VPC ID, subnet ID, and so on for our end-to-end instance creation. For example, when we created the resource group, we needed its name for future use, so we can call it in our next code as we used in the VM creation role.

Let us use a register module, save the content in a variable here, and parse it in the **debug** module:

```
[root@ip-172-31-8-19 ansible]# cat roles/testing/tasks/main.yml
---
- name: Demo VM
  azure_rm_resourcegroup:
    name: myResourceGroup
    location: westus
  register: variable
- debug:
    msg: "{{variable}}"
[root@ip-172-31-8-19 ansible]#
```

Figure 6.33: Role with variable saved and further used for debugging

Let us see the output of the execution and see what useful information we can find in it:

```
TASK [testing : debug] *************************************************************
ok: [localhost] => {
    "msg": {
        "changed": false,
        "contains_resources": false,
        "failed": false,
        "state": {
            "id": "/subscriptions/51a23039-7d9b-4900-837f-84d8e83a5591/resourceGroups/
            "location": "westus",
            "name": "myResourceGroup",
            "provisioning_state": "Succeeded",
            "tags": {}
        }
    }
}
```

Figure 6.34: Play recap with debug module

As we can see under the state, we have the name field which gives us the information of the resource group name. We can fetch these details very easily. Let us try it:

```
[root@ip-172-31-8-19 ansible]# cat roles/testing/tasks/main.yml
---
- name: Demo VM
  azure_rm_resourcegroup:
    name: myResourceGroup
    location: westus
  register: variable
- debug:
    msg: "{{variable.state.name}}"
[root@ip-172-31-8-19 ansible]#  ansible-playbook firtplay.yaml -e 'a
/usr/local/lib/python3.6/site-packages/ansible/parsing/vault/__init_
r it is deprecated in cryptography. The next release of cryptography
  from cryptography.exceptions import InvalidSignature

PLAY [test] *******************************************************

TASK [Gathering Facts] ********************************************
ok: [localhost]

TASK [testing : Demo VM] ******************************************
ok: [localhost]

TASK [testing : debug] ********************************************
ok: [localhost] => {
    "msg": "myResourceGroup"
}

PLAY RECAP ********************************************************
localhost                  : ok=3    changed=0    unreachable=0    f
```

Figure 6.35: *Role where we have fetched the name of the resource group and displayed it on the terminal*

This is how we can fetch the information and use it in the future. Let us create a role right here and use it:

```
[root@ip-172-31-8-19 ansible]# cat roles/testing/tasks/main.yml
---
- name: Demo VM
  azure_rm_resourcegroup:
    name: myResourceGroup
    location: westus
  register: variable

- name: Demo VM
  azure_rm_virtualmachine:
    resource_group: "{{variable.state.name}}"
    name: DummmyVM
    admin_username: demouser
    admin_password: demouser@1234demo
    image:
      offer: CentOS
      publisher: OpenLogic
      sku: '7.7'
      version: latest
    vm_size: Standard_DS3_v2

[root@ip-172-31-8-19 ansible]#
```

Figure 6.36: *Fetching and using the resource group name in our code*

Let us run and see the output:

```
[root@ip-172-31-8-19 ansible]# ansible-playbook firtplay.yaml -e 'ansible_python_interpreter=/usr/bin/python3.6'
/usr/local/lib/python3.6/site-packages/ansible/parsing/vault/__init__.py:44: CryptographyDeprecationWarning: Python 3.6 is no longe
r it is deprecated in cryptography. The next release of cryptography will remove support for Python 3.6.
  from cryptography.exceptions import InvalidSignature

PLAY [test] *********************************************************************************************************

TASK [Gathering Facts] *********************************************************************************************
ok: [localhost]

TASK [testing : Demo VM] *******************************************************************************************
ok: [localhost]

TASK [testing : Demo VM] *******************************************************************************************
fatal: [localhost]: FAILED! => {"changed": false, "msg": "Unable unable to find virtual network in resource group myResourceGroup
 des to create a NIC for the virtual machine."}

PLAY RECAP *********************************************************************************************************
localhost                  : ok=2    changed=0    unreachable=0    failed=1    skipped=0    rescued=0    ignored=0
```

Figure 6.37: Successful playbook execution with a variable used in the code

The error clearly says it cannot find the virtual network in our resource group, so let us create it programmatically and use it further. This will give us the chance to explore one more module together.

Let us add the code for the VNet creation in the same role and see the results. We do not get any subnet from the VNet creation. We need to use the different module to make subnets.

Let us have a look at the code now: We have used the **azure_rm_virtualnetwork** module to create the virtual network. We have defined the prefix CIDR here. Do not get confused with CIDR defined here, it is not a subnet. Subnet will be created in the range of CIDR we defined here only however, that will be all together a different Ansible module.

The code is as follows:

```
[root@ip-172-31-8-19 ansible]# cat roles/testing/tasks/main.yml
---
- name: Demo VM
  azure_rm_resourcegroup:
    name: myResourceGroup
    location: westus
  register: variable

- name: Create a virtual network
  azure_rm_virtualnetwork:
    resource_group: "{{variable.state.name}}"
    name: myVirtualNetwork
    address_prefixes_cidr:
      - "10.10.0.0/16"
      - "172.100.0.0/16"

- name: Create a subnet
  azure_rm_subnet:
    resource_group: "{{variable.state.name}}"
    virtual_network_name: myVirtualNetwork
    name: mySubnet
    address_prefix_cidr: "10.10.0.0/24"

- name: Demo VM
  azure_rm_virtualmachine:
    resource_group: "{{variable.state.name}}"
    name: DummmyVM
    admin_username: demouser
    admin_password: demouser@1234demo
    image:
      offer: CentOS
      publisher: OpenLogic
      sku: '7.7'
      version: latest
    vm_size: Standard_DS3_v2
```

Figure 6.38: Consolidated role that creates resource group, virtual network, subnet, and VM using a variable

For subnet creation, we have used the **azure_rm_subnet** module. We have used the name of the virtual network and resource group. We could have saved the value of the virtual network in a variable again here using the register module and called that variable in the code. However, it is ok to call the name too, since it is the same name we have used. Let us run our code this time and see the result:

```
        "resource_group": "myResourceGroup",
        "restarted": false,
        "secret": null,
        "security_profile": null,
        "short_hostname": null,
        "ssh_password_enabled": true,
        "ssh_public_keys": null,
        "started": null,
        "state": "present",
        "storage_account_name": null,
        "storage_blob_name": null,
        "storage_container_name": "vhds",
        "subnet_name": null,
        "subscription_id": null,
        "tags": null,
        "tenant": null,
        "thumbprint": null,
        "virtual_network_name": null,
        "virtual_network_resource_group": null,
        "vm_identity": null,
        "vm_size": "Standard_DS3_v2",
        "windows_config": null,
        "winrm": null,
        "x509_certificate_path": null,
        "zones": null
        }
    },
    "powerstate_change": null
}

PLAY RECAP *********************************************************************************************************
localhost                  : ok=5    changed=2    unreachable=0    failed=0    skipped=0    rescued=0    ignored=0
```

Figure 6.39: Play recap shows the successful execution of the code

As we can see, it is a successful execution. All the parameters were right, and we have created a VM in Azure. Similarly, we should start navigating to the module of your choice and work and practice it.

Ansible using Microsoft Azure Cloud Shell

First of all, we need to navigate to the Azure portal and click on **Cloud Shell**. The following figure will give you an idea of where to find it on screen:

Figure 6.40: Finding the place for Cloud Shell

For the first-time user, it is going to offer a few options. You can choose the PowerShell there. Just for your information second option is Bash. Once you have chosen PowerShell, it will show you the **Subscription** you have. Very next to that, you have **Show advanced settings**. Click on that:

Figure 6.41: Selecting the right advanced settings

It will open a new window which will have the following listed options:

- **Subscription**: Keep the same
- **Cloud shell region**: Choose your nearest one
- **Resource group**: Click on create new and give it a name
- **Storage account**: Click on create new and give it a name
- **File share**: Click on create new and give it a name

At the last click on create storage, it will start the process. This is how it will look once everything is created. As you can see on the terminal, it has authenticated to the Azure, which means you will not need to provide the authentication parameters to the Ansible code:

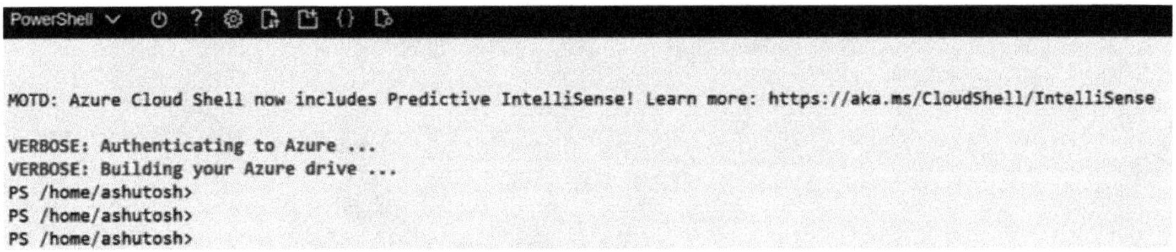

Figure 6.42: View of Azure PowerShell

Let us try and create our first playbook here. Here you can start using the **vi** editor to create your playbook. Refer to the following figure for a better understanding:

Figure 6.43: vi editor is present in PowerShell, like our Linux host

Content of **FirstAzure.yaml**:

```
PowerShell ∨    ⏻  ?  ⚙  ⬚  ⬚  {}  ⬚

---
- name: Create a resource Group
  connection: local
  hosts: localhost
  tasks:
    - name: Creating resource group
      azure_rm_resourcegroup:
        name: DumbRGAs
        location: eastus
      register: output
    - debug:
        msg: "{{output}}"
```

Figure 6.44: View of our playbook created in PowerShell using the vi editor

Let us run the code now in PowerShell and see if it works:

```
PS /home/ashutosh> ansible-playbook FirstAzure.yml
[WARNING]: No inventory was parsed, only implicit localhost is available
[WARNING]: provided hosts list is empty, only localhost is available. Note that the implicit localhost does not match

PLAY [Create a resource Group] ****************************************************************

TASK [Gathering Facts] ************************************************************************
ok: [localhost]

TASK [Creating resource group] ****************************************************************
ok: [localhost]

TASK [debug] **********************************************************************************
ok: [localhost] => {
    "msg": {
        "changed": false,
        "contains_resources": false,
        "failed": false,
        "state": {
            "id": "/subscriptions/51a23039-7d9b-4900-837f-84d8e83a5591/resourceGroups/DumbRGAs",
            "location": "eastus",
            "name": "DumbRGAs",
            "provisioning_state": "Succeeded",
            "tags": {}
        }
    }
}

PLAY RECAP ************************************************************************************
localhost                  : ok=3    changed=0    unreachable=0    failed=0    skipped=0    rescued=0    ignored=0
```

Figure 6.45: Playbook recap in Azure PowerShell

As we can see, it works fine with the Microsoft Azure PowerShell, too. The good thing about it is that it has all the Python SDK and requirements installed. You simply need to start using it.

Other Linux commands also work fine. We can also try the Bash here.

In the dropdown menu, we can see the Bash. Click on it and see what happens when we try the same code from the Bash.

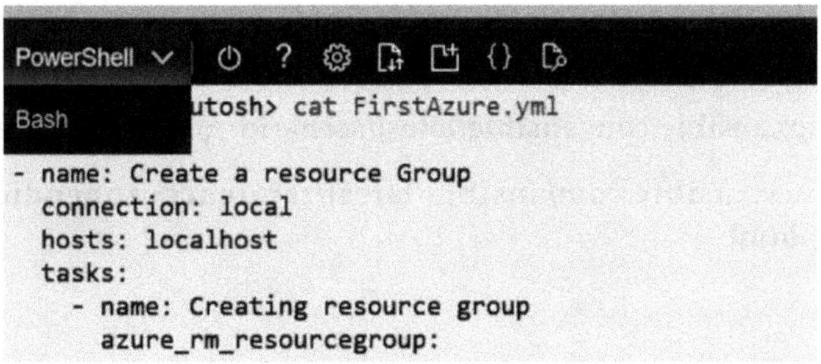

Figure 6.46: Playbook view from the Bash terminal of Azure Cloud

Right now, we will not give you the results of the test on Bash. You need to do it on your own for now.

Similarly, you can create the VNet, subnet, and VM all things from here. This is good for those who like Ansible but do not have an Ansible environment available in their organization. This is also for those who already have a stable version of the Ansible control machine and do not want to disturb it. It is also good for those who do not want to install the Azure SDK on their box. For all these people, Azure PowerShell is a good option.

Conclusion

Just to summarize what we learned so far, we have seen what an IT automation engine like Ansible can do with the cloud, like AWS and Microsoft Azure. The best thing about Azure is that we do not even need our control machine if we want to use Ansible with Azure. We can directly start using PowerShell and deploy our Ansible playbooks. However, if you want to run the code from your Ansible control machine, then it is the best way to use it. We can create a service principal and install the Python SDK for Microsoft Azure, and after a few dependencies, we are ready to work efficiently with Microsoft Azure.

In the next chapter, we will start focusing on our day-to-day tasks. As our motive is reducing our daily repetitive tasks and focusing on the productive work, we will focus on a few Linux modules and then navigate to the Windows module of Ansible.

References

- **https://www.ansible.com/**

- **https://docs.ansible.com/ansible/2.9/modules/azure_rm_subnet_module. html#azure-rm-subnet-module**

- **https://learn.microsoft.com/en-us/azure/developer/ansible/getting-started-cloud-shell?tabs=ansible**

- https://learn.microsoft.com/en-us/azure/developer/ansible/install-on-linux-vm?tabs=azure-cli

- https://docs.ansible.com/ansible/latest/scenario_guides/guide_azure.html

- https://docs.ansible.com/ansible/latest/reference_appendices/interpreter_discovery.html

Join our Discord space

Join our Discord workspace for latest updates, offers, tech happenings around the world, new releases, and sessions with the authors:

https://discord.bpbonline.com

CHAPTER 7

Configuration Management

Introduction

So far, we have learnt that Ansible is a configuration management tool. Finally, we are ready to perform configuration changes to the target hosts. In this chapter, we will configure a few servers. We will try to focus on our day-to-day activities and how we can achieve them using Ansible.

Structure

This chapter includes the following topics:

- Ansible for Linux hosts
- Ansible command module
- Ansible for Windows

Objectives

By the end of this chapter, you will learn how you can manage your servers using Ansible and how you can perform various configuration changes to them. Now, in this chapter, we have focused on the servers only, but in the next few chapters, we will cover a lot more topics.

Ansible for Linux hosts

Ansible is mainly designed for server configuration management. This is why we have a huge amount of development from Ansible on the configuration management of Windows and Linux servers. As we know, Ansible works on top of SSH, and it is not different from the Linux hosts; it establishes the connection with the target host on SSH or port 22 and pushes the commands to the target host. Whether they have an Ubuntu host or RHEL, the modules are there for all flavors of Linux. Let us start with a few basic modules of Linux, which can be used for executing a few frequently used commands on the target host.

Ansible command module

Ansible command module is a built-in module for Ansible. It comes installed with almost all versions of Ansible. It is a very helpful and easy-to-use module. It simply executes the commands on the target host. A sample role for the Ansible command module is as follows:

```
[root@ip-172-31-8-19 ansible]# cat roles/newlinux/tasks/main.yml
---
- name: Return motd to registered var
  ansible.builtin.command: cat /etc/hosts
[root@ip-172-31-8-19 ansible]#
```

Figure 7.1: Example of a command module

Just like any other module, we need to specify the name of the module. Once this is done, we need to put the command we want to push on the target host. In this case, we want to execute the **cat /etc/hosts** command on the target host.

Let us execute the command and see the results:

```
        "start": "2023-04-26 22:45:51.778350",
        "stderr": "",
        "stderr_lines": [],
        "stdout": "127.0.0.1   localhost localhost.localdomain localhost4 localhost4.localdomain4\n::1        localhost localhost.localdomain localhost6 localhost6.localdomain6",
        "stdout_lines": [
            "127.0.0.1   localhost localhost.localdomain localhost4 localhost4.localdomain4",
            "::1         localhost localhost.localdomain localhost6 localhost6.localdomain6"
        ]
}

PLAY RECAP *********************************************************************************************************************
20.245.227.241             : ok=2    changed=1    unreachable=0    failed=0    skipped=0    rescued=0    ignored=0
localhost                  : ok=2    changed=1    unreachable=0    failed=0    skipped=0    rescued=0    ignored=0

[root@ip-172-31-8-19 ansible]#
```

Figure 7.2: Play recap with newly created playbook

As we can see, it works fine with the target host. Let us try another command like **uptime**, as follows:

```
    "invocation": {
        "module_args": {
            "_raw_params": "uptime",
            "_uses_shell": false,
            "argv": null,
            "chdir": null,
            "creates": null,
            "executable": null,
            "removes": null,
            "stdin": null,
            "stdin_add_newline": true,
            "strip_empty_ends": true,
            "warn": true
        }
    },
    "msg": "",
    "rc": 0,
    "start": "2023-04-26 22:57:10.698216",
    "stderr": "",
    "stderr_lines": [],
    "stdout": " 22:57:10 up 3 days,  9:05,  1 user,  load average: 0.01, 0.02, 0.05",
    "stdout_lines": [
        " 22:57:10 up 3 days,  9:05,  1 user,  load average: 0.01, 0.02, 0.05"
    ]
}
META: ran handlers
META: ran handlers

PLAY RECAP ***********************************************************************
20.245.227.241             : ok=2    changed=1    unreachable=0    failed=0    skipped=
localhost                  : ok=2    changed=1    unreachable=0    failed=0    skipped=

[root@ip-172-31-8-19 ansible]#
[root@ip-172-31-8-19 ansible]#
[root@ip-172-31-8-19 ansible]#
[root@ip-172-31-8-19 ansible]# cat roles/newlinux/tasks/main.yml
---
- name: Return motd to registered var
  ansible.builtin.command: uptime
[root@ip-172-31-8-19 ansible]#
```

Figure 7.3: Second example of a command module that runs a command on target hosts

With this, we can conclude that we can simply send any command and get it executed on the target host. However, this module has some limitations too. Let us demonstrate the same with a very small example here. We know we can redirect the output of any command to a file very easily in the Linux shell. For example, if we want to redirect the output of the command **uptime** to a file named **output.txt**, it can be done as follows:

```
[root@ip-172-31-8-19 ansible]# uptime
 22:19:17 up 4 days,  8:27,  1 user,  load average: 0.00, 0.01, 0.05
[root@ip-172-31-8-19 ansible]# uptime > output.txt
[root@ip-172-31-8-19 ansible]# cat output.txt
 22:19:19 up 4 days,  8:27,  1 user,  load average: 0.00, 0.01, 0.05
[root@ip-172-31-8-19 ansible]#
```

Figure 7.4: Example with redirection in Linux

So, as we can see, the **>** is used for the redirect here. However, let us try that in our module and see the result:

```
[root@ip-172-31-8-19 ansible]# cat roles/newlinux/tasks/main.yml
---
- name: Return motd to registered var
  ansible.builtin.command: uptime > saveuptime.txt
[root@ip-172-31-8-19 ansible]#
```

Figure 7.5: Example redirection used in the command module

In this situation, **uptime** is getting redirected to the **saveuptime.txt** file. The execution will happen in both the local server and one remote server.

We will verify them as follows:

```
[root@ip-172-31-8-19 ansible]# ansible-playbook firtplay.yaml -u demouser -k
/usr/local/lib/python3.6/site-packages/ansible/parsing/vault/__init__.py:44: CryptographyDeprecationWarning: Python 3.6 is
r it is deprecated in cryptography. The next release of cryptography will remove support for Python 3.6.
  from cryptography.exceptions import InvalidSignature
SSH password:

PLAY [test] ***********************************************************************************

TASK [Gathering Facts] ************************************************************************
ok: [localhost]
ok: [20.245.227.241]

TASK [newlinux : Return motd to registered var] ***********************************************
changed: [20.245.227.241]
changed: [localhost]

PLAY RECAP ************************************************************************************
20.245.227.241             : ok=2    changed=1    unreachable=0    failed=0    skipped=0    rescued=0    ignored=0
localhost                  : ok=2    changed=1    unreachable=0    failed=0    skipped=0    rescued=0    ignored=0

[root@ip-172-31-8-19 ansible]# ll
total 64
-rw-r--r--. 1 root root 20025 Apr 23 14:33 1
-rw-r--r--. 1 root root 20027 Apr 23 14:35 ansible.cfg
-rwxr-xr-x. 1 root root   210 Apr 23 18:07 credentials
-rw-r--r--. 1 root root    73 Apr 26 22:42 firtplay.yaml
-rw-r--r--. 1 root root  1039 Apr 26 22:43 hosts
-rw-r--r--. 1 root root   275 Apr 23 15:03 newtest.yaml
-rw-r--r--. 1 root root    69 Apr 27 22:19 output.txt
drwxr-xr-x. 4 root root    37 Apr 26 22:41 roles
drwxr-xr-x. 5 root root   100 Apr 23 15:03 venv-test
-rw-r--r--. 1 root root   287 Apr 23 23:14 vmcreate.yaml
```

Figure 7.6: The list shows the redirected file is missing even after successful playbook execution

As we can see, the local server does not contain any file with the name **saveuptime.txt**. Let us log in to the remote server and see if that has any text files created there:

```
[root@ip-172-31-8-19 ansible]# ssh demouser@20.245.227.241
demouser@20.245.227.241's password:
Last login: Thu Apr 27 22:27:36 2023 from ec2-13-50-242-159.eu-north-1.compute.amazonaws.com
[demouser@DummmyVM ~]$ ll
total 0
```

Figure 7.7: The redirected file is missing from the target host

We can see that we did not find any text file here. This means that the commands are not getting processed through the Linux shell. So, the redirect option does not work using the command module. Redirect is not the only thing that will not work here. Operations such as **&**, **|**, **;**, *****, **<**, and **>** will also fail. Similarly, variables like **$hostname** will not work in this context.

Now, you might have started thinking about how we can work without them. This might become a big problem in our daily work; what is the solution now? We have another module in Ansible that executes the commands in the Linux shell. The name of that module is the shell module itself. So let us have a look at it next.

Ansible shell module

Now you will find all the functionality of the shell module and the command module itself. The major difference is how commands get executed on the target hosts. Shell module pushes the commands on the target host through a shell, which is **/bin/sh**. This means that all the functions, like redirect and variables like hostname, are going to work here without any hassle. Now, let us try the redirect function first with the shell module and look at the worthiness of this module:

```
[root@ip-172-31-8-19 ansible]#
[root@ip-172-31-8-19 ansible]# cat roles/newlinux/tasks/main.yml
---
- name: Return motd to registered var
  ansible.builtin.shell: uptime > saveuptime.txt

[root@ip-172-31-8-19 ansible]#
```

Figure 7.8: Example of shell module with redirection

As highlighted in the module used here, let us execute this role and see the result. We should see the file named **saveuptime.txt** in the target host:

```
[root@ip-172-31-8-19 ansible]#
[root@ip-172-31-8-19 ansible]# ansible-playbook firtplay.yaml -u demouser -k
/usr/local/lib/python3.6/site-packages/ansible/parsing/vault/__init__.py:44: CryptographyDeprecationWarning: Python
r it is deprecated in cryptography. The next release of cryptography will remove support for Python 3.6.
  from cryptography.exceptions import InvalidSignature
SSH password:

PLAY [test] **********************************************************************

TASK [Gathering Facts] **********************************************************
ok: [20.245.227.241]

TASK [newlinux : Return motd to registered var] *********************************
changed: [20.245.227.241]

PLAY RECAP **********************************************************************
20.245.227.241             : ok=2    changed=1    unreachable=0    failed=0    skipped=0    rescued=0    ignored=0

[root@ip-172-31-8-19 ansible]# ssh demouser@20.245.227.241
demouser@20.245.227.241's password:
Last login: Thu Apr 27 22:41:43 2023 from ec2-13-50-242-159.eu-north-1.compute.amazonaws.com
[demouser@DummmyVM ~]$ ll
total 4
-rw-rw-r--. 1 demouser demouser 68 Apr 27 22:41 saveuptime.txt
[demouser@DummmyVM ~]$ 
```

Figure 7.9: Redirected file present after use of the shell module

We have written a small code to print **hello world!** on execution. We will use Ansible to execute that Python code on the target host. You can make it complex Python code or any

Bash code you want to execute or trigger on the target host. You can even create a code inline and execute that using the Linux shell module, as shown in *Figure 7.10*:

```
[root@ip-172-31-8-19 ansible]# cat roles/newlinux/tasks/main.yml
---
- name: Return motd to registered var
  ansible.builtin.shell: /usr/bin/python hello.py
```

Figure 7.10: Sample Python code to run using Ansible

Let us execute it and see the results:

```
[root@ip-172-31-8-19 ansible]# ansible-playbook firtplay.yaml -u demouser -k -v
/usr/local/lib/python3.6/site-packages/ansible/parsing/vault/__init__.py:44: CryptographyDeprecationWarning: Pyt
r it is deprecated in cryptography. The next release of cryptography will remove support for Python 3.6.
  from cryptography.exceptions import InvalidSignature
Using /etc/ansible/ansible.cfg as config file
SSH password:

PLAY [test] ************************************************************************

TASK [Gathering Facts] ************************************************************
ok: [20.245.227.241]

TASK [newlinux : Return motd to registered var] ***********************************
changed: [20.245.227.241] => {"changed": true, "cmd": "/usr/bin/python hello.py", "delta": "0:00:00.017966", "en
:55:41.346907", "stderr": "", "stderr_lines": [], "stdout": "Hello world", "stdout_lines": ["Hello world"]}

PLAY RECAP ************************************************************************
20.245.227.241             : ok=2    changed=1    unreachable=0    failed=0    skipped=0    rescued=0    ignored

[root@ip-172-31-8-19 ansible]# cat roles/newlinux/tasks/main.yml
---
- name: Return motd to registered var
  ansible.builtin.shell: /usr/bin/python hello.py

[root@ip-172-31-8-19 ansible]#
```

Figure 7.11: Successful execution of the Python code on the target host using an Ansible playbook

As we can see, we can execute any executables on the target host using Ansible. However, what if we want to push a bunch of the commands on the target host? Well, that is also easy, and let us see how we can do that. You just need a pipe | to start with, and you can push any many commands as you want:

```
[root@ip-172-31-8-19 ansible]# cat roles/newlinux/tasks/main.yml
---
- name: Return motd to registered var
  ansible.builtin.shell: |
    uptime
    cat /etc/hosts
    ls -ltr

[root@ip-172-31-8-19 ansible]#
```

Figure 7.12: Sample playbook to send multiple commands on the target host

You just have to make sure that there is a right indentation of two spaces. The rest will be good.

Let us run our code and see the results:

Figure 7.13: Output of multiple commands executed on the target host

As we can seein *Figure 7.13*, the output shows that the multiple commands were correctly executed on the target host.

Now, you will be working a lot with the variables in the real-life situation, and this is the right time to begin with the variables.

Let us see something tricky here. It might look good to the developers, but for first-time viewers, it might be a little cryptic. Let us try to execute this code and see what we get in return:

Figure 7.14: Print the variable information on the terminal

Basically, the **gather_facts** will gather the information about the target hosts and will store that in variables. Now, the version information is saved under the variable named **ansible_distribution_version**:

```
[root@ip-172-31-8-19 ansible]# ansible-playbook firtplay.yaml -u demouser -k -v
/usr/local/lib/python3.6/site-packages/ansible/parsing/vault/__init__.py:44: Crypt
r it is deprecated in cryptography. The next release of cryptography will remove s
  from cryptography.exceptions import InvalidSignature
Using /etc/ansible/ansible.cfg as config file
SSH password:

PLAY [test] *******************************************************************

TASK [Gathering Facts] ********************************************************
ok: [20.245.227.241]

TASK [newlinux : Return motd to registered var] ******************************
changed: [20.245.227.241] => {"changed": true, "cmd": "echo \"7.7\"\n", "delta": "
650", "stderr": "", "stderr_lines": [], "stdout": "7.7", "stdout_lines": ["7.7"]}

PLAY RECAP ********************************************************************
20.245.227.241             : ok=2    changed=1    unreachable=0    failed=0    ski
```

Figure 7.15: Debug of playbook execution, which shows the distribution version of CentOS

The output shows the version of CentOS on the target host, which is 7.7. You can have a look at our old code for Microsoft Azure and see which version of CentOS we created on Azure using our playbook. So, this is showing the right thing. Now, let us see how it shows with cryptic lines. Think and try to understand why.

"{{ansible_distribution_version}}"

This means we are parsing a variable. Whatever the value is of the variable **ansible_distribution_version**, we will replace that with this variable name:

```
[root@ip-172-31-8-19 ansible]# cat roles/newlinux/tasks/main.yml
---
- name: Return motd to registered var
  ansible.builtin.shell: |
    echo "{{ansible_distribution_version}}" # This means echo the value of Ansible_distribution_version.
  Which is 7.7 in this case.
[root@ip-172-31-8-19 ansible]#
```

Figure 7.16: Role that shows the distribution version of CentOS

However, we have not created any variables so far. Then, from where did this **ansible_distribution_version** come into the picture? Well, that brings us to the very useful module of Ansible, which is **gather_facts**. So, let us talk and learn about the **gather_facts** module. The **gather_facts** will gather the information about the target hosts and will store that in variables. Now, the version information is saved under the variable named **ansible_distribution_version**, and we have called that variable in our code.

Before we do that, how many of you have realized that we have run two extra tasks so far in our execution? Let us see what is happening here. Let us have a look at the following figure:

```
[root@ip-172-31-8-19 ansible]# ansible-playbook firtplay.yaml -u demouser -k
/usr/local/lib/python3.6/site-packages/ansible/parsing/vault/__init__.py:44:
r it is deprecated in cryptography. The next release of cryptography will rem
  from cryptography.exceptions import InvalidSignature
SSH password:

PLAY [test] ************************************************************

TASK [Gathering Facts] ************************************************
ok: [localhost]
ok: [20.245.227.241]

TASK [newlinux : Return motd to registered var] *********************
changed: [20.245.227.241]
changed: [localhost]

PLAY RECAP **********************************************************
20.245.227.241             : ok=2    changed=1    unreachable=0    failed=0
localhost                  : ok=2    changed=1    unreachable=0    failed=0
```

Figure 7.17: Play recap of successful execution

Whenever we ran a single role in our playbook, we always got two extra execution responses, except for the obvious one:

- One is **PLAY [name of our play]**:

```
PLAY [test] ****************************
```

Figure 7.18: Play execution with no error

When everything is good in our play, we get **ok=1** for this play execution.

- The second is **ok**:

```
TASK [Gathering Facts] ***
ok: [localhost]
ok: [20.245.227.241]
```

Figure 7.19: gather_facts of Ansible

The second uninvited execution is of **gather_facts**. This is visible to us all the time when we run our code.

- The third is **changed/ok,** which we always expected since we ran it. (Depending on the situation, whether our code performs any changes on the target host or not, it will be **ok** or **changed** in the play recap summary.):

```
TASK [newlinux : Return motd to registered var] **
changed: [20.245.227.241]
changed: [localhost]
```

Figure 7.20: Play recap of task execution

So, all the time when we saw a few extra **ok=2** in our code. They were the execution of play and **gather_facts**. Play execution is obvious, but **gather_facts** is something special that we had not expected.

Ansible gather_facts module

The **gather_facts** module is an auto-enabled module of Ansible. Anytime you run any of your playbooks, it automatically triggers for all target hosts. This is by design, and it tries to collect all the information about the target host, like its distribution, version, hardware IP address, etc. Now, this information is stored in a temporary place, which is known as a variable. There are different names assigned to different variables. For example, **ansible_distribution_version** is one Ansible variable name that stores the information about the version of the target host. Now this information is very useful when we try to write our code or playbooks.

For example, you want to install Ansible on all your target hosts. If the target host is CentOS or Linux, then you will use **yum install ansible**, but what if that is Ubuntu? The command will be **apt install ansible,** and this is where the problem starts. Now, you will deal with this kind of situation as follows:

- First of all, find out what distribution it is.
- Then, create an if condition on the basis of that distribution.
- Then, command it if that condition is met.

This is how we manage the conditions in any programming language. So, to find out the Linux distribution, you need to log in to the target host, run a few commands, and get the distribution and version information. This information is already collected by Ansible when you run your playbook. You simply need to call that variable and use it.

This will look like the best thing to you when it saves lots of time and energy. This means that half of your work is already done by Ansible; you just need to put the conditions and fire the command on that target host. This is all about the **gather_facts** module. Now, you must know the syntax for the conditions in Ansible. Let us have some basic idea about the syntax right now. We will cover the conditions in detail later. The syntax is as follows:

> **- name:** Install Ansible if version is debian
> **ansible.builtin.command:** apt install ansible
> **when:** ansible_facts['os_family'] == "Debian"

Figure 7.21: Role with the use of the command module

There are specific modules for installing any package or software in Windows, but this was just an example. We will put multiple conditions in the future. We will see the code where multiple conditions need to be fulfilled before execution.

Ansible register module

We have already used the register module a couple of times in our book, but now we will deep dive into the register module. The register module is an Ansible module that helps us save the output of execution in a variable. Once we save the output of execution in a variable, we can use that later in our code, and this helps us a lot in production:

```
- name: Install Ansible if version is debian
  ansible.builtin.command: uptime
  register: varoutput
```

Figure 7.22: Role with the use of the register module to capture the execution content

As you can see in the preceding example, we have used the register module, which will store the entire output of execution in a variable named **varoutput**. We can use the same variable and debug the content of that variable. We need to use the **debug** module to print the content of the variable. So let us focus on the debug module of Ansible.

Ansible debug module

The Ansible **debug** module is an important module of Ansible. If you wish to print the statement during execution, this is your preferred choice. However, statement printing is not the only useful thing we can do using this module. Debugging the variables and printing variable content can be another useful feature of the **debug** module. In the following example, we have printed the content stored in the variable **varoutput**:

```
- name: Install Ansible if version is debian
  ansible.builtin.command: uptime
  register: varoutput
- debug:
    msg: "{{ varoutput }}"
```

Figure 7.23: Role with use of register module and debug module

Ansible copy module

Ansible **copy** module is another important module of Ansible. It gives us the option to save/copy the content of execution to a file. If you want to copy the content of a variable to a file, that is possible. This module is very useful when you want to take a backup of any configuration on the device. Yes, there are other Ansible modules in the market, and you can still use the sync using the Ansible command or **shell** modules. However, this is another option you get with Ansible.

```
---
# tasks file for democopy
- name: test
  shell: uptime
  register: output

- name: copy uptime result to file
  ansible.builtin.copy:
    content: "{{ output.stdout }}"
    dest: temp.txt
```

Figure 7.24: Role with the use of the copy module

The **shell** module is used in *Figure 7.24* to view the uptime of this device, but the output only stays inline, and it will not be displayed to us. So, to view the uptime of the device, we have stored the content of execution in the variable named output using the register module. Once the value was stored in the variable, we used the copy module to save the content of the variable in the destination file.

Let us run the code now and see the results:

```
[root@ip-172-31-1-184 ansible]# cat roles/democopy/tasks/main.yml
---
# tasks file for democopy
- name: test
  shell: uptime
  register: output
- ansible.builtin.copy:
    content: "{{output}}"
    dest: temp.txt
[root@ip-172-31-1-184 ansible]# ansible-playbook playbook.yaml

PLAY [test] ************************************************************************

TASK [Gathering Facts] ************************************************************
ok: [localhost]

TASK [democopy : test] ************************************************************
changed: [localhost]

TASK [democopy : ansible.builtin.copy] ********************************************
changed: [localhost]

PLAY RECAP ************************************************************************
localhost                  : ok=3    changed=2    unreachable=0    failed=0    skipped=0    rescued=0    ignored=0

[root@ip-172-31-1-184 ansible]# ls -lt
total 36
-rw-r--r--. 1 root root   355 May 13 22:01 temp.txt
-rw-r--r--. 1 root root    72 May 13 21:55 playbook.yaml
```

Figure 7.25: Play recap shows the successful execution with the copy module

As we can see from the output, the file **temp.txt** has been created successfully on the server. This contains the information about the variable. In this case, it is the uptime of the host. However, the variable can contain any information, and we can always save that in a file using the **copy** module.

If your target folder is not the default local folder, ensure you have enough permission given to save the content to the destination folder/directory.

Similarly, we can copy the content of any file or the entire file to the destination we want. Let us have a look at another example where we took the backup of **/etc/hosts** file:

```
[root@ip-172-31-1-184 ansible]# cat roles/democopy/tasks/main.yml
---
- name:
  ansible.builtin.copy:
    src: /etc/hosts
    dest: backup
    follow: no
[root@ip-172-31-1-184 ansible]# ansible-playbook playbook.yaml

PLAY [test] ***********************************************************************

TASK [Gathering Facts] ***********************************************************
ok: [localhost]

TASK [democopy : ansible.builtin.copy] *******************************************
ok: [localhost]

PLAY RECAP ***********************************************************************
localhost                  : ok=2    changed=0    unreachable=0    failed=0    skipped=0    rescue

[root@ip-172-31-1-184 ansible]# ls -lt
total 40
-rw-r--r--. 1 root root    159 May 13 22:05 backup
-rw-r--r--. 1 root root    355 May 13 22:01 temp.txt
```

Figure 7.26: Sample role for the backup of a file

As we can see, the new backup file has been created in the **/etc/Ansible** folder. Similarly, we can use it for more work.

Ansible for Windows

As we have seen the Ansible has a lot of modules for all technologies. Windows hosts are no different. We have Ansible modules specifically defined for Windows. **WinRM** is one of the most famous and versatile Ansible modules for Windows clients. However, we need to correct one sentence that we have been using since the start of our book. We wrote that we do not need any additional configuration on the target hosts. However, we have an exception here. In case of a Windows machine, we need to log in to the target hosts and perform some configuration on them. Once we make the required configuration changes in the target hosts, we can start managing the target hosts using Ansible. Let us talk about the host's requirement for Windows hosts, where the first requirement will be to have the right Windows OS version.

The host requirements for Windows are as follows:

- We need to make sure we are using Windows Server 2012, 2012 R2, 2016, 2019, and 2022. Ansible supports a lot more than these mentioned server OS, and we can even manage a Windows PC running Windows 10. So, for the latest information on the supported platform, refer their website as there will be new addition and deletion of supported platforms.

- If you use Windows, you must know how good PowerShell is, and we cannot run our target host without PowerShell. We need the 3.0+ version of PowerShell and .Net 4.0+ on the Windows target hosts.

- Just like other IT automation engines (which need the installation of clients on the target host), we need to enable the WinRM listener in our target host. In this case, we need to install and activate it.

Ansible WinRM module

First of all, we need to enable TLS 1.2 on our target host by running the following command:

```
[Net.ServicePointManager]::SecurityProtocol          =          [Net.
SecurityProtocolType]::Tls12
```

Once that is done we need to install powershell in our Windows host. Use the below configuration to make the powershell working.

```
$url   =   &quot;https://raw.githubusercontent.com/jborean93/ansible-windows/
master/scripts/Upgrade-
PowerShell.ps1&quot;
$file = &quot;$env:temp\Upgrade-PowerShell.ps1&quot;
$username = &quot;Administrator&quot;
$password = &quot;PJOG@VR4pksLYpF)C4.32O8bYn0Khp0p&quot;
(New-Object -TypeName System.Net.WebClient).DownloadFile($url, $file)
Set-ExecutionPolicy -ExecutionPolicy Unrestricted -Force
&amp;$file -Version 5.1 -Username $username -Password $password -Verbose
```

Once this is done, we need to verify our WinRM listener is working. Use the following command to verify the status of WinRM:

```
Enable-PSRemoting -Force
Set-Item -Path WSMan:\localhost\Service\Auth\Certificate -Value $true
Set-Item  -Path  &#39;WSMan:\localhost\Service\AllowUnencrypted&#39;  -Value
$true
Set-Item -Path &#39;WSMan:\localhost\Service\Auth\Basic&#39; -Value $true
Set-Item -Path &#39;WSMan:\localhost\Service\Auth\CredSSP&#39; -Value $true

winrm enumerate winrm/config/Listener
```

You should be able to see a listener, which is running on HTTP. If you see the HTTPS as well, then you are good to proceed further with the Windows host.

In this case, we need to perform the additional configuration as we have been using the latest version of Windows Server.

```
PS C:\Users\Administrator>
PS C:\Users\Administrator> winrm enumerate winrm/config/Listener
Listener
    Address = *
    Transport = HTTP
    Port = 5985
    Hostname
    Enabled = true
    URLPrefix = wsman
    CertificateThumbprint
    ListeningOn = 127.0.0.1, 172.31.1.4, ::1, 2001:0:2851:782c:3099:3ae0:53e0:fefb, fe80::5efe:172.31.1.4%7, fe80::21ce:1f5a:2f28:220c%3, fe80::3099:3ae0:53e0:fe

PS C:\Users\Administrator>
```

Figure 7.27: *HTTP listener on the server*

Let us run the following command and see the error:

winrm quickconfig -transport:https

If you do not understand what the preceding command does, then to explain in short, basically, this command tries to run the **winrm** over the **https**.

After executing the command, if you find an error, **cannot find the certificate**, then you have your problem right in front of you. You need to find your DN and generate the certificate on the server (if it is not there).

```
PS C:\Users\Administrator> winrm quickconfig -transport:https
WinRM service is already running on this machine.
WSManFault
    Message
        ProviderFault
            WSManFault
                Message = Cannot create a WinRM listener on HTTPS because this machine does not have an appropriate certificate. To be used for SSL, a certificate must have a
iate for Server Authentication, and not be expired, revoked, or self-signed.

Error number:  -2144108267 0x80338115
Cannot create a WinRM listener on HTTPS because this machine does not have an appropriate certificate. To be used for SSL, a certificate must have a CN matching the hostname,
tion, and not be expired, revoked, or self-signed.
PS C:\Users\Administrator>
```

Figure 7.28: *Attempt to activate the HTTPS service on the Windows host*

Since we are just working with the demo environment, we will create a self-signed certificate, but in production, it is suggested to use a proper certificate.

Let us see how to generate the self-signed certificate:

$cert = New-SelfSignedCertificate -DnsName $(Invoke-RestMethod -Uri http://169.254.169.254/latest/meta-data/public-hostname) -CertStoreLocation "cert:\LocalMachine\My"

Now, you need to re-run the same command, and things should be operational. If it is not, then we need to manually configure the listener. Use the following command to do the same:

winrm create winrm/config/Listener?Address=*+Transport=HTTPS "@

```
{Hostname=`"$(Invoke-RestMethod    -Uri    http://169.254.169.254/latest/meta-
data/public-hostname)`";CertificateThumbprint=`"$($cert.Thumbprint)`"}"
```

```
PS C:\Users\Administrator>
PS C:\Users\Administrator> $cert = New-SelfSignedCertificate -DnsName $(Invoke-RestMethod -Uri http://169.254.169.254/la
test/meta-data/public-hostname) -CertStoreLocation "cert:\LocalMachine\My"
PS C:\Users\Administrator> winrm create winrm/config/Listener?Address=*+Transport=HTTPS "@{Hostname=`"$(Invoke-RestMetho
d -Uri http://169.254.169.254/latest/meta-data/public-hostname)`";CertificateThumbprint=`"$($cert.Thumbprint)`"}"
ResourceCreated
    Address = http://schemas.xmlsoap.org/ws/2004/08/addressing/role/anonymous
    ReferenceParameters
        ResourceURI = http://schemas.microsoft.com/wbem/wsman/1/config/listener
        SelectorSet
            Selector: Address = *, Transport = HTTPS
```

Figure 7.29: Listener activation on the Windows host

As we can see, the **winrm** services started on transport HTTPS, and that is what we were trying to achieve. Let us run the command again and see the status of the listers:

```
winrm enumerate winrm/config/Listener
```

```
PS C:\Users\Administrator> winrm enumerate winrm/config/Listener
Listener
    Address = *
    Transport = HTTP
    Port = 5985
    Hostname
    Enabled = true
    URLPrefix = wsman
    CertificateThumbprint
    ListeningOn = 127.0.0.1, 172.31.1.40, ::1, fe80::9bc0:4279:e849:da41%7

Listener
    Address = *
    Transport = HTTPS
    Port = 5986
    Hostname = ec2-13-233-163-2.ap-south-1.compute.amazonaws.com
    Enabled = true
    URLPrefix = wsman
    CertificateThumbprint = DBB5E8D5A68CF627F6822C0799DB291F2E47F1E0
    ListeningOn = 127.0.0.1, 172.31.1.40, ::1, fe80::9bc0:4279:e849:da41%7
```

Figure 7.30: Output shows now both listeners are now active on the Windows host

Once that is done, we need to enable the firewall rule on our Windows host. By default, the communication is blocked on ports 5986 and 5985. In our lab case, we disabled the firewall but you can use the GUI or CLI command to do so. If you do not like CLI, you can do it using the GUI as well:

```
New-NetFirewallRule -DisplayName "TCP HTTPS" -Direction Inbound -LocalPort
5986 -Protocol TCP -Action Allow
```

```
New-NetFirewallRule -DisplayName "TCP HTTPS" -Direction Inbound -LocalPort
5985 -Protocol TCP -Action Allow
```

Now, a few of our engineers might want to run it on the http, and for those people, they need to add the control machine to the trusted host list. This can be done using the following steps:

1. First, check the current list:

   ```
   Get-Item WSMan:\localhost\Client\TrustedHosts
   ```

2. Now, use the following command to add the host to the list:

```
Set-Item WSMan:\localhost\Client\TrustedHosts -Value 10.20.30.40
```

3. If you are facing any issue, to test it, you can use the following command. Just remember, this is just for the testing and not the best practice:

```
Set-Item WSMan:\localhost\Client\TrustedHosts -Value "*"
```

At last, you can restart the **winrm** services.

4. You might need to apply a token filter policy:

```
New-ItemProperty    -Name    LocalAccountTokenFilterPolicy    -Path
HKLM:\SOFTWARE\Microsoft\Windows\CurrentVersion\Policies\System
-PropertyTypeDWord -Value 1 -Force
```

Restart-service WinRM

Once services are restarted, check the listener again, and you should be good and be able to see two listeners, http and https, there. Now, if you are testing this lab in a cloud environment, make sure ports 5985 and 5986 are opened from your control machine. Otherwise, the communication is going to fail. Just because of time constraints, we have enabled any in this case, but you should get the source IP details and configure it over there.

Figure 7.31 shows that we have allowed any TCP communication for the Windows host. Remember, our requirement was only ports 5985 and 5986:

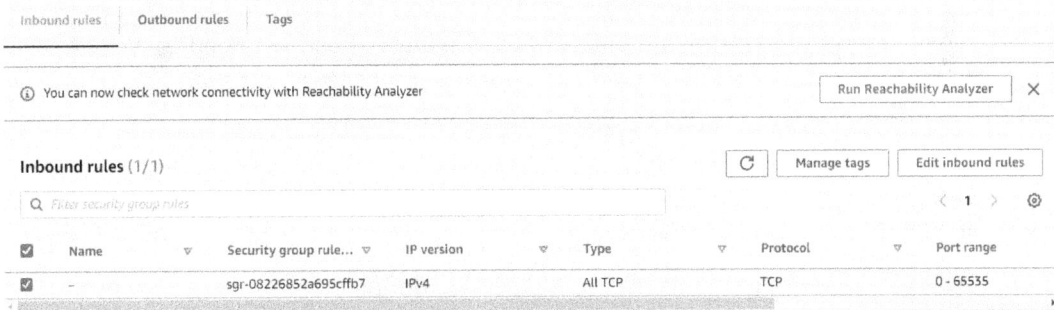

Figure 7.31: Network security group with allow any TCP communication

Now, navigate back to our Ansible control machine and perform the required configuration there. So, just like the installation of the Python SDK of AWS and Microsoft Azure, we need to perform some additional installation. In the case of Windows, it is a Python library for Windows remote management. The command for the installation is as follows:

```
pip3 install "pywinrm>=0.3.0" -user
```

This command will install the **winrm** Python package on our control machine. For a few people, it might require additional dependencies. You can install them and get through it.

We had to install two additional packages before it started working. Here is the list of them:

```
pip3 install --upgrade pip
pip3 install setuptools_rust
pip3 install rust
```

Now, we need to navigate to our home directory, which is **/etc/ansible,** and create an inventory file to run a test (we will use the variable file in case of a playbook).

Let us create an inventory file named **demoserver.ini**:

```
vi demoserver.ini

[demoserver]
x.x.x.x

[demoserver:vars] # These are the group variables
ansible_user=usernameofWindows
ansible_password="password"
ansible_port=5986
ansible_connection=winrm
ansible_winrm_scheme=https
ansible_winrm_server_cert_validation=ignore
ansible_winrm_kerberos_delegation=true
```

Any time we want to communicate with any of the target host, we need to authenticate our credentials. In this case, we use **ansible_user** and **ansible_password** to define our username and password:

- **ansible_port=5986**: This is the port on which the Windows host is listening. If it is **http**, it will be 5985, and for **https**, it is 5986. In our case, we are using **https**, hence, it is configured as 5986.

- **Ansible_connection**: This is mandatory to define the **winrm** connection type, otherwise, Ansible will try its default method. Does anyone remember what is the default connection method of Ansible? Well, if you are thinking of SSH, you are absolutely right about it. By default, Ansible uses OpenSSH as a connection method and tries to SSH to the target host. So, if we want to differ from that, we need to define the connection method here. Generally, we define that in the playbook, but since we are using ad-hoc commands here, we will define that in the inventory file.

- **ansible_winrm_scheme=https**: Now, we need to define the **winrm** parameters. Since we have two options in **winrm**, **http** and **https**. The https is more secure and recommended. Hence, we have used **https** here, but we can also use **http** if you want.

- **ansible_winrm_server_cert_validation=ignore**: Now, the certificate is self-signed in our case and will cause the error while execution. This is why we have disabled the certificate validation using this command.

- **ansible_winrm_kerberos_delegation=true**: This allows the credentials to traverse multiple hops.

Now you will see one more option in many places, that is, **ansible_winrm_transport**. Right now, we have five possible transport methods. The following are the methods available to us:

- Basic
- Certificate
- Kerberos
- NTLM
- CredSSP

These are the five options available for us to configure as a transport method for authentication in Windows Server. Just like we have certificate and password authentication in our Linux host, we have these five methods. Let us talk about each one of them and understand which one should be used when:

- **Basic**: Basic authentication is best suited for the lab environment. If you have created a lab in your local computer using VMware Workstation or VirtualBox and you have local authentication set up for your lab, then this is the right type for you. In general, this is used when we have local authentication set up for our hosts. However, this is not a very safe and secure method as the credentials are b64 encoded. Let us take an example here:

```
ansible_user: user
ansible_password: passwd
ansible_connection: winrm
ansible_winrm_transport: basic
```

Now, you might need to enable the basic authentication if you messed with authentication methods in the past. Here is how you can set it:

```
Set-Item -Path WSMan:\localhost\Service\Auth\Basic -Value $true
```

- **Certificate**: The most secure one, according to the author, is the certificate-based authentication. Just like a normal Linux host, we can use certificate authentication here as well. Let us have a look at an example of how we can achieve it:

```
ansible_connection: winrm
```

```
ansible_winrm_cert_pem: /tmp/key.pem
ansible_winrm_cert_key_pem: /tmp/certificate/private/key.pem
ansible_winrm_transport: certificate
```

Now, we need to enable the certificate-based authentication in Windows. Here is how you can set it. Remember, this will be executed from PowerShell and not the normal command prompt.

```
Set-Item -Path WSMan:\localhost\Service\Auth\Certificate -Value $true
```

- **Kerberos**: If you are running an AD in your environment, then this is the recommended method. So, for all the domain environments, you have two options: one is Kerberos and the second is **New Technology LAN Manager** (**NTLM**). Kerberos is the best among them, and that is what you should always choose for the domain environment. Kerberos needs some additional configuration, which is listed as follows:

```
yum-yinstallgccpython-develkrb5-develkrb5-libskrb5-workstation
pip install pywinrm[kerberos]
```

Now, since we have been using CentOS in our environment, we have used the commands of Centos for the installation of Kerberos. However, you need to use your Linux-specific commands.

- **NTLM**: NTLM is the old authentication method that can be used with both local credentials and domain-based authentication. We will use Kerberos over NTLM. By default, NTLM is enabled when we enable the WinRM services. Hence, we do not need to enable NTLM additionally with commands. However, let us look at the command to check whether it is enabled or not on your host:

```
winrm get winrm/config/Service
```

This is how the output of the command will look:

```
PS C:\Users\Administrator>
PS C:\Users\Administrator> winrm get winrm/config/Service
Service
    RootSDDL = O:NSG:BAD:P(A;;GA;;;BA)(A;;GR;;;IU)S:P(AU;FA;GA;;;WD)(AU;SA;GXGW;;;WD)
    MaxConcurrentOperations = 4294967295
    MaxConcurrentOperationsPerUser = 1500
    EnumerationTimeoutms = 240000
    MaxConnections = 300
    MaxPacketRetrievalTimeSeconds = 120
    AllowUnencrypted = true
    Auth
        Basic = true
        Kerberos = true
        Negotiate = true
        Certificate = true
        CredSSP = true
        CbtHardeningLevel = Relaxed
    DefaultPorts
        HTTP = 5985
        HTTPS = 5986
    IPv4Filter = *
    IPv6Filter = *
    EnableCompatibilityHttpListener = false
    EnableCompatibilityHttpsListener = false
    CertificateThumbprint
    AllowRemoteAccess = true

PS C:\Users\Administrator> _
```

Figure 7.32: WinRM service status

As we can see, **winrm** is already enabled.

- **CredSSP**: CredSSP is the newest authentication protocol. This encrypts the credentials after the authentication has succeeded and sends them to the server over the CredSSP protocol. It supports both local and domain account-based authentication. Here is how we can set up the variable for the CredSSP:

```
ansible_user: Username
ansible_password: Password
ansible_connection:winrm
ansible_winrm_transport:credssp
```

Once this is sorted and we have saved the inventory file, we can run the ad-hoc command to test the connectivity using **win_ping** module.

```
root@ip-172-31-2-134:/etc/ansible# cat demoserver.ini
[demoserver]
ip-172-31-2-182.ap-south-1.compute.internal

[demoserver:vars]
ansible_user=Administrator
ansible_password="UfvrGC12M(4fd&j@Mi.nJylga-B=gcAF"
ansible_port=5986
ansible_connection=winrm
ansible_winrm_scheme=https
ansible_winrm_server_cert_validation=ignore
ansible_winrm_kerberos_delegation=true

root@ip-172-31-2-134:/etc/ansible#
root@ip-172-31-2-134:/etc/ansible#
root@ip-172-31-2-134:/etc/ansible#
```

Figure 7.33: Successful ping for the target host

As we can see, the pong response to our ping request. This means we have successfully established communication with the target host. Now, we can create the playbooks and play with the other modules of Windows.

Now, we will create a playbook and a role, which will help us create a directory or file in a directory. Let us navigate to the roles and create a role using Ansible Galaxy:

```
root@ip-172-31-2-134:/etc/ansible/roles# ansible-galaxy init createDirectory
- Role createDirectory was created successfully
root@ip-172-31-2-134:/etc/ansible/roles# cat createDirectory/tasks/main.yml
---
# tasks file for createDirectory
root@ip-172-31-2-134:/etc/ansible/roles#
```

Figure 7.34: Creation of a new role using ansible-galaxy

Let us start our journey with **win_file** module of Ansible:

```
root@ip-172-31-2-134:/etc/ansible# cat roles/createDirectory/tasks/main.yml
---
# tasks file for createDirectory
- name: Create a file
  ansible.windows.win_file:
    path: C:\Users\Administrator\Abcd.txt
    state: touch

root@ip-172-31-2-134:/etc/ansible#
```

Figure 7.35: New role using win_file module

As we can see in this module, we have created a file named **Abcd.txt** in the directory **C/**

users/Administrator. Now, let us go ahead and create a playbook and use it. In this example, we have used the existing inventory that we used while ad-hoc command. In the next example, we will use our traditional method of defining all parameters in roles and playbook:

```
root@ip-172-31-2-134:/etc/ansible#
root@ip-172-31-2-134:/etc/ansible# cat roles/createDirectory/tasks/main.yml
---
# tasks file for createDirectory
- name: Create a file
  ansible.windows.win_file:
    path: C:\Users\Administrator\Abcd.txt
    state: touch

root@ip-172-31-2-134:/etc/ansible# ansible-playbook firplaybook.yaml -i demoserver.ini

PLAY [demo] ************************************************************************

TASK [Gathering Facts] ************************************************************
ok: [ip-172-31-2-182.ap-south-1.compute.internal]

TASK [createDirectory : Create a file] ********************************************
changed: [ip-172-31-2-182.ap-south-1.compute.internal]

PLAY RECAP ************************************************************************
ip-172-31-2-182.ap-south-1.compute.internal : ok=2    changed=1    unreachable=0    failed=0

root@ip-172-31-2-134:/etc/ansible#
```

Figure 7.36: Successful execution on the target host, which creates a text file

The code successfully executed on the target host. Let us go back to the Windows host and see if the file has been created:

```
PS C:\Users\Administrator> dir


    Directory: C:\Users\Administrator


Mode                 LastWriteTime         Length Name
----                 -------------         ------ ----
d-r---        6/18/2023   5:36 PM                3D Objects
d-r---        6/18/2023   5:36 PM                Contacts
d-r---        6/18/2023   5:36 PM                Desktop
d-r---        6/18/2023   5:36 PM                Documents
d-r---        6/18/2023   5:36 PM                Downloads
d-r---        6/18/2023   5:36 PM                Favorites
d-r---        6/18/2023   5:36 PM                Links
d-r---        6/18/2023   5:36 PM                Music
d-r---        6/18/2023   5:36 PM                Pictures
d-r---        6/18/2023   5:36 PM                Saved Games
d-r---        6/18/2023   5:36 PM                Searches
d-r---        6/18/2023   5:36 PM                Videos
-a----        6/18/2023   9:05 PM              0 Abcd.txt


PS C:\Users\Administrator>
```

Figure 7.37: Text file Abcd.txt successfully created on the target host

As we can see, we have a file named **Abcd.txt** at the bottom of the list. This shows us that the file has been created at the required target location.

win_copy module

Just like our copy module, we have **win_copy** module. This module helps us copy the files from our control machine to the target host. In this example, we have created a text file, **Ashutosh.txt**. Now, we will copy this file to the Windows host using **win_copy** module:

```
root@ip-172-31-2-134:/etc/ansible#
root@ip-172-31-2-134:/etc/ansible# cat ashutosh.txt
hi i want this content to go to the destination server
root@ip-172-31-2-134:/etc/ansible#
```

Figure 7.38: We can see the file ashutosh.txt present on the control machine

Let us modify the Ansible module to incorporate the changes and use **ansible.windows. win_copy** module to copy this content. This is how the module will look:

```
root@ip-172-31-2-134:/etc/ansible#
root@ip-172-31-2-134:/etc/ansible# cat roles/createDirectory/tasks/main.yml
---
# tasks file for createDirectory
- name: Copy a single file
  ansible.windows.win_copy:
    src: ashutosh.txt
    dest: C:\Users\Administrator\ashuDemo.txt
root@ip-172-31-2-134:/etc/ansible#
```

Figure 7.39: Role to copy the file from control machine to the target host

Let us run it and see the result:

```
root@ip-172-31-2-134:/etc/ansible#
root@ip-172-31-2-134:/etc/ansible# ansible-playbook firplaybook.yaml -i demoserver.ini

PLAY [demo] ********************************************************************

TASK [Gathering Facts] ********************************************************
ok: [ip-172-31-2-182.ap-south-1.compute.internal]

TASK [createDirectory : Copy a single file] **********************************
changed: [ip-172-31-2-182.ap-south-1.compute.internal]

PLAY RECAP ********************************************************************
ip-172-31-2-182.ap-south-1.compute.internal : ok=2    changed=1    unreachable=0    failed=0    skipped=0

root@ip-172-31-2-134:/etc/ansible#
```

Figure 7.40: Successful execution of playbook

As we can see, the execution was successful now, we will navigate to the target server and see if the file is present on the target host or not:

Figure 7.41: File successfully copied to the target host

win_shell module

`win_shell` module is another important module of Ansible. We can execute any PowerShell script code and all other commands of the PowerShell terminal using this module. In the following example, we will simply use the **dir** command with the register and **debug** module of Ansible. This means that we will execute the **dir** command on the Windows host. The content of that execution will be saved in a variable named **output,** and that variable will be printed on the terminal using **debug** module. Refer to *Figure 7.42*:

```
root@ip-172-31-2-134:/etc/ansible# cat roles/createDirectory/tasks/main.yml
---
# tasks file for createDirectory
- name: Copy a single file
  win_shell: dir
  register: output
- debug:
    msg: "{{output}}"
root@ip-172-31-2-134:/etc/ansible#
```

Figure 7.42: Role with example of win_shell module

One more important thing we need to do is get rid of that inventory file and add the variable into the roles themselves:

```
root@ip-172-31-2-134:/etc/ansible#
root@ip-172-31-2-134:/etc/ansible#
root@ip-172-31-2-134:/etc/ansible#
root@ip-172-31-2-134:/etc/ansible# cat /etc/ansible/roles/createDirectory/vars/main.yml
ansible_user: Administrator
ansible_password: "UfvrGC12M(4fd&j@Mi.nJylga-B=gcAF"
ansible_port: 5986
ansible_connection: winrm
ansible_winrm_scheme: https
ansible_winrm_server_cert_validation: ignore
ansible_winrm_kerberos_delegation: true

root@ip-172-31-2-134:/etc/ansible#
```

Figure 7.43: Variable file for the Windows target host with extra parameters

This is how our vars file will look in our roles. As we need to define the dictionaries of variables, we have used the key: value format and removed the INI format from here.

Let us run it and see the results:

```
    "d-r---        6/18/2023   5:36 PM                 Favorites                        ",
    "d-r---        6/18/2023   5:36 PM                 Links                            ",
    "d-r---        6/18/2023   5:36 PM                 Music                            ",
    "d-r---        6/18/2023   5:36 PM                 Pictures                         ",
    "d-r---        6/18/2023   5:36 PM                 Saved Games                      ",
    "d-r---        6/18/2023   5:36 PM                 Searches                         ",
    "d-r---        6/18/2023   5:36 PM                 Videos                           ",
    "-a----        6/18/2023   9:05 PM              0  Abcd.txt                         ",
    "-a----        6/18/2023   9:18 PM             55  ashuDemo.txt                     ",
    "",
    ""
   ]
  }
 )
}

PLAY RECAP ************************************************************************************************************
ip-172-31-2-192.ap-south-1.compute.internal : ok=3     changed=1    unreachable=0    failed=0    skipped=0    rescued=0    ignored=0
```

Figure 7.44: Successful execution of code that prints the output of dir command

Since the output of our last command was huge, we will try to run a small command where we can use the execution properly and make sure our variable file is working as expected, without the inventory file. Also, for your information, we have to add the host DNS in our hosts file:

```
root@ip-172-31-2-134:/etc/ansible# cat /etc/ansible/roles/createDirectory/tasks/main.yml
---
# tasks file for createDirectory
- name: Copy a single file
  win_shell: date
  register: output
- debug:
    msg: "{{output}}"
root@ip-172-31-2-134:/etc/ansible# ansible-playbook firplaybook.yaml

PLAY [demo] ************************************************************************************

TASK [Gathering Facts] ************************************************************************
ok: [ip-172-31-2-182.ap-south-1.compute.internal]

TASK [createDirectory : Copy a single file] *************************************************
changed: [ip-172-31-2-182.ap-south-1.compute.internal]

TASK [createDirectory : debug] ***************************************************************
ok: [ip-172-31-2-182.ap-south-1.compute.internal] => {
    "msg": {
        "changed": true,
        "cmd": "date",
        "delta": "0:00:00.718766",
        "end": "2023-06-18 21:44:43.297830",
        "failed": false,
        "rc": 0,
        "start": "2023-06-18 21:44:42.579064",
        "stderr": "",
        "stderr_lines": [],
        "stdout": "\r\nSunday, June 18, 2023 9:44:43 PM\r\n\r\n\r\n",
        "stdout_lines": [
            "",
            "Sunday, June 18, 2023 9:44:43 PM",
            "",
            ""
        ]
    }
}

PLAY RECAP ************************************************************************************
ip-172-31-2-182.ap-south-1.compute.internal : ok=3    changed=1    unreachable=0    failed=0

root@ip-172-31-2-134:/etc/ansible# █
```

Figure 7.45: Example of date command executed on the target host using win_shell module

As we see the results of execution, we can see the output of the command visible on the terminal.

Playbook for Windows updates

We had committed the fully working playbook and role for the Windows updates. We will use the `win_updates` module of Ansible to update the critical updates of the Windows host. We will modify the same role and make it useful for the Windows update, as follows:

```
root@ip-172-31-2-134:/etc/ansible#
root@ip-172-31-2-134:/etc/ansible# cat /etc/ansible/roles/createDirectory/tasks/main.ym
---
# tasks file for createDirectory
- name: Install the updates
  win_updates:
    category_names:
      - CriticalUpdates
root@ip-172-31-2-134:/etc/ansible#
```

Figure 7.46: Role to update the critical updates of Windows

As you all know, we can use the same playbook again and see the results:

```
root@ip-172-31-2-134:/etc/ansible#
root@ip-172-31-2-134:/etc/ansible# ansible-playbook firplaybook.yaml

PLAY [demo] ************************************************************************

TASK [Gathering Facts] ***********************************************************
ok: [ip-172-31-2-182.ap-south-1.compute.internal]

TASK [createDirectory : Install the updates] ************************************
ok: [ip-172-31-2-182.ap-south-1.compute.internal]

PLAY RECAP *********************************************************************
ip-172-31-2-182.ap-south-1.compute.internal : ok=2    changed=0    unreachable=0

root@ip-172-31-2-134:/etc/ansible# 
```

Figure 7.47: Successful execution of playbook

We can see that the execution was successful. Ansible could find the device up to the latest version of updates and had to perform no changes on the target host. That is why we see the **ok=2**. If it could have been outdated, you would have seen **changed=1**, and the updates would have been installed on the target host.

This is how we can start getting familiar with the Windows module and learn more about it. You can see the demo of 10 more modules, but the important thing is to use them while reading their documents. So, use the following link to navigate to the rest of the Ansible Windows module and use your useful Ansible modules:

https://docs.ansible.com/ansible/2.9/modules/list_of_windows_modules.html

Conclusion

To conclude, we have seen what an IT automation engine like Ansible can do with the different kinds of operating systems and platforms. Whether it is Linux or Windows, Ansible works great with both. However, you will need to configure some additional settings with the Windows host. You should try a few more modules of Ansible for Windows. Read their documents and become a master of them.

In the next chapter, we will work with IIS and nginx. We will try to create a small page where we will try to print a small keyword on the browser.

References

- https://docs.ansible.com/ansible/latest/os_guide/windows_winrm.html#id3
- https://docs.ansible.com/ansible/latest/collections/ansible/windows/win_file_module.html
- https://docs.ansible.com/ansible/latest/collections/ansible/windows/win_copy_module.html
- https://docs.ansible.com/ansible/2.9/modules/win_updates_module.html#win-updates-module

Join our Discord space

Join our Discord workspace for latest updates, offers, tech happenings around the world, new releases, and sessions with the authors:

https://discord.bpbonline.com

CHAPTER 8
App Deployment

Introduction

In this chapter, we will focus on the process of deploying an application on Windows and Linux hosts. We will start by deploying various required packages on the target hosts. Then, we will create playbooks to deploy the application and restart the services.

Structure

This chapter contains the following topics:

- Demo website and installing Apache server
- Creating an IIS server on Windows hosts
- Playbook for NGINX installation and configuration
- Deployment of applications on Linux
- Cloning code from GitHub
- Installing multiple packages

Objectives

By the end of this chapter, you will learn how to deploy various packages on the new servers. Once the package installation is sorted, we will learn about application deployment on Windows and Linux platforms. At last, you will learn how to activate the web application services. We will learn how we can deploy **Internet Information Services (IIS)** using Ansible and use Git to clone the required file from the public repository.

Demo website and installing Apache server

Ansible is a good tool to deploy your application. You can keep your applications in Git and pull them from there. If you have your demo environment and the code is saved on S3, then you can copy it from there too. The initial plan was to create a single script that would create an EC2 instance from scratch, then install the Apache server, and then build the application. However, since we have already taken care of the EC2 instance from scratch, let us not spend more time on it and focus on the deployment of the application. This is going to be a very easy task for us, so let us go ahead and do it.

Additionally, we do not have an application handy with us. Since this is not an app development book, we have simply created an **index.html** file on the Ansible control machine. This simply says hello to the entire world.

Now, first, let us try to understand what we need to do to run an application on a normal Linux server:

1. The first requirement is to install the Apache server on a Linux host. We will use the **yum** module of Ansible to install it.

2. Once the Apache server is installed, we need to assign the right permissions to it. We have used the command module here, but you can use the shell module too. The best option for us will be **ansible.builtin.file.**

3. At last, we need to copy the application (which is the **index.html** file on the control machine) to the web server.

4. Then, we need to start the Apache server, and we should be good to go. We are using the service module of Ansible to start the Apache services:

```
root@ip-172-31-2-134:/etc/ansible# cat roles/createapache/tasks/main.yml
---
- name: Installing the package for the apache server
  ansible.builtin.yum:
    name: httpd
    state: latest
  become: yes
- name: change the permission for the folders
  ansible.builtin.command: /usr/bin/chmod -R 777 /var
  become: yes
```

Figure 8.1: Role to install the httpd services in the Linux host

```
root@ip-172-31-2-134:/etc/ansible# cat roles/copywebsite/tasks/main.yml
---
- name: Copy file with owner and permissions
  ansible.builtin.copy:
    src: index.html
    dest: /var/www/html/index.html
    owner: ashutmch
    group: ashutmch
    mode: '0644'
- name: Start service httpd, if not started
  ansible.builtin.service:
    name: httpd
    state: started
```

Figure 8.2: Role to assign the right permission to the target host and activate services

Now, let us run this code and see the results:

```
root@ip-172-31-2-134:/etc/ansible#
root@ip-172-31-2-134:/etc/ansible# ansible-playbook  firplaybook.yaml -u ashutmch -k -K
SSH password:
BECOME password[defaults to SSH password]:

PLAY [demo] ***********************************************************************

TASK [Gathering Facts] ***********************************************************
ok: [172.31.6.75]

TASK [createapache : Installing the package for the apache server] ***************
ok: [172.31.6.75]

TASK [createapache : change the permission for the folders] **********************
changed: [172.31.6.75]

TASK [copywebsite : Copy file with owner and permissions] ************************
changed: [172.31.6.75]

TASK [copywebsite : Start service httpd, if not started] *************************
ok: [172.31.6.75]

PLAY RECAP ***********************************************************************
172.31.6.75                : ok=5    changed=2    unreachable=0    failed=0    skipped=0    rescued=0
```

Figure 8.3: Play recap shows the successful execution of roles

Let us try to access the services and see if we can see **Hello World!** in action:

← → C ⚠ Not secure | 3.108.53.227

Avocent   Study & research   MAERSK

Hello World!

Figure 8.4: Demo app live after playbook execution

So, our webpage is up, and similarly, you can deploy your code. You can use Git anytime you want and copy your code to the target host, and deploy it. One very important thing is exploring more and more Ansible modules. You might find 3-4 modules for doing the same thing, but you need to find the best one that runs the validation in the end.

Creating an IIS server on Windows hosts

Just like we used Apache server on the Linux platform to create a small webpage, we can create a small web page on the Windows platform using IIS. Now, the names might be different; however, the results in both these cases are the same. Both features help us bring the web page up. So, let us have a look at the **win_feature** module of the Ansible which will help us create the web page using IIS on the Windows server.

win_feature

Ansible can help you create your own webpage using IIS on a Windows server. We will use the Ansible **win_featue** to make the IIS server up on the host. Let us go back to the Windows server and see whether IIS is enabled on the server or not and navigate to the **Server Manager Dashboard** and see if IIS is enabled:

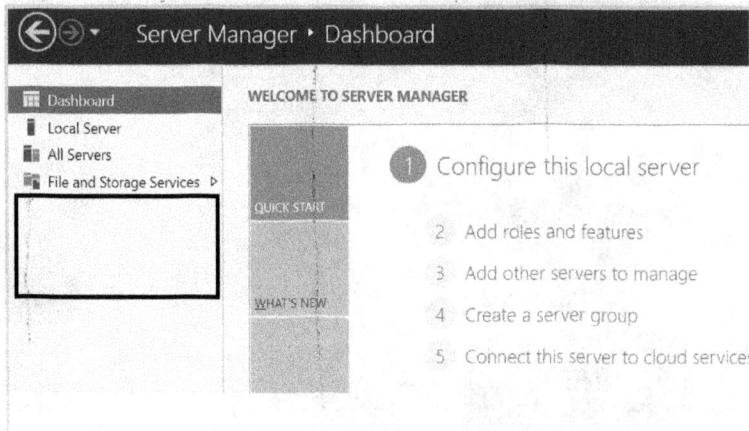

Figure 8.5: Current status of services

As we can see, there is no IIS working on the host, we will go back to the control machine and create a playbook which will activate the IIS service on the Windows host by using the following code:

```
root@ip-172-31-2-134:/etc/ansible#
root@ip-172-31-2-134:/etc/ansible#
root@ip-172-31-2-134:/etc/ansible# cat roles/createDirectory/tasks/main.yml
---
# tasks file for createDirectory
- name: Test website
  win_feature:
    name: "Web-Server"
    state: present
    restart: yes
    include_sub_feature: yes
    include_management_tools: yes
root@ip-172-31-2-134:/etc/ansible#
root@ip-172-31-2-134:/etc/ansible#
```

Figure 8.6: Role for activating the IIS

Let us discuss the code or role one by one after **win_feature** module.

- We need to define the name of the service we want to enable.

- **State**: Will be set to present as we want to enable the service, we need to mention present. The alternative option is absent, which is used for removing the service. We want Ansible to restart the services, and that is why we see: **restart: yes**. At last, we want to enable the sub-features and management tools, and that is why we see a yes there. Now, in this demo, we have used the old Ansible module; the latest has some differences there. We have created and run the playbook in the back-end. Now, we want you to create the playbook and call the role shown in *Figure 8.6* in a playbook. Once it is ready run the playbook. this should bring up the IIS services like shown in *Figure 8.7* and web page should start loading like *Figure 8.8*:

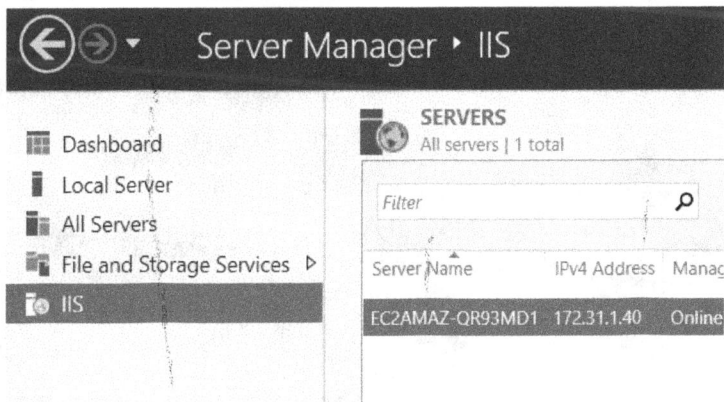

Figure 8.7: Services are online after playbook execution

As we can see, IIS is enabled, so we will try to access it:

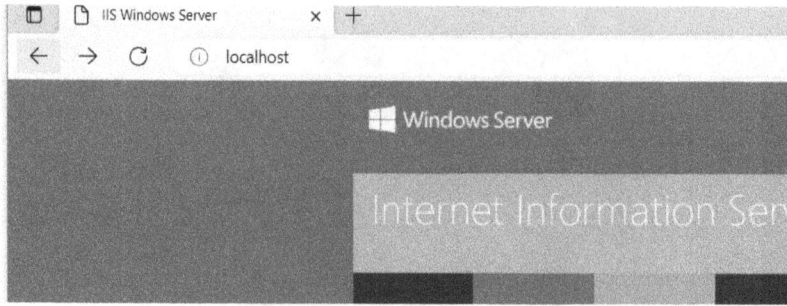

Figure 8.8: Services are active now

Finally, we can see that the server is up and running. Let us remove it using a new Ansible module.

Code:

```
root@ip-172-31-2-134:/etc/ansible# cat roles/createDirectory/tasks/main.yml
---
# tasks file for createDirectory
- name: Test website
  ansible.windows.win_feature:
    name: Web-Server
    state: absent
root@ip-172-31-2-134:/etc/ansible#
```

Figure 8.9: Role to deactivate the IIS services

As we can see, we have used the latest **win_feature** module of Ansible. This time, we have asked it to remove the web server from there. Let us execute it and see the results:

Output:

```
root@ip-172-31-2-134:/etc/ansible#
root@ip-172-31-2-134:/etc/ansible# ansible-playbook firplaybook.yaml

PLAY [demo] *********************************************************************

TASK [Gathering Facts] *********************************************************
ok: [ip-172-31-1-40.ap-south-1.compute.internal]

TASK [createDirectory : Test website] *****************************************
changed: [ip-172-31-1-40.ap-south-1.compute.internal]

PLAY RECAP ********************************************************************
ip-172-31-1-40.ap-south-1.compute.internal : ok=2    changed=1    unreachable=0
```

Figure 8.10: Play recap shows successful execution

The execution is successful. Let us go back and see the result on the webpage. Refer to *Figure 8.8:*

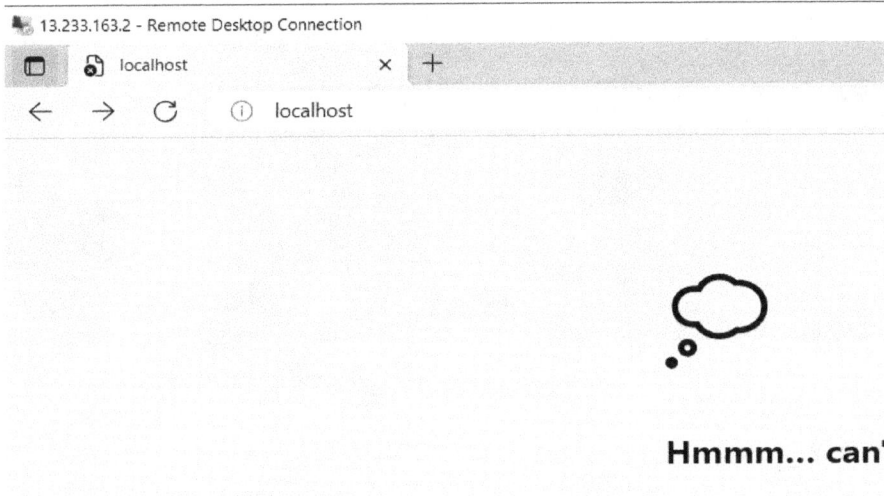

Figure 8.11: Services successfully removed using IIS

We can see in the output that the webpage is down again.

Now, let us enable the IIS again and remove the default page from there. Then, we will see how we can deploy the other code to the IIS.

WIN_IIS_Website module

The first thing we do is remove the default page from IIS when we deploy our actual page. Let us see how this can be done. The web page is named the default website, and that can be viewed from the manager. Since we want to remove it, we need to use the **state: absent**.

Code:

```
root@ip-172-31-2-134:/etc/ansible#
root@ip-172-31-2-134:/etc/ansible# cat roles/createDirectory/tasks/main.yml
---
# tasks file for createDirectory
- name: Test website
  win_iis_website:
    name: "Default Web Site"
    state: absent
root@ip-172-31-2-134:/etc/ansible#
```

Figure 8.12: Role using the win IIS module to remove the default page

Execution:

```
root@ip-172-31-2-134:/etc/ansible#
root@ip-172-31-2-134:/etc/ansible# ansible-playbook firplaybook.yaml

PLAY [demo] ************************************************************

TASK [Gathering Facts] ***********************************************
ok: [ip-172-31-1-40.ap-south-1.compute.internal]

TASK [createDirectory : Test website] ******************************
changed: [ip-172-31-1-40.ap-south-1.compute.internal]

PLAY RECAP ***********************************************************
ip-172-31-1-40.ap-south-1.compute.internal : ok=2    changed=1    unreachable=0

root@ip-172-31-2-134:/etc/ansible#
```

Figure 8.13: Play recap shows successful removal of default page

Unfortunately, we do not have a live website with us, so we cannot demo hosting a website. However, if you have it handy, then it is an easy task. You simply need to follow the guidelines and remember what we have learned so far. Yes, we have our **index.html** ready with us. Just do some simple research and find out how we can achieve that here. You can consider this your assignment for today.

Playbook for NGINX installation and configuration

Just like the installation of the Apache server, we will perform the NGINX installation. This is going to be a very easy task. Just like we used the **yum** module to install the Apache server, you can use the **yum** module to install the NGINX server. In the end, all we will use is the service module to start the services. We have used the legacy service module, so we can cover both the latest and the old service modules in our book.

Code:

```
root@ip-172-31-2-134:/etc/ansible# cat roles/copywebsite/tasks/main.yml
---
- name: Start service httpd, if not started
  service:
    name: nginx
    state: started
  become: yes
root@ip-172-31-2-134:/etc/ansible#
root@ip-172-31-2-134:/etc/ansible#
root@ip-172-31-2-134:/etc/ansible# cat roles/createapache/tasks/main.yml
---
- name: Installing the package for the apache server
  ansible.builtin.yum:
    name: nginx
    state: latest
  become: yes
root@ip-172-31-2-134:/etc/ansible#
```

Figure 8.14: Role to install NGINX using yum module

```
root@ip-172-31-2-134:/etc/ansible# ansible-playbook firplaybook.yaml -u ashutmch -k -K
SSH password:
BECOME password[defaults to SSH password]:

PLAY [demo] ************************************************************************

TASK [Gathering Facts] ************************************************************
ok: [172.31.6.75]

TASK [createapache : Installing the package for the apache server] ****************
ok: [172.31.6.75]

TASK [copywebsite : Start service httpd, if not started] **************************
changed: [172.31.6.75]

PLAY RECAP ************************************************************************
172.31.6.75              : ok=3    changed=1    unreachable=0    failed=0    skipped=0
```

Figure 8.15: Play recap shows successful installation and activation of NGINX

Let us go back to the browser and see if things are operational. Refer to the following *Figure 8.16*:

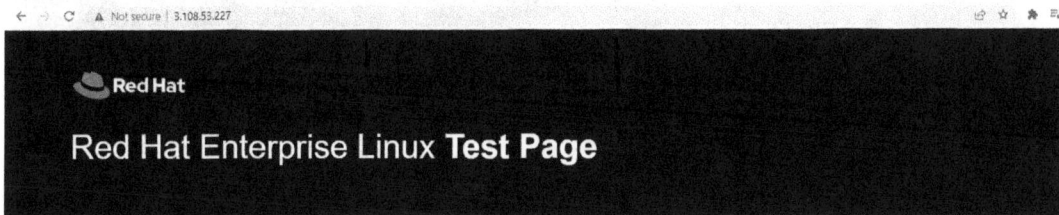

This page is used to test the proper operation of the HTTP server after it has been installed. If you can read this page, it means that the HTTP server installed at this site is working properly.

Figure 8.16: Web page is up after NGINX installation

As we can see, the web page is loading after starting NGINX on the target host.

Deployment of applications on Linux

So far, we have tried NGINX and Apache server installations on the Linux host. The next step is the installation of PHP. The process is going to be the same, where we will use the **yum** module for the installation.

The roles will be as follows:

```
root@ip-172-31-2-134:/etc/ansible# cat roles/createapache/tasks/main.yml
---
- name: Installing the package for the apache server
  ansible.builtin.yum:
    name: php-*
    state: latest
  become: yes
root@ip-172-31-2-134:/etc/ansible#
```

Figure 8.17: Role to install PHP on the target host using Ansible

Let us run our playbook and see the results:

```
root@ip-172-31-2-134:/etc/ansible# ansible-playbook firplaybook.yaml -u ashutmch -k -K
SSH password:
BECOME password[defaults to SSH password]:

PLAY [demo] ************************************************************************

TASK [Gathering Facts] ************************************************************
ok: [172.31.6.75]

TASK [createapache : Installing the package for the apache server] ****************
changed: [172.31.6.75]

TASK [copywebsite : Start service httpd, if not started] *************************
ok: [172.31.6.75]

PLAY RECAP ************************************************************************
172.31.6.75                : ok=3    changed=1    unreachable=0    failed=0    skipped=0    rescued=0    ignored=0

root@ip-172-31-2-134:/etc/ansible#
```

Figure 8.18: Playbook execution with new role

As shown in *Figure 8.18*, we can see that the execution was successful. Now, you can create the **index.php** file and copy it from your control machine to the target host. Once everything is in place, we need to simply start the services, and we should be good. A demo of how we can copy the files to the destination and start the service is shown in the preceding example. Please refer to that, and you should be good to go.

So far, we have been keeping our **index.html** or **index.php** file in our control machine, but that will not be the case in production. All industries nowadays use Git for version control. So, there are 99.99% chances that you will need to clone your code from Git. So, let us go ahead and have a look at how we can install Git using Ansible and clone our repo.

Cloning code from GitHub

Git is a very basic requirement nowadays in the IT industry. Many of you might be working on it for years, and therefore, there will be nothing new for you here. However, some of you might have come across this for the first time. Now, it is suggested that all of you should pause here and start searching for it on *Google*. It is also recommended that you create your own account on GitHub and see how you can clone any repo to the Linux host. This will help you understand what we are going to do in the following section. So, let us go ahead and see how we will install Git in a Linux host using Ansible. Once again, we will use the **yum** packaging module to install Git.

We have modified our last code, and there we have performed just one change, i.e., the name of the new package, which is Git in this case. (For your information, **yum install git** is the command from the terminal):

```
root@ip-172-31-2-134:/etc/ansible# cat roles/createapache/tasks/main.yml
---
- name: Installing the package for the apache server
  ansible.builtin.yum:
    name: git
    state: latest
  become: yes
root@ip-172-31-2-134:/etc/ansible#
```

Figure 8.19: Installation of Git using Ansible

Now, let us go back to our playbook and re-run it. The result will be as follows:

```
root@ip-172-31-2-134:/etc/ansible# ansible-playbook firplaybook.yaml -u ashutmch -k -K
SSH password:
BECOME password[defaults to SSH password]:

PLAY [demo] ********************************************************************

TASK [Gathering Facts] ********************************************************
ok: [172.31.6.75]

TASK [createapache : Installing the package for the apache server] ***********
changed: [172.31.6.75]

TASK [copywebsite : Start service httpd, if not started] *********************
ok: [172.31.6.75]

PLAY RECAP ********************************************************************
172.31.6.75                : ok=3    changed=1    unreachable=0    failed=0    skipped=0

root@ip-172-31-2-134:/etc/ansible#
```

Figure 8.20: Play recap shows successful installation of Git

We can see the **changed=1** for the process installing the package for the Apache server. Since we have not changed the name in the role, it is showing the same name, and the **git** package has been installed in the target host. Let us go back to the server and verify the same:

```
[root@ip-172-31-6-75 Copy-the-Running-config-to-Blob-storage]# git --version
git version 2.39.3
[root@ip-172-31-6-75 Copy-the-Running-config-to-Blob-storage]#
```

Figure 8.21: Successful installation of version 2.39.3 after playbook execution

We can see that **version 2.39.3** is installed in the target Linux host. Now, the next thing is cloning our code from the Git Repo. Now we have our own account and repo created on GitHub. You all can create your account and clone your Git Repo to the target host. Do not use our public repo, create your own. That way you will learn a few more things.

Now, we need to do two things. Clone the Git Repo to the target host, and once that is done, we need to copy the code to the **/var/www/html** directory. After this, we will restart the **httpd** services.

Now, we have multiple options for **git clone**. We can use the shell module, we can also use the command module, and a dedicated **git** module from Ansible, too. If you want to use the command module, then the code will be as follows:

```
---
- name: Clone the git branch
  ansible.builtin.command: git clone https://github.com/ashutoshc1234/ashutoshc1234.git
```

However, in this case, we have used the **git** module of Ansible since we wanted to see as many modules of Ansible as possible:

```
root@ip-172-31-2-134:/etc/ansible# cat roles/copywebsite/tasks/main.yml
---
- name: Example clone of a single branch
  ansible.builtin.git:
    repo:  https://github.com/ashutoshc1234/ashutoshc1234.git
    dest: /tmp/demo
    single_branch: yes
- name: copy the index.html to the right directory
  ansible.builtin.command: cp /tmp/demo/index.html /var/www/html/
    become: yes

root@ip-172-31-2-134:/etc/ansible#
```

Figure 8.22: Git clone using Ansible from public repo

It is time to run the code. Now, you can see the code was executed successfully. Let us go back to the server and check whether **index.html** and **index.php** are both files in that target folder:

```
root@ip-172-31-2-134:/etc/ansible# ansible-playbook firplaybook.yaml -u ashutmch -k -K
SSH password:
BECOME password[defaults to SSH password]:

PLAY [demo] ********************************************************************

TASK [Gathering Facts] ********************************************************
ok: [172.31.6.75]

TASK [createapache : Installing the package for the apache server] ***********
ok: [172.31.6.75]

TASK [copywebsite : Example clone of a single branch] ***********************
ok: [172.31.6.75]

TASK [copywebsite : Start service httpd, if not started] *******************
changed: [172.31.6.75]

PLAY RECAP ******************************************************************
172.31.6.75                : ok=4    changed=1    unreachable=0    failed=0    skipped=0

root@ip-172-31-2-134:/etc/ansible#
```

Figure 8.23: Play recap shows successful execution of code

Here, we can see in *Figure 8.24*, the **index.html** file is now present in the target host and in the right directory:

```
[root@ip-172-31-6-75 html]# ll
total 8
-rw-r--r--. 1 root root 13 Jun 22 18:05 index.html
-rw-r--r--. 1 root root 18 Jun 21 15:04 info.php
```

Figure 8.24: List of files in html directory

We can also navigate to the folder where the files were copied using **git clone**:

```
[root@ip-172-31-6-75 html]# cd /tmp/demo/
[root@ip-172-31-6-75 demo]# ll
total 4
-rw-r--r--. 1 ashutmch ashutmch 13 Jun 22 17:58 index.html
[root@ip-172-31-6-75 demo]#
```

Figure 8.25: Successfully fetched the file from the Git Repo

So, the next thing will be restarting the **httpd** services using Ansible. Let us consider this your assignment for today. If you still struggle, you can turn back a few pages, and you will see how it is done in the same chapter.

What if you have multiple packages to install? Let us learn how to achieve it.

Installing multiple packages

As soon as you land in a company, the production environment will demand you to install 10+ packages using **yum** in one shot. So, let us now see how we can install multiple packages in the target host using a single playbook. This time, we will create a variable and iterate over a list of packages so Ansible can install all of those packages on the target host:

```
root@ASHU:/etc/ansible# cat roles/createapache/tasks/main.yml
---
- name: Installing the package for the apache server
  ansible.builtin.yum:
    name: "{{item}}"
    state: latest
  loop:
    - git
    - nginx
    - httpd
    - php
  become: yes
```

Figure 8.26: Role to install multiple packages on the target host

This is how we used to create a loop in the case of Ansible. We have defined the variable named item with values—**git**, **nginx**, **http,** and **php**. This will be parsed one by one, and those packages will be installed on the target host. If you have 100 more packages, add them to this list, and you will be good to install all of them. Let us run it now. The result will be as follows:

```
root@ip-172-31-2-134:/etc/ansible# ansible-playbook firplaybook.yaml -u ashutmch -k -K
SSH password:
BECOME password[defaults to SSH password]:

PLAY [demo] ************************************************************************

TASK [Gathering Facts] ************************************************************
ok: [172.31.6.75]

TASK [createapache : Installing the package for the apache server] ****************
ok: [172.31.6.75] => (item=git)
ok: [172.31.6.75] => (item=nginx)
ok: [172.31.6.75] => (item=httpd)
changed: [172.31.6.75] => (item=php)

PLAY RECAP ************************************************************************
172.31.6.75                : ok=2    changed=1    unreachable=0    failed=0    skipped=0
```

Figure 8.27: Successful installation of services on the target host

Conclusion

To conclude, we have learned how to install various web applications on the target host, create a web server from scratch, and install various packages on those servers. Once packages are installed, we can copy our application code from various platforms. The most famous one is Git, which we can use using Ansible easily. If you do not use Git, then you can copy your code from any server. In this case, we kept the code on our control machine, and you could do the same. However, the best solution is GitHub. Keep your code there, install the packages, and clone the code. Finally, we learned how to create a list of packages and iterate over that in any of the Ansible modules, as well as the task of restarting the services. Do not forget that we can do all of this in Windows, too. In this chapter, we also looked at how we can install IIS in Windows.

In our next chapter, we will focus on a few regular operational usages of Ansible. We will see how we can use Ansible in our daily tasks so we can save some time. If we talk about our daily operations, then lots of teams take the regular backup of their devices. Now, there are many paid tools that are present in the market to take the configuration backup of the devices, however why should we spend any money if we can achieve the same using ansible.

References

- https://docs.ansible.com/ansible/latest/collections/ansible/builtin/git_module.html
- https://docs.ansible.com/ansible/latest/collections/ansible/builtin/command_module.html
- https://github.com/git-guides/git-clone
- https://www.digitalocean.com/community/tutorials/how-to-install-git-on-centos-7
- https://docs.ansible.com/ansible/2.9/modules/service_module.html

Join our Discord space

Join our Discord workspace for latest updates, offers, tech happenings around the world, new releases, and sessions with the authors:

https://discord.bpbonline.com

CHAPTER 9
Routine Use of Ansible

Introduction

In this chapter, we will focus on a few daily tasks performed in the IT industry. For example, the configuration backup. This chapter will have tasks that range from starting a VM to deleting it.

Structure

This chapter contains the following topics:

- Taking configuration backup of devices
- Taking database backup
- Installing packages in the Linux host
- Adding new users to the target host

Objectives

By the end of this chapter, you will learn how to perform daily tasks using Ansible. We regularly perform tasks like VM build, server patch, package installation, and backups, so we will learn all these topics in this chapter. By the end of the chapter, you will be able to perform all your regular tasks using Ansible.

Taking configuration backup of devices

We know there are tons of tools available in the market for taking configuration backups of the devices, and they work great for this task. However, you might work in a company that does not want to invest in those tools and wants you to develop an in-house code to take the regular backup. For this, you should not think about logging into all the hundreds of devices manually and copying the files to the folder, as that is not the efficient and right way of doing things. For this, we will use Ansible to perform this regular configuration backup.

Now, there are multiple ways of doing the configuration backup. We can use the **shell** module or the **command** module to take a backup of the code. **Remote sync** or **remote synchronization** (**RSYNC**) is another thing that can help us achieve it, and we will try to offer a demo for most of them. So, let us start and write our configuration backup plan on paper, and then we will execute the plan.

Strategy

The step-by-step configuration plan is divided into three major steps:

1. Decide what we want to back up. In our case, we will go ahead with **/tmp/demo/index.html** file.

2. Finalize your backup server and enable SSH communication between them. In our lab scenario, we do not want to spin up a new VM, so we will use the Ansible control machine as our backup server. Now, you can also do that, but it is suggested that you keep a different server as a backup server.

3. Write a code using an appropriate Ansible module (command/shell/file or any other module).

4. Write a cronjob and schedule it for execution on a weekly, daily, or monthly basis (whatever your company policies are).

Let us use the **copy** module to start with.

> **Note: The last time we copied the file from the control machine to the target host. This time, the file is present on the target host itself.**

In this case, we are taking the backup of the file on the target host. You will encounter this situation many times, where you will try to modify the configuration file and might want to take a backup of the file before you modify it. In that situation, you can take a backup of the old file and modify the file after that. If something goes wrong, you will still have the old file handy.

Let us take a look at the following example, where we will take the backup of the file **index.html** from the remote server:

```
root@ip-172-31-2-134:/etc/ansible# cat roles/createapache/tasks/main.yml
---
- name: Installing the package for the apache server
  ansible.builtin.copy:
    src: /tmp/demo/index.html
    dest: /tmp/
    remote_src: yes
    backup: yes
  become: yes
root@ip-172-31-2-134:/etc/ansible#
```

Figure 9.1: Role to take the backup of any remote file

Now, what we have done here is that we took the backup of the index.html file to the new location. Since the source file was on the remote host, we have defined the **remote_src: yes**, in our role. We are defining the **backup: yes**, that simply means the backup file will be created, and this file can be easily restored in case of any issue with the original file.

Let us run the code and see the results:

```
root@ip-172-31-2-134:/etc/ansible# ansible-playbook firplaybook.yaml -u ashutmch -k -K
SSH password:
BECOME password[defaults to SSH password]:

PLAY [demo] **********************************************************************

TASK [Gathering Facts] **********************************************************
ok: [172.31.6.75]

TASK [createapache : Installing the package for the apache server] **********************
changed: [172.31.6.75]

PLAY RECAP **********************************************************************
172.31.6.75                : ok=2    changed=1    unreachable=0    failed=0    skipped=0
```

Figure 9.2: Playbook execution with backup role

We can see that the execution was successful. Let us go back to the target host and see if the file is present in the **/tmp** folder.

```
[ec2-user@ip-172-31-6-75 demo]$ cd /tmp/
[ec2-user@ip-172-31-6-75 tmp]$ ll
total 4
drwxr-xr-x. 3 ashutmch ashutmch 36 Jun 22 17:58 demo
-rw-r--r--. 1 root     root     13 Jun 22 17:58 index.html
drwx------. 3 root     root     17 Jun 20 19:58 systemd-priv
drwx------. 3 root     root     17 Jun 20 19:58 systemd-priv
drwx------. 3 root     root     17 Jun 21 15:06 systemd-priv
drwx------. 3 root     root     17 Jun 20 19:58 systemd-priv
[ec2-user@ip-172-31-6-75 tmp]$ cat index.html
Hello World!
[ec2-user@ip-172-31-6-75 tmp]$
```

Figure 9.3: Successful backup after playbook execution

According to *Figure 9.3*, we have found the file as we were expecting.

Now, let us go ahead and try to send this file to the control machine. We will use the **posix.synchronize** module to achieve this. In the backend, this will use **rsync**. The other option is using the command/shell module and calling the **rsync** module using these modules. However, let us go ahead with the native modules of Ansible for this work, and later, we will use the shell and command modules too.

Since this module uses **rsync** in the backend, we need to make sure that **rsync** is already present on both servers. If it is not, then we need to install it:

```
[ec2-user@ip-172-31-6-75 ~]$ rsync --version
rsync  version 3.2.3  protocol version 31
Copyright (C) 1996-2020 by Andrew Tridgell, Wa
```

Figure 9.4: Current version of rsync in our demo environment

As you can see, the **rsync** is present in our host. Let us go ahead with the code. The synchronized module works in the following two modes:

- Push
- Pull

Push

The push option is used when you want to sync your local file to the target host. Simply put, the source is on the control machine or localhost.

Let us try a playbook that can copy/sync the content of a local directory. We will try to sync the **/etc/ansible** directory in this demo.

Ansible role:

```
[root@ip-172-31-2-117 ansible]# cat roles/rsync/tasks/main.yml
---
- name: Synchronization
  ansible.posix.synchronize:
    src: /etc/ansible
    dest: /tmp
[root@ip-172-31-2-117 ansible]#
[root@ip-172-31-2-117 ansible]#
```

Figure 9.5: Role to sync a local directory to the target host

Execution:

Let us execute and see the results for the **rsync** role:

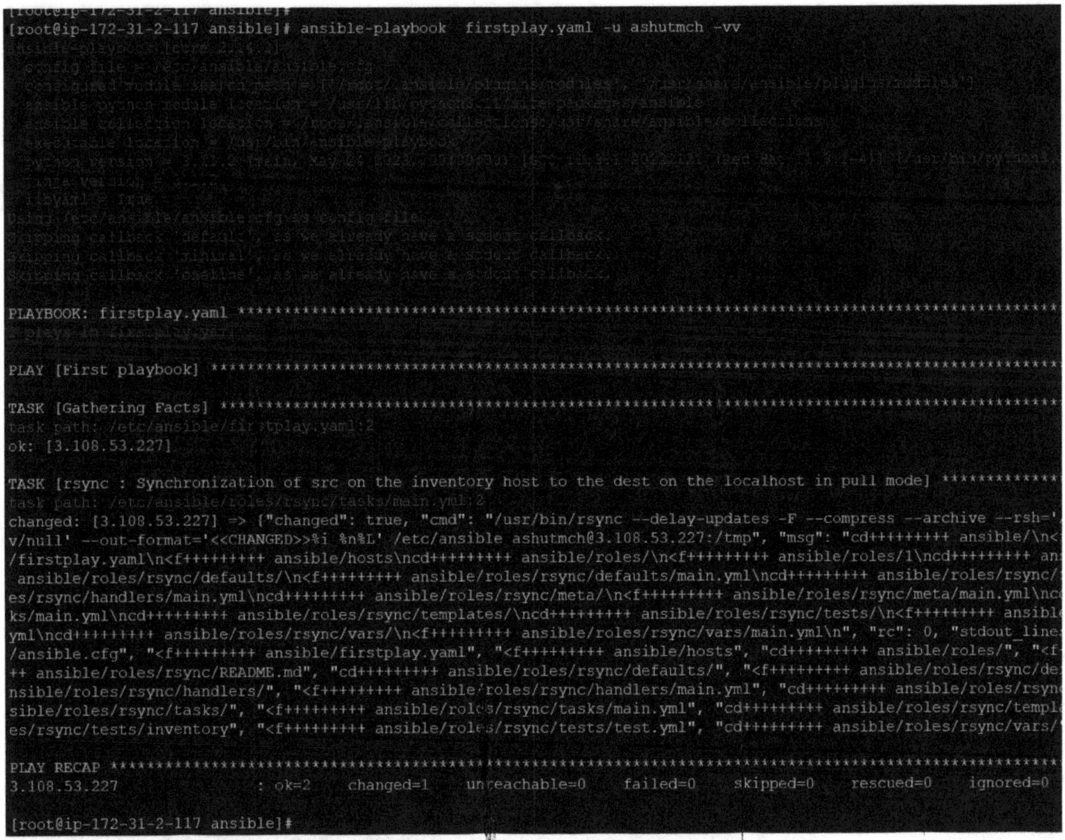

Figure 9.6: Successful execution of playbook in debug mode

Pull

The pull option is used when you want the directories on the target host to be synchronized to the control machine. In simple words, the source file is present on the target host. Now, since we have to pull the configuration from the target host, we need to change the mode to the pull mode, and this is why you will find the **mode: pull** in our roles.

Note: **We had not defined any mode in our last roles where we sync the file of the control machine to the target host. The reason is very simple, since push is the default mode, it was not necessary to define it. However, there is no harm in defining it if you wish to do so.**

```
[root@ip-172-31-2-117 ansible]# cat roles/rsync/tasks/main.yml
---
- name: Synchronization of src on the inventory host to the dest on the localhost in pull mode
  ansible.posix.synchronize:
    mode: pull
    src: /tmp/demo
    dest: /tmp
[root@ip-172-31-2-117 ansible]#
```

Figure 9.7: Role to sync of remote file to the control machine

Here is our new playbook, as the old VM has been deleted:

```
[root@ip-172-31-2-117 ansible]# cat firstplay.yaml
---
- name: First playbook
  hosts: all
  roles:
    - rsync
[root@ip-172-31-2-117 ansible]#
```

Figure 9.8: New playbook with new role

Let us execute it now and see the results:

```
[root@ip-172-31-2-117 ansible]# ansible-playbook  firstplay.yaml -u ashutmch -vv

PLAYBOOK: firstplay.yaml ************************************************************

PLAY [First playbook] **************************************************************

TASK [Gathering Facts] *************************************************************
ok: [3.108.53.227]

TASK [rsync : Synchronization of src on the inventory host to the dest on the localhost in pull mode] ***************
changed: [3.108.53.227] => {"changed": true, "cmd": "/usr/bin/rsync --delay-updates -F --compress --archive --rsh='/
v/null' --out-format='<<CHANGED>>%i %n%L' ashutmch@3.108.53.227:/tmp/demo /tmp", "msg": "cd+++++++++ demo/\n>f++++++++
HEAD\n>f+++++++++ demo/.git/HEAD\n>f+++++++++ demo/.git/ORIG_HEAD\n>f+++++++++ demo/.git/config\n>f+++++++++ demo/.gi
-refs\ncd+++++++++ demo/.git/branches/\ncd+++++++++ demo/.git/hooks\n>f+++++++++ demo/.git/hooks/applypatch-msg.samp
/hooks/fsmonitor-watchman.sample\n>f+++++++++ demo/.git/hooks/post-update.sample\n>f+++++++++ demo/.git/hooks/pre-app
++ demo/.git/hooks/pre-merge-commit.sample\n>f+++++++++ demo/.git/hooks/pre-push.sample\n>f+++++++++ demo/.git/hooks
```

Figure 9.9: Playbook execution successful

Now, let us go back to the target host and see if the directory demo has been copied to our control machine.

```
[root@ip-172-31-2-117 ansible]# ls -ltr /tmp/
total 0
drwxr-xr-x. 4 1001 1001 51 Jun 23 21:23 demo
```

Figure 9.10: New folder present after execution

As we can see, the folder demo is now present as expected, and this contains all the data that it had.

Taking database backup

Now we are trying to create a script that can help us take a backup of the database. Let us go ahead and take the example of the PostgreSQL DB.

In this case, we are using Ansible Core right now in our free tier account. Let us go ahead and install the Ansible module for the DB. The command to install it is as follows:

```
ansible-galaxy collection install community.postgresql
```

```
[root@ip-172-31-2-117 ansible]# ansible-galaxy collection install community.postgresql
Starting galaxy collection install process
Process install dependency map
Starting collection install process
Downloading https://galaxy.ansible.com/download/community-postgresql-3.0.0.tar.gz to /r
Installing 'community.postgresql:3.0.0' to '/root/.ansible/collections/ansible_collecti
community.postgresql:3.0.0 was installed successfully
[root@ip-172-31-2-117 ansible]#
```

Figure 9.11: Installation of PostgreSQL

As we can see, the packages are installed successfully.

Note: You do not need to install the package if you are running Ansible on your device. This is only needed if you are using Ansible Core.

Now, let us go ahead and have a look at how we can dump an existing database to a file:

```
- name: Create a Dump
  community.postgresql.postgresql_db:
    name: acme
    state: dump
    target: /tmp/acme.sql.gz
```

Figure 9.12: Role to create a dump of an existing database to a file

Here, the functions are as follows:

- **Name**: This parameter is used for the database, which needs to be added/removed.
- **State**: State has multiple options like present, absent; however, since we wanted to create the DB backup, we have chosen this option.
- **Target**: File where we want to backup.

Now, we do not have any DB running with us, and therefore, the demo execution is not available. However, we suggest that you spin up a DB and run the commands on your own.

Installing packages in the Linux host

As soon as you build any server, the first thing you do is install the required packages on it. Whether it is a Windows host or a Linux host, all of them need some packages or installations. So, installing packages or software is an essential part of any job profile. Hence, we will focus on how we can achieve it and what the different packaging modules available are to make our lives easier.

So far, we have already seen the **yum** module for the installation of the packages in the Linux host. We should always remember **yum** is not the only packaging module in RHEL/CentOS. Many times, we also use the **pip** for the installation of a few modules. We will have a deep dive into all of those modules one by one. Let us go back to the first module that we tried, which was the **yum** module.

YUM module of Ansible

We use the **YUM** and **Dandified YUM (DNF)** on the CentOS/RHEL platform. The older version of RHEL uses **yum**, however, the newer version of RHEL supports both DNF and **yum** packaging modules. We will have a close look at the **yum** module first, and then we will talk about the DNF module.

The main functionality of the **yum** module is to install, remove, list, upgrade, or downgrade packages with the help of the **yum** package manager.

Now, we need to note that this module only works with Python 2, and anytime you need Python 3, start looking towards the latest package manager like **dnf**.

Example:

```
- name: Name of module
  ansible.builtin.yum:
    name: httpd
    state:present
```

Figure 9.13: Role to install the latest httpd using the yum module

Let us go ahead and try to understand the roles in detail. We will have a look at all the lines present in the code. Starting from name:

- **-name: Name of module:** Name of the role this can be anything.

- **ansible.builtin.yum**: Name of module.

- **name: httpd**: Package name. If you want to install Ansible, write Ansible after 'name:'.

- **state:present**: At the last, we need to tell Ansible what we want to do with the package. This is where we define whether we want to install this package or remove it from the device. In this example, we have chosen the present, which means we want to install this package in the target host. Now, this is not the only option offered by Ansible, we also have a few more options with us. Those options are as follows:

- o **Present**: This simply means we want this package to be installed on our target host.

- o **Installed**: This is the same thing as present. It also makes sure the package is installed in the target host.

- o **Absent and remove**: These two options are used to uninstall the package from the target host.

- o **Latest**: This means the latest package will be installed in your target host, but in actuality, the package is installed on the target host, and then it tries to upgrade the package to the latest version. This is like cit in our normal Linux terminology.

So, these are the four options available to us. So far, we have used the single package name and variables to install the package, however, we can also use a list of packages and install the packages on the target host. Let us have a look at the example and execute it as follows:

```
[root@ip-172-31-2-117 ansible]# cat roles/rsync/tasks/main.yml
---
- name: Install a list of packages (suitable replacement for 2.11 loop deprecation warning)
  ansible.builtin.yum:
    name:
      - postgresql
      - postgresql-server
    state: present
  become: yes

- name: Install bottle python package
  ansible.builtin.pip:
    name: ansible

[root@ip-172-31-2-117 ansible]#
```

Figure 9.14: Role to install multiple packages on the target host

Playbook execution:

```
[root@ip-172-31-2-117 ansible]# ansible-playbook  firstplay.yaml -K -u ashutmch
BECOME password:

PLAY [First playbook] **********************************************************

TASK [Gathering Facts] **********************************************************
ok: [3.108.53.227]

TASK [rsync : Install a list of packages (suitable replacement for 2.11 loop dep
ok: [3.108.53.227]

TASK [rsync : Install bottle python package] **********************************
changed: [3.108.53.227]

PLAY RECAP **********************************************************
3.108.53.227                    : ok=3    changed=1    unreachable=0    failed=0
```

Figure 9.15: Successful execution of code that installs multiple packages

Now, there will be times when your security team will come to you and tell you that we need the **httpd** package higher than 2.3, in that condition, you should know how we can define that in our role:

```
[root@ip-172-31-2-117 ansible]# cat roles/rsync/tasks/main.yml
---
- name: Install a package
  ansible.builtin.yum:
    name: httpd  >=2
    state: present
  become: yes
```

Figure 9.16: Role to install a specific package version

Another example:

```
[root@ip-172-31-2-117 ansible]# cat roles/rsync/tasks/main.yml
---
- name: Install a package
  ansible.builtin.yum:
    name: python >=2.8
    state: present
  become: yes
```

Figure 9.17: Another example of installing version specific package

Let us execute the code. The playbook execution will be successful; however, we will not see **changed=1/2**. Since Python is already installed on the target hosts:

```
[root@ip-172-31-2-117 ansible]# vi roles/rsync/tasks/main.yml
[root@ip-172-31-2-117 ansible]#  ansible-playbook  firstplay.yaml -u ashutmch -K
BECOME password:

PLAY [First playbook] ***************************************************************

TASK [Gathering Facts] **************************************************************
ok: [3.108.53.227]

TASK [rsync : Install a package] ****************************************************
ok: [3.108.53.227]

PLAY RECAP **************************************************************************
3.108.53.227                : ok=2    changed=0    unreachable=0    failed=0    skipped=0

[root@ip-172-31-2-117 ansible]#
```

Figure 9.18: Successful execution of playbook

Let us have a look at one more thing, which is defining your repository. Since things like Ansible installation require a repository like **epel-release**, let us try putting it in place and see if the code is functional or not:

```
[root@ip-172-31-2-117 ansible]# cat roles/rsync/tasks/main.yml
---
- name: Install a package
  ansible.builtin.yum:
    name: python >=2.0
    state: present
    enablerepo: "epel-release"
  become: yes
```

Figure 9.19: Installing a package using a specific repository

The playbook is successfully executed:

```
[root@ip-172-31-2-117 ansible]#  ansible-playbook  firstplay.yaml -u ashutmch -K
BECOME password:

PLAY [First playbook] ***************************************************************

TASK [Gathering Facts] **************************************************************
ok: [3.108.53.227]

TASK [rsync : Install a package] ****************************************************
ok: [3.108.53.227]

PLAY RECAP **************************************************************************
3.108.53.227                : ok=2    changed=0    unreachable=0    failed=0    skipped=0

[root@ip-172-31-2-117 ansible]#
```

Figure 9.20: Successful playbook execution with new role

Similarly, you can define any repository that has your package. Now, we need to cover one more important thing here, and that is, **pip** usage. As we know, we need the **pip** installer for many additional Python packages. Let us see an example and see how we can install different packages using **pip**.

Using the **pip** module is also very easy. You simply need to define the name of the package you want to install under the Ansible module:

```
[root@ip-172-31-2-117 ansible]# cat roles/rsync/tasks/main.yml
---
- name: Install bottle python package
  ansible.builtin.pip:
    name: pandas

[root@ip-172-31-2-117 ansible]#
```

Figure 9.21: Role to install the package using the pip module

Let us execute the code. The result will be as follows:

```
[root@ip-172-31-2-117 ansible]# ansible-playbook firstplay.yaml -u ashutmch

PLAY [First playbook] **********************************************************

TASK [Gathering Facts] *********************************************************
ok: [3.108.53.227]

TASK [rsync : Install bottle python package] **********************************
changed: [3.108.53.227]

PLAY RECAP *********************************************************************
3.108.53.227               : ok=2    changed=1    unreachable=0    failed=0

[root@ip-172-31-2-117 ansible]#
```

Figure 9.22: Successful playbook execution

As we can see, the execution was successful.

Just like the **yum** module, the **pip** module also has four options. They are as follows:

- present
- latest
- forceinstall
- absent

Present is the default state, and this is why we do not need to define it there. However, if you want to remove a package or force install it, then we will use the state option. Let us use it to remove the package from the target host. Just now we installed Pandas, let us try to remove it from there:

```
[root@ip-172-31-2-117 ansible]# cat roles/rsync/tasks/main.yml
---
- name: Install bottle python package
  ansible.builtin.pip:
    name: pandas
    state: absent
[root@ip-172-31-2-117 ansible]#
[root@ip-172-31-2-117 ansible]#
[root@ip-172-31-2-117 ansible]#  ansible-playbook  firstplay.yaml -u ashutmch

PLAY [First playbook] ****************************************************

TASK [Gathering Facts] **************************************************
ok: [3.108.53.227]

TASK [rsync : Install bottle python package] ****************************
changed: [3.108.53.227]

PLAY RECAP **************************************************************
3.108.53.227              : ok=2    changed=1    unreachable=0    failed=0

[root@ip-172-31-2-117 ansible]#
```

Figure 9.23: Role to remove the Pandas from the target host

DNF module of Ansible

The DNF module is just like the **yum** module of Ansible. The only difference will be that we will replace the name of the module from **yum** to **dnf,** and the rest is going to be the same. If you want to install any package, you will provide the name of that package in the name option. If you want to install the latest package, you will set the state to latest.

Let us go ahead and have a look at the code and execution:

```
[root@ip-172-31-2-117 ashutoshc1234]#  ansible-playbook  firstplay.yaml -u ashutmch -K
BECOME password:

PLAY [First playbook] ****************************************************

TASK [Gathering Facts] **************************************************
ok: [3.108.53.227]

TASK [dnf : Install bottle python package] ******************************
changed: [3.108.53.227]

PLAY RECAP **************************************************************
3.108.53.227              : ok=2    changed=1    unreachable=0    failed=0    skipped=0

[root@ip-172-31-2-117 ashutoshc1234]# cat firstplay.yaml
---
- name: First playbook
  hosts: all
  roles:
  - dnf
[root@ip-172-31-2-117 ashutoshc1234]# cat roles/dnf/tasks/main.yml
---
- name: Install bottle python package
  ansible.builtin.dnf:
    name: httpd
    state: latest
  become: yes
[root@ip-172-31-2-117 ashutoshc1234]#
```

Figure 9.24: Role and playbook for the dnf module of Ansible

As we can see, our playbook is successful. The playbook contains the role **dnf,** which we created right here. Let us discuss the role.

The first line is the name of the module we used here, **ansible.builtin.dnf**. In the second line, we have defined the name of the package, which is httpd, and the state is set as latest, as we wanted the latest package to be installed. If you want to uninstall the package from the target host, then we simply need to use the option absent or remove.

There are many similarities in **yum** and **dnf** module usage. We need to use **dnf** in the latest version of RHEL and CentOS, as the older versions do not support **dnf**.

Just like the **yum** module, we can create a list of packages we want to install on the target host. We can create a variable and iterate over the list of packages and all those things we tried and tested in the **yum** module are supported here.

APT module of Ansible

Just like we have **yum** and **dnf** modules for the CentOS/RHEL, similarly, we have the APT module for the Ubuntu platform. Now, many things are the same, like the **yum** module here. For installing the package, we choose **state:present,** and for removing the package, we need to choose **state:absent**. Let us go ahead and have a closer look at the different features of this module.

Roles will be as follows:

```
- name: Install HTTPD
  ansible.builtin.apt:
    name: apache2
    state: latest
```

Figure 9.25: Role to install Apache2 in Ubuntu host

For the first and the second lines, we already know that they are names and module names. The third thing that is also well-known to us is the package name we want to install on the target host. The last line is the state, and you will see the same latest option there, which does the same thing it does in the **yum** module, that is, installation of the latest package on the target host. However, we have a few extra options in the APT module, which we should discuss in detail, so let us cover them. They are as follows:

- Present
- Absent
- Latest
- Build-dep
- Fixed

We will now focus on all these options individually:

- **Present**: This indicates that the package should be in the present or installed state.

- **Absent**: This parameter removes the package from the target Linux distribution

- **Latest**: This parameter makes sure the desired state of the package is the latest version.

- **Build-dep**: Build-dep is a nice and useful feature as it takes care of all the dependencies and installs them on the target host. So, build-dep makes sure that dependencies are taken care of in the target host.

- **Fixed**: As the name suggests, it tries to fix something, but the question is what? Well, it tries to fix the broken dependencies on the target host.

Let us now create a role in the control host:

```
[root@ip-172-31-2-117 ashutoshc1234]# cat roles/ubuntu/tasks/main.yml
---
- name: HTTPD installation
  ansible.builtin.apt:
    name: apache2
    state: latest
  become: yes
[root@ip-172-31-2-117 ashutoshc1234]#
```

Figure 9.26: Role to install Apache2 in Ubuntu

Now, we need to modify the playbook too:

```
[root@ip-172-31-2-117 ashutoshc1234]#
[root@ip-172-31-2-117 ashutoshc1234]# cat firstplay.yaml
---
- name: First playbook
  hosts: all
  roles:
    - ubuntu
[root@ip-172-31-2-117 ashutoshc1234]#
```

Figure 9.27: Playbook with new role for Ubuntu target host

Here, we have called the new role which is Ubuntu. Let us go ahead and run our code and wait for the result:

```
[root@ip-172-31-2-117 ashutoshc1234]# ansible-playbook firstplay.yaml -u ashutmch -k -K
SSH password:
BECOME password[defaults to SSH password]:

PLAY [First playbook] ********************************************************

TASK [Gathering Facts] ******************************************************
ok: [13.127.53.212]

TASK [ubuntu : HTTPD installation] ******************************************
changed: [13.127.53.212]

PLAY RECAP ******************************************************************
13.127.53.212              : ok=2    changed=1    unreachable=0    failed=0    skipped=0

[root@ip-172-31-2-117 ashutoshc1234]#
```

Figure 9.28: Playbook execution successful with new role

We can see the execution is successful. We can see the **changed=1,** which means one change was performed on the target host, and that was the installation of the httpd on the target host. If we run it again this time, it will come with **changed=0**.

The simple reason is that Ansible checks the configuration on the target host first and only then performs the changes. If it finds that the **httpd** is already installed on the target host, then it does not perform any of the additional changes on the target host.

Let us re-run it and refresh our concept:

```
[root@ip-172-31-2-117 ashutoshc1234]# ansible-playbook firstplay.yaml -u ashutmch -k -K
SSH password:
BECOME password[defaults to SSH password]:

PLAY [First playbook] ********************************************************

TASK [Gathering Facts] ******************************************************
ok: [13.127.53.212]

TASK [ubuntu : HTTPD installation] ******************************************
ok: [13.127.53.212]

PLAY RECAP ******************************************************************
13.127.53.212              : ok=2    changed=0    unreachable=0    failed=0    skipped=0

[root@ip-172-31-2-117 ashutoshc1234]#
```

Figure 9.29: Re-execution of the same playbook 9.24 with changed=0

Our theory is correct, and we see **changed=0** in the results.

Now, let us go ahead and see the code to upgrade the packages. The same module will be used, but there will be a few modifications.

Let us use another feature of Ansible, which will update the Linux distribution:

```
[root@ip-172-31-2-117 ashutoshc1234]# cat roles/ubuntu/tasks/main.yml
---
- name: upgrade
  ansible.builtin.apt:
    upgrade: dist
  become: yes
[root@ip-172-31-2-117 ashutoshc1234]#
```

Figure 9.30: *Role to upgrade the package in the Ubuntu target host*

If we wish to upgrade the packages to the latest version, then we have some useful options available in the Ansible APT module for us:

The default is no upgrade, so let us explore the rest of the four choices:

- **Full**: The full option will perform the **apt** full upgrade on the target host.

- **Dist**: Dist will perform **apt-get dist-upgrade** on the target host. As we know, **apt-get upgrade** only upgrades existing packages, which means no new packages will be installed or removed.

- **Safe and Yes**: Both these options perform a safe upgrade on the target host.

Let us assume that you all are familiar with the kind of things the upgrade option does, now since this is not a Linux session, we will not deep dive into what each of these option does. However, if you do not know what these options are, it is recommended that you spend some time learning them. Now, you need to explore a few more options available in this module. This will be a good learning experience for you to explore the option on your own.

In this topic, **installing packages**, we will just cover these three platforms of Linux. If you are using any other Linux distribution, remember the concept and apply it in the next Ansible module, and you should be good with it.

Adding new users to the target host

Well, the user management will be part of any IT system, but that majorly happens using AD and Azure AD nowadays. To be realistic, you do not need to have a 1000 AD server in the environment. So, we do not have a realistic use case here for the user addition on the target AD server, but for a few cases, you will still need the local user. Now, you might have thousands of devices where you want to perform the changes, and you do not want to manually do it. So, let us see how Ansible can help you achieve it. Ansible has offered us the user module, and that will help us configure things. Let us go and have a look at the role:

```
[root@ip-172-31-2-117 ashutoshc1234]# cat roles/ubuntu/tasks/main.yml
- name: Add the user demo
  ansible.builtin.user:
    name: demouser
    comment: Ashue
    uid: 200
    group: admin
    password: "$6$ashusalt$g1QjIFdlQ.p3EjrI3B6PksGnS3TIn.rwXKHItq7aIzVU7VAa28P7kt7gUk4At64sxoYq2qGZIet9aQu3i.296/"
  become: yes
```

Figure 9.31: Role to add a user in the Ubuntu target host

As we know, user is the name of the module. The first parameter is the name, and that simply means the name of the user we want to add to the target host. In this case, we have added the user **demouser. comment** and **uid** are two common things we all know. At last, we have an important option, that is, the **group**. We need to define what level of access we want to offer to this user. Since we wanted our **demouser** to get enough privileges, we have added it to the **admin group**.

At last, we see the **password: 'hash'**. Here, we need to put the hash value of our **password**. There are tons of tools available in the market that allow us to generate the **password** hash. You can use that alternatively, or you can use the following method of Ansible:

```
[root@ip-172-31-2-117 ashutoshc1234]#
[root@ip-172-31-2-117 ashutoshc1234]# ansible all -i localhost, -m debug -a "msg={{ 'Abcd@1234' | password_hash('sha512', 'ashusalt') }}"
[DEPRECATION WARNING]: Encryption using the Python crypt module is deprecated. The Python crypt module is deprecated and will be removed
continued encryption functionality. This feature will be removed in version 2.17. Deprecation warnings can be disabled by setting depreca
localhost | SUCCESS => {
    "msg": "$6$ashusalt$g1QjIFdlQ.p3EjrI3B6PksGnS3TIn.rwXKHItq7aIzVU7VAa28P7kt7gUk4At64sxoYq2qGZIet9aQu3i.296/"
}
[root@ip-172-31-2-117 ashutoshc1234]#
```

Figure 9.32: Ad-hoc command to generate hash value

Here, we have defined the password, hashing algorithm, and salt to create the password. If you are unaware of any one of them, then please pause here and read about the hash and salt, and resume the course after. This command has generated the hash, and the same hash is used in the roles that you see.

Now, the next thing we need to do is execute this code. So, let us try it now:

```
[root@ip-172-31-2-117 ashutoshc1234]# ansible-playbook firstplay.yaml -k -K
SSH password:
BECOME password[defaults to SSH password]:

PLAY [First playbook] ***********************************************************

TASK [Gathering Facts] **********************************************************
ok: [13.127.53.212]

TASK [ubuntu : Add the user demo] ***********************************************
changed: [13.127.53.212]

PLAY RECAP **********************************************************************
13.127.53.212              : ok=2    changed=1    unreachable=0    failed=0
```

Figure 9.33: Successful playbook execution

We can see that the execution is successful. Let us try to log into the target host using the **demouser** credentials:

```
[root@ip-172-31-2-117 ashutoshc1234]# ssh demouser@13.127.53.212
demouser@13.127.53.212's password:
Permission denied, please try again.
demouser@13.127.53.212's password:
Welcome to Ubuntu 22.04.2 LTS (GNU/Linux 5.19.0-1025-aws x86_64)

 * Documentation:  https://help.ubuntu.com
 * Management:     https://landscape.canonical.com
 * Support:        https://ubuntu.com/advantage

  System information as of Mon Jun 26 20:32:55 UTC 2023

  System load:  0.0               Processes:             102
  Usage of /:   32.4% of 7.57GB   Users logged in:       0
  Memory usage: 35%               IPv4 address for eth0: 172.31.47.238
  Swap usage:   0%

 * Ubuntu Pro delivers the most comprehensive open source security and
   compliance features.

   https://ubuntu.com/aws/pro

Expanded Security Maintenance for Applications is not enabled.

0 updates can be applied immediately.

Enable ESM Apps to receive additional future security updates.
See https://ubuntu.com/esm or run: sudo pro status


*** System restart required ***

The programs included with the Ubuntu system are free software;
the exact distribution terms for each program are described in the
individual files in /usr/share/doc/*/copyright.

Ubuntu comes with ABSOLUTELY NO WARRANTY, to the extent permitted by
applicable law.

$
$
$
```

Figure 9.34: Successful login attempt to the target host using the last user password

We can see that we have successfully logged into the target host. That host is an Ubuntu machine, clearly visible from the output. In the first attempt, we entered the wrong password, and in the second attempt, it worked correctly.

Note: **Spinning up a new VM in the cloud and shutting down an old VM and starting it in the cloud is also covered in detail in the chapter dedicated to the clouds.** *Chapters 5, Automating AWS Cloud Provisioning with Ansible* **and 6, Ansible for Cloud Provisioning Microsoft Azure have all the details available for us. So this is already covered.**

Conclusion

In this chapter, we learned how to perform and improve our daily tasks. This chapter will definitely make your daily IT life much easier. You will save quality time if you automate most of your routine tasks.

In the next chapter, we will focus on DevOps. We will deep dive into a few of the advanced features of Ansible. We will have a look at jinja2 template as well and understand a bit more about it.

Join our Discord space

Join our Discord workspace for latest updates, offers, tech happenings around the world, new releases, and sessions with the authors:

https://discord.bpbonline.com

## CHAPTER 10

Ansible for DevOps

Introduction

In this chapter, we will try to focus in-depth on roles and playbooks, how Ansible Vault is used, and at the last, we will look at things which are recommended and things which we should not do ever in production.

Structure

This chapter contains the following topics:

- Preparatory work for running a playbook
- Creating a role
- Creating a playbook
- Playbook execution and walkthrough
- Creating an Ansible Vault
- Data manipulation
- Dos and do nots for DevSecOps environment

Objectives

In this chapter, we will learn lot more about the roles, playbook and other features of Ansible. We will learn how we can perform few complicated tasks in Ansible. At the end of the chapter, you will enhance your Ansible skills and will be able to perform the tasks securely.

Preparatory work for running a playbook

We know that there are tons of Ansible modules available in the market. Now, it is a good practice to read the official documents of that module. Here are a few things we should do before we create our code and run it in production.

We should always refer to the official documents of that module before running our playbook and creating roles.

> **Note: We have covered most of the latest things here but by the time your will read this book, there will be new changes in the modules, so refer to the documents before you proceed**

One should also make sure the SSH communication is already in place before trying to execute the code.

Before you run your code, initiate the SSH communication to the target host using that user. For example, if you run the Ansible playbook as a testing user, then you should establish the manual connection to the target host, and this way, the target host will be added to the known list, and you will not find the error. Now, some of you might still be confused, so let us see the live demo of it.

Just have a look at the following code. For demo, we have removed the hosts from the **.ssh/known_host** list. Now, we will try to ssh into the target host:

Figure 10.1: Error when host is not added to the known host list

In the preceding example, we can see the error properly as it says that host key checking is enabled, and because of that ssh is failing. The exact error is:

Using a SSH password instead of a key is not possible because Host Key checking is enabled and sshpass does not support this. Please add this host's fingerprint to your known_hosts file to manage this host.

This is why we manually initiated the communication to the target host and selected yes. Then, the device can be added into **known_host** list, as shown in the following code.

Now, since we want to fix the preceding error and get our host added into the **known_host** list, we are manually connecting the target host and then retrying:

```
[root@ip-172-31-2-117 ashutoshc1234]# ssh ashutmch@13.127.53.212
The authenticity of host '13.127.53.212 (13.127.53.212)' can't be established.
ED25519 key fingerprint is SHA256:UeNFow6g5323u7uq6GPJw7oC+K6vwqrJqCQ9JyNR7xM.
This key is not known by any other names
Are you sure you want to continue connecting (yes/no/[fingerprint])? yes
Warning: Permanently added '13.127.53.212' (ED25519) to the list of known hosts.
ashutmch@13.127.53.212's password:
Welcome to Ubuntu 22.04.2 LTS (GNU/Linux 5.19.0-1025-aws x86_64)

 * Documentation:  https://help.ubuntu.com
 * Management:     https://landscape.canonical.com
 * Support:        https://ubuntu.com/advantage

  System information as of Tue Jun 27 21:47:55 UTC 2023

  System load:  0.0              Processes:               102
  Usage of /:   32.4% of 7.57GB  Users logged in:         0
  Memory usage: 35%              IPv4 address for eth0: 172.31.47.238
  Swap usage:   0%

 * Ubuntu Pro delivers the most comprehensive open source security and
   compliance features.

   https://ubuntu.com/aws/pro

Expanded Security Maintenance for Applications is not enabled.

0 updates can be applied immediately.

Enable ESM Apps to receive additional future security updates.
See https://ubuntu.com/esm or run: sudo pro status


*** System restart required ***
Last login: Tue Jun 27 21:43:13 2023 from 3.110.174.224
ashutmch@ip-172-31-47-238:~$ exit
logout
Connection to 13.127.53.212 closed.
[root@ip-172-31-2-117 ashutoshc1234]# ansible-playbook  firstplay.yaml -k -K
SSH password:
BECOME password[defaults to SSH password]:

PLAY [First playbook] *********************************************************

TASK [Gathering Facts] ********************************************************
ok: [13.127.53.212]
```

Figure 10.2: Manual connection initiation and working playbook post device added to the known host

We can see that it has started working this time. Let us go back to the **known_host** list, delete it again, and see what other options we have.

Another easy option is using the **ssh-keyscan** option. The **keyscan** is a command that gathers information about the public host key. We can easily redirect that information in the **known_list**, and we should be good to go.

Example:

```
[root@ip-172-31-2-117 ashutoshc1234]# ssh-keyscan -H 13.127.53.212 >> ~/.ssh/known_hosts
# 13.127.53.212:22 SSH-2.0-OpenSSH_8.9p1 Ubuntu-3ubuntu0.1
# 13.127.53.212:22 SSH-2.0-OpenSSH_8.9p1 Ubuntu-3ubuntu0.1
# 13.127.53.212:22 SSH-2.0-OpenSSH_8.9p1 Ubuntu-3ubuntu0.1
# 13.127.53.212:22 SSH-2.0-OpenSSH_8.9p1 Ubuntu-3ubuntu0.1
# 13.127.53.212:22 SSH-2.0-OpenSSH_8.9p1 Ubuntu-3ubuntu0.1
[root@ip-172-31-2-117 ashutoshc1234]#
[root@ip-172-31-2-117 ashutoshc1234]#
[root@ip-172-31-2-117 ashutoshc1234]#
[root@ip-172-31-2-117 ashutoshc1234]#
[root@ip-172-31-2-117 ashutoshc1234]#
[root@ip-172-31-2-117 ashutoshc1234]# ansible-playbook  firstplay.yaml -k -K
SSH password:
BECOME password[defaults to SSH password]:

PLAY [First playbook] *************************************************************

TASK [Gathering Facts] ************************************************************
ok: [13.127.53.212]

TASK [ubuntu : Add the user demo] *************************************************
ok: [13.127.53.212]

PLAY RECAP ************************************************************************
13.127.53.212              : ok=2    changed=0    unreachable=0    failed=0    skipped=0    rescued=0
```

Figure 10.3: SSH keyscan and working playbook

We can see that as soon as we used this command, the device was added to the **known_hosts** list, and when we tried the playbook again, it started working.

However, this does not look like our way of working. What if we have 1000 hosts? We cannot manually connect all target hosts and add them to the **known_hosts** file. Our preference should be automating that, now we must start thinking and try adding all new target hosts to the **known_hosts** file using automation. We have already shown the way of achieving it using Ansible and we have written a simple playbook to add all servers in **known_hosts** file in a single playbook. Let us have a look at it:

```
[root@ip-172-31-2-117 ashutoshc1234]# cat addknown.yaml
---
# ansible playbook that adds ssh fingerprints to known_hosts
- hosts: all
  connection: local
  gather_facts: no
  tasks:
  - shell: "/usr/bin/ssh-keyscan -H {{ ansible_host }} >> ~/.ssh/known_hosts"
[root@ip-172-31-2-117 ashutoshc1234]#
[root@ip-172-31-2-117 ashutoshc1234]#
```

Figure 10.4: Playbook to add all new target host in the known_hosts file

We have used the variable which is **ansible_host** information. So, for target host, it will execute the same command locally and add them in the **known_hosts** list. This way, all the hosts will be added to the **known_ hosts** list, and you will be able to proceed with your actual playbook:

```
PLAYBOOK: addknown.yaml ****************************************************

PLAY [all] ******************************************************************

TASK [shell] ****************************************************************
changed: [13.127.53.212] => {"ansible_facts": {"discovered_interpreter_python": "/usr/bin/
delta": "0:00:00.103703", "end": "2023-06-27 22:21:40.836027", "msg": "", "rc": 0, "start"
.1\n# 13.127.53.212:22 SSH-2.0-OpenSSH_8.9p1 Ubuntu-3ubuntu0.1\n# 13.127.53.212:22 SSH-2.0
127.53.212:22 SSH-2.0-OpenSSH_8.9p1 Ubuntu-3ubuntu0.1", "stderr_lines": ["# 13.127.53.212:
tu0.1", "# 13.127.53.212:22 SSH-2.0-OpenSSH_8.9p1 Ubuntu-3ubuntu0.1", "# 13.127.53.212:22
.1"], "stdout": "", "stdout_lines": []}

PLAY RECAP ******************************************************************
13.127.53.212          : ok=1    changed=1    unreachable=0    failed=0    skipped=0
```

Figure 10.5: Successful execution of playbook which adds the new host to the kown_hosts file

Now, let us have a look at a task. Try running the same playbook using the **command** module of Ansible. It will fail since the commands executed using the Ansible **command** module does not processed through the shell, and that is the reason why the operation like *****, **>**, **&** and **;** does not work.

Now, if you have a huge host list or you are working in a disconnected environment where the latency is very high, then connection timeout might be a big concern. If your commands take a lot of time to execute, you will again face a connection timeout error. So, to get over this problem, modify the **ansible.cfg** as per your requirement. You should increase the timeout as per your need; for example, if your command takes one minute to execute, you may change the connection timeout to 75 seconds. If you are working in a slow, disconnected environment, then you might want to change the retires option too. You should modify that from the **ansible.cfg** file.

Creating a role

This topic has been covered in detail in *Chapter 3, Working with Ansible*. We will not duplicate the content here. However, we will look at something that has not been covered there. Let us have a look at the following hosts file:

```
[root@ip-172-31-2-117 ansible]# cat hosts
# This is the default ansible 'hosts' file.
#
# It should live in /etc/ansible/hosts
[ubuntu]
13.127.53.212
[root@ip-172-31-2-117 ansible]#
```

Figure 10.6: Example of host file with Group

We can see that we have created a group of hosts which is ubuntu. Now, we can also define group variables here only like we have learned in *Chapter 3, Working with Ansible*. However, this is not how you will see the things in the production. You will see a new directory named as **group_vars** which will contain different group variable files. The group we have created in our case is Ubuntu.

Let us look at how things are used in a production environment:

1. We will create a directory named as **group_vars**, and a file named Ubuntu in that directory (Since we created a group named as **ubuntu** in the host file. If your group is Linux, you need to create the file named Linux):

```
mkdir group_vars
cd group_vars
vi ubuntu
```

```
[root@ip-172-31-2-117 ansible]# mkdir group_vars
mkdir: cannot create directory 'group_vars': File exists
[root@ip-172-31-2-117 ansible]#
[root@ip-172-31-2-117 ansible]#
[root@ip-172-31-2-117 ansible]# cd group_vars/
[root@ip-172-31-2-117 group_vars]# vi ubuntu
```

Figure 10.7: Creation of group variables

Since we already have the **group_vars**, you can see the file is showing an error. We have navigated to the directory and created a file named **ubuntu**. Inside that file, we have defined the username and password parameters.

Note: This is just for demo. Never use the clear text password in production. In the next chapter, we will go ahead with the encryption of this file and password.

```
---
ansible_user: ashutmch
ansible_ssh_pass: abcd1123
~
~
```

Figure 10.8: How to define username and password

For now, let us run this code and see the results:

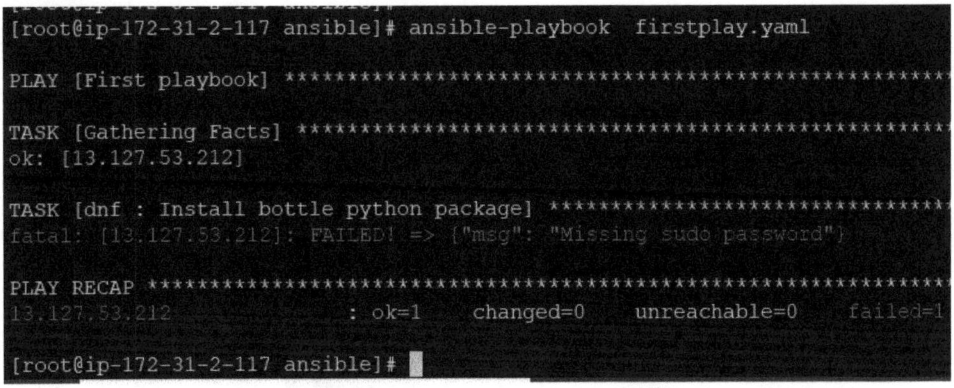

Figure 10.9: Playbook execution with sudo password error

As we can see, the **gather_facts** were successful; however, we see the error of sudo password missing. So, let us fix that too:

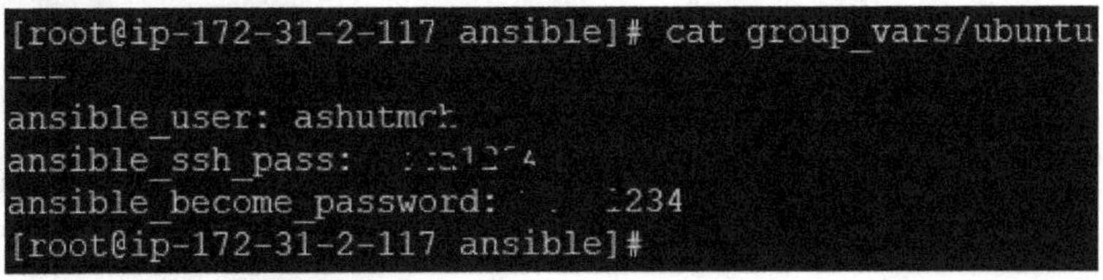

Figure 10.10: Group variable defining username and password

This is how the new **group_vars** will look. Execute it again and see the results, as shown in the following figure:

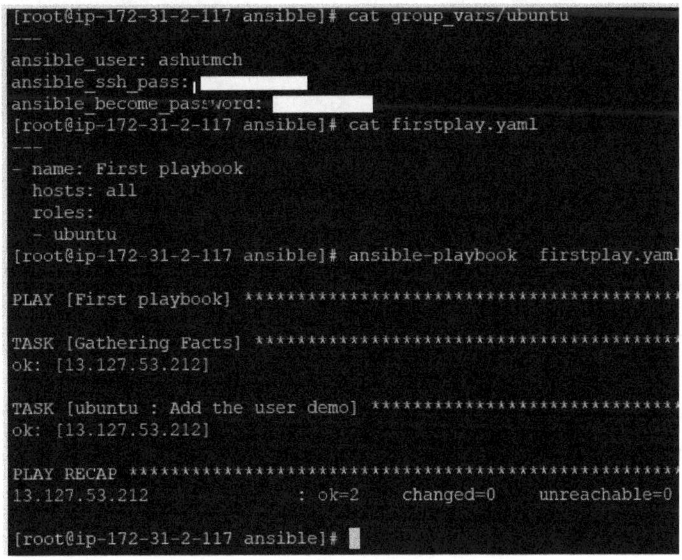

Figure 10.11: Play recap with group variables containing credentials

This time the execution was successful. Similarly, we can save the password in the **roles/ubuntu/vars/main.yaml** file too. So, let us move the content of our **group_vars** to the new destination:

```
[root@ip-172-31-2-117 ansible]# cat roles/ubuntu/vars/main.yml
---
ansible_user: ashutmch
ansible_ssh_pass:
ansible_become_password:
[root@ip-172-31-2-117 ansible]#
```

Figure 10.12: Example of roles variable containing the credentials

We can see that our new location has username and password. Now, let us try to run it again and see the results. We can see in the output that the **group_vars** directory does not contain those credentials anymore, as they were moved to the vars of roles:

```
[root@ip-172-31-2-117 ansible]#
[root@ip-172-31-2-117 ansible]# ls -ltr  group_vars/
total 4
-rw-r--r--. 1 root root 54 Jun 28 16:28 1
[root@ip-172-31-2-117 ansible]#
[root@ip-172-31-2-117 ansible]#
[root@ip-172-31-2-117 ansible]#
[root@ip-172-31-2-117 ansible]# ansible-playbook  firstplay.yaml

PLAY [First playbook] ************************************************

TASK [Gathering Facts] **********************************************
ok: [13.127.53.212]

TASK [ubuntu : Add the user demo] ***********************************
ok: [13.127.53.212]

PLAY RECAP **********************************************************
13.127.53.212                : ok=2    changed=0    unreachable=0    failed=0

[root@ip-172-31-2-117 ansible]#
```

Figure 10.13: Playbook execution with role's variable file

The execution is successful.

Creating a playbook

Since this topic has been covered in detail in *Chapter 3, Working with Ansible,* we will not duplicate the content here. Let us have a look at advanced things we can do in Ansible. In this section, we will look at how to use the conditions in Ansible. Let us see a practical situation where you need to update the security patches on target hosts. All of them are Linux hosts, however, a few of them are ubuntu and a few of them are RHEL.

Now, commands are different in both target hosts, so, you have to use different modules. Let us think about how we can handle this kind of situation.

The solution can be achieved in multiple ways, and you should think about your solution once and then look for the solution shown as follows. We will use the magic variables to find out the target host information, and then, based on the OS, the command and modules will be chosen. Let us see the practical here:

1. We have created an Ansible role that gathers information about the target host. Let us have a look at the code:

```
[root@ip-172-31-2-117 ansible]# cat roles/facts/tasks/main.yml
---
# tasks file for facts
- name: Gather the information about the target host
  ansible.builtin.gather_facts:
  register: output
- debug:
    msg: "{{output}}"
[root@ip-172-31-2-117 ansible]#
[root@ip-172-31-2-117 ansible]#
```

Figure 10.14: Role with gather_facts and its debug

2. Now we have registered the output of the **gather_facts** into the variable named **output**, and later we have used the **debug** module to show the content of that variable. Let us execute the code on the target host. Remember, we need to find the OS category here in this case:

```
[root@ip-172-31-2-117 ansible]# ansible-playbook firstplay.yaml -u ashutmch -k
SSH password:

PLAY [First playbook] *******************************************************

TASK [Gathering Facts] *******************************************************
ok: [13.127.53.212]
ok: [3.108.53.227]

TASK [facts : Gather the information about the target host] ******************
ok: [13.127.53.212]
ok: [3.108.53.227]

TASK [facts : debug] *********************************************************
ok: [3.108.53.227] => {
    "msg": {
        "ansible_facts": {
            "ansible_all_ipv4_addresses": [
                "172.31.6.75"
            ],
            "ansible_all_ipv6_addresses": [
                "fe80::8f8:8bff:fe4c:4892"
            ],
            "ansible_apparmor": {
                "status": "disabled"
            },
            "ansible_architecture": "x86_64",
            "ansible_bios_date": "08/24/2006",
            "ansible_bios_vendor": "Xen",
            "ansible_bios_version": "4.11.amazon",
            "ansible_board_asset_tag": "NA",
            "ansible_board_name": "NA",
            "ansible_board_serial": "NA",
```

Figure 10.15: Debug of gather_facts in playbook execution

The output continues. We can see the output is huge and we want to refer the **os_family** of the target host from this output. Let us put the output down and drill down it again.

This time, we have simply used the grep option to find the OS details. As we can see, one OS is **Debian**, and another one is **RedHat**. Let us go ahead and write our role on the basis of that information. The commands of **Debian** will be pushed on the **Debian**, and commands of **RedHat** will be pushed on the respective target host:

```
[root@ip-172-31-2-117 ansible]#
[root@ip-172-31-2-117 ansible]# ansible-playbook  firstplay.yaml -u ashutmch -k | grep ansible_os_family
SSH password:
        "ansible_os_family": "RedHat",
        "ansible_os_family": "Debian",
[root@ip-172-31-2-117 ansible]#
[root@ip-172-31-2-117 ansible]#
```

Figure 10.16: Different commands for the target hosts on the basis of OS Family

Since we have a way of knowing the OS family, let us use it to send different commands to different devices. Now, we will create a role that contains the code for both **Debian** and **RedHat**. In *Figure 10.17*, we are updating the distribution version if the OS is **Debian**; however, for **RedHat**, we are updating all packages to the latest release.

- If the OS family is **Debian**, the package distribution should be updated on the target host.
- If the OS family is **RedHat**, all the packages should be upgraded to the latest version. (Avoid using it in production at any cost. Always specify the specific package you want to upgrade. This might be a disruptive change.)

Let us have a look at the role and how we could specify the variables in it:

```
[root@ip-172-31-2-117 ansible]#
[root@ip-172-31-2-117 ansible]# cat roles/ubuntu/tasks/main.yml
---
- name: Add the user demo
  ansible.builtin.apt:
    upgrade: dist
  become: yes
  when: ansible_facts['os_family'] == "Debian"


- name: Install bottle python package
  ansible.builtin.dnf:
    name: '*'
    state: latest
  become: yes
  when: ansible_facts['os_family'] == "RedHat"
[root@ip-172-31-2-117 ansible]#
```

Figure 10.17: Role with use of magic variables and conditions

Let us go ahead and decode the code in parts:

```
---

- name: Add the user demo
  ansible.builtin.apt:
    upgrade: dist
  become: yes
  when: ansible_facts['os_family'] == "Debian"
```

The **when** statement simply says check for the **ansible_facts** and inside those **ansible_facts**, search for the **os_family**. If you find the **os_family** to be **Debian**, then execute the preceding five commands. Generally, tasks are executed top to bottom, line by line; however, in the case of a **when** statement, it will be different. First of all, Ansible will look for the condition and try to match that. If that succeeds, then only the task will be executed ; otherwise, it will be skipped, and you will see **skipped=1** at the result for that task.

Similarly, the second task will be executed. The only difference will be in the commands and OS family that it will search for:

```
- name: Install bottle python package
  ansible.builtin.dnf:
    name: '*'
    state: latest
  become: yes
  when: ansible_facts['os_family'] == "RedHat"   -- In this case
```

It will check for the **os_family** as **RedHat** and if that is the case, then only the following four lines will be executed:

```
- name: Install bottle python package
  ansible.builtin.dnf:
    name: *
    state: latest
  become: yes
```

Let us go ahead and execute this code and wait for the results:

```
[root@ip-172-31-2-117 ansible]#
[root@ip-172-31-2-117 ansible]#
[root@ip-172-31-2-117 ansible]# ansible-playbook  firstplay.yaml

PLAY [First playbook] ***********************************************************

TASK [Gathering Facts] **********************************************************
ok: [3.108.53.227]
ok: [13.127.53.212]

TASK [ubuntu : Add the user demo] ***********************************************
skipping: [3.108.53.227]
changed: [13.127.53.212]

TASK [ubuntu : Install bottle python package] ***********************************
skipping: [13.127.53.212]
ok: [3.108.53.227]

PLAY RECAP **********************************************************************
13.127.53.212              : ok=2    changed=1    unreachable=0    failed=0    skipped=1
3.108.53.227               : ok=2    changed=0    unreachable=0    failed=0    skipped=1
```

Figure 10.18: Successful playbook execution where one target is skipped for a task

As we can see in the results, a few things were skipped while others were executed successfully. Since the conditions were not matching, Ansible had to skip that task and move ahead with the next one.

Let us go back to the **when** statement and what else we can do using it. Right now, we have just one condition, but what do you have a bunch of them? You can use multiple conditions too in Ansible. Let us have a look at the code and see how we can achieve it:

```
-name:Upgrade the OS It is less than 6
 ansible.builtin.dnf:
     name: '*'
     state: latest
   when: (ansible_facts['distribution'] == "CentOS" and ansible_facts['distribution_major_version'] == "6")
```

So, this is how you can match multiple conditions and if they match the preceding code, the condition will be executed. In this condition, **dnf** module will be used to upgrade all packages. If you have multiple conditions that need to be true or matched before we send our commands on the target host, then we can match such conditions for the target hosts. We can look for the list of conditions and once all conditions are true or matched, then only the command will be executed on the target host. If the condition fails, then the task will be skipped for the target host:

```
- name: Upgrade the OS if CentOS version is less than 6
  ansible.builtin.dnf:
    name: '*'
    state: latest
```

```
when:
  - ansible_facts['distribution'] == "CentOS"
  - ansible_facts['distribution_major_version'] | int < 6
```

There will be a time when you would want to run a command on the target host, and on the basis of the output, you want to decide the next command. That is also well possible in Ansible. Let us see a small example here.

Let us take a situation where you want to add a user in the target host. What you want to do is check if the user is already present on the target host. If the user is already present on the target host, then print **The user is already present on the target host**. If it is not there, then add the new user on the target host. Let us have a look at the role for that code:

```
[root@ip-172-31-2-117 ansible]#
[root@ip-172-31-2-117 ansible]# cat roles/whencon/tasks/main.yml
---
- name: Add the user demo
  command: cat /etc/passwd
  register: output
- name: Print it is there
  command: echo "Yes demo user is there"
  become: yes
  when: output.stdout.find('demo') != -1
[root@ip-172-31-2-117 ansible]#
```

Figure 10.19: Code to check and print if the user is present on the target host

In this example, we use the command module and send the command **cat /etc/passwd**. Now, this command helps us check the users on the target host. The output is then saved on the variable named **output**. Then once again, we are using the command module to print **yes demo user is there** if the demo user is found in the target host.

Overall, task two will first check the condition in which it will try to find the keyword **demo**. If it is found on the target host, then only the **yes demo user is there** will be printed on the screen.

Let us run our code and see the result:

```
[root@ip-172-31-2-117 ansible]# ansible-playbook firstplay.yaml

PLAY [First playbook] ***********************************************************

TASK [Gathering Facts] **********************************************************
ok: [13.127.53.212]
ok: [3.108.53.227]

TASK [whencon : Add the user demo] **********************************************
changed: [13.127.53.212]
changed: [3.108.53.227]

TASK [whencon : Print it is there] **********************************************
skipping: [3.108.53.227]
changed: [13.127.53.212]

PLAY RECAP **********************************************************************
13.127.53.212              : ok=3    changed=2    unreachable=0    failed=0    skipped=0
3.108.53.227               : ok=2    changed=1    unreachable=0    failed=0    skipped=1

[root@ip-172-31-2-117 ansible]#
```

***Figure 10.20**: Successful execution shows the demo user is present on one host and task skipped on the other host*

The result says that the execution is skipping on the target host 3.108.53.227. This should ideally mean that the user demo is not present on the target host. Let us log in to the target host 3.108.53.227, manually enter the `cat /etc/passwd` command, and verify if this user is not there:

```
[root@ip-172-31-2-117 ansible]# ssh ashutmch@3.108.53.227
Register this system with Red Hat Insights: insights-client --register
Create an account or view all your systems at https://red.ht/insights-dashboard
Last login: Thu Jun 29 18:18:15 2023 from 3.110.174.224
[ashutmch@ip-172-31-6-75 ~]$ cat /etc/passwd
root:x:0:0:root:/root:/bin/bash
bin:x:1:1:bin:/bin:/sbin/nologin
daemon:x:2:2:daemon:/sbin:/sbin/nologin
adm:x:3:4:adm:/var/adm:/sbin/nologin
lp:x:4:7:lp:/var/spool/lpd:/sbin/nologin
sync:x:5:0:sync:/sbin:/bin/sync
shutdown:x:6:0:shutdown:/sbin:/sbin/shutdown
halt:x:7:0:halt:/sbin:/sbin/halt
mail:x:8:12:mail:/var/spool/mail:/sbin/nologin
operator:x:11:0:operator:/root:/sbin/nologin
games:x:12:100:games:/usr/games:/sbin/nologin
ftp:x:14:50:FTP User:/var/ftp:/sbin/nologin
nobody:x:65534:65534:Kernel Overflow User:/:/sbin/nologin
systemd-coredump:x:999:997:systemd Core Dumper:/:/sbin/nologin
dbus:x:81:81:System message bus:/:/sbin/nologin
polkitd:x:998:996:User for polkitd:/:/sbin/nologin
tss:x:59:59:Account used for TPM access:/dev/null:/sbin/nologin
sssd:x:997:994:User for sssd:/:/sbin/nologin
sshd:x:74:74:Privilege-separated SSH:/usr/share/empty.sshd:/sbin/nologin
chrony:x:996:993:chrony system user:/var/lib/chrony:/sbin/nologin
systemd-oom:x:991:991:systemd Userspace OOM Killer:/:/usr/sbin/nologin
ec2-user:x:1000:1000:Cloud User:/home/ec2-user:/bin/bash
ashutmch:x:1001:1001::/home/ashutmch:/bin/bash
apache:x:48:48:Apache:/usr/share/httpd:/sbin/nologin
nginx:x:990:990:Nginx web server:/var/lib/nginx:/sbin/nologin
postgres:x:26:26:PostgreSQL Server:/var/lib/pgsql:/bin/bash
rtkit:x:172:172:RealtimeKit:/proc:/sbin/nologin
pipewire:x:989:989:PipeWire System Daemon:/var/run/pipewire:/sbin/nologin
geoclue:x:988:988:User for geoclue:/var/lib/geoclue:/sbin/nologin
flatpak:x:987:987:User for flatpak system helper:/:/sbin/nologin
pesign:x:986:986:Group for the pesign signing daemon:/run/pesign:/sbin/nologin
[ashutmch@ip-172-31-6-75 ~]$
[ashutmch@ip-172-31-6-75 ~]$
```

Figure 10.21: The output clearly shows the demo user is not present on this host

As we can see, the demo user is not there. Let us login to the other target host and see if this demo user is present on the other host. As expected, the demo user is present on the target host 13.127.53.212:

```
See https://ubuntu.com/esm or run: sudo pro status


*** System restart required ***
Last login: Thu Jun 29 18:26:03 2023 from 3.110.174.224
ashutmch@ip-172-31-47-238:~$ cat /etc/passwd | grep demo
demouser:x:200:118:Ashue:/home/demouser:/bin/sh
ashutmch@ip-172-31-47-238:~$
ashutmch@ip-172-31-47-238:~$
ashutmch@ip-172-31-47-238:~$
```

Figure 10.22: Demouser present on the second host

The entire output is as follows:

```
backup:x:34:34:backup:/var/backups:/usr/sbin/nologin
list:x:38:38:Mailing List Manager:/var/list:/usr/sbi
irc:x:39:39:ircd:/run/ircd:/usr/sbin/nologin
gnats:x:41:41:Gnats Bug-Reporting System (admin):/va
nobody:x:65534:65534:nobody:/nonexistent:/usr/sbin/n
systemd-network:x:100:102:systemd Network Management
systemd-resolve:x:101:103:systemd Resolver,,,:/run/s
messagebus:x:102:105::/nonexistent:/usr/sbin/nologin
systemd-timesync:x:103:106:systemd Time Synchronizat
syslog:x:104:111::/home/syslog:/usr/sbin/nologin
_apt:x:105:65534::/nonexistent:/usr/sbin/nologin
tss:x:106:112:TPM software stack,,,:/var/lib/tpm:/bi
uuidd:x:107:113::/run/uuidd:/usr/sbin/nologin
tcpdump:x:108:114::/nonexistent:/usr/sbin/nologin
sshd:x:109:65534::/run/sshd:/usr/sbin/nologin
pollinate:x:110:1::/var/cache/pollinate:/bin/false
landscape:x:111:116::/var/lib/landscape:/usr/sbin/no
fwupd-refresh:x:112:117:fwupd-refresh user,,,:/run/s
ec2-instance-connect:x:113:65534::/nonexistent:/usr/
chrony:x:114:121:Chrony daemon,,,:/var/lib/chrony:/
ubuntu:x:1000:1000:Ubuntu:/home/ubuntu:/bin/bash
lxd:x:999:100::/var/snap/lxd/common/lxd:/bin/false
ashutmch:x:1001:1001:ashu,,,:/home/ashutmch:/bin/bas
demouser:x:200:118:Ashue:/home/demouser:/bin/sh
```

Figure 10.23: All users list in the host

Let us go ahead and use the regular expression now. Try to find the **demo** keyword using that:

```
[root@ip-172-31-2-117 ansible]# cat roles/whencon/tasks/main.yml
---
- name: Add the user demo
  command: cat /etc/passwd
  register: output
- name: Print it is there
  command: echo "Yes demo user is there"
  become: yes
  when: output.stdout is regex("demo")
```

Figure 10.24: Code to find the user using regular expression in Ansible role

As you can see, we are searching for the word **demo** in that file. If it finds the demo, then the message is displayed, or any command can be executed on the target host.

Now, you might be thinking, if we have a simple option of **find('demo')**, which we used in *Figure 10.19*, then why go for the regular expression? Well, what if you want to find the keyword, which is complex, like **ec2-user:x:** or lot more complicated which has multiple special characters in it. In that condition, **find** will fail and **regex** will become your friend. That is why we are exploring options like **regex**, which works great with complex keywords too.

Let us go ahead and try other situations where we are searching for the user demo on the target host, but the target host does not contain the user **demouser**. If it does not contain that, we would want to add **demouser1** in the target host.

Let us create a role for that and then execute it:

```
[root@ip-172-31-2-117 ansible]# cat roles/whencon/tasks/main.yml
---
- name: Add the user demo
  command: cat /etc/passwd
  register: output
- name: Print it is there
  ansible.builtin.user:
    name: demouser
    comment: demouser1
    uid: 200
    group: admin
    password: "$6$ashusalt$g1QjIFdlQ.p3EjrI3B6PksGnS3TIn.rwXKHItq7a-
IzVU7VAa28P7kt7gUk4At64sxoYq2qGZIet9aQu3i.296/"
  become: yes
  when: output.stdout is not contains ("demo")
```

This time, we used the **contains** option rather than regex. This will search for that keyword in the output. In this case, the **demo** keyword. If we wanted to search for the demo user and print something like old cases, the condition would have been **when: output.stdout contains ("demo")**. Since we wanted to use the other way around and add the user if it is not there, this is why we have used the condition **not contains** and then action.

Let us go ahead and try to execute this code:

```
[root@ip-172-31-2-117 ansible]# ansible-playbook firstplay.yaml

PLAY [First playbook] ***********************************************************

TASK [Gathering Facts] **********************************************************
ok: [13.127.53.212]
ok: [3.108.53.227]

TASK [whencon : Add the user demo] **********************************************
changed: [13.127.53.212]
changed: [3.108.53.227]

TASK [whencon : Print it is there] **********************************************
skipping: [13.127.53.212]
changed: [3.108.53.227]

PLAY RECAP **********************************************************************
13.127.53.212              : ok=2    changed=1    unreachable=0    failed=0    skipped=1
3.108.53.227               : ok=3    changed=2    unreachable=0    failed=0    skipped=0
```

***Figure 10.25**: Successful playbook execution*

As we can see in *Figure 10.25*, the host 13.127.53.212 already had the user demo created in it. Hence, the task **whencon: Print it is there** is being skipped; however, since there was no **demouser** in the target host 3.108.53.227, it was created, and that is why you see the changed: [3.108.53.227] for the tasks **whencon: Print it is there**.

This is how you can match the different conditions and perform some actions accordingly. Let us also look by logging in to the target host and seeing the output. One host should contain the **demouser**, and the second should also contain the **demouser1**.

Let us login and see it. As expected, one device contains the **demouser** and another contains the **demouser1** now:

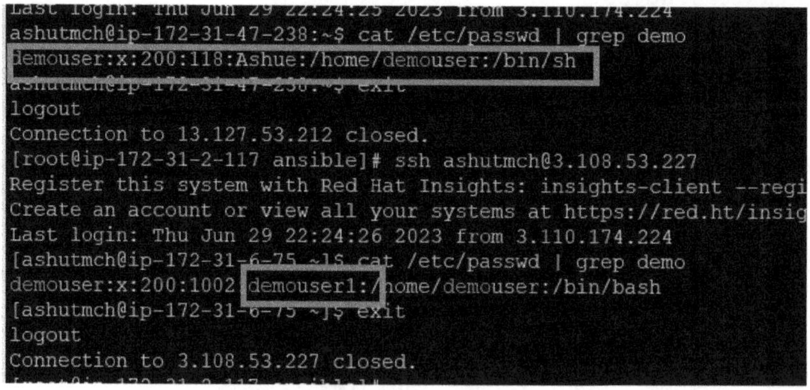

Figure 10.26: Demouser and demouser1 present in respective host

Let us go ahead and talk about one more important feature of Ansible, which is **block**. Let us learn more about this in the next section:

Block

Block is a local group of multiple tasks. Blocks are just like exception handling in many programming languages. However, if you do not know any of the programming languages, then do not worry. Just think of it as a tool which will logically group your multiple tasks, and then, Ansible will start handing the block as a single entity. Block generally offers two things. Let us write them one by one and then talk about them in detail.

Grouping multiple tasks together

So far, we have seen how a when condition is used for a single task. However, if we have 10 tasks that need the same when condition, repeating it for each task becomes tedious and inefficient. For example, consider the following use case where we have two tasks required on the target host, if they are **Debian**:

```
[root@ip-172-31-2-117 ansible]# cat roles/ubuntu/tasks/main.yml
---
- name: Add the user demo
  ansible.builtin.apt:
    upgrade: dist
  become: yes
  when: ansible_facts['os_family'] == "Debian"

- name: Add the user demo
  ansible.builtin.apt:
    name: ansible
    state: present
  become: yes
  when: ansible_facts['os_family'] == "Debian"

- name: Install bottle python package
  ansible.builtin.dnf:
    name: '*'
    state: latest
  become: yes
  when: ansible_facts['os_family'] == "RedHat"
[root@ip-172-31-2-117 ansible]#
```

Figure 10.27: Role where we will use block option and make it more efficient

The role simply says apply dist update if the OS family is Debian and at the same time install Ansible in the target host.

Now, as a developer, this will sound like an inferior style of coding, so we need to see how we can fix it using an Ansible block. In this case, we can combine these two tasks and apply a when statement to the entire block of these two tasks. So, we can create a new logical task that will be checked against the when statement. Let us do it now and see how it looks in real:

```
[root@ip-172-31-2-117 ansible]# cat roles/ubuntu/tasks/main.yml
---
- name: Add the user demo
  block:
    - name: Update dist
      ansible.builtin.apt:
        upgrade: dist
      become: yes

    - name: Add the user demo
      ansible.builtin.apt:
        name: ansible
        state: present
      become: yes
  when: ansible_facts['os_family'] == "Debian"

- name: Install bottle python package
  ansible.builtin.dnf:
    name: '*'
    state: latest
  become: yes
  when: ansible_facts['os_family'] == "RedHat"
[root@ip-172-31-2-117 ansible]#
```

Figure 10.28: Role with use of block which performs two tasks if condition matched

So now what we have done is created a logical group using a block and applied when statement against the block. If you are still confused, then think of this block as a task. Just like we are using a when statement for a task, we can use it for the block. Inside that block, we need to use the code with indentation. Since the indentation in YAML is of two spaces, we are seeing two space, and then the—name statement starts inside the block. All the other rules of YAML will be applied as it is. Let us go ahead and execute our code:

```
[root@ip-172-31-2-117 ansible]# ansible-playbook firstplay.yaml

PLAY [First playbook] ***********************************************************

TASK [Gathering Facts] **********************************************************
ok: [13.127.53.212]
ok: [3.108.53.227]

TASK [ubuntu : Update dist] *****************************************************
skipping: [3.108.53.227]
changed: [13.127.53.212]

TASK [ubuntu : Add the user demo] ***********************************************
skipping: [3.108.53.227]
changed: [13.127.53.212]

TASK [ubuntu : Install bottle python package] **********************************
skipping: [13.127.53.212]
ok: [3.108.53.227]

PLAY RECAP **********************************************************************
13.127.53.212              : ok=3    changed=2    unreachable=0    failed=0    skipped=1
3.108.53.227               : ok=2    changed=0    unreachable=0    failed=0    skipped=2
```

Figure 10.29: Successful playbook execution

We can see that the execution is successful. Similarly, you can keep many tasks inside that block. You can even create another block inside the existing block.

Using block for error handling

Let us go ahead and talk about the situation where you want all stages to succeed at every cost, and if any fail, you want the rollback configuration to be pushed to the target host.

In this case, we used it to create a block just like the preceding one, but if any of the task fails in that condition, we can put the rescue configuration on the target host. If all things go well then, the rescue configuration code is skipped. So, in simple words, rescue only comes into the picture and get executed if any task in the earlier block fails:

```
[root@ip-172-31-2-117 ansible]# cat roles/block/tasks/main.yml
---
- name: Task two generate the error
  block:
    - name: Debug module
      ansible.builtin.debug:
        msg: 'Normal execution'

    - name: Failure
      ansible.builtin.command: /bin/false

    - name: skipped
      ansible.builtin.debug:
        msg: 'since the task two failed i will be skipped'
  rescue:
    - name: Rescue code on the target host
      ansible.builtin.debug:
        msg: 'There is an error'
[root@ip-172-31-2-117 ansible]#
```

Figure 10.30: Error handling using block

In the preceding example, we have used the debug module, and in task two, we have induced the failure. Since block mode is created for error handling, and we generated an error, the rescue configuration will be pushed to the target host.

Let us go ahead and try the execution of the preceding role. Once that is done, we will try to put all the green things in place and see if the rescue configuration is skipped:

```
[root@ip-172-31-2-117 ansible]# ansible-playbook firstplay.yaml

PLAY [First playbook] ***************************************************

TASK [Gathering Facts] *************************************************
ok: [13.127.53.212]
ok: [3.108.53.227]

TASK [block : Debug module] *********************************************
ok: [3.108.53.227] => {
    "msg": "Normal execution"
}
ok: [13.127.53.212] => {
    "msg": "Normal execution"
}

TASK [block : Failure] *************************************************
fatal: [13.127.53.212]: FAILED! => {"changed": true, "cmd": ["/bin/false"], "delta": "0:00:00.003079",
"2023-06-30 22:32:51.192168", "stderr": "", "stderr_lines": [], "stdout": "", "stdout_lines": []}
fatal: [3.108.53.227]: FAILED! => {"changed": true, "cmd": ["/bin/false"], "delta": "0:00:00.003304",
2023-06-30 22:32:51.252308", "stderr": "", "stderr_lines": [], "stdout": "", "stdout_lines": []}

TASK [block : Rescue code on the target host] ***************************
ok: [3.108.53.227] => {
    "msg": "There is an error"
}
ok: [13.127.53.212] => {
    "msg": "There is an error"
}

PLAY RECAP *************************************************************
13.127.53.212           : ok=3    changed=0    unreachable=0    failed=0    skipped=0    rescued=1
3.108.53.227            : ok=3    changed=0    unreachable=0    failed=0    skipped=0    rescued=1

[root@ip-172-31-2-117 ansible]#
```

Figure 10.31: Successfully generated fake error and aborted the execution

We can see that task one was successful, the second one failed, and the third one was never executed. For the first time in this book, you see **rescued=1** since the rescue configuration was pushed on the target host. You can see the rescue code is being pushed on the devices. Let us go ahead and make everything green there.

Now, what we have done in the following role is to remove the failure with the uptime command. So, this time, rather than a fake failed error, we have sent a genuine Linux command on the target host, the uptime command will be sent to the target host and will be executed on the target host. This time, the third task will also be executed, but the rescue operation should not come into the picture, and in the **PLAY RECAP** as well, you should not see any entry for the rescued:

```
[root@ip-172-31-2-117 ansible]# cat roles/block/tasks/main.yml
---
- name: Task two generate the error
  block:
    - name: Debug module
      ansible.builtin.debug:
        msg: 'Normal execution'

    - name: Failure
      ansible.builtin.command: uptime

    - name: skipped
      ansible.builtin.debug:
        msg: 'since the task two failed i will be skipped'
  rescue:
    - name: Rescue code on the target host
      ansible.builtin.debug:
        msg: 'There is an error'
[root@ip-172-31-2-117 ansible]#
```

Figure 10.32: Updated code with fixing the error

Execution: Now, let us have a look at the execution summary and understand it in detail:

```
[root@ip-172-31-2-117 ansible]# ansible-playbook firstplay.yaml

PLAY [First playbook] *******************************************************

TASK [Gathering Facts] ******************************************************
ok: [13.127.53.212]
ok: [3.108.53.227]

TASK [block : Debug module] *************************************************
ok: [3.108.53.227] => {
    "msg": "Normal execution"
}
ok: [13.127.53.212] => {
    "msg": "Normal execution"
}

TASK [block : Failure] ******************************************************
changed: [13.127.53.212]
changed: [3.108.53.227]

TASK [block : skipped] ******************************************************
ok: [3.108.53.227] => {
    "msg": "since the task two failed i will be skipped"
}
ok: [13.127.53.212] => {
    "msg": "since the task two failed i will be skipped"
}

PLAY RECAP ******************************************************************
13.127.53.212              : ok=4    changed=1    unreachable=0    failed=0    skipped=0    rescued=0
3.108.53.227               : ok=4    changed=1    unreachable=0    failed=0    skipped=0    rescued=0

[root@ip-172-31-2-117 ansible]#
```

Figure 10.33: Successful playbook execution with no errors

As we can see, the third task skipped is also executed this time, and the rescued configuration was not there in the picture. This is how you can use the block feature of Ansible and keep your rescue configuration handy if something goes wrong. For example, if you are trying to apply a new application on the target host and the services are not coming up with the new application, then in the rescue configuration, you can put the old application. So, if things go as per the plan, the old application will not be restored, but if there is any failure in the new application, then the rescue code will be executed, and the old application should come up.

Now, there will be some code that we always want to execute, whether the preceding steps fail or not. So, in that condition, we should be using the always feature. As its name suggests, it will be always executed.

Let us go back to the example of the new application deployment. The rescue configuration was of redeploying the old application, but one thing we always want to do is restart the Apache services (Just for the example, it can be any other service). For that kind of situation, we can use the always option, and that will be executed whether the block fails or not.

This is how the role will look like, as shown in *Figure 10.34*. Since we have terminated the httpd services after the demo, we have entered the command to check the status of the

sshd service. However, you can change the command to any command you want, and that will be executed on the target host:

```
[root@ip-172-31-2-117 ansible]# cat roles/block/tasks/main.yml
---
- name: Task two generate the error
  block:
    - name: Debug module
      ansible.builtin.debug:
        msg: 'Normal execution'

    - name: Failure
      ansible.builtin.command: uptime

    - name: skipped
      ansible.builtin.debug:
        msg: 'since the task two failed i will be skipped'
  rescue:
    - name: Rescue code on the target host
      ansible.builtin.debug:
        msg: 'There is an error'
  always:
    - name: restart the httpd services
      command: service sshd status
[root@ip-172-31-2-117 ansible]#
```

Figure10.34: Role with use of always with block

Let us go ahead and execute the command:

```
[root@ip-172-31-2-117 ansible]# ansible-playbook firstplay.yaml

PLAY [First playbook] *********************************************

TASK [Gathering Facts] *********************************************
ok: [13.127.53.212]
ok: [3.108.53.227]

TASK [block : Debug module] *********************************************
ok: [3.108.53.227] => {
    "msg": "Normal execution"
}
ok: [13.127.53.212] => {
    "msg": "Normal execution"
}

TASK [block : Failure] *********************************************
changed: [13.127.53.212]
changed: [3.108.53.227]

TASK [block : skipped] *********************************************
ok: [3.108.53.227] => {
    "msg": "since the task two failed i will be skipped"
}
ok: [13.127.53.212] => {
    "msg": "since the task two failed i will be skipped"
}

TASK [block : restart the httpd services] *********************************************
changed: [13.127.53.212]
changed: [3.108.53.227]

PLAY RECAP *********************************************
13.127.53.212              : ok=5    changed=2    unreachable=0
3.108.53.227               : ok=5    changed=2    unreachable=0
```

Figure 10.35: Successful playbook execution

We can see the execution was successful, and we have successfully executed the **always** command.

The preceding four tasks are the same; the last one, **restart the httpd services**, is the latest one, and that is successfully executed. Now, let us go ahead and try to simulate the failure of the second task again and see if the rescue and always both configuration gets executed:

```
[root@ip-172-31-2-117 ansible]#
[root@ip-172-31-2-117 ansible]# ansible-playbook firstplay.yaml

PLAY [First playbook] ***************************************************************

TASK [Gathering Facts] *************************************************************
ok: [13.127.53.212]
ok: [3.108.53.227]

TASK [block : Debug module] *********************************************************
ok: [3.108.53.227] => {
    "msg": "Normal execution"
}
ok: [13.127.53.212] => {
    "msg": "Normal execution"
}

TASK [block : Failure] **************************************************************
[WARNING]: Module invocation had junk after the JSON data: polkit-agent-helper-1: pam_authenticate fai
fatal: [13.127.53.212]: FAILED! => {"changed": true, "cmd": ["service", "httpd", "restart"], "delta":
rc": 1, "start": "2023-07-01 16:49:21.051667", "stderr": "Failed to restart httpd.service: Connection
lines": ["Failed to restart httpd.service: Connection timed out", "See system logs and 'systemctl stat
fatal: [3.108.53.227]: FAILED! => {"changed": true, "cmd": ["service", "httpd", "restart"], "delta": "
c": 1, "start": "2023-07-01 16:49:21.159771", "stderr": "Redirecting to /bin/systemctl restart httpd.s
temctl status httpd.service' for details.", "stderr_lines": ["Redirecting to /bin/systemctl restart ht
and 'systemctl status httpd.service' for details."], "stdout": "", "stdout_lines": []}

TASK [block : Rescue code on the target host] **************************************
ok: [3.108.53.227] => {
    "msg": "There is an error"
}
ok: [13.127.53.212] => {
    "msg": "There is an error"
}

TASK [block : restart the httpd services] *****************************************
changed: [13.127.53.212]
changed: [3.108.53.227]

PLAY RECAP *************************************************************************
13.127.53.212              : ok=4    changed=1    unreachable=0    failed=0    skipped=0    rescued=1
3.108.53.227               : ok=4    changed=1    unreachable=0    failed=0    skipped=0    rescued=1

[root@ip-172-31-2-117 ansible]#
```

Figure 10.36: Regenerated the error however always was still executed

Playbook execution and walkthrough

In this section, we will go ahead and talk about the preceding execution:

```
[root@ip-172-31-2-117 ansible]#
[root@ip-172-31-2-117 ansible]#
[root@ip-172-31-2-117 ansible]# cat firstplay.yaml
---
- name: First playbook
  hosts: all
  roles:
  - ubuntu
[root@ip-172-31-2-117 ansible]#
[root@ip-172-31-2-117 ansible]#
[root@ip-172-31-2-117 ansible]# cat hosts
# This is the default ansible 'hosts' file.
#
# It should live in /etc/ansible/hosts
3.108.53.227
[ubuntu]
13.127.53.212
[root@ip-172-31-2-117 ansible]#
```

Figure 10.37: Simple playbook with host information

Let us talk about the playbook. It is a very small playbook that will be executed on the all-target host. In our case, they are two: 3.108.53.227 is a Redhat Linux host, and 13.127.53.212 is an Ubuntu host. The first task will be attempted on both target hosts:

```
---
- name: Add the user demo
  ansible.builtin.apt:
    upgrade: dist
  become: yes
  when: ansible_facts['os_family'] == "Debian"
```

First of all, our Ansible will check the OS family of host 3.108.53.227, and since it is Red-Hat, the task will be skipped on the target host 3.108.53.227. Now, Ansible will try to attempt the same task on the host 13.127.53.212. When it checks the OS family of this host, it will find that it is Debian OS, and the apt distribution upgrade is performed in this case:

```
TASK [ubuntu : Add the user demo] *******
skipping: [3.108.53.227]
changed: [13.127.53.212]
```

Figure 10.38: First host is skipped and task is performed on the second host

This is why task one, which is to add the user demo, contains skipping **3.108.53.227,** as that is a RedHat family member, and when it finds the Debian family host **13.127.53.212**, the changes were performed on the target host. This is also the reason why you see the **changed:[13.127.53.212]**. Now, if the Debian family host had the latest version, then you would have seen output, like the following *Figure 10.39,* because the target host was already with the latest version, so none of the changes could have been performed on the target host:

```
TASK [ubuntu : Add the user demo]
skipping: [3.108.53.227]
ok: [13.127.53.212]
```

Figure 10.39: Task is skipped on first host and successfully executed on second host

Most times, Ansible checks whether the device is already running with the required configuration, and if the changes are already there, it does not perform any further changes on the target host and gives us **ok:[Host]** and **ok=+1** in the play recap:

Similarly, for the second task:

```
- name: Install bottle python package
  ansible.builtin.dnf:
    name: '*'
    state: latest
  become: yes
  when: ansible_facts['os_family'] == "RedHat"
```

Ansible tries to execute the task on both target hosts. First, it tries on the first host (3.108.53.227) which is a RHEL host and as soon as it finds it is **RedHat** Linux host the condition matches and it attempts to perform the upgrade on the target host. However, the RHEL server is already running with the latest packages and that is why it gives us **ok** for the host **3.108.53.227** since it does not perform the additional changes:

```
TASK [ubuntu : Install bottle python package]
skipping: [13.127.53.212]
ok: [3.108.53.227]
```

Figure 10.40: Task is skipped on the first target host and successfully executed on the second host

Just after attempting the changes on the first host, it tries to execute the task on the second host, which is 13.127.53.212. It once again checks the family of that server, and it finds it is Debian and not RHEL:

```
When: ansible_facts['os_family'] == "RedHat"
```

That is why it skips the execution on the second host 13.127.53.212, which is why you see **skipping: [13.127.53.212]**.

Now, apart from this condition, rest all the other things were covered in the *Chapter 3, Working with Ansible.*

ignore_errors: true

This is another very important feature of Ansible. When Ansible executes the tasks top to bottom and any of the task fails, Ansible stops there and does not perform the next task, but if you want that behavior to change, then you can use this option. You will use it mostly with the block:

```
[root@ip-172-31-2-117 ansible]# cat roles/whencon/tasks/main.yml
---
- name: Add the user demo
  command: cat /etc/passwd
  register: output

- name: Fail simulation
  ansible.builtin.command: /bin/false

- name: Print it is there
  ansible.builtin.user:
    name: demouser
    comment: demouser1
    uid: 200
```

Figure 10.41: Demo playbo.ok which is used for showing use of ignore_errors

So, in task two, we have simulated the failure. Let us see what happens at the execution and how we can fix it:

```
[root@ip-172-31-2-117 ansible]# ansible-playbook firstplay.yaml

PLAY [First playbook] ******************************************************

TASK [Gathering Facts] *****************************************************
ok: [3.108.53.227]

TASK [whencon : Add the user demo] *****************************************
changed: [3.108.53.227]

TASK [whencon : Fail simulation] *******************************************
fatal: [3.108.53.227]: FAILED! => {"changed": true, "cmd": ["/bin/false"], "de
2023-07-03 08:53:19.723743", "stderr": "", "stderr_lines": [], "stdout": "", ".

PLAY RECAP *****************************************************************
3.108.53.227               : ok=2    changed=1    unreachable=0    failed=1
```

Figure 10.42: Successfully generated the error which stopped the playbook after error

We can see that task two failed. Once Ansible had a failure, it did not go for task three. What if you want to execute task three irrespective of past failures?

Let us try to get that done:

```
[root@ip-172-31-2-117 ansible]# cat roles/whencon/tasks/main.yml
---
- name: Add the user demo
  command: cat /etc/passwd
  register: output

- name: Fail simulation
  ansible.builtin.command: /bin/false
  ignore_errors: true
- name: Print it is there
  ansible.builtin.user:
    name: demouser
    comment: demouser1
    uid: 200
```

Figure 10.43: Role with use of ignore_error in task two

We have simply configured the **ignore_errors: true** so any error in that task can be ignored and next task can be executed. Let us run the code now:

```
[root@ip-172-31-2-117 ansible]# ansible-playbook firstplay.yaml

PLAY [First playbook] ********************************************************

TASK [Gathering Facts] ******************************************************
ok: [3.108.53.227]

TASK [whencon : Add the user demo] ******************************************
changed: [3.108.53.227]

TASK [whencon : Fail simulation] ********************************************
fatal: [3.108.53.227]: FAILED! => {"changed": true, "cmd": ["/bin/false"], "delta": "0:00:00.003289", "end": "2023
2023-07-03 09:04:53.529386", "stderr": "", "stderr_lines": [], "stdout": "", "stdout_lines": []}
...ignoring

TASK [whencon : Print it is there] ******************************************
changed: [3.108.53.227]

PLAY RECAP ******************************************************************
3.108.53.227               : ok=4    changed=3    unreachable=0    failed=0    skipped=0    rescued=0    ignored=1

[root@ip-172-31-2-117 ansible]#
```

Figure 10.44: Task 3 executed successfully even after failed task

We can see that task two failed and was ignored immediately. Ansible still went for task three and it was successful. When we say task three, we are ignoring the **gather_facts**. If you include that as task one, then the sequence will increase by 1.

One might think that we can configure this option in block level. Well, you can, without any issue. The only point is that all the failures will be ignored in that case, and the next task will be executed since we asked the Ansible to ignore the errors on the task level.

Let us see the role will this feature:

```
[root@ip-172-31-2-117 ansible]# cat roles/block/tasks/main.yml
---
- name: Task two generate the error
  block:
    - name: Debug module
      ansible.builtin.debug:
        msg: 'Normal execution'

    - name: Failure
      ansible.builtin.command: /bin/false

    - name: skipped
      ansible.builtin.debug:
        msg: 'since the task two failed i will be skipped'
  when: ansible_facts['os_family'] == "RedHat"
  ignore_errors: true
[root@ip-172-31-2-117 ansible]#
[root@ip-172-31-2-117 ansible]#
```

Figure 10.45: ignore_error usage with block

We can see the code we applied **ignore_errors** for the entire block and all the task which fails in this block will be ignored and the next task will be executed.

Let us run it now and see it in the action:

```
[root@ip-172-31-2-117 ansible]# ansible-playbook firstplay.yaml

PLAY [First playbook] *************************************************************

TASK [Gathering Facts] ***********************************************************
ok: [3.108.53.227]

TASK [block : Debug module] ******************************************************
ok: [3.108.53.227] => {
    "msg": "Normal execution"
}

TASK [block : Failure] ***********************************************************
fatal: [3.108.53.227]: FAILED! => {"changed": true, "cmd": ["/bin/false"], "delt
2023-07-03 09:14:34.514662", "stderr": "", "stderr_lines": [], "stdout": "", "st
...ignoring

TASK [block : skipped] **********************************************************
ok: [3.108.53.227] => {
    "msg": "since the task two failed i will be skipped"
}

PLAY RECAP **********************************************************************
3.108.53.227               : ok=4    changed=1    unreachable=0    failed=0    s
```

Figure 10.46: Successful playbook execution with ignore errors and block

Notice that you have started seeing another option in the **PLAY RECAP** which is ignored.

Jinja templating

For templating, we use the jinja2 template in Ansible. For those who have not used jinja2, let us see what it is. In simple language, jinja2 is a text file that is widely used in many programming languages, and it can generate any text-based format whether it is HTML, CSV, XML, etc. So, to summarize the definition jinja2 is a templating language which is used in many platforms.

In order to make jinja work, we need two things:

- The template itself, as it is a templating language.
- The actual data.

jinja2 engine renders the data, and the final output is in place.

All this templating thing happens in the Ansible controller itself, and then only it is sent to the target host. So, the overall well-generated code is sent to the target host.

Let us now go ahead and take an example where we can use templates. The simplest use case is a situation where you have a deployment of 100 server. The configuration for all servers are the same except their host name and IP address. So, in that condition, you can create a jinja2 template containing the configuration of common commands/configuration. For the IP address and hostname, we will define a variable for those two values, which will be rendered on the basis of the variable files. It does not matter how those variables are rendered. The final configuration file will be generated locally and then pushed to the target host. Let us take an example here.

We will start from the very basics. In this simple example, we will push a jinja2 file to the target host. The jinja2 file will be index.html code with variables defined in it. So, let us go ahead and write it now:

```
[root@ip-172-31-2-117 ansible]#
[root@ip-172-31-2-117 ansible]# cat jinjatemplate.j2
Hello World from {{ hostname }}
[root@ip-172-31-2-117 ansible]#
[root@ip-172-31-2-117 ansible]#
[root@ip-172-31-2-117 ansible]# cat hosts
# This is the default ansible 'hosts' file.
#
# It should live in /etc/ansible/hosts
#3.108.53.227
[ubuntu]
3.108.53.227
[ubuntu:vars]
hostname= testingtarget1
ipaddress= 111.11.111.111

[root@ip-172-31-2-117 ansible]#
```

Figure 10.47: jinja2 template with variables

As we can see, the jinja2 template contains message **Hello world from VARIABLE**. Now, that variable will be rendered during the execution and will be replaced with the value of hostname:

```
[ubuntu]
3.108.53.227
[ubuntu:vars]
hostname= testingtarget1
ipaddress= 111.11.111.111
```

Figure 10.48: Variable defined under host vars

The hostname is simply **testingtarget1**. Overall, the output will be converted into the **Hello World from testingtarget1**.

Let us have a look at our code now:

```
[root@ip-172-31-2-117 ansible]# cat roles/demojinja/tasks/main.yml
---
- name: Add the user demo
  ansible.builtin.template:
    src: jinjatemplate.j2
    dest: /var/www/html/index.html

[root@ip-172-31-2-117 ansible]#
```

Figure 10.49: Role with use of jinja2 template

The role will be very simple; we need to call the template module. The template module needs two simple things:

- src
- dest

Both of them will send the data to the target host, and we should be good to go.

Since this is a template module, the source will be the jinja2 template we created previously and the destination will be the file location where we want to transfer the file. In this case, it is **index.html** file.

Let us execute our code:

```
[root@ip-172-31-2-117 ansible]# ansible-playbook firstplay.yaml

PLAY [First playbook] ***************************************

TASK [Gathering Facts] **************************************
ok: [3.108.53.227]

TASK [demojinja : Add the user demo] ************************
changed: [3.108.53.227]

PLAY RECAP **************************************************
3.108.53.227                 : ok=2     changed=1     unreachable=0
```

Figure 10.50: Successful playbook execution

The execution was successful. Let us login to the target host and see the result:

```
[root@ip-172-31-2-117 ansible]#
[root@ip-172-31-2-117 ansible]# ssh ashutmch@3.108.53.227
Register this system with Red Hat Insights: insights-clier
Create an account or view all your systems at https://red.
Last login: Sun Jul  2 21:23:18 2023 from 3.110.174.224
[ashutmch@ip-172-31-6-75 ~]$ cat /var/www/html/index.html
Hello World from testingtarget1
[ashutmch@ip-172-31-6-75 ~]$
```

Figure 10.51: Variable parsed successfully using jinja2 template

We can see that the result clearly shows the value is parsed correctly, and we are able to see the desired result. This was our simplest demo for the jinja2 template. Let us go ahead and try to do a bit of a complex thing.

So, let us go ahead and define a list in the host's file. You can create your own inventory in production, but since we are in a lab environment, we have the liberty to manipulate the hosts file itself:

```
[ubuntu]
3.108.53.227
[ubuntu:vars]
hostname= testingtarge1
product= ['Burger', 'Pizza', 'Vegan', 'Vegetarian','Italian']
day = ['Monday', 'Tuesday', 'Wednesday', 'Thursday','Friday']
[root@ip-172-31-2-117 ansible]#
[root@ip-172-31-2-117 ansible]#
```

Figure 10.52: Example with few more variables

So, assume we are in the food industry, and these are the only products we sell. They need to be displayed on our website. So, we will send these food products in **index.html** file in the target host, but not like the last example. This time, we will use the **for** loop and iterate the list of products. After this, we should be good. The **for** loop simply says for the **item** (variable) in products, print the item in our next line, and at the last, end **for** loop we see:

```
[root@ip-172-31-2-117 ansible]# cat jinjatemplate.j2
Hello World from {{ hostname }}
{% for item in product %}
  our menu are {{ item }}
{% endfor %}
[root@ip-172-31-2-117 ansible]#
```

Figure 10.53: Jinja2 template with variables

Let us go ahead and run the code now to see the result:

```
[root@ip-172-31-2-117 ansible]# ansible-playbook firstplay.yaml

PLAY [First playbook] ****************************************

TASK [Gathering Facts] ****************************************
ok: [3.108.53.227]

TASK [demojinja : Add the user demo] ****************************************
changed: [3.108.53.227]

PLAY RECAP ****************************************
3.108.53.227               : ok=2    changed=1    unreachable=0

[root@ip-172-31-2-117 ansible]#
```

Figure 10.54: Successful playbook execution

The execution is successful. Let us go ahead and verify from the target host:

```
[root@ip-172-31-2-117 ansible]# ssh ashutmch@3.108.53.227
Register this system with Red Hat Insights: insights-client --register
Create an account or view all your systems at https://red.ht/insights-dashboard
Last login: Sun Jul  2 22:11:52 2023 from 3.110.174.224
[ashutmch@ip-172-31-6-75 ~]$ cat /var/www/html/index.html
Hello World from testingtarge1
  our menu are Burger
  our menu are Pizza
  our menu are Vegan
  our menu are Vegetarian
  our menu are Italian
[ashutmch@ip-172-31-6-75 ~]$
```

Figure 10.55: As expected all desired values are there in place

In our next example, we want to write a menu on the basis of day. If we want to say our menu for Monday is burgers, then let us do it.

In this case, we need to use the **zip** option:

```
[root@ip-172-31-2-117 ansible]# cat jinjatemplate.j2
Hello World from {{ hostname }}
our Product for {{ (day | zip(product)) }}
[root@ip-172-31-2-117 ansible]#
```

Figure 10.56: Jinja2 template with zip option

Let us go ahead and execute it. At last, we will verify from the target host:

```
[root@ip-172-31-2-117 ansible]# ansible-playbook firstplay.yaml

PLAY [First playbook] ***************************************************************

TASK [Gathering Facts] **************************************************************
ok: [3.108.53.227]

TASK [demojinja : Add the user demo] ***********************************************
changed: [3.108.53.227]

PLAY RECAP **************************************************************************
3.108.53.227               : ok=2    changed=1    unreachable=0    failed=0    skipped=0

[root@ip-172-31-2-117 ansible]#
[root@ip-172-31-2-117 ansible]#
[root@ip-172-31-2-117 ansible]# ssh ashutmch@3.108.53.227
Register this system with Red Hat Insights: insights-client --register
Create an account or view all your systems at https://red.ht/insights-dashboard
Last login: Sun Jul  2 22:58:48 2023 from 3.110.174.224
[ashutmch@ip-172-31-6-75 ~]$ cat /var/www/html/index.html
Hello World from testingtarge1
our Product for [('Monday', 'Burger'), ('Tuesday', 'Pizza'), ('Wednesday', 'Vegan'), ('Th
[ashutmch@ip-172-31-6-75 ~]$
```

Figure 10.57: Successful execution and desired dishes on the basis of days

The execution is successful and as we can see we got the desired result. We had no requirement of **for** loop. In this case the **zip** option is a good alternative for that.

Creating an Ansible Vault

This is very important for you and your team to hide the credentials at any cost. Somehow, if your system gets compromised, then your credentials will be easily accessible to the hackers, and you do not want that to happen ever.

In the *Roles* section of the chapter, we had created the group variable and defined the variables in the roles itself, but those details were in the clear text. So, let us see how we can fix it:

```
[root@ip-172-31-2-117 ansible]#
[root@ip-172-31-2-117 ansible]# cat roles/ubuntu/vars/main.yml
---
ansible_user: ashutmch
ansible_ssh_pass: Abcd1234
ansible_become_password: Abcd1234
[root@ip-172-31-2-117 ansible]#
[root@ip-172-31-2-117 ansible]#
```

Figure 10.58: Variable file with clear text password

As we can see the file is still in the clear text and the password is visible and everyone can read it. Now, we will encrypt the entire file. Let us see how we can do it.

This will be done using the Ansible Vault. Ansible Vault is a great feature of Ansible which helps us encrypt the confidential information like password and other sensitive information.

Let us go ahead and use it to encrypt our variable files:

ansible-vault encrypt FILENAME

In our case, it is **roles/ubuntu/vars/main.yml**. If you want to encrypt the **group_vars/ ubuntu** file, then you can put the name of that file after encrypt. Once we enter, this will ask us for the master password. We need to enter the password and confirm it. After that, the encryption will be done:

```
[root@ip-172-31-2-117 ansible]#
[root@ip-172-31-2-117 ansible]# ansible-vault encrypt roles/ubuntu/vars/main.yml
New Vault password:
Confirm New Vault password:
Encryption successful
[root@ip-172-31-2-117 ansible]# cat roles/ubuntu/vars/main.yml
$ANSIBLE_VAULT;1.1;AES256
66376361653566663935383932666564366331386636656631323530303737393363333931383633
63386339323165613739336136386663653861623462313330a623537383234636664303638653266
34336538616334303833313032366461666446663343839613763326564313162646338363064663
31363366626633363650a623536393061306163631346563366133666663643436163373939303956531
646139373465323235316339326630303031363832306565353465663566663262366663336161653
62336565373931383239333061663838386166396663161623166356139636232613835343436266
396638633832383033353334303030643866333861306635626264343539373538313431383466383
3831346237646161366536343435323131366664656639663938333538355303461636323939396565393
3236
[root@ip-172-31-2-117 ansible]#
```

Figure 10.59: How to encrypt the file and encrypted file content

Let us try, and execute our code using Ansible playbook.

Note: Our variable files of this role is encrypted, so let us see if that is going to create any issue.

```
[root@ip-172-31-2-117 ansible]# ansible-playbook  firstplay.yaml
[root@ip-172-31-2-117 ansible]# ansible-playbook  firstplay.yaml
ERROR! Attempting to decrypt but no vault secrets found
[root@ip-172-31-2-117 ansible]#
```

Figure 10.60: Error shows playbook will not work without vault secret

Well, the execution is failing, and Ansible has detected that encryption is used somewhere, but it does not find any vault password to decrypt it.

We have three options to decrypt it, which are described in the following sections.

First option

Just like we had the option of **-u** to define the username, **-k** to prompt for the password, we have **–ask-vault-pass** option in Ansible. Let us have a look at the code and then learn more about it:

```
[root@ip-172-31-2-117 ansible]# ansible-playbook  firstplay.yaml --ask-vault-pass
Vault password:

PLAY [First playbook] **********************************************************

TASK [Gathering Facts] *********************************************************
ok: [13.127.53.212]

TASK [ubuntu : Add the user demo] **********************************************
ok: [13.127.53.212]

PLAY RECAP *********************************************************************
13.127.53.212              : ok=2    changed=0    unreachable=0    failed=0    skipped

[root@ip-172-31-2-117 ansible]#
```

Figure 10.61: Playbook execution with vault password defined as ad-hoc command

Now, once this option is used in the Ansible playbook command, the Ansible control machine will prompt us for the master password we used to encrypt our variable files (**roles/ubuntu/vars/main.yml**). Once the password is entered, the Ansible will decrypt the secret values and start executing the playbook.

Second option

--vault-password-file is out second option. In this option, we need to create a file where we will store the master password. Once that is done, we need to use the **--vault-password-file** and name the master file after that.

Example:

```
[root@ip-172-31-2-117 ansible]# ansible-playbook  firstplay.yaml --vault-password-file masterpassword.txt

PLAY [First playbook] ****************************************************************************

TASK [Gathering Facts] ****************************************************************************
ok: [13.127.53.212]

TASK [ubuntu : Add the user demo] ****************************************************************
ok: [13.127.53.212]

PLAY RECAP ***************************************************************************************
13.127.53.212              : ok=2    changed=0    unreachable=0    failed=0    skipped=0    rescued=0

[root@ip-172-31-2-117 ansible]#
```

Figure 10.62: Playbook with vault password saved in text file

As we can see from the execution after playbook name, we used the option **-vault-password-file** and then wrote the name of the master password file name, and execution was successful.

Third option

In the third option, we need to go to the **ansible.cfg** file and hardcode the password file location. That way, it will find out the master password and use it to decrypt the file and execute the code.

Let us see where it is located in the **ansible.cfg** file and hardcode it:

```
[root@ip-172-31-2-117 ansible]# cat ansible.cfg | grep vault
# specifying --vault-password-file on the command line.
#vault_password_file = /path/to/vault_password_file
[root@ip-172-31-2-117 ansible]#
```

Figure 10.63: Enabling default vault password file

As we can see, the option for the **vault_password_file** is hashed right now. We will enable and provide the right location of the master password file.

Let us do it now:

```
[root@ip-172-31-2-117 ansible]#
[root@ip-172-31-2-117 ansible]# cat ansible.cfg | grep vault
# specifying --vault-password-file on the command line.
vault_password_file = masterpassword.txt
[root@ip-172-31-2-117 ansible]# ansible-playbook  firstplay.yaml

PLAY [First playbook] ****************************************

TASK [Gathering Facts] ****************************************
ok: [13.127.53.212]

TASK [ubuntu : Add the user demo] *****************************
ok: [13.127.53.212]

PLAY RECAP ***************************************************
13.127.53.212              : ok=2    changed=0    unreachable=0

[root@ip-172-31-2-117 ansible]#
```

Figure 10.64: Configured the vault password file and successfully executed code after that

As you can see, we have provided the location of **masterpssword.txt** file. Once that is saved, we have rerun the code without any additional parameters and things are good to go.

Now, encrypting a variable file and a group variable is not the only option we have. We can create a brand new file too.

Use the following command to create a new file:

```
[root@ip-172-31-2-117 ansible]# ansible-vault create newvault.yaml
[root@ip-172-31-2-117 ansible]#
```

Once that is done, we can enter our password there and call it later in the Ansible variable files.

If you want to view the content of the vault file, then the **cat** command will not help. We need to use the following command to view it:

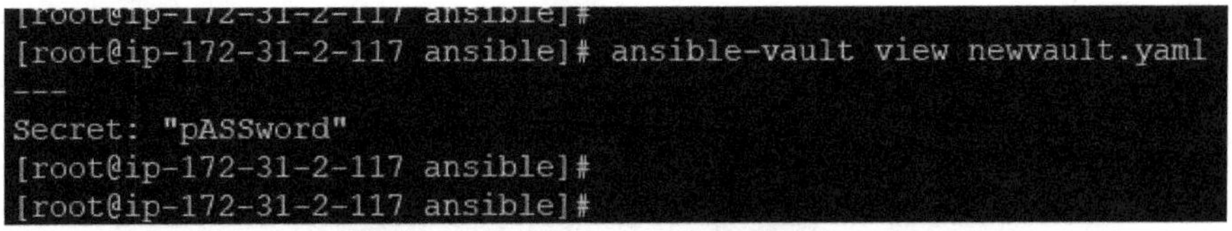

Figure 10.65: Command to view the vault content

If you want to edit the file, use the following command to do so:

```
[root@ip-172-31-2-117 ansible]#
[root@ip-172-31-2-117 ansible]# ansible-vault edit newvault.yaml
```

This is going to be the master password that you set while creating the file. Enter that password, and you will be able to edit its content. If some day you feel like decrypting it again, then the command is easy and will ask you for the password. Once entered, you should be good. The command is as follows:

```
ansible-vault decrypt newvault.yaml
```

So, these were the few options of Ansible Vault. Now let us have a look at a task.

We want you to save the master password on the Azure vault, use automation to bring that to the Ansible control machine, and use it in your playbook to decrypt the code. This will be a bit difficult, but not impossible. Try this very practical situation, which will happen in the production all the time so try it.

Data manipulation

While working in any developing environment, data manipulation is required and Ansible is no different. There are many features in Ansible that can help us manipulate the data. We will cover filter in this topic which can convert the JSON data to YAML using filters, and at the same time, we can split the bulky content and fetch the required data, like the hostname, hash of string, and so on. There are many filters and different ways of data manipulation. Unfortunately, we will not be able to cover all of them, but we will try to cover a few of them, which are a must for us to work in the IT industry.

The first requirement for anyone reading the book will be to change the data format. The very basic one will be JSON to YAML conversion. So, let us go ahead and first of all learn what our data type is, so we can manipulate it. Many of you might already know what a data type is, but it is always good to cross-check if you are confused.

The way of checking is very simple. We just need to use the **typ_debug** filter to check the right type of the variable:

`{{ variable|type_debug }}`

Let us go ahead and put it in the **gather_facts** role we had created:

```
---
# tasks file for facts
- name: Gather the information about the target host
  ansible.builtin.gather_facts:
  register: output
- debug:
    msg: "{{output | type_debug }}"
```

Figure 10.66: Role with use of filter

Now, before we execute this code, try to guess the variable type, and then we will match that with the result. In the end, if it matches what you guessed, it is good, but if it does not, you will find the importance of this feature:

```
[root@ip-172-31-2-117 ansible]#
[root@ip-172-31-2-117 ansible]# ansible-playbook firstplay.yaml -u ashutmch

PLAY [First playbook] ***************************************************

TASK [Gathering Facts] **************************************************
ok: [3.108.53.227]

TASK [facts : Gather the information about the target host] *************
ok: [3.108.53.227]

TASK [facts : debug] ****************************************************
ok: [3.108.53.227] => {
    "msg": "dict"
}

PLAY RECAP **************************************************************
3.108.53.227              : ok=3    changed=0    unreachable=0    failed=0
```

Figure 10.67: Successful playbook execution shows the variable type is dictionaries

We can find it to be dictionaries.

So now you have to find the dictionary type variable, so let us try to convert it into a list. The way of conversion is simple. We can use the filter **{{ variable|dict2items }}** to convert it to a list of the items, which we can use later to loop the content of the dictionary:

```
[root@ip-172-31-2-117 ansible]# cat roles/facts/tasks/main.yml
---
# tasks file for facts
- name: Gather the information about the target host
  ansible.builtin.gather_facts:
  register: output
- debug:
    msg: "{{output | dict2items}}"
```

Figure 10.68: Role to convert the variable to the list of items

Let us go ahead and execute our code as follows:

```
[root@ip-172-31-2-117 ansible]# ansible-playbook firstplay.yaml -u ashutmch

PLAY [First playbook] ******************************************************************

TASK [Gathering Facts] *****************************************************************
ok: [3.108.53.227]

TASK [facts : Gather the information about the target host] ****************************
ok: [3.108.53.227]

TASK [facts : debug] *******************************************************************
ok: [3.108.53.227] => {
    "msg": [
        {
            "key": "ansible_facts",
            "value": {
                "ansible_all_ipv4_addresses": [
                    "172.31.6.75"
                ],
                "ansible_all_ipv6_addresses": [
                    "fe80::8f8:8bff:fe4c:4892"
                ],
                "ansible_apparmor": {
```

Figure 10.69: Successful playbook execution

As we can see, the output is in the form of a key: value, and this is what we wanted to achieve, and the content can be easily used for the loop.

Similarly, we can do the opposite, and convert the list into a dictionary. The filter is as following:

{{ name | items2dict }}

Now, let us take a case where you want to upgrade the OS, if the distribution version is outdated. We have a simple logic for now, which will echo the message if the device has the latest distribution. However, you can modify this logic to upgrade the OS:

```
[root@ip-172-31-2-117 ansible]# cat roles/facts/tasks/main
---
# tasks file for facts
- name: Gather the information about the target host
  ansible.builtin.gather_facts:
- shell: echo "The version is latest no need of upgrade"
  when: ansible_facts['distribution_version']  | int >=8
  register: output
- debug:
    msg: "{{output.stdout_lines}}"
```

Figure 10.70: Role with condition to check for the OS distribution version and upgrade

It checks for the **dist_version** of the target host, if that is more than 8, we do not need an upgrade. Now, you cannot directly write the logic against the value received from the **ansible_facts**, as that is not an integer value. That is a dictionary, and we need to write the logic with the mathematical operation to check whether the version is higher than 8. In order to do that, we have forcefully converted the output to the integer, and now we can easily perform any mathematical operation:

```
[root@ip-172-31-2-117 ansible]# ansible-playbook firstplay.yaml

PLAY [First playbook] ****************************************

TASK [Gathering Facts] ****************************************
ok: [localhost]

TASK [facts : Gather the information about the target host] *****
ok: [localhost]

TASK [facts : shell] ****************************************
changed: [localhost]

TASK [facts : debug] ****************************************
ok: [localhost] => {
    "msg": [
        "The version is latest no need of upgrade"
    ]
}

PLAY RECAP ****************************************
localhost                  : ok=4    changed=1    unreachable=0
```

Figure 10.71: Successful playbook execution shows the device has the latest version

The next thing we should do is change the format to JSON. We will use the preceding role and modify the variable to the JSON:

```
[root@ip-172-31-2-117 ansible]# cat roles/facts/tasks/main.yml
---
# tasks file for facts
- name: Gather the information about the target host
  ansible.builtin.gather_facts:
- shell: echo "The version is latest no need of upgrade"
  when: ansible_facts['distribution_version']   | int >=8
  register: output
- debug:
    msg: "{{output | to_json}}"
```

Figure 10.72: Filter to convert the variable to the JSON

In the **debug** message, we have used the filter **to_json**, and this will change the message to the JSON. Let us go ahead and execute it:

```
[root@ip-172-31-2-117 ansible]# ansible-playbook firstplay.yaml

PLAY [First playbook] ************************************************

TASK [Gathering Facts] ************************************************
ok: [localhost]

TASK [facts : Gather the information about the target host] ****************
ok: [localhost]

TASK [facts : shell] ************************************************
changed: [localhost]

TASK [facts : debug] ************************************************
ok: [localhost] => {
    "msg": "{\"changed\": true, \"stdout\": \"The version is latest no need o
start\": \"2023-07-03 19:29:31.619908\", \"end\": \"2023-07-03 19:29:31.62430
\"], \"stderr_lines\": [], \"failed\": false}"
}

PLAY RECAP ************************************************
localhost                  : ok=4    changed=1    unreachable=0    failed=0
```

Figure 10.73: Playbook execution shows successful conversion to the JSON

Let us go ahead and do the same thing to convert it to YAML. The filter will be **to_yaml** as expected. Let us modify the role and execute it to see the result:

```
---
# tasks file for facts
- name: Gather the information about the target host
  ansible.builtin.gather_facts:
- shell: echo "The version is latest no need of upgrade"
  when: ansible_facts['distribution_version']  | int >=8
  register: output
- debug:
    msg: "{{output | to_yaml}}"
```

Figure 10.74: *Role to convert the variable to the YAML*

Execution:

```
[root@ip-172-31-2-117 ansible]# ansible-playbook firstplay.yaml

PLAY [First playbook] ******************************************************

TASK [Gathering Facts] ******************************************************
ok: [localhost]

TASK [facts : Gather the information about the target host] ***************
ok: [localhost]

TASK [facts : shell] ******************************************************
changed: [localhost]

TASK [facts : debug] ******************************************************
ok: [localhost] => {
    "msg": "changed: true\ncmd: echo \"The version is latest no need of upgrade\'
-03 19:32:29.847460'\nstderr: ''\nstderr_lines: []\nstdout: The version is latest
}

PLAY RECAP ******************************************************************
localhost                    : ok=4    changed=1    unreachable=0    failed=0    s
```

Figure 10.75: *Successful playbook execution*

Merge, combing, and split are a few more things that are required to read and understand. There are also a few filters specific to the network, and if you belong to that field, you should read them. We have few Ansible filters for the XML too. So, based on your requirements you can go ahead and read more about those filters.

Dos and do nots for DevSecOps environment

Everyday, hackers come with new ideas of intruding into the servers. They keep innovatin,g and it is our duty to keep our environment a safes as possible. Here are a few suggestions for all the new engineers:

- **Dos:**
  - o Always save the master key in a safe location like Azure vault and the rest all vaults.
  - o Regularly upgrade the server and install security patches.
  - o Always take the backup of the configuration file before you modify them.
  - o Always run your code in the pre-production environment first, and then only use it in the production, as code misbehaves sometimes, and you do not want the things to go bad in production.

- **Do nots:**
  - o We should never save the password in the control machine.
  - o Even if there is any need of saving the password in the control machine, use the Ansible Vault.
  - o Saving the Ansible Vault file on the right location is also important. Never keep the vault file in the Git Repo. You need to keep it separate.
  - o Do not share secrets on email and chat.
  - o Never use old unmanaged Ansible modules. Always try to use the latest version of the Ansible module.
  - o Upgrade the server and install security patches.
  - o Never use the settings shown on the internet if you do not understand them. For example, a few articles will suggest that you disable the strict **hostkey-checking** for the new users. This will work for you and will automatically add the new host into the **known_hosts** list, but this is dangerous. If you do not understand something, read more about it to understand it better and use it if it is safe:

Set the `StrictHostKeyChecking` option to `no`, either in the config file or via `-o` :

`ssh -o StrictHostKeyChecking=no username@hostname.com`

Figure 10.76: Avoid this kind of setting

Conclusion

In this chapter, we covered various topics like playbooks, blocks, etc. This chapter will help you become a much more efficient automation engineer. Now, you might need some time to learn all these topics. So, take your time and read it again if needed. Practice is very important, so perform all these tasks in a lab environment.

In the next chapter, we will learn how to use Ansible for network automation.

Join our Discord space

Join our Discord workspace for latest updates, offers, tech happenings around the world, new releases, and sessions with the authors:

https://discord.bpbonline.com

CHAPTER 11
Ansible with Network Automation

Introduction

Manually logging into the Cisco router and configuring devices is the part of history. Today is the age of automation. Whether you have Cisco **Internetwork Operating System (IOS)** router or Juniper **security, routing, and switching (SRX)** device, whether you want to manage your firewall or wish to automate the load balancer, all of them can be managed using Ansible. Ansible works differently for networking equipment. For all normal Linux managed nodes, the execution happens on the target host. However, that is not the case with the networking gears, the task execution happens on the control machine.

Also, things are different here for the modules like backup, which offers backup on the target hosts itself. In case of Linux/Unix systems, the backup file is created on them itself, however, that is not the case with the network devices. For example, if we talk about the Cisco IOS device, that is not a customizable OS. Cisco does not allow you to modify or create any directory on their router so all the backups are taken in the control machines itself.

So just to summarize how networking modules work, the task is executed locally on the control machine and the backup is also taken on the control machine.

Structure

This chapter contains the following topics:

- Connection protocol
- Juniper junos_os automation
- Cumulus Linux NCLU module

Objectives

In this chapter, we will learn how to manage networking devices. If you are an automation engineer someday, your networking team will approach you and ask for automation assistance. Since Ansible works differently with network devices, it is necessary to cover this topic. After completing this chapter, you will be able to automate any networking device and network.

Connection protocol

As discussed, by default, Ansible uses ssh to communicate with the target host, and if it is something else, then we need to define the connection protocol, which will be used to communicate with the target host.

If you remember it correctly, we used the WinRM module, and **winrm** was the connection method.

So, the settings for Windows were:

```
ansible_connection: winrm
```

Well, CLI will be there for sure, so the connection type is **network_cli**. Now, Cisco is not the only giant in the market today in the field of networking. Many vendors are there in the market that support a huge range of protocols. A few of them are accessible using an API call and that is why we have **httpapi** as another connection type. A few of them support the XML, which is why we have **netconf** connection type for them. Just to list down the possible options, look at the list as follows:

- network_cli
- netconf
- httpapi
- local

Now, let us go ahead with one more difference. If we talk about the Cisco router and switches, then there is nothing like **sudo su–** in Cisco IOS legacy devices. Privilege escalation is done using the enable mode. So, this time we will need to define the **become_method** when we configure the privilege escalation.

So, the variable file should look as follows:

```
ansible_connection: network_cli
ansible_network_os: ios
ansible_become: yes
ansible_become_method: enable
```

Let us have a look at the entire playbook and how different it will look from the other target host:

Playbook we used so far for all devices	Playbook for the networking devices

<pre>--- 	
 	
- name: First playbook
  hosts: all
  roles:
  - facts</pre>
	<pre>--- 	
	
	- name: First playbook
	  hosts: all
	  connection: network_cli
	  gather_facts: false
	  roles:
	  - ciscorouter</pre>

Table 11.1: Normal Linux devices vs. networking devices

Now, if you look at the preceding comparison, we have two additional changes here. Let us go ahead and discuss both:

- **Connection: network_cli**: This is a networking device, which is managed from the CLI hence we use **network_cli** here.

- **Gather_facts**: By default, **gather_facts** are enabled in the playbook. If you see the preceding playbook, which we executed, then you will see there is no option like **gather_facts: true** configured, however, still **gather_facts** was being executed. *Figure 11.1* is for those who have ignored it so far.

Just look at the number of tasks configured in the role and see the playbook execution. The first task is shown as **Gathering Facts**. Also, look at the **PLAY RECAP**. You do not see the third task in the result, but rather you see the fourth task there because the first task is **gather_facts**:

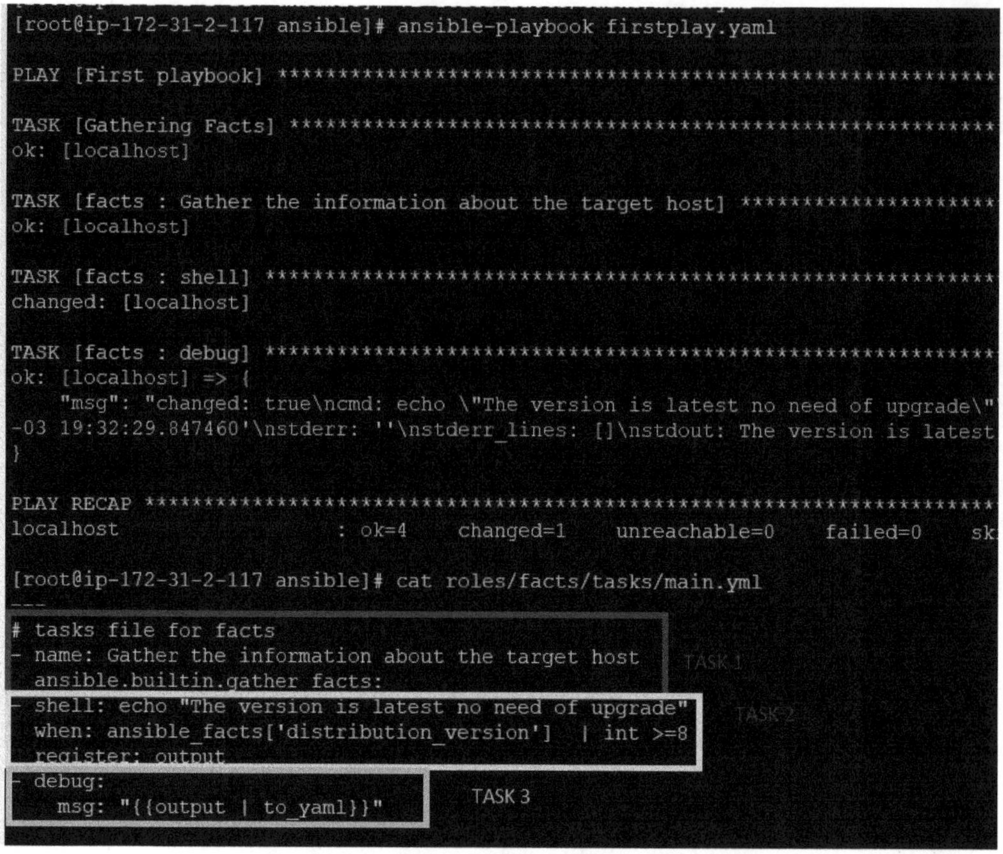

Figure 11.1: Tasks information in role and playbook execution

Now, you must have understood that by default, Ansible goes ahead with the **gather_facts** and executes the task for the target host when it is a Linux/Unix host, but this feature does not work with the networking devices. If you keep this feature enabled, your playbook will fail. So, we need to disable the **gather_facts** feature, which is done using **gather_facts: false**.

Now, one might think that if **gather_facts** is not there, how would we collect the information about the target host? For example, we were using the **os_family** of the target host in the when statement of Ansible.

Example of the condition we used in the past:

```
when: ansible_facts['os_family'] == "Debian"
```

So now, how can we gather the information about the target host? Well, do not worry, Ansible has another module for your help, which is **ios_facts**. The **ios_facts** module can give us all the information we need about the target host and then we can play around with that.

We are in a position where we can start working on our real Ansible modules. Let us start our journey with Cisco itself. The first module we have picked is Cisco IOS_Command module. This module is used to run the show command on the Cisco target host, which is a router/switch in this case. If you want to configure something on the router/switch, then we have the Cisco **ios_config** module.

Cisco IOS_Command module

The IOS_Command module is dedicatedly designed for the Cisco IOS devices. Anytime you want to run the show commands on the router/switch, you need to use the IOS_Command module. Now, this module is not 100% compatible with the **Nexus Operating System** (**NXOS**) and other Cisco devices. For NXOS, we have **cisco.nxos** module, and we can use that with the NXOS devices. So, remember this module is only designed for the show commands on the Cisco IOS target hosts.

Now, let us go ahead and have a look at the role. The first command we are going to execute on our target host is **show version | i uptime**.

Role:

```
---

- name: Run our first command on the network devices
  cisco.ios.ios_command:
    commands:
      - show version | i uptime
```

As we know, the first two things are the names of the role, and the second line is that of the module we have used. In the third line, we have defined the commands we want to send to the target hosts. Just below that, we can define the lists of commands. If you have 10 commands to execute on the target host, you can add them below. Refer to the following figure:

```
root@ip-172-31-33-97:/etc/ansible# cat roles/ciscorouter/tasks/main.yml
---
- name: Run our first command on the network devices
  cisco.ios.ios_command:
    commands:
      - show version | i uptime
```

Figure 11.2: Example of show command on the Cisco IOS router

Example of multiple commands is as follows:

```
root@ip-172-31-33-97:/etc/ansible# cat roles/ciscorouter/tasks/main.yml
---
- name: Run our first command on the network devices
  cisco.ios.ios_command:
    commands:
      - show version | i uptime
      - show clock
root@ip-172-31-33-97:/etc/ansible#
```

Figure 11.3: Role to send multiple commands on the target host

Now, let us go ahead and write our playbook, and as we know, the playbook has some extra things for the network gears:

```
root@ip-172-31-33-97:/etc/ansible# cat networkplay.yaml
---
- name: First playbook
  hosts: all
  connection: network_cli
  gather_facts: false
  roles:
  - ciscorouter

root@ip-172-31-33-97:/etc/ansible#
```

Figure 11.4: Playbook for the Cisco target hosts

As discussed, it will contain the extra connection settings and **gather_facts** will be disabled. Rest all the things should be good.

Let us run our playbook now:

```
root@ip-172-31-33-97:/etc/ansible# ansible-playbook networkplay.yaml -u ashutmch -k
SSH password:

PLAY [First playbook] *********************************************************

TASK [ciscorouter : Run multiple commands and evaluate the output] ************
fatal: [13.234.29.231]: FAILED! => {"msg": "Unable to automatically determine host network os.

PLAY RECAP ********************************************************************
13.234.29.231              : ok=0    changed=0    unreachable=0    failed=1    skipped=0    res
```

Figure 11.5: Expected error shows the OS information cannot be determined automatically

As soon as we ran the code, we received an error. Now, you might not get it in your environment and that is fine, but let us see the entire error:

msg": "Unable to automatically determine host network os. Please manually configure ansible_network_os value for this host"}

If you read the error, it says Ansible is not able to get the network OS information and it asks us to manually input the network OS details. As we know, our target host is IOS device, so, let us make modifications to the host's file, as shown in the following figure:

```
root@ip-172-31-33-97:/etc/ansible#
root@ip-172-31-33-97:/etc/ansible# cat hosts
[router]
13.234.29.231
[router:vars]
 ansible_network_os = ios
```

Figure 11.6: Manually defined the network OS in the host variables

We have made the modification as suggested by the error. So, let us go ahead and execute the code again:

```
root@ip-172-31-33-97:/etc/ansible# ansible-playbook networkplay.yaml -u ashutmch -k -v

SSH password:

PLAY [First playbook] ********************************************************

TASK [ciscorouter : Run multiple commands and evaluate the output] ***********
[WARNING]: ansible-pylibssh not installed, falling back to paramiko
ok: [13.234.29.231] => {"changed": false, "stdout": ["ip-172-31-13-14 uptime is 4 hours, 0 minutes"]

PLAY RECAP *******************************************************************
13.234.29.231              : ok=1    changed=0    unreachable=0    failed=0    skipped=0    rescued=
```

Figure 11.7: Successful playbook execution after OS defined

We can see the execution is successful this time. So, we ran our first ever code on the networking devices. Now, let us go ahead and execute the second role with multiple commands in the role, as shown in the following figure:

```
root@ip-172-31-33-97:/etc/ansible#
root@ip-172-31-33-97:/etc/ansible# ansible-playbook networkplay.yaml -u ashutmch -k -v

SSH password:

PLAY [First playbook] ********************************************************

TASK [ciscorouter : Run our first command on the network devices] ***********
[WARNING]: ansible-pylibssh not installed, falling back to paramiko
ok: [13.234.29.231] => {"changed": false, "stdout": ["ip-172-31-13-14 uptime is 4 hours, 15 minutes"
rs, 15 minutes"], ["*21:09:59.375 UTC Wed Jul 5 2023"]]}

PLAY RECAP *******************************************************************
13.234.29.231              : ok=1    changed=0    unreachable=0    failed=0    skipped=0    rescued=

root@ip-172-31-33-97:/etc/ansible#
```

Figure 11.8: Multiple commands execution on the target host

We can see the execution was successful. Now, can we use the register module here and debug the content of the execution? Do those things work with the networking gears and network modules? Well, let us try it ourselves and see it.

So, just like our Linux **shell** and **command** module, we have used the **register** and **debug** module here. Please have a look at the role given as follows, and then we will execute it:

```
root@ip-172-31-33-97:/etc/ansible# cat roles/ciscorouter/tasks/main.yml
---
- name: Run our first command on the network devices
  cisco.ios.ios_command:
    commands:
      - show version | i uptime
      - show clock
    register: output
- debug:
    msg: "{{output.stdout}}"
root@ip-172-31-33-97:/etc/ansible#
```

Figure 11.9: Register module and debug module with IOS command module

We can see that we have created a variable named as **output** which captures the execution output of the two commands above. Then, we used the **debug** module to print the content of that variable. We have also used the **stdout** filter to see the neat and clean output. You can simply use output there (**msg: "{{output}}"**), and that too is fine. If you want, you can also use **output.stdout_lines** to find the output of your choice.

So, let us go ahead and execute the code as follows:

```
root@ip-172-31-33-97:/etc/ansible# ansible-playbook networkplay.yaml -u ashutmch -k
SSH password:

PLAY [First playbook] ********************************************************

TASK [ciscorouter : Run our first command on the network devices] ***********
[WARNING]: ansible-pylibssh not installed, falling back to paramiko
ok: [13.234.29.231]

TASK [ciscorouter : debug] **************************************************
ok: [13.234.29.231] => {
    "msg": [
        "ip-172-31-13-14 uptime is 4 hours, 22 minutes",
        "*21:17:11.371 UTC Wed Jul 5 2023"
    ]
}

PLAY RECAP ******************************************************************
13.234.29.231              : ok=2    changed=0    unreachable=0    failed=0    skipp
root@ip-172-31-33-97:/etc/ansible#
```

Figure 11.10: Debug output shows us the uptime and clock information

Now, let us go ahead with a few commands with bigger output and see what happens in the terminal:

```
root@ip-172-31-33-97:/etc/ansible# cat roles/ciscorouter/tasks/main.yml
---
- name: Run our first command on the network devices
  cisco.ios.ios_command:
    commands:
      - show tech
      - show clock
  register: output
- debug:
    msg: "{{output.stdout}}"
root@ip-172-31-33-97:/etc/ansible#
root@ip-172-31-33-97:/etc/ansible#
```

Figure 11.11: Example with a command which has huge output

So, what we have done here is use a command with a huge output, and that has shown some error on the screen. Let us read the error and see what is happening here:

```
root@ip-172-31-33-97:/etc/ansible# ansible-playbook networkplay.yaml --ask-vault-pass
Vault password:

PLAY [First playbook] ****************************************************************

TASK [ciscorouter : Run our first command on the network devices] ********************
[WARNING]: ansible-pylibssh not installed, falling back to paramiko
fatal: [13.234.29.231]: FAILED! => {"changed": false, "msg": "command timeout triggered,
Guide."}

PLAY RECAP ***************************************************************************
13.234.29.231              : ok=0    changed=0    unreachable=0    failed=1    skipped=0
```

Figure 11.12: Error with commands which has huge output

Now, if you know the Cisco gears well, then you know the show tech takes forever to execute and that has created the command timeout. The default timeout for the command execution is 30 seconds, and show tech takes a lot more than that. Now, what is the solution here?

There are a few ways of dealing with this issue. Let us go ahead and change the setting for this playbook, as shown in *Figure 11.13,* and later, we will see how to change it globally:

```
root@ip-172-31-33-97:/etc/ansible# cat networkplay.yaml
---
- name: First playbook
  hosts: all
  connection: network_cli
  vars:
    ansible_command_timeout: 300
  gather_facts: false
  roles:
  - ciscorouter

root@ip-172-31-33-97:/etc/ansible#
```

Figure 11.13: Command timeout fix for the commands that contains large output

What we have done is configure a variable for this playbook. In that variable, we have configured the **ansible_command_timeout** to be 300 seconds, which is 5 mins. So, if your show tech takes up to 5 minutes, it will succeed. However, if it takes more than that, change the setting to a bigger number per your requirement.

We have modified the role here as well, as there will be errors in the show tech for sure, which will result in the failure of the playbook. So, we have excluded the errors:

```
root@ip-172-31-33-97:/etc/ansible# cat roles/ciscorouter/tasks/main.yml
---
- name: Run our first command on the network devices
  cisco.ios.ios_command:
    commands: show tech-support | exclude rror
  register: output
- debug:
    msg: "{{output}}"
root@ip-172-31-33-97:/etc/ansible#
```

Figure 11.14: Role after increasing command timeout

Let us execute the following code:

```
"    Drops after proc'ed: 0",
"        Pending messages: 0",
" Pending message refs: 0",
"      Conf queue status: up (true), ready (true), s
" SA stats err ignored: 0",
"",
"Crypto counter.",
"   Pending crypto reqs: 0",
"Total crypto req done: 2",
" Avg crypto req ticks: 1 (100 msec/tick)",
" Total crypto throttled: 0",
"",
"   -------------------------------------------------
"   BOOT             2              2
"   IKE-DEF-KGRP     6              6
"   CFGMON           4              4
            ]
        ]
    }
}
PLAY RECAP *******************************************************
13.234.29.231           : ok=2    changed=0    unreachable=0
```

Figure 11.15: Successful playbook execution after increasing command timeout

As we can see, the execution is successful. Since the screen is not able to capture the entire output, here is a suppressed output.

The other way of changing the execution timeout is from the **ansible.cfg** file. We have already modified the file here, so let us grep the content of it:

```
root@ip-172-31-33-97:/etc/ansible#
root@ip-172-31-33-97:/etc/ansible# cat ansible.cfg | grep command_t
command_timeout = 300
root@ip-172-31-33-97:/etc/ansible#
root@ip-172-31-33-97:/etc/ansible#
```

Figure 11.16: Location to change the timeout for all execution

We can see that the value has changed from 30 seconds to 300 seconds, and once that is done this will apply to all roles and playbook.

Now, let us go ahead and look on the scenarios of the interactive commands. For example:

ip-172-31-13-14#reload

Proceed with reload? [confirm]

When we try to reload the router/switch, it does not directly start and reload the devices. It provides us a prompt which has the options yes/no. If we hit yes, then the reload will start, but the point the device interactively asks for the input from the user. So how would we handle this kind of situation? Well, we have some option here with us.

We can define the prompt and answer options after the command is sent to the target host:

```
---

- name: Run commands that require answering a prompt
  cisco.ios.ios_command:
    commands:
      - command: "reload"
        prompt: ' \[confirm\]'
        answer: "n"
```

The router prompts us **Proceed with reload? [confirm]**. Now, we can write in the prompt the entire message, or alternatively, we can enter the last word it asks in the prompt. You might be thinking the last word is **[confirm]** but why do we see **\[confirm\]** in the role? So, let us try the execution of the entire prompt, which is **Proceed with reload? [confirm]** and see if we get the desired result:

```
root@ip-172-31-33-97:/etc/ansible# cat roles/ciscorouter/tasks/main.yml
---
- name: Run commands that require answering a prompt
  cisco.ios.ios_command:
    commands:
      - command: "reload"
        prompt: 'Proceed with reload? [confirm]'
        answer: "n"
root@ip-172-31-33-97:/etc/ansible#
```

Figure 11.17: Role with code issues for demo purpose

Now, let us execute our code:

```
root@ip-172-31-33-97:/etc/ansible# ansible-playbook networkplay.yaml --ask-vault-pass
Vault password:

PLAY [First playbook] ***********************************************************

TASK [ciscorouter : Run commands that require answering a prompt] ***************
[WARNING]: ansible-pylibssh not installed, falling back to paramiko
fatal: [13.234.29.231]: FAILED! => {"changed": false, "msg": "command timeout triggered, timeout value is 30
Guide."}

PLAY RECAP **********************************************************************
13.234.29.231              : ok=0    changed=0    unreachable=0    failed=1    skipped=0    rescued=0    ign
```

Figure 11.18: Expected execution error

As you can see on the screen, there is an error of command timeout because Ansible is not getting what it was supposed to get. However, why? Well, the prompt message **Proceed with reload? [confirm]** has some special characters in it and that is treated differently by Ansible. It has the character like **?** and **[]**. So, how do we fix it? Well, we need to escape those special character.

If you do not know the meaning of the escape character, let us have a look at it. It simply means that we are telling Ansible to treat it like a normal English character and not like some filter or some different operation in Ansible. For example, we use double curly braces for rendering a value in Ansible, but if we had the prompt from Cisco, which had the curly braces in it, then we could have asked Ansible to treat it like a normal prompt. The way of telling Ansible is using an escape character. So, this **** you had seen in the command was actually the escape character. In the future, if you wish to escape the special character in Ansible, then backslash is your buddy.

Regex_escape filter is also a good option try playing with that in free time.

Now, let us go ahead and fix the code using backslash and re-run the code, as follows:

```
root@ip-172-31-33-97:/etc/ansible# cat roles/ciscorouter/tasks/main.yml
---
- name: Run commands that require answering a prompt
  cisco.ios.ios_command:
    commands:
      - command: "reload"
        prompt: 'Proceed with reload\? \[confirm\]'
        answer: "n"
root@ip-172-31-33-97:/etc/ansible#
root@ip-172-31-33-97:/etc/ansible#
root@ip-172-31-33-97:/etc/ansible# ansible-playbook networkplay.yaml --ask-va
Vault password:

PLAY [First playbook] ***********************************************************

TASK [ciscorouter : Run commands that require answering a prompt] ***********
[WARNING]: ansible-pylibssh not installed, falling back to paramiko
ok: [13.234.29.231]

PLAY RECAP **********************************************************************
13.234.29.231              : ok=1    changed=0    unreachable=0    failed=0

root@ip-172-31-33-97:/etc/ansible#
```

Figure 11.19: Playbook successfully executed after using escape character for special characters

As we can see, we have put the backslash on the three spots. One is before question mark; second one is before square bracket opening and the last one is before square bracket closing and that has informed the Ansible to escape these three characters and not execute them for regular expressions.

Once that was done, our code was successfully executed since we do not have the liberty to restart the box. Hence, we will go ahead with the interface counter. We will clear it and see the result as follows:

```
root@ip-172-31-33-97:/etc/ansible# cat roles/ciscorouter/tasks/main.yml
---
- name: Run commands that require answering a prompt
  cisco.ios.ios_command:
    commands:
      - command: "clear counters Gi1"
        prompt: ' \[confirm\]'
        answer: "y"

root@ip-172-31-33-97:/etc/ansible#
root@ip-172-31-33-97:/etc/ansible#
root@ip-172-31-33-97:/etc/ansible# ansible-playbook networkplay.yaml --as
Vault password:

PLAY [First playbook] ***********************************************

TASK [ciscorouter : Run commands that require answering a prompt] ******
[WARNING]: ansible-pylibssh not installed, falling back to paramiko
ok: [13.234.29.231]

PLAY RECAP **********************************************************
13.234.29.231              : ok=1    changed=0    unreachable=0    failed

root@ip-172-31-33-97:/etc/ansible#
```

Figure 11.20: Role with prompt and answer for the Cisco commands

We have used the clear counter **gi1** command here. Where the device asks us whether we want to clear the counters, confirm. We answered as **y** or yes at the end, and the execution was successful. So, let us log in to the target host and see the result:

```
ip-172-31-13-14#sh int gi 1
GigabitEthernet1 is up, line protocol is up
  Hardware is CSR vNIC, address is 0a42.fbe3.95a8 (bia 0a42.fbe3.95a8)
  Internet address is 172.31.13.14/20
  MTU 1500 bytes, BW 1000000 Kbit/sec, DLY 10 usec,
     reliability 255/255, txload 1/255, rxload 1/255
  Encapsulation ARPA, loopback not set
  Keepalive set (10 sec)
  Full Duplex, 1000Mbps, link type is auto, media type is Virtual
  output flow-control is unsupported, input flow-control is unsupported
  ARP type: ARPA, ARP Timeout 04:00:00
  Last input 00:00:00, output 00:00:00, output hang never
  Last clearing of "show interface" counters 00:01:48
```

Figure 11.21: Device output can confirm that our clear counter executed successfully using Ansible

As you can see, we spent 1 min and 48 seconds in writing our book and then checked this router. As we can see, the counters were clear recently (1.48 SECONDS ago).

Now, entering y/n is not the only option here. We can enter **/r** as well and that will simply put an enter command on the terminal. If the default enter is yes, then it will be yes applied to the target host, and if the default enter is no, then no will be executed to the target host.

Just like any other Ansible module, we can use the variables in this **command** module, and they get rendered well.

Note: If your control machine is taking forever to execute some command on the router/switch, that means something is wrong and command execution timeout is not letting prompt you error. If you have, changed the value to 5 mins then you will get the error after 5 mins. So, avoid changing the values globally the best way of doing it is per playbook basis.

There is one more thing about subtends, and that is how backup modules works in networking modules. Let us use the **copy** module for this time and see what happens here.

If you recall our last few chapters and copy modules, then it used to take the backup of files locally on the target host. However, this will not be the case in case of networking gears. Since we cannot modify anything in the Cisco IOS router/switch, the configuration backup or copied file will be saved on the control machine.

Let us go ahead and run the show version command on a router, register the output of the command on a variable, and copy the content of variable in the file:

```
root@ip-172-31-33-97:/etc/ansible# cat roles/ciscorouter/tasks/main.yml
---
- name: Run commands that require answering a prompt
  cisco.ios.ios_command:
    commands: show ver
  register: output
- copy:
    content: "{{output}}"
    dest: "showversion"

root@ip-172-31-33-97:/etc/ansible#
```

Figure 11.22: Copy module with Cisco IOS devices

Our role will look like the preceding where we have used the content feature of the copy module. The content of the variable **output** should be copied to the destination file **showversion**. Let us execute and see the result now:

```
root@ip-172-31-33-97:/etc/ansible# ansible-playbook networkplay.yaml --ask-vault-pass
Vault password:

PLAY [First playbook] ***********************************************************

TASK [ciscorouter : Run commands that require answering a prompt] ******************
[WARNING]: ansible-pylibssh not installed, falling back to paramiko
ok: [13.234.29.231]

TASK [ciscorouter : copy] *******************************************************
changed: [13.234.29.231]

PLAY RECAP **********************************************************************
13.234.29.231              : ok=2    changed=1    unreachable=0    failed=0    skippe
```

Figure 11.23: Successful playbook execution

Let us find the file and see the content of it:

```
root@ip-172-31-33-97:/etc/ansible# ll
total 52
drwxr-xr-x  3 root root  4096 Jul  6 16:19 ./
drwxr-xr-x 95 root root  4096 Jul  6 06:21 ../
-rw-r--r--  1 root root   204 Jul  5 21:12 1
-rw-r--r--  1 root root 19982 Jul  6 12:27 ansible.cfg
-rw-r--r--  1 root root   283 Jul  5 20:53 hosts
-rw-r--r--  1 root root   154 Jul  6 13:10 networkplay.yaml
drwxr-xr-x  3 root root  4096 Jul  5 20:48 roles/
-rw-r--r--  1 root root  5211 Jul  6 16:19 showversion
root@ip-172-31-33-97:/etc/ansible# cat showversion
{"changed": false, "stdout": ["Cisco IOS XE Software, Version 17.03.03\nCisco IOS Softw
RE (fc7)\nTechnical Support: http://www.cisco.com/techsupport\nCopyright (c) 1986-2021
) 2005-2021 by cisco Systems, Inc.\nAll rights reserved.  Certain components of Cisco
e code licensed under GPL Version 2.0 is free software that comes\nwith ABSOLUTELY NO W
ore details, see the\ndocumentation or \"License Notice\" file accompanying the IOS-XE
S-XE ROMMON\n\nip-172-31-13-14 uptime is 23 hours, 24 minutes\nUptime for this control
packages.conf\"\nLast reload reason: Unknown reason\n\n\nThis product contains crypto
nsfer and\nuse. Delivery of Cisco cryptographic products does not imply\nthird-party au
are responsible for\ncompliance with U.S. and local country laws. By using this produc
d local laws, return this product immediately.\n\nA summary of U.S. laws governing Cisc
f you require further assistance please contact us by sending email to\nexport@cisco.cc
e current throughput level is 1000 kbps \n\n\nSmart Licensing Status: UNREGISTERED/No
Processor board ID 95QH1J3C74U\nRouter operating mode: Autonomous\n1 Gigabit Ethernet
032K bytes of virtual hard disk at bootflash:.\n\nConfiguration register is 0x2102"],
E Software (X86_64_LINUX_IOSD-UNIVERSALK9-M), Version 17.3.3, RELEASE SOFTWARE (fc7)",
", "Compiled Thu 04-Mar-21 12:49 by mcpre", "", "", "Cisco IOS-XE software, Copyright
re are", "licensed under the GNU General Public License (\"GPL\") Version 2.0.  The",
Y.  You can redistribute and/or modify such", "GPL code under the terms of GPL Version
ftware,", "or the applicable URL provided on the flyer accompanying the IOS-XE", "softw
this control processor is 23 hours, 26 minutes", "System returned to ROM by reload",
This product contains cryptographic features and is subject to United", "States and lo
s does not imply", "third-party authority to import, export, distribute or use encrypt
cal country laws. By using this product you", "agree to comply with applicable laws an
.", "", "A summary of U.S. laws governing Cisco cryptographic products may be found at
ease contact us by sending email to", "export@cisco.com.", "", "License Level: ax", "L
level is 1000 kbps ", "", "", "Smart Licensing Status: UNREGISTERED/No Licenses in Use
 board ID 95QH1J3C74U", "Router operating mode: Autonomous", "1 Gigabit Ethernet inter
8032K bytes of virtual hard disk at bootflash:.", "", "Configuration register is 0x210
root@ip-172-31-33-97:/etc/ansible#
root@ip-172-31-33-97:/etc/ansible#
```

Figure 11.24: File created on the control machine which shows the output of command

This is how the copy module behaves differently for the networking gears in Ansible.

Cisco ios_config module

Cisco **ios_config** is one of the most important modules for configuration of the Cisco target hosts. As we learned in the previous topic, if we want to run any of the show command in the target hosts (Cisco router/switch), we need to use the **ios_command** module but if we wish to configure the device, then we need to use the **ios_conifg** module.

Let us go ahead and have a look on the role and understand that bit more. Refer to the following code:

```
root@ip-172-31-33-97:/etc/ansible# cat roles/iosconfig/tasks/main.yml
---
- name: Configure the hostname of the target host
  ios_config:
    lines: hostname DemoIOSConfig
  register: output
- debug:
    msg: "{{output}}"
```

Figure 11.25: Register and debug module with Cisco devices

ios_config is the name of the module, as you would have understood by now. The next line contains the parameter of this module. Here, we have used the lines parameter. In the lines, we define the commands in the ordered way.

In this case, we wanted to change the hostname of the target host, which is why we used the hostname **DemoIOSConfig**. So, this command will change the hostname of the target host to the **DemoIOSConfig**. Now, this was just a command, but if you have a list of commands, we can put them as shown in the following code:

```
root@ip-172-31-33-97:/etc/ansible# cat roles/iosconfig/tasks/main.yml
---
- name: Configure the hostname of the target host
  ios_config:
    lines:
    - hostname DemoIOSConfig
    - line vty 4 15
  register: output
- debug:
    msg: "{{output}}"
```

Figure 11.26: Sending multiple commands to the target host

Let us go ahead and execute the code and see the results:

```
root@ip-172-31-33-97:/etc/ansible#
root@ip-172-31-33-97:/etc/ansible# ansible-playbook networkplay.yaml --ask-vault-pass
Vault password:

PLAY [First playbook] ********************************************************

TASK [iosconfig : Configure the hostname of the target host] ****************
[WARNING]: ansible-pylibssh not installed, falling back to paramiko
[WARNING]: To ensure idempotency and correct diff the input configuration lines should
changed: [13.234.29.231]

TASK [iosconfig : debug] ****************************************************
ok: [13.234.29.231] => {
    "msg": {
        "banners": {},
        "changed": true,
        "commands": [
            "hostname DemoIOSConfiG"
        ],
        "failed": false,
        "updates": [
            "hostname DemoIOSConfiG"
        ],
        "warnings": [
            "To ensure idempotency and correct diff the input configuration lines shou
        ]
    }
}

PLAY RECAP ******************************************************************
13.234.29.231                 : ok=2    changed=1    unreachable=0    failed=0    skipped
```

Figure 11.27: Successful playbook execution

We can see that the command was executed successfully on the target host and changes were performed on the target host. Debug also shows what command was executed on the target host. Let us manually log in to the target host and see the device in action:

```
root@ip-172-31-33-97:/etc/ansible# ssh ashutmch@13.234.29.231
(ashutmch@13.234.29.231) Password:


DemoIOSConfiG#
```

Figure 11.28: Login prompt of router clearly shows device name updated successfully

We can see the hostname of the device is changed successfully.

Now, let us go ahead and have a look at the features like parent and child commands. When we try to go to configuration mode, the device prompt shows where exactly we are:

```
DemoIOSConfiG#
DemoIOSConfiG#
DemoIOSConfiG#conf t
Enter configuration commands, one per lin
DemoIOSConfiG(config)#no ruo
```

Figure 11.29: Current configuration mode of device

When we entered the **conf t** command the device prompt changed from **DemoIOSConfiG#** to **DemoIOSConfiG(config)#**. Similarly, if we enter router **bgp 65000**, the prompt changes from **Devicename(config)#** to **Devicename(config-router)#**. The command **router bgp 65000** is used for the configuration of **bgp**:

```
R1#
R1#conf t
Enter configuration commands, one per line.  End with CNTL/Z.
R1(config)#
R1(config)#
R1(config)#router bg
R1(config)#router bgp 65001
R1(config-router)#nie
```

Figure 11.30: Entering router configuration mode changes the device prompt

As soon as we go to the **bgp** configuration, the privilege mode will show us different prompt changes from **R1(config)#** to **R1(config-router)#**. So, anytime you see a command which is going to result in a change of configuration mode prompt on the target router, that command will be considered as a parent command. **int gi1** is a parent command as we will enter the interface configuration mode. All the further commands inside the **int gi1** will be child commands, like shut/no shut, description, ip address. All these commands will be entered inside the interface configuration mode, so all those commands will be child commands.

Since the **router bgp 65000** commands will take you to the router configuration mode, which is a parent command. Since all the neighbor commands will be executed inside that mode, we can put them as child commands:

```
root@ip-172-31-33-97:/etc/ansible# cat roles/iosconfig/tasks/main.yml
---
- name: Configure the hostname of the target host
  ios_config:
    lines:
    - nei 10.10.10.12 remote-as 65002
    parents: router bgp 65001
  register: output
- debug:
    msg: "{{output}}"
root@ip-172-31-33-97:/etc/ansible#
```

Figure 11.31: Role to configure the bgp in Cisco routers

Let us execute it now and see the result:

```
root@ip-172-31-33-97:/etc/ansible# ansible-playbook networkplay.yaml --ask-vault-pass
Vault password:

PLAY [First playbook] ****************************************************************

TASK [iosconfig : Configure the hostname of the target host] ************************
[WARNING]: ansible-pylibssh not installed, falling back to paramiko
[WARNING]: To ensure idempotency and correct diff the input configuration lines should b
changed: [13.234.29.231]

TASK [iosconfig : debug] ************************************************************
ok: [13.234.29.231] => {
    "msg": {
        "banners": {},
        "changed": true,
        "commands": [
            "router bgp 65001",
            "nei 10.10.10.12 remote-as 65002"
        ],
        "failed": false,
        "updates": [
            "router bgp 65001",
            "nei 10.10.10.12 remote-as 65002"
        ],
        "warnings": [
            "To ensure idempotency and correct diff the input configuration lines should
        ]
    }
}

PLAY RECAP *************************************************************************
13.234.29.231              : ok=2    changed=1    unreachable=0    failed=0    skipped=0
```

Figure 11.32: Successful configuration of bgp on the target router

We can see the execution is successful. If you have more than one command inside the child, you can put them all in there:

```
root@ip-172-31-33-97:/etc/ansible# cat roles/iosconfig/tasks/main.yml
---
- name: Configure the hostname of the target host
  ios_config:
    lines:
      - nei 10.10.10.12 remote-as 65002
      - nei 10.10.10.12 ebgp-mul 5
    parents: router bgp 65001
  register: output
- debug:
    msg: "{{output}}"
```

Figure 11.33: Role to send multiple child commands under parent

This is how you can manage the multiple commands inside the child.

Just like any other Ansible module, loops are also supported in the **ios_config** module.

Let us have a look at the example where we have used the option of a loop. We have defined the variable named as **item** and created a list of items to be rendered. At last, **register** module is used to capture the output of the execution, and then the **debug** module to show the debug on the terminal:

```
root@ip-172-31-33-97:/etc/ansible# cat roles/ciscorouter/tasks/main.yml
---
- name: configure ip helpers on multiple interfaces
  ios_config:
    lines:
      - desc testing123
    parents: "{{ item }}"
  with_items:
    - inter lo0
    - inter lo1
  register: output
- debug:
    msg: "{{output}}"
```

Figure 11.34: Loops for Cisco IOS_Command module

In the preceding example, we will create two loopback interfaces on the target host and change the description for both of them.

Let us go ahead and execute the code as follows:

```
root@ip-172-31-33-97:/etc/ansible# ansible-playbook  networkplay.yaml --ask-vault-password
Vault password:

PLAY [First playbook] ****************************************************************

TASK [ciscorouter : configure ip helpers on multiple interfaces] ********************
[WARNING]: ansible-pylibssh not installed, falling back to paramiko
changed: [13.234.29.231] => (item=inter lo0)
changed: [13.234.29.231] => (item=inter lo1)
[WARNING]: To ensure idempotency and correct diff the input configuration lines should be
TASK [ciscorouter : debug] **********************************************************
ok: [13.234.29.231] => {
    "msg": {
        "changed": true,
        "msg": "All items completed",
        "results": [
            {
                "ansible_loop_var": "item",
                "banners": {},
                "changed": true,
                "commands": [
                    "inter lo0",
                    "desc testing123"
```

Figure 11.35: Successful playbook execution

The extra lines of output are suppressed to keep the output clean. As we can see, the execution was successful. Let us login to the router:

```
root@ip-172-31-33-97:/etc/ansible#
root@ip-172-31-33-97:/etc/ansible# vi roles/ciscorouter/tasks/main.yml ^C
root@ip-172-31-33-97:/etc/ansible# ssh ashutmch@13.234.29.231
(ashutmch@13.234.29.231) Password:



DemoIOSConfiG#sh int des
Interface                    Status              Protocol Description
Gi1                          up                  up        testing123
Lo0                          up                  up        testing123
Lo1                          up                  up        testing123
Vi0                          up                  up
```

Figure 11.36: Successfully changed the interface descriptions

We can see on the router loop 0 and loopback 1 has been created. Both have been named as **testing123**. The only reason you see **Gi1** as the same name is because we tried the same code with the **Gi1** first, and then used two loopback interfaces.

Now, one important thing for all of you is to save the configuration. The configuration will wipe-out at the restart, so we need to save the configuration. The configuration will not be saved by default. We need to use **save_when** parameter of this module.

We basically have four options with us. They are as follows:

- Always
- Never
- Modified
- Changed

Unfortunately, the default option is never and because of that, the configuration is not saved in the target router. The reason why it is like this, is not clear. However, let us go ahead and have a look at the options as follows:

- **Always**: As the name suggests, the configuration will be saved always where any changes were performed on the target router or not.

- **Modified**: In this option, the configuration changes are only saved to the target hosts if Ansible finds there are changes in the running configuration since last save or write in Cisco's language. In simple words, Ansible will check if there are some changes in the running configuration since last save if there are some uncommitted or unsaved changes then the configuration will be saved.

- **Changed**: In this option, the configuration will be only saved if our task has performed some changes in the target router.

- **Never**: Never is the default option and it simply means—do not write the configuration.

Let us go ahead and use another feature of this module which allows us to compare the configuration to the intended configuration or start-up configuration:

```
root@ip-172-31-33-97:/etc/ansible# cat roles/ciscorouter/tasks/main.yml
---
- name: check the diff
  ios_config:
    diff_against: startup
root@ip-172-31-33-97:/etc/ansible#
```

Figure 11.37: Checking the difference between the running config and current config in Cisco router

We need to use an extra switch here. Just like we have used **-u** to define the username, we need to use the **--diff** to show the difference on the terminal. If we do not do that, nothing will be visible on the terminal:

```
root@ip-172-31-33-97:/etc/ansible# ansible-playbook networkplay.yaml --ask-vault-password --dif
Vault password:

PLAY [First playbook] ***********************************************************

TASK [ciscorouter : check the diff] *********************************************
[WARNING]: ansible-pylibssh not installed, falling back to paramiko
--- before
+++ after
@@ -6,7 +6,7 @@
 platform qfp utilization monitor load 80
 platform punt-keepalive disable-kernel-core
 platform console virtual
-hostname ip-172-31-13-14
+hostname DemoIOSConfiG
 boot-start-marker
 boot-end-marker
 vrf definition GS
@@ -27,9 +27,63 @@
   enrollment pkcs12
   revocation-check crl
```

Figure 11.38: Output shows the difference on terminal

As we can see, the old configuration is visible in the red font and the new configuration in the green font. This is how we can see the difference between the running configuration and the start-up configuration.

Let us go ahead and do something important now. Assume you have an ACL with you in your target host/router. An example is as follows:

```
DemoIOSConfiG#sh ip access-lists
Standard IP access list GS_NAT_ACL
    10 permit 192.168.35.0, wildcard bits 0.0.0.255
Extended IP access list meraki-fqdn-dns
Extended IP access list test
    10 permit ip host 1.1.1.1 any log
    20 permit ip host 2.2.2.2 any log
    30 permit ip host 3.3.3.3 any log
    40 permit ip host 4.4.4.4 any log
    50 permit ip host 5.5.5.5 any log
DemoIOSConfiG#
```

Figure 11.39: *Demo ACL of Cisco router*

Now, what you wish to do is update that to the new ACL and restructure the entire ACL. Since you wanted to restructure the entire ACL, you decided to go ahead with the **no ip access-list extended test** first and then later re-configured the ACL. Here is your new list of what you want in your target host. You tried changing the sequence number 30 and add a new line there as **30 permit ip host 30.30.30.30 any log**. Your new ACL should look as follows:

Extended IP access list test:

```
    10 permit ip host 1.1.1.1 any log
    20 permit ip host 2.2.2.2 any log
    30 permit ip host 30.30.30.30 any log
    40 permit ip host 4.4.4.4 any log
    50 permit ip host 5.5.5.5 any log
```

So, first command is:

```
no ip access-list extended test
```

Then:

```
ip access-list extended test
    10 permit ip host 1.1.1.1 any log
    20 permit ip host 2.2.2.2 any log
    30 permit ip host 30.30.30.30 any log
    40 permit ip host 4.4.4.4 any log
    50 permit ip host 5.5.5.5 any log
```

If you want to configure an access list on a Cisco device using Ansible, we can do it using the ios_config module, which allows us to manage device settings with structured commands. In this example, we use the **before** parameter to remove any existing access list named test before creating a new one. This ensures that the configuration starts clean. The main command **ip access-list extended test** is known as the parent command, which creates a new access list named **test**. Under this parent, we define several child commands that specify the access rules, such as allowing traffic from specific IP addresses. Each child command is assigned a sequence number (like 10, 20, 30, etc.) to control the order in which the rules are applied. In Cisco's configuration hierarchy, commands are structured into different levels or modes, such as User EXEC mode, Global Configuration mode, and Router Configuration mode. When we enter the access list mode using the parent command **ip access-list extended test**, all the rules defined inside it are considered child commands. The following Ansible code demonstrates this structure clearly by first removing any existing access list and then creating a new one with specific permit rules under the defined parent command. Let us run the following code in the control machine:

```
ios_config:
lines:
-10 permit ip host 1.1.1.1 any log
-20 permit ip host 2.2.2.2 any log
-30 permit ip host 30.30.30.30 any log
-40 permit ip host 4.4.4.4 any log
-50 permit ip host 5.5.5.5 any log
parents:ip access-list extended test
before:no ip access-list extended test
```

```
root@ip-172-31-33-97:/etc/ansible# cat roles/ciscorouter/tasks/main.yml
---
- name: load new acl into device
  ios_config:
    lines:
      - 10 permit ip host 1.1.1.1 any log
      - 20 permit ip host 2.2.2.2 any log
      - 30 permit ip host 30.30.30.30 any log
      - 40 permit ip host 4.4.4.4 any log
      - 50 permit ip host 5.5.5.5 any log
    parents: ip access-list extended test
    before: no ip access-list extended test
root@ip-172-31-33-97:/etc/ansible#
```

Figure 11.40: Demo role to configure the ACLs in Cisco router

Let us execute the code and have a look at the output of execution:

```
root@ip-172-31-33-97:/etc/ansible# ansible-playbook  networkplay.yam
Vault password:

PLAY [First playbook] ******************************************

TASK [ciscorouter : load new acl into device] *******************
[WARNING]: ansible-pylibssh not installed, falling back to paramiko
[WARNING]: To ensure idempotency and correct diff the input configur
changed: [13.234.29.231]

PLAY RECAP ******************************************************
13.234.29.231                   : ok=1     changed=1    unreachable=0    f
```

Figure 11.41: Successful playbook execution

It looks like the execution is good, but there is something wrong here. Let us have a look at something strange:

```
root@ip-172-31-33-97:/etc/ansible# ansible-playbook  networkplay.yaml
Vault password:

PLAY [First playbook] ********************************************

TASK [ciscorouter : load new acl into device] ********************
[WARNING]: ansible-pylibssh not installed, falling back to paramiko
[WARNING]: To ensure idempotency and correct diff the input configurat
changed: [13.234.29.231]

PLAY RECAP *******************************************************
13.234.29.231                   : ok=1     changed=1    unreachable=0    fai

root@ip-172-31-33-97:/etc/ansible# ssh ashutmch@13.234.29.231
(ashutmch@13.234.29.231) Password:



DemoIOSConfiG#sh ip acc
DemoIOSConfiG#sh ip access-lists
Standard IP access list GS_NAT_ACL
    10 permit 192.168.35.0, wildcard bits 0.0.0.255
Extended IP access list meraki-fqdn-dns
Extended IP access list test
    30 permit ip host 30.30.30.30 any log
DemoIOSConfiG#
```

Figure 11.42: Router output confirms there is some problem

Now, if you realize the ACL test, it just shows our newly modified sequence 30 entry only, but where are the other ACL entries? It is not a good thing. If it could have been your production, then you would have cost a huge outage in your production environment. So, lesson 1 to remember: Always test your code in the pre-production environment first, then run it in production.

Ansible checks for the existing configuration of the target hosts first, and changes are only configured on the target host if they are not already present on the target host. In this case, Ansible verified the existing configuration and realized that all configuration is present on the target host, so it only pushed the line which was not present on the target host.

First, it sent the command:

`no ip access-list extended test`

Then, the parent command was pushed to the target host, which was:

`ip access-list extended test`

At last, the child command was pushed to the target host, which was just line 30 as per Ansible:

`30 permit ip host 30.30.30.30 any log`

Now, we know the problem and what caused it. But how do we fix it? Well, by default, Ansible checks the configuration on the target host line by line, but we can change this behaviour. Let us see what our options are. The parameter that we have been offered by the `ios_command` module is the `match` parameter. We have the following choices:

- **Line**: If the match parameter is set to the line, then commands are matched line by line and that is what caused us the issue in our last execution as line is our default option.

- **Strict**: If we set the match to strict, then the command lines will be matched even with respect to their position.

- **Exact**: If we set the match statement to the exact, then the commands will be exactly matched to the source configuration with the running configuration on the target host.

- **None**: If we set it to none, no match operation will be performed. Irrespective of the current configuration on the target host the commands will be pushed always.

So, let us go ahead and set it to the exact and get the ACL fixed:

```
root@ip-172-31-33-97:/etc/ansible# cat roles/ciscorouter/tasks/main.yml
---
- name: load new acl into device
  ios_config:
    lines:
      - 10 permit ip host 1.1.1.1 any log
      - 20 permit ip host 2.2.2.2 any log
      - 30 permit ip host 30.30.30.30 any log
      - 40 permit ip host 4.4.4.4 any log
      - 50 permit ip host 5.5.5.5 any log
    parents: ip access-list extended test
    before: no ip access-list extended test
    match: exact
root@ip-172-31-33-97:/etc/ansible#
```

Figure 11.43: *Role with before and match options which fix the issue*

Execution results:

```
root@ip-172-31-33-97:/etc/ansible# cat roles/ciscorouter/tasks/main.yml
---
- name: load new acl into device
  ios_config:
    lines:
      - 10 permit ip host 1.1.1.1 any log
      - 20 permit ip host 2.2.2.2 any log
      - 30 permit ip host 30.30.30.30 any log
      - 40 permit ip host 4.4.4.4 any log
      - 50 permit ip host 5.5.5.5 any log
    parents: ip access-list extended test
    before: no ip access-list extended test
    match: exact
root@ip-172-31-33-97:/etc/ansible#
root@ip-172-31-33-97:/etc/ansible#
root@ip-172-31-33-97:/etc/ansible# ansible-playbook networkplay.yaml --ask
Vault password:

PLAY [First playbook] ***********************************************

TASK [ciscorouter : load new acl into device] **********************
[WARNING]: ansible-pylibssh not installed, falling back to paramiko
[WARNING]: To ensure idempotency and correct diff the input configuration
changed: [13.234.29.231]

PLAY RECAP *********************************************************
13.234.29.231              : ok=1      changed=1    unreachable=0    failed=0

root@ip-172-31-33-97:/etc/ansible# ssh ashutmch@13.234.29.231
(ashutmch@13.234.29.231) Password:


DemoIOSConfiG#sh ip acc
DemoIOSConfiG#sh ip access-lists
Standard IP access list GS_NAT_ACL
    10 permit 192.168.35.0, wildcard bits 0.0.0.255
Extended IP access list meraki-fqdn-dns
Extended IP access list test
    10 permit ip host 1.1.1.1 any log
    20 permit ip host 2.2.2.2 any log
    30 permit ip host 30.30.30.30 any log
    40 permit ip host 4.4.4.4 any log
    50 permit ip host 5.5.5.5 any log
DemoIOSConfiG##
```

Figure 11.44: *Successful playbook execution and desired output*

We can see the things are sorted this time. The configuration is pushed the way it was supposed to be configured in the target router. This is how we can perform few complicated operations. It is advised to always prepare and test your code in the pre-production first and never use it directly in the production.

Cisco ios_facts module

As discussed at the beginning of the chapter, the **ansible_facts** command does not work with the networking devices. So, the question arises, how do we gather the information about the networking devices? Well, the answer is **ios_facts** module. This module helps us collect the information about the target router and saves it into the magic variables, which can be further used in the roles and playbooks.

Let us go ahead with the role and parameters we get with this module:

```
root@ip-172-31-33-97:/etc/ansible# cat roles/facts/tasks/main.yml
---
- name: Information about the IOS router
  cisco.ios.ios_facts:
    gather_subset: all
root@ip-172-31-33-97:/etc/ansible#
```

Figure 11.45: Demo role for ios_facts

As we know, **cisco.ios.ios_facts** is the name of the Ansible module. We need to let this module know what we want to gather. If you want to collect all information, then simply say **gather_subset: all**. Let us go ahead and execute this code, after that we will explore more choices which we get with the **gather_subset** parameter.

Code:

```
root@ip-172-31-33-97:/etc/ansible#
root@ip-172-31-33-97:/etc/ansible# cat networkplay.yaml
---
- name: First playbook
  hosts: all
  connection: network_cli
  vars:
    ansible_command_timeout: 30
  gather_facts: false
  roles:
  - facts

root@ip-172-31-33-97:/etc/ansible#
root@ip-172-31-33-97:/etc/ansible# ansible-playbook  networkplay.yaml
Vault password:

PLAY [First playbook] ********************************************

TASK [facts : Information about the IOS router] *****************
[WARNING]: ansible-pylibssh not installed, falling back to paramiko
ok: [13.234.29.231]

PLAY RECAP ******************************************************
13.234.29.231              : ok=1    changed=0    unreachable=0    fai
```

Figure 11.46: Successful playbook execution

The execution is successful. However, we need to run the debug mode. Alternatively, we can use the register and **debug** module to print the content of execution. So, let us go ahead with the register and **debug** module, as follows:

```
root@ip-172-31-33-97:/etc/ansible# cat roles/facts/tasks/main.yml
---
- name: Information about the IOS router
  cisco.ios.ios_facts:
    gather_subset: all
  register: output
- debug:
    msg: "{{output}}"
root@ip-172-31-33-97:/etc/ansible#
```

Figure 11.47: Debug the content of ios_facts

Let us execute the code again and see the results:

```
root@ip-172-31-33-97:/etc/ansible# ansible-playbook  networkpla
Vault password:

PLAY [First playbook] ********************************

TASK [facts : Information about the IOS router] **************
[WARNING]: ansible-pylibssh not installed, falling back to para
ok: [13.234.29.231]

TASK [facts : debug] ********************************
ok: [13.234.29.231] => {
    "msg": {
        "ansible_facts": {
            "ansible_net_all_ipv4_addresses": [
                "172.31.13.14",
                "192.168.35.101"
            ],
            "ansible_net_all_ipv6_addresses": [],
            "ansible_net_api": "cliconf",
            "ansible_net_config": "Building configuration...\n\
3\nservice timestamps debug datetime msec\nservice timestamps l
```

Figure 11.48: ios_facts debug part 1

Output suppressed. The result is shown as follows, since the information was huge:

```
         "ansible_net_iostype": "IOS-XE",
         "ansible_net_memfree_mb": 1774.6016464233398,
         "ansible_net_memtotal_mb": 2020.2203178405762,
         "ansible_net_model": "CSR1000V",
         "ansible_net_neighbors": {},
         "ansible_net_operatingmode": "autonomous",
         "ansible_net_python_version": "3.10.6",
         "ansible_net_serialnum": "95QH1J3C74U",
         "ansible_net_system": "ios",
         "ansible_net_version": "17.03.03",
         "ansible_network_resources": {}
     },
     "changed": false,
     "failed": false
  }
}

PLAY RECAP ***********************************************************
13.234.29.231                    : ok=2      changed=0     unreachable=0
```

Figure 11.49: ios_facts debug part 2

We can see we are getting the information like current IOS information about the target router. If you want to send the upgrade commands, if the IOS version is less than 15 or so, then you can do that easily. Let us try to print the IOS version on the terminal first, and then we will go ahead with the other information.

Let us have a look at the role to print the value of the version. Things are a bit different in the **ios_facts** modul and you can notice that easily, as shown in the following code:

```
root@ip-172-31-33-97:/etc/ansible# cat roles/facts/tasks/main.yml
---
- name: Information about the IOS router
  cisco.ios.ios_facts:
    gather_subset: all
  register: output
- debug:
    msg: "{{output.ansible_facts.ansible_net_version}}"
root@ip-172-31-33-97:/etc/ansible#
root@ip-172-31-33-97:/etc/ansible#
```

Figure 11.50: Fetching the IOS version information from ios_facts

Let us run our code. The result will be as follows:

```
root@ip-172-31-33-97:/etc/ansible# ansible-playbook   networkplay.yaml
Vault password:

PLAY [First playbook] ***********************************************

TASK [facts : Information about the IOS router] *********************
[WARNING]: ansible-pylibssh not installed, falling back to paramiko
ok: [13.234.29.231]

TASK [facts : debug] ***********************************************
ok: [13.234.29.231] => {
    "msg": "17.03.03"
}

PLAY RECAP ***********************************************************
13.234.29.231                    : ok=2      changed=0     unreachable=0    fa
```

Figure 11.51: Playbook output clearly shows the version 17.03.03 on the router

Let us assume you have been assigned to upgrade the versions of both IOS and IOS-XE devices. You have different images for the different devices. How would you figure out which image should be uploaded to which device? Well, the **when** statement will help here again.

The code will be as follows:

```
root@ip-172-31-33-97:/etc/ansible# cat roles/whencond/tasks/main.yml
---
- name: Information about the IOS router
  cisco.ios.ios_facts:
    gather_subset: all
  register: output
- ansible.builtin.debug:
    msg: Version is IOS xe uplod the XE image
    when:  ansible_facts['net_iostype'] == "IOS-XE"
root@ip-172-31-33-97:/etc/ansible#
```

Figure 11.52: Using IOS facts for conditions

Let us run the code. The result will be as follows:

```
root@ip-172-31-33-97:/etc/ansible#
root@ip-172-31-33-97:/etc/ansible# ansible-playbook  networkplay.yaml --
Vault password:

PLAY [First playbook] ********************************************

TASK [whencond : Information about the IOS router] ****************
[WARNING]: ansible-pylibssh not installed, falling back to paramiko
ok: [13.234.29.231] => {"ansible_facts": {"ansible_net_all_ipv4_addresse
net_config": "Building configuration...\n\nCurrent configuration : 7526
  debug datetime msec\nservice timestamps log datetime msec\nservice pass
  80\nplatform punt-keepalive disable-kernel-core\nplatform console virtu
ess-family ipv4\n exit-address-family\n!\nlogging persistent size 100000
n!\nsubscriber templating\n! \n! \n! \n! \n!\n!\nmultilink bundle-name a
t selfsigned\n subject-name cn=IOS-Self-Signed-Certificate-268555362\n 
12\n revocation-check crl\n!\n!\ncrypto pki certificate chain TP-self-si
```

Figure 11.53: Successful playbook execution

Figure 11.54 shows us the debug output when condition **when** was found true. It finds out a magic variable values and matches compares that with keyword IOS-XE, when it was found true, it gives us the debug output stating **Version is IOS xe upload the XE image**:

```
TASK [whencond : ansible.builtin.debug] ***********************************
ok: [13.234.29.231] => {
    "msg": "Version is IOS xe uplod the XE image"
}

PLAY RECAP ****************************************************************
13.234.29.231              : ok=2    changed=0    unreachable=0    failed=0

root@ip-172-31-33-97:/etc/ansible#
```

Figure 11.54: Condition matches and gives us the expected result

We can see the desired result here. Let us try something better next:

```
root@ip-172-31-33-97:/etc/ansible# cat roles/whencond/tasks/main.yml
---
- name: Information about the IOS router
  cisco.ios.ios_facts:
    gather_subset: all
- name: Let's upgrade
  block:
  - name: Copy the image
    cisco.ios.ios_command:
      commands:
        - command: "copy tftp://172.31.33.97/abcd.txt bootflash://newabcd.txt"
          prompt: '\[newabcd\.txt\]\?'
          answer: "\r"
  - name: change the boot menu
    ios_config:
      lines: hostname Newbootimage
      save_when: modified
  when: ansible_facts['net_iostype'] == "IOS-XE"
  register: output
- debug:
    msg: "{{output}}"
root@ip-172-31-33-97:/etc/ansible#
```

Figure 11.55: IOS upgrade preparation and how we can send any command to the target host

In the preceding role, we have copied the file **abcd.txt** from **tftp** to the **bootflash** in the CSR router. You need to change the name from abcd.txt to the **iosimage.iso** file name. Since we do not have the real image with us, we cannot change the boot option here, but in your real upgrade, you need to change the commands to the correct one to change the boot menu. At last, we need to save the configuration and reboot the host.

Note: **The important thing is to change the timeout since the IOS image copy will take lot of time and the obvious reason is the huge size of the IOS file. So, change the timeout to 3600 or any significant you feel like. The way of changing it is already shown in this book.**

```
root@ip-172-31-33-97:/etc/ansible# ansible-playbook  networkplay.yaml -
Vault password:

PLAY [First playbook] ****************************************************

TASK [whencond : Information about the IOS router] *********************
[WARNING]: ansible-pylibssh not installed, falling back to paramiko
ok: [13.234.29.231]

TASK [whencond : Copy the image] **************************************
ok: [13.234.29.231]

TASK [whencond : change the boot menu] ********************************
[WARNING]: To ensure idempotency and correct diff the input configurati
changed: [13.234.29.231]

PLAY RECAP ************************************************************
13.234.29.231              : ok=3    changed=1    unreachable=0    fail

root@ip-172-31-33-97:/etc/ansible#
```

Figure 11.56: Successful playbook execution

We can see that the execution is successful here.

Let us go back to the target host and see if the file is copied and the hostname is changed, by following the given code:

```
NewbootImage#
Newbootimage#dir
Directory of bootflash:/

24        -rw-            21    Jul 9 2023 20:20:06 +00:00  newabcd.txt
298369    drwx        65536    Jul 9 2023 20:19:04 +00:00  tracelogs
56449     drwx         4096    Jul 9 2023 14:19:27 +00:00  syslog
```

Figure 11.57: The file we tried coping using Ansible is present on the target host

We can see the new host name and the copied file are both present on the target router. So, this was a working example of the script for the router OS upgrade. Now, this was just an example. You can use this example to build your own script for your pre-prod and then production environment. Always test your code in pre-production first, as you will always see some weird behaviour from the code. Sometimes they are human errors, sometimes it is a lack of knowledge, and sometimes they are bugs as well. Hence, always run your code in the pre-production environment or test environment first, and then only use it in production.

We have discussed only three Cisco IOS module in this chapter, but there are many IOS module for us. These three modules are enough for doing any task in the Cisco IOS devices. However, you can choose a more specific module based on your requirement.

A list of the modules available for IOS devices is as follows:

- ios_acl_interfaces module – Resource module to configure ACL interfaces.
- ios_acls module – Resource module to configure ACLs.
- ios_banner module – Module to configure multiline banners.
- ios_bgp module – Module to configure BGP protocol settings.
- ios_bgp_address_family module – Resource module to configure BGP Address family.
- ios_bgp_global module – Resource module to configure BGP.
- ios_command module – Module to run commands on remote devices.
- ios_config module – Module to manage configuration sections.
- ios_facts module – Module to collect facts from remote devices.

Figure 11.58: List of the modules available for IOS devices

The list continues. Here is the document for the list of all Cisco IOS modules:

https://docs.ansible.com/ansible/latest/collections/cisco/ios/index.html

Juniper junos_os automation

As we have learned about the modules available for the Cisco IOS gears. Similarly, we have many Juniper modules of Ansible. Just like we have **command**, **config** and **facts** module for the Cisco IOS gears, similarly, we have these three modules available specifically designed for the JUNOS devices.

junos_command module

We will start our journey of Juniper from **junos_command** module, just like Cisco IOS devices. For beginners to understand, **junos_command** module is an Ansible module designed for the Juniper devices. This module sends the commands on the target host and captures the output and reflect that on the terminal.

Let us go ahead and create a rule as follows:

```
root@ip-172-31-33-97:/etc/ansible# cat roles/junos/tasks/main.yml
- name: run first junos command
  junipernetworks.junos.junos_command:
    commands: show version
root@ip-172-31-33-97:/etc/ansible#
root@ip-172-31-33-97:/etc/ansible#
```

Figure 11.59: Show command using junos command module for Juniper hosts

This is no different than the **ios_command** module. The first line after the name is the name of the module, the second line simply asks for the commands we want to execute on the target hosts.

Let us execute it and wait for the result:

```
root@ip-172-31-33-97:/etc/ansible# cat hosts
[router]
13.233.131.40
[router:vars]
  ansible_network_os = junos
```

Figure 11.60: Network OS needs to be changed from IOS to junos for Juniper

You must remember we had to modify the hosts file and change the OS type to junos as this is not an IOS device.

```
root@ip-172-31-33-97:/etc/ansible# ansible-playbook networkplay.yaml
Vault password:

PLAY [First playbook] ***********************************************

TASK [junos : run first junos command] *****************************
[WARNING]: ansible-pylibssh not installed, falling back to paramiko
[WARNING]: arguments wait_for, match, rpcs are not supported when usin
ok: [13.233.131.40]

PLAY RECAP **********************************************************
13.233.131.40               : ok=1    changed=0    unreachable=0    fai
```

Figure 11.61: Successful playbook execution with few modifications

As we can see, the execution is successful.

Let us run it in the verbose mode and see something on the terminal:

```
root@ip-172-31-33-97:/etc/ansible# ansible-playbook  networkplay.yaml --ask-vault-password -v
Using /etc/ansible/ansible.cfg as config file
Vault password:

PLAY [First playbook] *******************************************************************

TASK [junos : run first junos command] *************************************************
[WARNING]: ansible-pylibssh not installed, falling back to paramiko
[WARNING]: arguments wait_for, match, rpcs are not supported when using transport=cli
ok: [13.233.131.40] => {"changed": false, "stdout": ["Model: vSRX\nJunos: 22.3R2.12\nJUNOS OS
lder_stable_12_223]\nJUNOS OS runtime [20221212.98a33a0_builder_stable_12_223]\nJUNOS OS time
33a0_builder_stable_12_223]\nJUNOS OS 32-bit compatibility [20221212.98a33a0_builder_stable_12
05_builder_junos_223_r2]\nJUNOS OS vmguest [20221212.98a33a0_builder_stable_12_223]\nJUNOS OS
2_223]\nJUNOS OS boot-ve files [20221212.98a33a0_builder_stable_12_223]\nJUNOS network stack a
223_r2]\nJUNOS libs compat32 [20230223.221505_builder_junos_223_r2]\nJUNOS runtime [20230223.2
age [20230223.221505_builder_junos_223_r2]\nJUNOS vsrx modules [20230223.221505_builder_junos_
30223.221505_builder_junos_223_r2]\nJUNOS srx platform support [20230223.221505_builder_junos_
me [20230223.221505_builder_junos_223_r2]\nJUNOS Routing mpls-oam-basic [20230223.221505_build
it Compatible Version [20230223.221505_builder_junos_223_r2]\nJUNOS Routing aggregated [202302
NOS pppoe [20230223.221505_builder_junos_223_r2]\nJUNOS Openconfig [22.3R2.12]\nJUNOS mtx netw
s_223_r2]\nJUNOS srx libs [20230223.221505_builder_junos_223_r2]\nJUNOS L2 RSI Scripts [202302
```

Figure 11.62: Debug output clearly gives us the show version output on the terminal

The output is suppressed, as the output of the show version command is huge.

This is how you can run the show commands in the Juniper routers/devices. The concept is going to be the same for the **command** and **config** module, so we are not going to spent lot of time in the same sort of module this time.

Let us go ahead and try running a show configuration on the target router. The concept is going to be the same, and all the things like **register** module and **debug** will run in the same way. Let us have a look at the role:

```
root@ip-172-31-33-97:/etc/ansible# cat roles/junos/tasks/main.yml
- name: run first junos command
  junipernetworks.junos.junos_command:
    commands: show configuration
  register: output
- debug:
    msg: "{{output}}"
root@ip-172-31-33-97:/etc/ansible#
```

Figure 11.63: Use of register and debug module with junos command module

Let us run our code. The result will be as follows:

```
root@ip-172-31-33-97:/etc/ansible# vi roles/junos/tasks/main.yml
root@ip-172-31-33-97:/etc/ansible# ansible-playbook  networkplay.yaml --ask-vault-password
Vault password:

PLAY [First playbook] ********************************************************

TASK [junos : run first junos command] ********************************************
[WARNING]: ansible-pylibssh not installed, falling back to paramiko
[WARNING]: arguments wait_for, match, rpcs are not supported when using transport=cli
ok: [43.204.230.55]

TASK [junos : debug] ********************************************************
ok: [43.204.230.55] => {
    "msg": [
        [
            "## Last commit: 2023-07-10 11:11:39 UTC by ec2-user",
            "version 22.3R2.12;",
            "#junos-config",
            "groups {",
            "    aws-default {",
            "        system {",
            "            root-authentication {",
            "                encrypted-password *disabled*; ## SECRET-DATA",
            "            }",
            "            scripts {",
            "                translation {",
            "                    max-datasize 512m;",
            "                }",
            "            }",
            "            login {",
            "                user ec2-user {",
            "                    full-name juniper-aws-ec2-user;",
            "                    uid 100;",
            "                    class super-user;",
            "                    authentication {",
```

Figure 11.64: Debug successful for the show version configuration

We can see the execution was successful. We personally like the set of commands in the Juniper devices, so let us see how you can achieve that. The following code is an example if you wish to get the configuration that way:

```
root@ip-172-31-33-97:/etc/ansible# cat roles/junos/tasks/main.yml
- name: run first junos command
  junipernetworks.junos.junos_command:
    commands: show configuration
    display: set
  register: output
- debug:
    msg: "{{output.stdout_lines}}"
root@ip-172-31-33-97:/etc/ansible#
```

Figure 11.65: Role to show the device output in display set mode

The parameter to configure is displayed. We have a bunch of options, like text, JSON, set, and XML. So, we can choose any of them. We personally like the set, so we have chosen in example, as follows:

```
root@ip-172-31-33-97:/etc/ansible# ansible-playbook  networkplay.yaml --ask-vault-password
Vault password:

PLAY [First playbook] *********************************************************************

TASK [junos : run first junos command] ***************************************************
[WARNING]: ansible-pylibssh not installed, falling back to paramiko
[WARNING]: arguments wait_for, match, rpcs are not supported when using transport=cli
ok: [43.204.230.55]

TASK [junos : debug] *********************************************************************
ok: [43.204.230.55] => {
    "msg": [
        [
            "set version 22.3R2.12",
            "set groups aws-default system root-authentication encrypted-password *disabled*",
            "set groups aws-default system scripts translation max-datasize 512m",
            "set groups aws-default system login user ec2-user full-name juniper-aws-ec2-user",
            "set groups aws-default system login user ec2-user uid 100",
            "set groups aws-default system login user ec2-user class super-user",
            "set groups aws-default system login user ec2-user authentication ssh-rsa \"ssh-rsa A
0BEJxmz19pQkJdjvvITojyjCkd3zaFcvvBYdfaXvnSaoUffUDBYOozr7CRH1A8mkmFkCBEycbJZaUYf7AQW50G5h64aiqCuW0
8ofU193tM/LoOz9NZ9tmN1gNFqleQnwrlgyH+UMUOL6CGfAlgbbwnnxxY/wwUqpFw6iC7fGFVX1XPNSN+p45N9hxEH Ansibl
            "set groups aws-default system login user ashutmch uid 2000",
            "set groups aws-default system login user ashutmch class super-user",
            "set groups aws-default system login user ashutmch authentication encrypted-password
LFcSZbF.\"",
            "set groups aws-default system services ssh",
            "set groups aws-default system services netconf ssh",
            "set groups aws-default system services web-management https system-generated-certifi
            "set groups aws-default system license autoupdate url https://ae1.juniper.net/junos/k
            "set groups aws-default interfaces fxp0 unit 0 family inet dhcp",
            "set apply-groups aws-default"
        ]
    ]
}

PLAY RECAP *******************************************************************************
43.204.230.55              : ok=2    changed=0    unreachable=0    failed=0    skipped=0    rescu
```

Figure 11.66: Debug is successful in display set mode of Ansible

Now the configuration looks much neater. You can choose any type you like most.

junos_hostname module

The next important topic we want to cover here is **junos_config** module, but before we do that, let us look at some additional modules available for us. As discussed earlier, you can do everything using **facts**, **command**, and **config** modules, but someday you might want to use a specific module, so you let us prepare well for that day.

Now, we need to perform some changes in our control machine to use this module. However, how do we figure out if we need something for this module? Well, we need to follow the official document of that module.

While reading the official document of this module, we found two additional requirements for this module. They are as follows:

- **ncclient** (>=v0.6.4)
- **xmltodict** (>=0.12.0)

The requirement is quite clear, we need to install the **ncclient** and **xmltodict** Python library. Let us go ahead and install them. The simple command to install the library is:

```
pip3 install ncclient
```

xmltodict can be installed using the following command:

```
pip3 install xmltodict
```

```
No VM guests are running outdated hypervisor (qemu) binaries on this host.
root@ip-172-31-33-97:/etc/ansible# pip3 install ncclient
Collecting ncclient
  Downloading ncclient-0.6.13.tar.gz (105 kB)
                                          105.7/105.7 KB 2.1 MB/s eta 0:00:00
  Preparing metadata (setup.py) ... done
Collecting lxml>=3.3.0
  Downloading lxml-4.9.3-cp310-cp310-manylinux_2_28_x86_64.whl (7.9 MB)
                                          7.9/7.9 MB 28.9 MB/s eta 0:00:00
Requirement already satisfied: paramiko>=1.15.0 in /usr/lib/python3/dist-packages (from ncclient) (2.9.3)
Requirement already satisfied: setuptools>0.6 in /usr/lib/python3/dist-packages (from ncclient) (59.6.0)
Requirement already satisfied: six in /usr/lib/python3/dist-packages (from ncclient) (1.16.0)
Building wheels for collected packages: ncclient
  Building wheel for ncclient (setup.py) ... done
  Created wheel for ncclient: filename=ncclient-0.6.13-py2.py3-none-any.whl size=84643 sha256=5cc61ba8cc0
  Stored in directory: /root/.cache/pip/wheels/86/9b/b4/27799df81d6faea66359dfb4843c099c8d486e2f064cbf9d5
Successfully built ncclient
Installing collected packages: lxml, ncclient
Successfully installed lxml-4.9.3 ncclient-0.6.13
```

Figure 11.67: Successfully installed the dependencies

Let us install few dependencies and packages:

```
root@ip-172-31-33-97:/etc/ansible# c
root@ip-172-31-33-97:/etc/ansible# pip3 install xmltodict
Requirement already satisfied: xmltodict in /usr/lib/python3/dist-packages (0.12.0)
```

Figure 11.68: Other package is already up to the mark

We can see that one package was installed in the control machine, and the second one was already enabled. So, let us go ahead and have a look at the role:

```
root@ip-172-31-33-97:/etc/ansible# cat roles/junos/tasks/main.yml
- name: Demo of Hostname
  junipernetworks.junos.junos_hostname:
    config:
      hostname: 'ashutosh'
root@ip-172-31-33-97:/etc/ansible#
root@ip-172-31-33-97:/etc/ansible#
```

Figure 11.69: Role to change the device host name the junos target host

We also need to modify the playbook as the connection type is going to be changed for this hostname module of Ansible. This will be the case with the **junos_config** module too:

```
root@ip-172-31-33-97:/etc/ansible# cat networkplay.yaml
---
- name: First playbook
  hosts: all
  connection: ansible.netcommon.netconf
  vars:
    ansible_command_timeout: 300
  gather_facts: false
  roles:
  - junos
root@ip-172-31-33-97:/etc/ansible#
```

Figure 11.70: Playbook with new role and command timeout

So we have changed my connection to **ansible.netcommon.netconf** for the junos configuration. Let us go ahead and run our playbook now, as follows:

```
root@ip-172-31-33-97:/etc/ansible# ansible-playbook  networkplay.yaml --ask-vault-password
Vault password:

PLAY [First playbook] ***********************************************************

TASK [junos : Merge provided HOSTNAME configuration into running configuration.] ***
fatal: [3.109.211.151]: FAILED! => {"changed": false, "msg": "Could not open socket to 3.109.211.151:830"}

PLAY RECAP ***********************************************************
3.109.211.151              : ok=0    changed=0    unreachable=0    failed=1    skipped=0    rescued=0    ig
```

Figure 11.71: Unexpected error on the execution

Note: **Since fonts are small enough, hence we are pasting the error below so all of us can read it correctly:**

Error: fatal: [3.109.211.151]: FAILED! => {"changed": false, "msg": "Could not open socket to 3.109.211.151:830"}

It is unusual that Ansible is trying to communicate on the port number 830, so let us open that port on the firewall and then we will re execute the code, as follows:

```
root@ip-172-31-33-97:/etc/ansible#
root@ip-172-31-33-97:/etc/ansible# ansible-playbook  networkplay.yaml
Vault password:

PLAY [First playbook] *********************************************

TASK [junos : Demo of Hostname] **********************************
changed: [3.109.211.151]

PLAY RECAP *******************************************************
3.109.211.151              : ok=1    changed=1    unreachable=0    fai
```

Figure 11.72: Playbook execution successful after opening port 830

As expected, this time it worked. So, we had a few extra things to do in this Ansible module and this was a good learning for us. Let us go ahead with the new Juniper module.

junos_config module

The next important topic we want to cover here is **junos_config** module of Ansible. Now, you can configure almost everything with this module of Ansible. However, there are specific modules for your requirements which might be more suitable for you, but the **config** module is able to do almost everything in the Juniper router:

```
root@ip-172-31-33-97:/etc/ansible# cat roles/junosconfig/tasks/main.yml
- name: Check correctness of commit configuration
  junipernetworks.junos.junos_config:
    lines:
      - set groups aws-default system login user demo authentication encrypted-password "$6$8OcN
      - set groups aws-default system login user demo class super-user
root@ip-172-31-33-97:/etc/ansible#
```

Figure 11.73: Demo role to send the configuration on the junos target host

As we can see, the parameters looks similar to **ios_config** module. Now, we have the parameter comment available in the **junos_config** module to put the commit comment. Since we had no option of commit in the IOS devices, this option was not needed and is not present there. However, with **junos_config** module, we can put the commit comments; however, this is not mandatory.

Let us go ahead with the execution of our code as follows:

```
root@ip-172-31-33-97:/etc/ansible#
root@ip-172-31-33-97:/etc/ansible# ansible-playbook  networkplay.yaml --ask-vault-password
Vault password:

PLAY [First playbook] **************************************************************

TASK [junosconfig : Check correctness of commit configuration] ********************
changed: [3.109.211.151]

PLAY RECAP ***********************************************************************
3.109.211.151              : ok=1    changed=1    unreachable=0    failed=0    skipped=0

root@ip-172-31-33-97:/etc/ansible#
```

Figure 11.74: Successful playbook execution with code

As we can see, the execution is successful.

Let us go ahead and log into the target host, and see if the hostname is changed, and we have the required username in place, as shown in the following figure:

```
root@ip-172-31-33-97:/etc/ansible# ssh ashutmch@3.109.211.151
(ashutmch@3.109.211.151) Password:
Last login: Mon Jul 10 16:22:17 2023 from 13.126.31.37
--- JUNOS 21.4R3-S1.5 Kernel 64-bit XEN JNPR-12.1-20220922.ad9d8a5_buil
ashutmch@ashutosh> show configuration | display set
set version 21.4R3-S1.5
set groups aws-default system root-authentication encrypted-password *disabled*
set groups aws-default system scripts translation max-datasize 512m
set groups aws-default system login user ec2-user full-name juniper-aws-ec2-user
set groups aws-default system login user ec2-user uid 100
set groups aws-default system login user ec2-user class super-user
set groups aws-default system login user ec2-user authentication ssh-rsa "ssh-rsa AAAAE
jvvITojyjCkd3zaFcvvBYdfaXvnSaoUffUDBY0ozr7CRHlA8mkmFkCBEycbJZaUYf7AQW50G5h64aiqCuW0qQPI
9NZ9tmNlgNFqleQnwrlgyH+UMUOL6CGfAlgbbwnnxxY/wwUqpFw6iC7fGFVX1XPNSN+p45N9hxEH AnsibleHos
set groups aws-default system login user ashutmch uid 2000
set groups aws-default system login user ashutmch class super-user
set groups aws-default system login user ashutmch authentication encrypted-password "$6
set groups aws-default system login user demo uid 2001
set groups aws-default system login user demo class super-user
set groups aws-default system login user demo authentication encrypted-password "$6$80
set groups aws-default system services ssh
set groups aws-default system services netconf ssh
set groups aws-default system services web-management https system-generated-certificat
set groups aws-default system license autoupdate url https://ae1.juniper.net/junos/key_
set groups aws-default system interfaces fxp0 unit 0 family inet dhcp
set apply-groups aws-default
set system host-name ashutosh
```

Figure 11.75: Configuration pushed using Ansible is present on the target router

As we can see, the executed changes are present in the target host. So, this is how we can configure the Juniper target host. Similarly, we can use the **junos_facts** module too, as shown in the following figure:

```
root@ip-172-31-33-97:/etc/ansible# cat roles/junosconfig/tasks/main.yml
- name: collect default set of facts
  junipernetworks.junos.junos_facts:
root@ip-172-31-33-97:/etc/ansible#
```

Figure 11.76: junos_facts module of Ansible

Now, let us go ahead and execute our code and verify the results from the execution summary:

```
root@ip-172-31-33-97:/etc/ansible# ansible-playbook  networkplay.yaml --ask-vault-password -v
Using /etc/ansible/ansible.cfg as config file
Vault password:

PLAY [First playbook] ******************************************************************

TASK [junosconfig : collect default set of facts] *************************************
ok: [3 109.211.151] => {"ansible_facts": {"ansible_net_api": "netconf", "ansible_net_gather_netw
sh", "ansible_net_model": "vSRX", "ansible_net_python_version": "3.10.6", "ansible_net_serialnum
ble_network_resources": {}}, "changed": false}

PLAY RECAP **********************************************************************
3.109.211.151            : ok=1     changed=0    unreachable=0    failed=0    skipped=0    resc
```

Figure 11.77: Debug clearly shows the expected junos_facts

As we can see, the **junos_facts** are right in front of us. This can be used further in your playbook and roles as well, so feel free to combine all the knowledge and create your own playbooks and roles. As we all know, the best way to learn is by doing it ourselves. There will be a few failures while trying to read the error and understanding them, but always refer to the official documents for the latest update about the module. You can always use the **ansible-galaxy** to install the new module.

Cumulus Linux NCLU module

As we have seen, Ansible has a wide range of options for all sorts of target hosts. Whether it is Cisco, Juniper or even cumulus networking device, Ansible is there to help you. Now, for people who do not know anything about the cumulus Linux, it is basically a whitebox switching device. You can use any vendor's bare metal switch, assign cumulus Linux on top of that, and your switch is ready. Now, there are two ways of configuring the cumulus Linux. One is the traditional Linux way of working. If you want, you can use the **shell** module of Ansible, and things should be sorted. Alternatively, you can use the **Network Command Line Utility** (**NCLU**) module of Ansible. Since we have already used the shell module enough and we know how to use it this time, we will go ahead with the NCLU module of Ansible.

Since cumulus switch was not present in the AWS, we had to turn back to the personal computer and use the virtualization environment to create this lab.

Let us go ahead and have a look at the role and how we can use that:

We know that the first line is the **name** of the task, second is the name of module, and third parameter is the **commands**. Inside the **commands**, we have created a list of **commands** which will enable the switch port in the cumulus switch:

```
[root@localhost ansible]# cat roles/cumulus/tasks/main.yml
---
# tasks file for cumulus
- name: Demo of cumulus Module ansible
  nclu:
    commands:
       - add int swp2
       - add int swp3
[root@localhost ansible]#
```

Figure 11.78: Role to send commands on the cumulus target host using nclu module

Now, we as a user do not need to commit the changes as they will be done by the module itself. We just need to put the **commands** and remember to not use the **net** keyword in the **commands** when we use this module.

Let us have a look at the playbook, as shown in the following figure:

```
[root@localhost ansible]# cat cumulus.yaml
---
- name: demo
  #connection: local
  hosts: all
  roles:
   - cumulus
[root@localhost ansible]#
```

Figure 11.79: Playbook for the cumulus switch

Just remember that **connection: local** is commented/hashed so that is not being used. Rest all things are known to us.

Let us go ahead with the execution of our script as shown in the following figure:

```
PLAYBOOK: cumulus.yaml ***********************************************************
1 plays in cumulus.yaml

PLAY [demo] *********************************************************************

TASK [Gathering Facts] *********************************************************

[WARNING]: Platform linux on host 192.168.178.198 is using the discovered
Python interpreter at /usr/bin/python, but future installation of another
Python interpreter could change this. See https://docs.ansible.com/ansible/2
reference_appendices/interpreter_discovery.html for more information.
ok: [192.168.178.198]
META: ran handlers

TASK [Demo of cumulus Module ansible] ******************************************

changed: [192.168.178.198] => {"changed": true, "msg": "\n"}
META: ran handlers
META: ran handlers

PLAY RECAP *********************************************************************
192.168.178.198            : ok=2    changed=1    unreachable=0    failed=0
kipped=0    rescued=0    ignored=0
```

Figure 11.80: Playbook execution shows the changes perform on the target host

As we can see the execution was successful.

Since we were not able to see the execution on the terminal, we will run it in the debug mode this time:

```
changed: [192.168.178.198] => {
    "changed": true,
    "invocation": {
        "module_args": {
            "abort": false,
            "atomic": false,
            "commands": [
                "add int swp2",
                "add int swp3"
            ],
            "commit": false,
            "description": "Ansible-originated commit",
            "template": null
        }
    },
    "msg": "\n"
}
```

Figure 11.81: Debug of playbook execution shows the configuration pushed

As we can see, the commands being executed on the target hosts are visible and at last **commit** will be performed with the comment description. Right now, in the preceding example, you see the **commit: false**, since the changes were already pushed to the devices when we ran this code for the first time in demo.

So, this is how you can push and execute any NCLU command on the cumulus switch. Rest all modules like **register**, **debug** and **filters** are going to work in the same way in all Ansible modules.

Let us go ahead and try to run a show command on the cumulus switch this time, as shown in the following figure:

```
[root@localhost ansible]# cat roles/cumulus/tasks/main.yml
---
# tasks file for cumulus
- name: Demo of cumulus Module ansible
  nclu:
    commands:
      - show configuration
      - show interface
[root@localhost ansible]#
```

Figure 11.82: Sending the show commands on the target host

This time we will execute the show configuration and the show interface command on the target host. So, let us run these commands and see the output as follows:

```
[root@localhost ansible]# ansible-playbook cumulus.yaml -u cumulus -k -v
Using /etc/ansible/ansible.cfg as config file
SSH password:
```

Figure 11.83: Playbook execution

We have suppressed the extra lines from the output to make it neat and clean:

```
\n     priority1\n      255\n    \n    priority2\n      255\n    \n    domainNu
ber\n     0\n    \n    logging_level\n    5\n    \n    path_trace_enabled\n
   0\n    \n    use_syslog\n    1\n    \n    verbose\n     0\n    \n    sum
ary_interval\n      0\n    \n    time_stamping\n      hardware\n\nnlog syslog in
ormational\n\ninterface lo\n   # The primary network interface\n\ninterface eth0
n  address dhcp\n\ninterface swp1\n  address 192.168.178.198/24\n\nhostname nor
1234password\n\ndot1x\n    mab-activation-delay 30\n    eap-reauth-period 0\n   \n
adius\n     accounting-port 1813\n    authentication-port 1812\n\n\n# The above
utput is a summary of the configuration state of the switch.\n# Do not cut and
aste this output into /etc/network/interfaces or any other\n# configuration fil
.   This output is intended to be used for troubleshooting\n# when you need to s
e a summary of configuration settings.\n#\n# Please use \"net show configuratio
commands\" for a configuration that\n# you can back up or copy and paste into
new device.\n\nState  Name  Spd  MTU    Mode          LLDP  Summary\n----- --
- --- ----- ----------  ----  --------------------\nUP     lo    N/A   65
36  Loopback       IP: 127.0.0.1/8\n       lo
     IP: ::1/128\nUP     eth0  1G   1500   Mgmt          IP: 10.0.2.15/2
(DHCP)\nUP    swp1  1G   1500   Interface/L3   IP: 192.168.178.198/24\n\n
}

PLAY RECAP *********************************************************************
192.168.178.198            : ok=2    changed=1    unreachable=0    failed=0
kipped=0    rescued=0    ignored=0
```

Figure 11.84: Successful playbook execution shows us the output of the show commands

As we can see, the output is visible on the terminal. Now, we can use the **stdout** and **stdout_lines** with the variable. If we like the JSON or YAML, this can be achieved using filters too.

Conclusion

In this chapter, we have learned how we can automate the network using Ansible. We have covered two major vendors from the market. You might need to go through few basics of networking to understand this chapter.

In the next chapter, we will focus on security, and how we can secure our infrastructure using Ansible.

References

- https://docs.ansible.com/ansible/latest/playbook_guide/playbooks_delegation.html
- https://docs.ansible.com/ansible/latest/collections/cisco/ios/ios_facts_module.html
- https://docs.ansible.com/ansible/latest/playbook_guide/playbooks_conditionals.html
- https://docs.ansible.com/ansible/latest/playbook_guide/playbooks_error_handling.html#defining-failure
- https://docs.ansible.com/ansible/latest/collections/ansible/builtin/regex_escape_filter.html
- https://docs.ansible.com/ansible/latest/collections/cisco/ios/index.html
- https://docs.ansible.com/ansible/latest/collections/Junipernetworks/junos/junos_command_module.html#ansible-collections-Junipernetworks-junos-junos-command-module
- https://docs.ansible.com/archive/ansible/2.5/modules/ios_config_module.html
- https://docs.ansible.com/ansible/latest/collections/community/network/nclu_module.html

Join our Discord space

Join our Discord workspace for latest updates, offers, tech happenings around the world, new releases, and sessions with the authors:

https://discord.bpbonline.com

CHAPTER 12
Ansible for Security

Introduction

Security is not optional anymore. It is an essential part of any organization. As they say, data is new gold, and those with it are considered rich. Data breaches hurt every company badly, and financial loss is only a small part of that damage. Losing confidential customer data may result in losing faith from the customer, investors, and stakeholders, and regaining that faith can take years and years of hard work. So, security should be the number one priority of any company. Let us go ahead and look at how we can secure our infrastructure.

Structure

This chapter contains the following topics:

- Cisco Adaptive Security Appliance command module
- Cisco Adaptive Security Appliance config module
- Cisco Adaptive Security Appliance ACL module
- Checkpoint firewall modules
- Juniper SRX firewall
- Hardening of the server and infrastructure
- Making network gear security compliance

Objectives

In this chapter, we will focus on firewalls, the first line of defense for securing any infrastructure. Large enterprises may contain thousands of firewalls. So, managing them manually can be a time-consuming job. Hence, we will learn how to achieve this task using Ansible. By the end of this chapter, you will learn about the firewall and the tasks we can do at the server and host level.

To begin, we will pick the Cisco **Adaptive Security Appliance (ASA)** as our first firewall and will explore the modules of Cisco ASA.

Cisco Adaptive Security Appliance command module

Just like Cisco IOS router and switches, the Cisco ASA has the ASA command module. We can run any show command on the firewall. The parameters are just like the IOS command module, so we will not spend much time on it.

Let us go ahead and have a look at the role:

```
root@ip-172-31-33-97:/etc/ansible# cat roles/asa/tasks/main.yml
---
- name: Show commands on the ASA FW
  cisco.asa.asa_command:
    commands:
    - show version

root@ip-172-31-33-97:/etc/ansible#
```

Figure 12.1: Role to run show commands on Cisco ASA

Now, Cisco ASA will prompt us to enable password in this case, and we will need to change the become method to the enable and provide the enable password for the ASA.

Figure 12.2 shows how we can define the enable password for the Cisco ASA firewalls:

```
root@ip-172-31-33-97:/etc/ansible# cat roles/asa/vars/main.yml
---
ansible_user: ashutmch
ansible_password:
ansible_become_password:
root@ip-172-31-33-97:/etc/ansible#
```

Figure 12.2: Credentials in variable files

At the same time, we need to change the network OS type. In the case of Cisco IOS devices, it was IOS, but now it is an ASA firewall. We need to change the OS to ASA; otherwise, it will give us an error.

Figure 12.3 shows us how we can define the network OS information in Ansible using host vars. Now, based on your Ansible version, you might not even requires to define it, but if you get an error, then this is how you can achieve it:

```
root@ip-172-31-33-97:/etc/ansible# cat hosts
[router]
13.127.249.183
[router:vars]
  ansible_network_os = asa
```

Figure 12.3: Defining the network OS information from host vars

Let us run the following code now:

```
root@ip-172-31-33-97:/etc/ansible# ansible-playbook networkplay.yaml -v
Using /etc/ansible/ansible.cfg as config file

PLAY [First playbook] ********************************************************

TASK [asa : Show the ASA version] *******************************************
[WARNING]: ansible-pylibssh not installed, falling back to paramiko
ok: [13.127.249.183] => {"changed": false, "stdout": ["Cisco Adaptive Security
n\nCompiled on Mon 28-Nov-22 15:50 GMT by builders\nSystem image file is \"boo
me 28 secs\n\nHardware:   ASAv, 7680 MB RAM, CPU Xeon 4100/6100/8100 series 35
rmware Hub @ 0x0, 0KB\n\n\n 0: Ext: Management0/0      : address is 0ada.30a7
nASAv Platform License State: Unlicensed\nNo active entitlement: no feature ti
atform:\nMaximum VLANs            : 200          \nInside Hosts
     : Enabled          \nEncryption-3DES-AES          : Enabled
\nAnyConnect Premium Peers      : 2          \nAnyConnect Essentials
   : 750          \nAnyConnect for Mobile        : Disabled        \n
d License          : Disabled       \nTotal TLS Proxy Sessions
 Enabled        \n\nSerial Number: 9AD41QP7AF0\n\nImage type        : Releas
stdout_lines": [["Cisco Adaptive Security Appliance Software Version 9.19(1) "
15:50 GMT by builders", "System image file is \"boot:/asa9191-smp-k8.bin\"",  "
ardware:   ASAv, 7680 MB RAM, CPU Xeon 4100/6100/8100 series 3599 MHz, 1 CPU (
b @ 0x0, 0KB", "", "", " 0: Ext: Management0/0       : address is 0ada.30a7.c9
ng", "ASAv Platform License State: Unlicensed", "No active entitlement: no fea
s for this platform:", "Maximum VLANs             : 200           ",
Encryption-DES            : Enabled       ", "Encryption-3DES-AES
        : Disabled       ", "AnyConnect Premium Peers       : 2
   ", "Total VPN Peers              : 750           ", "AnyConnect for M
 Assessment     : Disabled       ", "Shared License            : Disa
ed       ", "Cluster             : Enabled       ", "", "Seria
 modified by enable_15 at 22:00:41.137 UTC Thu Jul 13 2023"]]}

PLAY RECAP ******************************************************************
13.127.249.183          : ok=1     changed=0    unreachable=0    failed=0
```

Figure 12.4: Debug shows us the output of show version command

We can see that the execution is successful. This is how we can run the show commands on the target host.

Now, the **register** and **debug** module will work here too. So, feel free to use the **register** module and name the variable. Then, you can either **copy** it or display the output on the terminal using **debug**.

Cisco Adaptive Security Appliance config module

Just like the ASA command module, the config module is also easy to use. We will cover a basic example of creating network objects, as you will be doing that very frequently while configuring your firewall.

The concept of parent and child lines is going to be the same here too. The object-group network **DemoNetwork**, the parent command, will be executed first, and then the lines will be added to the network object. Similarly, you can create many objects and **object-group**:

```
root@ip-172-31-33-97:/etc/ansible# cat roles/asa/tasks/main.yml
- cisco.asa.asa_config:
    lines:
    - network-object host 10.20.3.1
    - network-object host 10.30.70.1
    - network-object host 10.40.0.1
    parents: [object-group network DemoNetwork]
root@ip-172-31-33-97:/etc/ansible#
```

Figure 12.5: Demo role to configure the network objects

Let us run it now:

```
root@ip-172-31-33-97:/etc/ansible#
root@ip-172-31-33-97:/etc/ansible# ansible-playbook networkplay.yaml -v
Using /etc/ansible/ansible.cfg as config file

PLAY [First playbook] **********************************************************

TASK [asa : cisco.asa.asa_config] **********************************************
[WARNING]: ansible-pylibssh not installed, falling back to paramiko
changed: [13.127.249.183] => {"changed": true, "updates": ["object-group network DemoNetwork",
0.1"]}

PLAY RECAP *********************************************************************
13.127.249.183             : ok=1    changed=1    unreachable=0    failed=0    skipped=0    re
```

Figure 12.6: Play recap shows the successfully updated the object group

Execution output:

changed: [13.127.249.183] => {"changed": true, "updates": ["object-group network DemoNetwork", "network-object host 10.20.3.1", "network-object host 10.30.70.1", "network-object host 10.40.0.1"]}

Cisco Adaptive Security Appliance ACL module

In this section, we will have a look at the tasks you will need to do on a daily basis in your firewall, that is, the addition of a firewall rule. The main purpose of the firewall is to stop unauthorized access to your internal server, and we will need to put the **Access Control List** (**ACL**) in place for that. This is how we can achieve it.

So, let us go ahead and start using that:

```
root@ip-172-31-33-97:/etc/ansible# cat roles/asa/tasks/main.yml
- name: Merge provided configuration with device configuration
  cisco.asa.asa_acls:
    config:
      acls:
        - name: DemoACL
          acl_type: extended
          aces:
          - grant: permit
            line: 1
            protocol_options:
              tcp: true
            source:
              object_group: DemoNetwork
            destination:
              address: 192.0.3.0
              netmask: 255.255.255.0
              port_protocol:
                eq: www
            log: default
root@ip-172-31-33-97:/etc/ansible#
```

Figure 12.7: Role to create the firewall rule in Cisco ASA

In the following figure, a firewall access control list is being created:

```
root@ip-172-31-33-97:/etc/ansible#
root@ip-172-31-33-97:/etc/ansible# ansible-playbook networkplay.yaml -v
Using /etc/ansible/ansible.cfg as config file

PLAY [First playbook] ******************************************************

TASK [asa : Merge provided configuration with device configuration] *******
[WARNING]: ansible-pylibssh not installed, falling back to paramiko
changed: [13.127.249.183] => {"after": {"acls": [{"aces": [{"destination": {"address": "192.0.3.
, "log": "default", "protocol": "tcp", "protocol_options": {"tcp": true}, "source": {"object_gro
 true, "commands": ["access-list DemoACL line 1 extended permit tcp object-group DemoNetwork 19

PLAY RECAP *****************************************************************
13.127.249.183             : ok=1    changed=1    unreachable=0    failed=0    skipped=0    res
```

Figure 12.8: Play recap debug shows the successful creation of firewall rule

The execution is successful.

Let us go ahead and verify the same from the target firewall itself:

```
ciscoasa# sh run access-li
ciscoasa# sh run access-list
access-list DemoACL extended permit tcp object-group DemoNetwork 192.0.3.0 255.255.255.0 eq www log default
ciscoasa#
ciscoasa#
ciscoasa#
```

Figure 12.9: ASA output confirms the firewall rule is created in the ASA

We can also see the **object-group** created on the target ASA device:

```
ciscoasa# sh run object-group network
object-group network OG-MONITORED-SERVERS
 network-object host 10.80.30.18
 network-object host 10.80.30.19
 network-object host 10.80.30.20
object-group network DemoNetwork
 network-object host 10.20.3.1
 network-object host 10.30.70.1
 network-object host 10.40.0.1
ciscoasa#
```

Figure 12.10: Host defined under the network object DemoNetwork

Let us discuss these options in detail:

```
- name: Merge provided configuration with device configuration
  cisco.asa.asa_acls:
    config:
      acls:
        - name: DemoACL
          acl_type: extended        1
          aces:
          - grant: permit           2
            line: 1
            protocol_options:        3
              tcp: true
            source:                  4
              object_group: DemoNetwork
            destination:             5
              address: 192.0.3.0
              netmask: 255.255.255.0
              port_protocol:         6
                eq: www
            log: default
```

Figure 12.11: Decoding the firewall rule line by line

The ACL module has a lot of parameters, and you need networking skills to understand them a bit more. If you do not know much about networking, then ACLs are access control list that allows and block communication from source to destination. In general, the source is internet, and the destinations are your internal web server and database servers. There are a few terminologies which we are going to use here, which may be difficult at first.

Some terminologies are as follows:

- **ACL type**: There are two kinds of ACL options in this module of Ansible:
  - ○ Standard
  - ○ Extended

- **Grant**: Grant also has two options in this module. As expected, they are permit and deny. Now there are lot many things in the modern next gen firewall but in this module, we just have two options:
  - ○ Permit
  - ○ Deny

- **Protocol_options**: There are many options in this category, but there are few of them which are most used. They are:
  - ○ TCP
  - ○ UDP
  - ○ ICMP
  - ○ IP

  Now, there are more options than these four discussed previously. However, they are not frequently used. If you need to explore more of them, refer to the following link attached for more options:

  https://docs.ansible.com/ansible/latest/collections/cisco/asa/asa_acls_module. html#ansible-collections-cisco-asa-asa-acls-module

- **Source**: This is where we define the source address information. Now, this might be kept wide open from the internet, and we can choose from the many options available, but if you have IP address details, you can put the address and objects too. Let us have a look at a few mostly used options:
  - ○ Object-group
  - ○ Address
  - ○ Any/any4/any6 (Boolean, which means we need to configure the true/false option)
  - ○ Host/interface
  - ○ Netmask

- **Destination**: This the place where we provide the information about the target host. Now, the choices are the same as the source. All the object-group, address, and netmask, host, and interface options work great with it.

- **Port_options**: This is the place where we define the destination port information and the protocol information. Now, this is valid for just TCP/UDP, as the options like IP and ICM are not valid for the port numbers. Let us have a look at a few mostly used options:

o **Eq**: Match the given port number. For example, eq: 443 will allow only https.

o **Gt**: Match the port number greater than this port. Example: gt:80 all the ports above 80 will be allowed.

o **Lt**: Match the port number lesser than this port. Example: lt:443 which will allow all the ports smaller than 443. So, in simple words 0-443 range will be applied.

o **Range**: We can also define a range that has the start and end port number. Example:

```
- name: Merge provided configuration with device configuration
  cisco.asa.asa_acls:
    config:
      acls:
        - name: DemoACL
          acl_type: extended
          aces:
            - grant: permit
              line: 1
              protocol_options:
                tcp: true
              source:
                object_group: DemoNetwork
              destination:
                address: 192.0.3.0
                netmask: 255.255.255.0
                port_protocol:
                  range:
                    start: 80
                    end: 443
```

Figure 12.12: How to define the port range in asa acls module of Ansible

This is how we can assign the different parameters to the role and module. Once this is done, the playbook is ready to run. As we have seen, the successful execution, at the same time verify it on the target host that ACLs are available.

Checkpoint firewall modules

Cisco ASA has a limited number of modules, and they are able to do everything in ASA, however, for **Checkpoint (CP)**, things are quite different. CP has lot more modules and features than the ASA, but since this book is not focused entirely on Checkpoint and security, we will have a look at a few mostly used modules only. ACL is one of the most important things any security engineer has to build, so we will try focusing on that.

We know that the default way of connecting to the target host is SSH in Ansible, but we can use a connection method like WinRM too. There is one more category that we talked about when we were learning about the basics of Ansible. Now is the time when we should explore the third option too, that is, API calls. Ansible can be easily used to make the API calls to the target hosts.

Now, the Checkpoint can be configured using web API, and that is what we will use as a connection method when we try to connect the Checkpoint and configure it. Checkpoint has two components as follows:

- Security gateway
- Security management

We generally configure the policies from the security management server, and they are applied on the security gateways, but this time, we will use the web APIs to configure the policies, and we will verify the policy from the security management server. Let us go ahead and do some pre-requisites first.

We will start with the installation of a few packages which is required for the control machine to work efficiently with Checkpoint devices:

1. The first thing is installing a package for the Ansible Checkpoint management server. That can be done using the following command:

```
ansible-galaxy collection install check_point.mgmt
```

2. Once the required package is in place, we need to make sure the firewall ports are allowed to facilitate the web API communication.

3. Web API should be enabled from the Smart Console. So, we need to navigate the Smart Console of CP and navigate to the **MANAGE & SETTINGS** | **Blades** | **Management API** | **Advanced Settings**, as shown in *Figure 12.13* and *Figure 12.14*:

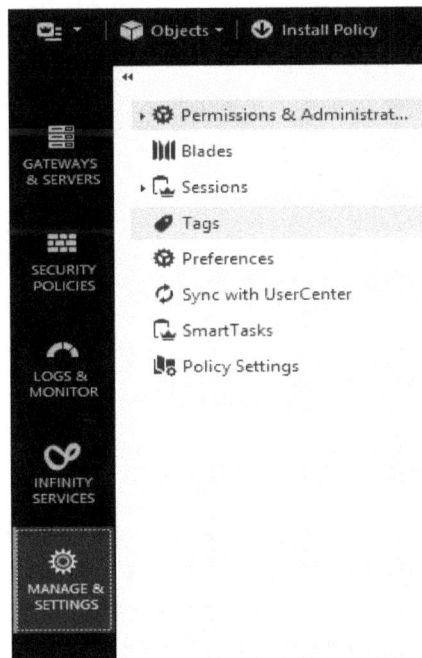

Figure 12.13: Navigate to the MANAGE & SETTINGS

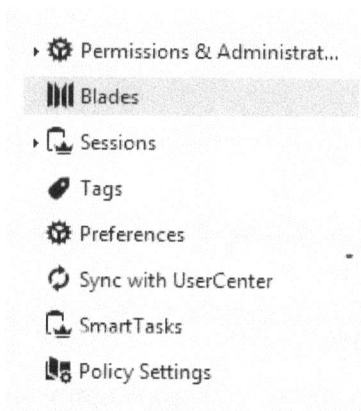

Figure 12.14: Selecting blades for Checkpoint firewall

In *Figure 12.14*, we have selected the required blades. You will select your blades based on requirements and license purchased by your organization:

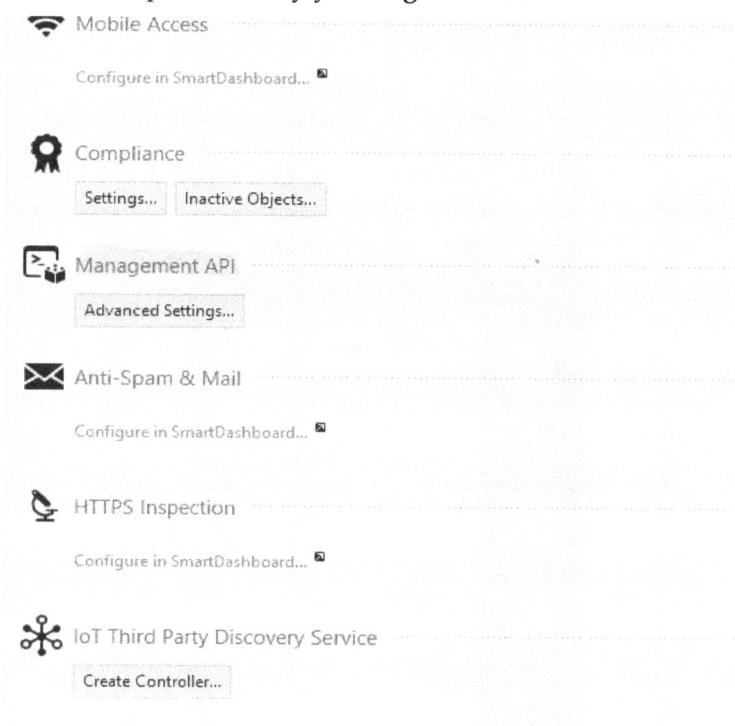

Figure 12.15: Navigate to the management API

We need to allow the API call from all the IP addresses in this example. You can choose the IP address based on your requirements:

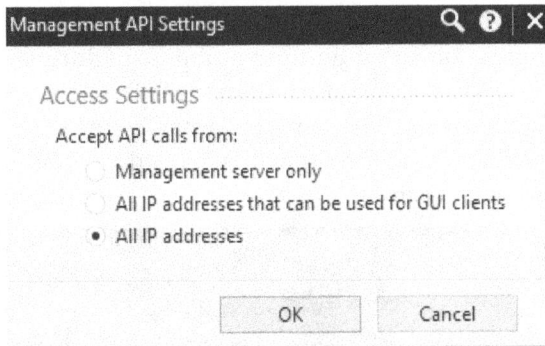

Figure 12.16: Allowing all IP addresses in access settings

The default selected value is the management server only. Change it to the **ALL IP addresses**/second option, whichever suits your organization.

4. Next, we need to set up the variable file, as shown in the following figure:

```
root@ip-172-31-33-97:/etc/ansible# cat hosts
[router]
#65.1.145.153
172.31.26.75
[router:vars]
ansible_httpapi_use_ssl=True
ansible_httpapi_validate_certs=False
ansible_network_os=check_point.mgmt.checkpoint
```

Figure 12.17: API configuration for the Checkpoint

5. Since it is a self-signed certificate, we have disabled the SSL cert validation. We have enabled the use of SSL at the first line, and at the last, we have defined the right network OS.

6. Remember that in the playbook, we need to modify the connection type. Since we will be using the web APIs, the connection type will be **httpapi** in this case:

```
root@ip-172-31-33-97:/etc/ansible# cat cpplaybook.yaml
---
- name: Testing
  hosts: all
  connection: httpapi
```

Figure 12.18: New option of httpapi in connection type

Now that we have done all the required work, we are good to proceed further with our first role of Checkpoint. Let us use the Ansible Galaxy and create it.

In the first module, we have used it to define the address range, and as we have to define the address range, there will be a first address and a last address. This is going to be an object we need to name, so we can call it further in the rule. In the end, we need to define a state where we will inform Ansible whether we want to create the object or delete it. Since we are performing some changes to the firewall, we need to publish the changes. We will see **auto_publish_session** as **true**:

```
root@ip-172-31-33-97:/etc/ansible# cat roles/checkpoint/tasks/main.yml
---
- name: Demo Objects
  cp_mgmt_address_range:
    auto_publish_session: true
    ip_address_first: 172.10.2.1
    ip_address_last: 172.10.2.10
    name: juniper
    state: present
- name: Demo policy push
  cp_mgmt_install_policy:
    access: true
    policy_package: standard
    targets:
    -  i-062f58f0f9324311c
    threat_prevention: true
```

Figure 12.19: Role to create object and push the policy

The second task is to install the policy, as the changes will not be reflected on the box automatically, we need to install the policy on the target router. There is a different module for installing the changes on the device, and we have used the same for our work here. Let us go ahead and execute our code:

```
root@ip-172-31-33-97:/etc/ansible# ansible-playbook networkplay.yaml -u admin -k
SSH password:

PLAY [First playbook] ********************************************************

TASK [checkpoint : Demo Objects] ********************************************
changed: [172.31.26.75]

TASK [checkpoint : Demo policy push] ****************************************
changed: [172.31.26.75]

PLAY RECAP ******************************************************************
172.31.26.75               : ok=2    changed=2    unreachable=0    failed=0    sk
```

Figure 12.20: Successful playbook execution

We can see the execution is successful. Now, either we can log into the target host and check the object from the smart console, or we can use the facts module of Ansible to verify the things:

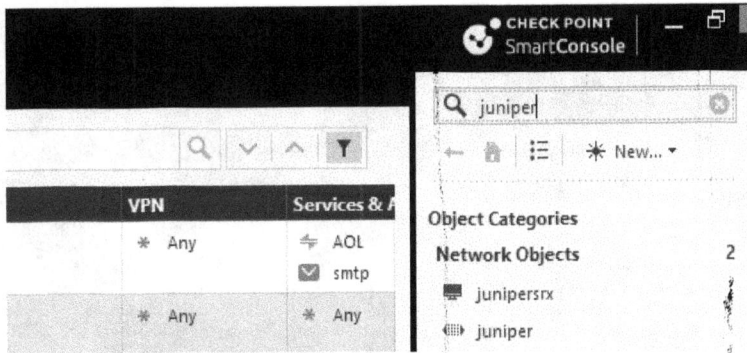

Figure 12.21: Object is successfully created on the target host

We can see the network object Juniper has been created on the target host. Let us go ahead and create a firewall rule. Now, offline, we have created two objects for our next firewall rule. The first one is **Junipersrx**, and the second one is **ciscoasa,** so we will call them in the rule now.

Let us have a look on the rule:

```
root@ip-172-31-33-97:/etc/ansible# cat roles/cprule/tasks/main.yml
---
- name: Create a permit rule
  cp_mgmt_access_rule:
    auto_publish_session: yes
    layer: Network
    position: top
    name: "permit_rule"
    source: ciscoasa
    destination: junipersrx
    service:
    - SMTP
    - AOL
    action: accept

- name: Demo policy push
  cp_mgmt_install_policy:
    access: true
    policy_package: standard
    targets:
    -  i-062f58f0f9324311c
    threat_prevention: true
```

Figure 12.22: Role to create the firewall rule and publish policy

It is important to read the role and understand it, as we have been creating many roles. We will start the execution and see the results:

Figure 12.23: Play recap shows the successful creation of firewall rule

The execution is successful on the target host. Let us go ahead and verify if the firewall rule is present on the firewall.

We can see in *Figure 12.23,* rule **1** is present in the firewall, and it is successfully added to our CP FW. This is how you can add any firewall rule in CP:

No.	Name	Source	Destination	VPN	Services & /
1	`permit_rule`	🖥 ciscoasa	🖥 junipersrx	✳ Any	⇴ AOL
					✉ smtp
⁃	… … …	—	—		

Figure 12.24: Firewall rule is created on the target host after playbook execution

You can also run the modules like facts. In the following output, we have used **cp_mgmt_access_rule_facts** module of Ansible.

We have intentionally not entered the rule details, as it is recommended that you should try it yourself and learn. Now, we are in that phase of our book where you should be reading the documents and understanding the Ansible modules by yourself.

```
root@ip-172-31-33-97:/etc/ansible# ansible-playbook backup.yaml -u admin -k -v
Using /etc/ansible/ansible.cfg as config file
SSH password:

PLAY [Testing] ************************************************************

TASK [Gathering Facts] ****************************************************
ok: [172.31.26.75]

TASK [show-access-rulebase] ***********************************************
ok: [172.31.26.75] => {"ansible_facts": {"access-rulebase": {"from": 1, "name":
oint Data", "uid": "a0bbbc99-adef-4ef8-bb6d-defdefdefdef"}, "icon": "Actions/ac
lor": "sienna", "domain": {"domain-type": "domain", "name": "SMC User", "uid":
last": "255.255.255.255", "name": "All_Internet", "type": "address-range", "uid
: "Check Point Data", "uid": "a0bbbc99-adef-4ef8-bb6d-defdefdefdef"}, "icon": "
"color": "red", "domain": {"domain-type": "data domain", "name": "Check Point D
190", "type": "service-tcp", "uid": "97aeb44f-9aea-11d5-bd16-0090272ccb30"}, {"
00c9fde"}, "icon": "Objects/host", "ipv4-address": "192.168.100.123", "name": "
n-type": "data domain", "name": "Check Point Data", "uid": "a0bbbc99-adef-4ef8-
-8eec-4103-ad21-cd461ac2c473"}, {"color": "black", "domain": {"domain-type": "d
ess": "9.9.9.9", "name": "junipersrx", "type": "host", "uid": "6a74c6fa-5411-46
 "uid": "a0bbbc99-adef-4ef8-bb6d-defdefdefdef"}, "icon": "Track/tracksLog", "na
ain-type": "data domain", "name": "Check Point Data", "uid": "a0bbbc99-adef-4ef
8fe-b6b1-d59bd88036f9"}, {"color": "none", "domain": {"domain-type": "data doma
 "name": "Policy Targets", "type": "Global", "uid": "6c488338-8eec-4103-ad21-cd
```

Figure 12.25: Output of Checkpoint access rule facts

Ansible has many modules for the Checkpoint and what we wanted to do is explore a few more modules of the Checkpoint. You can find more modules here:

https://galaxy.ansible.com/check_point/mgmt

Moving on, you can try things like snort and other blades of Checkpoint using Ansible. Believe us, the modules are there for the same. Also, you can write an entire code to upgrade the Checkpoint firewall from scratch. Just remember the basic concepts, and things will be good.

Juniper SRX firewall

The good news is that we have already covered the Juniper SRX in our networking modules. There, we used both the **config** and **command** module of Ansible. The same **config** module will be used for the configuration of the firewall, so we are not going to duplicate the content here again.

Assignment

Let us do an assignment. First of all, try adding the firewall rule using the config module of Ansible. Once that is done, we need to start exploring the `junos_security_policies_ module`.

Now, your task is to add a firewall rule that allows the traffic from 8.8.8.8 to your internal server, which is located at the 10.20.20.40 IP address. Use the logic and concept we learn so far in this book, as the concept is going to be the same.

Hardening of the server and infrastructure

We know security is an essential part of any organization. Enabling a few firewall rules is not going to secure our infrastructure completely. Yes, it would help a lot, but we still need to make sure that all the sections and layers of our organizations are secured and well-tightened. We need to ensure we do not have any bugs in our application, secure our server and database, and block unauthorized access to the devices.

Let us go ahead and see how we can harden the servers and infrastructure of our organization.

Now, Ansible Galaxy has some pre-developed collections of security modules for us. We can directly read and deploy them based on our requirements. At the time of writing this book, **ansible-os-hardening** was the highest rated OS hardening role available. So, let us go ahead and proceed further with it. Check the following documents about the things covered in this role:

https://galaxy.ansible.com/kmonticolo/ansible-os-hardening

In short, this module will offer security-related configuration. Now, this will not install the security packages on the target hosts, so we need to club it with the upgrade modules used in our last chapters.

Note: There are major chances that it will break a few things in production since we have habits of using unsecured things. Using this script, we will block those loopholes and break the things in production. So first we need to run this code in the pre-production, and analyze the impact. Once we know the impact, we need to mitigate the things one by one. For example, this role will remove the TFTP and if you are still using TFTP for something in your organization then you are writing welcome note to the hackers. You need to move to the SFTP and once all mitigations are done you can run it in the production.

Let us go ahead and use the following command to install the role:

```
ansible-galaxy install kmonticolo.ansible_os_hardening
```

```
root@ip-172-31-33-97:/etc/ansible# ansible-galaxy install dev-sec.os-hardening
Starting galaxy role install process
- downloading role 'os-hardening', owned by dev-sec
- downloading role from https://github.com/dev-sec/ansible-os-hardening/archive/6.2.0.tar.gz
- extracting dev-sec.os-hardening to /root/.ansible/roles/dev-sec.os-hardening
- dev-sec.os-hardening (6.2.0) was installed successfully
```

Figure 12.26: Command to download dev-sec or hardening package using Ansible Galaxy

We can see the role has been copied to the **/root/.ansible/roles** directory. We have copied it to our **/etc/ansible/roles** and modified it there:

```
root@ip-172-31-33-97:/etc/ansible/roles/dev-sec.os-hardening# ll
total 140
drwxr-xr-x 10 root root  4096 Jul 18 15:21 ./
drwxr-xr-x 12 root root  4096 Jul 18 15:21 ../
-rw-r--r--  1 root root   625 Jul 18 15:21 .gitattributes
drwxr-xr-x  4 root root  4096 Jul 18 15:21 .github/
-rw-r--r--  1 root root    28 Jul 18 15:21 .gitignore
-rw-r--r--  1 root root  1659 Jul 18 15:21 .kitchen.vagrant.yml
-rw-r--r--  1 root root  3616 Jul 18 15:21 .kitchen.yml
-rw-r--r--  1 root root  1496 Jul 18 15:21 .travis.yml
-rw-r--r--  1 root root 36564 Jul 18 15:21 CHANGELOG.md
-rw-r--r--  1 root root  4043 Jul 18 15:21 CONTRIBUTING.md
-rw-r--r--  1 root root   381 Jul 18 15:21 Gemfile
-rw-r--r--  1 root root 11759 Jul 18 15:21 README.md
-rw-r--r--  1 root root   335 Jul 18 15:21 Rakefile
-rw-r--r--  1 root root   197 Jul 18 15:21 TODO.md
-rw-r--r--  1 root root   564 Jul 18 15:21 ansible.cfg
drwxr-xr-x  2 root root  4096 Jul 18 15:21 defaults/
drwxr-xr-x  2 root root  4096 Jul 18 15:21 handlers/
-rw-r--r--  1 root root   164 Jul 18 15:21 kitchen_vagrant_block.r
drwxr-xr-x  2 root root  4096 Jul 18 15:21 meta/
-rw-r--r--  1 root root   290 Jul 18 15:21 rhel6_provision.rb
-rw-r--r--  1 root root   231 Jul 18 15:21 suse_provision.rb
drwxr-xr-x  2 root root  4096 Jul 18 15:22 tasks/
drwxr-xr-x  4 root root  4096 Jul 18 15:21 templates/
drwxr-xr-x  2 root root  4096 Jul 18 15:21 tests/
drwxr-xr-x  2 root root  4096 Jul 18 15:21 vars/
root@ip-172-31-33-97:/etc/ansible/roles/dev-sec.os-hardening#
root@ip-172-31-33-97:/etc/ansible/roles/dev-sec.os-hardening#
root@ip-172-31-33-97:/etc/ansible/roles/dev-sec.os-hardening# pwd
/etc/ansible/roles/dev-sec.os-hardening
root@ip-172-31-33-97:/etc/ansible/roles/dev-sec.os-hardening#
```

Figure 12.27: List of files and tasks in the hardening package

As we can see, it has multiple tasks we should read before executing them in the production:

```
root@ip-172-31-33-97:/etc/ansible/roles/dev-sec.os-hardening/tasks# ll
total 76
drwxr-xr-x  2 root root 4096 Jul 18 15:22 ./
drwxr-xr-x 10 root root 4096 Jul 18 15:21 ../
-rw-r--r--  1 root root  207 Jul 18 15:21 apt.yml
-rw-r--r--  1 root root  302 Jul 18 15:22 auditd.yml
-rw-r--r--  1 root root 1394 Jul 18 15:21 hardening.yml
-rw-r--r--  1 root root 1000 Jul 18 15:21 limits.yml
-rw-r--r--  1 root root  168 Jul 18 15:21 login_defs.yml
-rw-r--r--  1 root root   70 Jul 18 15:21 main.yml
-rw-r--r--  1 root root 1737 Jul 18 15:21 minimize_access.yml
-rw-r--r--  1 root root 1025 Jul 18 15:21 modprobe.yml
-rw-r--r--  1 root root 3804 Jul 18 15:21 pam.yml
-rw-r--r--  1 root root  430 Jul 18 15:21 profile.yml
-rw-r--r--  1 root root  611 Jul 18 15:21 rhosts.yml
-rw-r--r--  1 root root  149 Jul 18 15:21 securetty.yml
-rw-r--r--  1 root root  128 Jul 18 15:21 selinux.yml
-rw-r--r--  1 root root 1140 Jul 18 15:21 suid_sgid.yml
-rw-r--r--  1 root root 2326 Jul 18 15:21 sysctl.yml
-rw-r--r--  1 root root 1316 Jul 18 15:21 user_accounts.yml
-rw-r--r--  1 root root 1498 Jul 18 15:21 yum.yml
root@ip-172-31-33-97:/etc/ansible/roles/dev-sec.os-hardening/tasks#
```

Figure 12.28: List of YAML code for the hardening

Let us go ahead and create a rule and execute the same:

```
root@ip-172-31-33-97:/etc/ansible# cat devsec.yaml
- name: Dev-Sec work
  hosts: all
  roles:
    - dev-sec.os-hardening
  become: true
root@ip-172-31-33-97:/etc/ansible#
```

Figure 12.29: Playbook to run the hardening role

Execution results:

```
root@ip-172-31-33-97:/etc/ansible# ansible-playbook devsec.yaml -u ashutmch -k -K
SSH password:
BECOME password[defaults to SSH password]:

PLAY [Dev-Sec work] ********************************************************

TASK [Gathering Facts] ****************************************************
[WARNING]: Platform linux on host 172.31.5.52 is using the discovered Python interprete
meaning of that path. See https://docs.ansible.com/ansible-core/2.14/reference_appendic
ok: [172.31.5.52]

TASK [dev-sec.os-hardening : Set OS family dependent variables] ***********
ok: [172.31.5.52]

TASK [dev-sec.os-hardening : Set OS dependent variables] *****************
ok: [172.31.5.52] => (item=/etc/ansible/roles/dev-sec.os-hardening/vars/Amazon.yml)

TASK [dev-sec.os-hardening : install auditd package | package-08] ********
ok: [172.31.5.52]

TASK [dev-sec.os-hardening : configure auditd | package-08] **************
ok: [172.31.5.52]

TASK [dev-sec.os-hardening : create limits.d-directory if it does not exist | sysctl-31
ok: [172.31.5.52]
```

Figure 12.30: Playbook execution for the OS hardening

Output suppressed since it is going to perform 70+ tasks and we cannot show the execution status of all of them. Hence, the output is removed after a few tasks and shows only the results at the lasts:

```
ok: [172.31.5.52] => (item=/etc/dnf/dnf.conf)
ok: [172.31.5.52] => (item=/etc/yum/pluginconf.d/rhnplugin.conf)

PLAY RECAP *******************************************************************************
172.31.5.52                : ok=40    changed=17    unreachable=0    failed=1    skipped=25

root@ip-172-31-33-97:/etc/ansible#
```

Figure 12.31: Play recap summary which shows the 17 changes performed 1 failed and 25 skipped

A total of 17 changes were performed on the target hosts. A few of them were skipped, and one failed too. So, this is how we can perform the hardening of the server. Remember to test it in the pre-production first and mitigate the issues first and then use it in production in the maintenance window.

We can create our own role where we will disable things like TFTP, telnet and so on, and enable the features, like firewall, iptables, etc. Clubbing the preceding modules with the upgrade packages is a good idea as the security packages will be installed on the target host and that way the entire server will be secured and well tightened.

Apart from this, we need to make sure the users change their password frequently and never store the same in a clear text file. Remembering the password is always a good thing but if you cannot remember it, then you can still use things like password vault, which are secure and safe.

Always try the top command whenever you log into the host and see the top utilizing the process. If you have something suspicious going on in your network, then this is the point where you should focus.

Making network gear security compliance

One of the biggest problems we see in the network gear is permitting any policy, and that is as bad as removing the entire firewall. So, you can write an automation script to look for a wide permit policy and see if that permits any traffic.

The second most important thing is a weak enable password and a default SNMP string. Now, many people use the public as their SNMP string, and if you know that, hackers know it, too. So, keeping the default SNMP string is always a bad thing. You should write a code and search for the default configuration of SNMP. Now that the telnet and http are obsolete from the modern network, and if you still have those things enabled in your company, then you need to migrate to https and ssh.

Not changing the root/admin password for years is also a big loophole in any company. Our job should be to change that password frequently. You should write an automation script to change that password to the new one at a regular interval. You can use cronjob to automate things here.

Since we have already covered most of the network OS modules in Ansible, we will not create duplicate content here to show the demo of the compliance role for network gears.

Conclusion

In this chapter, we have learned how to configure the firewall rules and perform server hardening. However, this is not enough to secure infrastructure. We need to work hard every day to make our infrastructure safe and secure. Hackers come up with day 0 attack, and we cannot be prepared for the attack which is not yet created. So, we need to make sure all the patching is done on time. Make our teams aware of the security and stay updated about what hackers are doing nowadays.

In the next chapter, we will automate the Docker Kubernetes.

References

- **https://galaxy.ansible.com/check_point/mgmt**
- **https://galaxy.ansible.com/kmonticolo/ansible-os-hardening**
- **https://www.redhat.com/en/blog/implementing-security-benchmarks-red-hat-ansible-automation-platform**

Join our Discord space

Join our Discord workspace for latest updates, offers, tech happenings around the world, new releases, and sessions with the authors:

https://discord.bpbonline.com

CHAPTER 13

Installation of Kubernetes

Introduction

Kubernetes is a very important and essential thing for any DevOps engineer, so you need to spend some time to understand and learn K8. Once you have grabbed a good hold on it, we can start automating it. In this chapter, we will skip the learning Kubernetes or K8 part as this book is not focused on Kubernetes. So, let us directly jump into the process of installing Kubernetes on the target host first and, then, we can go ahead with the rest. Let us use Ansible to install it on the target host.

Structure

This chapter contains the following topics:

- Installation of Kubernetes and Docker
- Running K8 Pod for NGINX
- Installation of Docker APK
- Playbooks for gathering information about the image
- Playbook for container management
- Playbooks to execute commands in a Docker container

Objectives

At the end of this chapter, you will learn how you can manage your Kubernetes and Docker clusters using Ansible and how you can perform various configuration changes to them. You will learn how you can create a Kubernetes Pod and perform various operations.

Installation of Kubernetes and Docker

Kubernetes and Docker can be installed manually, but we do not want to do it. Let us use Ansible modules to install them. Now, we are not going to use anything new here; we will simply use the **yum** installer and **shell** module of Ansible to do this.

```
root@ip-172-31-33-97:/etc/ansible# cat roles/kuberpackage/tasks/main.yml
---
- name: Install the latest version of docker
  ansible.builtin.yum:
    name: docker
    state: latest

- name: Start the services of Docker
  ansible.builtin.shell: |
    systemctl start docker
    systemctl enable docker
    curl -LO "https://dl.k8s.io/release/$(curl -L -s https://dl.k8s.io/release/stable.txt)/bin/linux/amd64/kubectl"
    sudo install -o root -g root -m 0755 kubectl /usr/local/bin/kubectl


root@ip-172-31-33-97:/etc/ansible#
```

Figure 13.1: Role to install Docker and kubectl

So, in the first task, we have used the **yum** installer to install the latest package of Docker and in the second task, we have sent a bunch of commands. We can use the **|** to send multiple commands to the target host.

The first two commands are used for starting the service and enabling the docker, and the last two commands are used to download and install the **kubectl**. Now, for those of you who do not know what **kubectl** is, **kubectl** is a command line tool that helps us manage the K8 cluster.

Let us run the following code and see the result:

```
root@ip-172-31-33-97:/etc/ansible# ansible-playbook  devsec.yaml -u ashutmch -k -K
SSH password:
BECOME password[defaults to SSH password]:

PLAY [Dev-Sec work] *****************************************************************

TASK [Gathering Facts] **************************************************************
[WARNING]: Platform linux on host 172.31.5.52 is using the discovered Python interp
meaning of that path. See https://docs.ansible.com/ansible-core/2.14/reference_appe
ok: [172.31.5.52]

TASK [kuberpackage : Install the latest version of docker] **************************
changed: [172.31.5.52]

TASK [kuberpackage : Start the services of Docker] *********************************
changed: [172.31.5.52]

PLAY RECAP *************************************************************************
172.31.5.52              : ok=3    changed=2    unreachable=0    failed=0    skip
```

Figure 13.2: Successful playbook execution

We can see the execution was successful. Let us go back to the target host and verify whether both of these things are working or not:

```
[root@ip-172-31-5-52 ~]# kubectl version --client --output=yaml
clientVersion:
  buildDate: "2023-07-19T12:20:54Z"
  compiler: gc
  gitCommit: fa3d7990104d7c1f16943a67f11b154b71f6a132
  gitTreeState: clean
  gitVersion: v1.27.4
  goVersion: go1.20.6
  major: "1"
  minor: "27"
  platform: linux/amd64
kustomizeVersion: v5.0.1

[root@ip-172-31-5-52 ~]# service docker status
Redirecting to /bin/systemctl status docker.service
● docker.service - Docker Application Container Engine
   Loaded: loaded (/usr/lib/systemd/system/docker.service; enabled; vendor
   Active: active (running) since Sat 2023-07-22 21:45:46 UTC; 7min ago
     Docs: https://docs.docker.com
 Main PID: 11293 (dockerd)
   CGroup: /system.slice/docker.service
           └─11293 /usr/bin/dockerd -H fd:// --containerd=/run/containerd/c
```

Figure 13.3: Kubectl and docker installed successfully

We could have used the **`yum`** module to install the **`kubectl`**, but we wanted to see a way of pushing multiple commands using the **`shell`** module, so we chose this method. However, just for demo purposes, let us look at the installation of **`kubelet`** using **`yum`** installer:

```
root@ip-172-31-33-97:/etc/ansible# cat roles/kuberpackage/tasks/main.yml
---
- name: Install the latest version of docker
  ansible.builtin.yum:
    name: docker
    state: latest

- name: Install the latest version of docker
  ansible.builtin.yum:
    name: kubelet
    state: latest


- name: Start the services of Docker
  ansible.builtin.shell: |
    systemctl start docker
    systemctl enable docker
    curl -LO "https://dl.k8s.io/release/$(curl -L -s https://dl.k8s.io/release/stable.txt
    sudo install -o root -g root -m 0755 kubectl /usr/local/bin/kubectl
```

Figure 13.4: Role to install docker, kubelet and kubectl with activating services

Let us try to execute the code. For a few of you, this will prompt some errors but for rest, it might work:

```
root@ip-172-31-33-97:/etc/ansible#  ansible-playbook  devsec.yaml  -u ashutmch -k -K
SSH password:
BECOME password[defaults to SSH password]:

PLAY [Dev-Sec work] ***********************************************************************

TASK [Gathering Facts] ********************************************************************
[WARNING]: platform linux on host 172.31.5.52 is using the discovered Python interpreter at /usr/bin/python
meaning of that path. See https://docs.ansible.com/ansible-core/2.14/reference_appendices/interpreter_disco
ok: [172.31.5.52]

TASK [kube:package : Install the latest version of docker] ********************************
ok: [172.31.5.52]

TASK [kube:package : Install the latest version of docker] ********************************
fatal: [172.31.5.52]: FAILED! => {"changed": false, "msg": "No package matching 'kubelet' found available,
available, installed or updated"}]
```

Figure 13.5: Expected error of kubelet missing

We have found an error here, which says that there is no package as **kubelet**. Now, we need to offer the right **rpm** to the target host where it can find the right packages to install.

What we have done here is to search the official website of Kubernetes, find out their repo, and add the same in our shell module configuration:

```
---
- name: Install the latest version of docker
  ansible.builtin.yum:
    name: docker
    state: latest
- name: Start the services of Docker
  ansible.builtin.shell: |
    systemctl start docker
    systemctl enable docker
    curl -LO "https://dl.k8s.io/release/$(curl -L -s https://dl.k8s.i
    sudo install -o root -g root -m 0755 kubectl /usr/local/bin/kubect
    cat <<EOF | sudo tee /etc/yum.repos.d/kubernetes.repo
    [kubernetes]
    name=Kubernetes
    baseurl=https://packages.cloud.google.com/yum/repos/kubernetes-el7
    enabled=1
    gpgcheck=1
    gpgkey=https://packages.cloud.google.com/yum/doc/yum-key.gpg https
    EOF

- name: Install the latest version of kubelet
  ansible.builtin.yum:
    name: kubelet
    state: latest
  ignore_errors: true
```

Figure 13.6: Role to add Kubernetes repo using shell module

Specific configuration for the repo addition:

```
curl -LO "https://dl.k8s.io/release/$(curl -L -s https://dl.k8s.io/release/stable.txt)/bin/linux/amd64/kubectl"
sudo install -o root -g root -m 0755 kubectl /usr/local/bin/kubectl
cat <<EOF | sudo tee /etc/yum.repos.d/kubernetes.repo
[kubernetes]
name=Kubernetes
baseurl=https://packages.cloud.google.com/yum/repos/kubernetes-el7-\$basearch
enabled=1
gpgcheck=1
gpgkey=https://packages.cloud.google.com/yum/doc/yum-key.gpg https://packages.cloud.google.com/yum/doc/rpm-package-key.gpg
EOF

- name: Install the latest version of docker
```

Figure 13.7: Specific code from the role to add repo

Let us run the code and see if the things are working fine:

```
root@ip-172-31-33-97:/etc/ansible# ansible-playbook devsec.yaml
SSH password:
BECOME password[defaults to SSH password]:

PLAY [Dev-Sec work] ****************************************

TASK [Gathering Facts] ************************************
[WARNING]: Platform linux on host 172.31.5.52 is using the discov
meaning of that path. See https://docs.ansible.com/ansible-core/2
ok: [172.31.5.52]

TASK [kuberpackage : Install the latest version of docker] ******
ok: [172.31.5.52]

TASK [kuberpackage : Start the services of Docker] *************
changed: [172.31.5.52]

TASK [kuberpackage : Install the latest version of kubelet] *****
changed: [172.31.5.52]

PLAY RECAP ***********************************************
172.31.5.52                : ok=4    changed=2    unreachable=0
```

Figure 13.8: Successful playbook execution

This time, the installation was successful. Let us go back to the target host and see if the things are good:

```
[root@ip-172-31-5-52 ~]# service kubelet status
Redirecting to /bin/systemctl status kubelet.service
● kubelet.service - kubelet: The Kubernetes Node Agent
   Loaded: loaded (/usr/lib/systemd/system/kubelet.service;
   Active: inactive (dead)
     Docs: https://kubernetes.io/docs/
[root@ip-172-31-5-52 ~]#
```

Figure 13.9: kubelet is still inactive after successful playbook execution

When we see the status of services, we find them to be inactive. Let us go back to *Figure*

13.6 and see why the services are still inactive. If you have figured it out, then good, but if you have not, then the answer is very simple. We have not started the **kubelet** services, so let us do it now and wait for the result.

New role:

```
root@ip-172-31-33-97:/etc/ansible# cat roles/kuberpackage/tasks/main.yml
---
- name: Install the latest version of docker
  ansible.builtin.yum:
    name: docker
    state: latest
- name: Start the services of Docker
  ansible.builtin.shell: |
    systemctl start docker
    systemctl enable docker
    curl -LO "https://dl.k8s.io/release/$(curl -L -s https://dl.k8s.io/
    sudo install -o root -g root -m 0755 kubectl /usr/local/bin/kubectl
    cat <<EOF | sudo tee /etc/yum.repos.d/kubernetes.repo
    [kubernetes]
    name=Kubernetes
    baseurl=https://packages.cloud.google.com/yum/repos/kubernetes-el7-
    enabled=1
    gpgcheck=1
    gpgkey=https://packages.cloud.google.com/yum/doc/yum-key.gpg https:/
    EOF

- name: Install the latest version of kubelet
  ansible.builtin.yum:
    name: kubelet
    state: latest
  ignore_errors: true

- name: start kubelet services
  service:
    name: kubelet
    enabled: yes
    state: started
```

Figure 13.10: Service module to start the kubelet services

Now, we could use the old way of activating the services, where we can use the command or shell module, and that also works great. However, to use the variety of code and share a variety of options, we have used the service module to activate the services. So, let us now run it:

```
root@ip-172-31-33-97:/etc/ansible# ansible-playbook  devsec.yaml -u ashutmch
SSH password:
BECOME password[defaults to SSH password]:

PLAY [Dev-Sec work] **********************************************************

TASK [Gathering Facts] ******************************************************
[WARNING]: Platform linux on host 172.31.5.52 is using the discovered Python
meaning of that path. See https://docs.ansible.com/ansible-core/2.14/referenc
ok: [172.31.5.52]

TASK [kuberpackage : Install the latest version of docker] ******************
ok: [172.31.5.52]

TASK [kuberpackage : Start the services of Docker] **************************
changed: [172.31.5.52]

TASK [kuberpackage : Install the latest version of kubelet] *****************
ok: [172.31.5.52]

TASK [kuberpackage : start kubelet services] ********************************
changed: [172.31.5.52]

PLAY RECAP ******************************************************************
172.31.5.52                  : ok=5    changed=2    unreachable=0    failed=0
```

Figure 13.11: Successful playbook exeuction

This time the execution was successful. Let us go back to the target host and see if the things are operational:

```
[root@ip-172-31-5-52 ~]# service kubelet status
Redirecting to /bin/systemctl status kubelet.service
● kubelet.service - kubelet: The Kubernetes Node Agent
   Loaded: loaded (/usr/lib/systemd/system/kubelet.service; enabled; vendor pre
   Active: active (running) since Sun 2023-07-23 09:35:29 UTC; 1min 9s ago
     Docs: https://kubernetes.io/docs/
 Main PID: 18552 (kubelet)
    Tasks: 10
```

Figure 13.12: Kubelet services are finally active

As we can see, the services are up now. Now, we need to disable a few services, which may cause problems for us while execution. Now, we are not going to create the demo of that as we know the name of the modules and how to do that. So, you can do that yourself and consider that as your assignment. Let us have a look at the final role, which will be as follows:

```
root@ip-172-31-33-97:/etc/ansible# cat roles/kuberpackage/tasks/main.yml
---
- name: Start the services of Docker
  ansible.builtin.shell: |
    curl -LO "https://dl.k8s.io/release/$(curl -L -s https://dl.k8s.io/rel
    sudo install -o root -g root -m 0755 kubectl /usr/local/bin/kubectl
    cat <<EOF | sudo tee /etc/yum.repos.d/kubernetes.repo
    [kubernetes]
    name=Kubernetes
    baseurl=https://packages.cloud.google.com/yum/repos/kubernetes-el7-\$b
    enabled=1
    gpgcheck=1
    gpgkey=https://packages.cloud.google.com/yum/doc/yum-key.gpg https://p
    EOF

- name: Install the latest version of kubelet
  ansible.builtin.yum:
    name: "{{item}}"
    state: latest
  with_items:
    - kubelet
    - docker
    - kubeadm
    - kubernetes-cni
  ignore_errors: true

- name: start kubelet services
  service:
    name: "{{item}}"
    enabled: yes
    state: started
  with_items:
    - kubelet
    - docker

root@ip-172-31-33-97:/etc/ansible#
```

Figure 13.13: Installing few couple of services using loops with Ansible

Here, we can see that we have created two loops and iterated a list against that variable. Since we have many things to install in the target host, it will be a good idea to create a loop and parse the different package name to make our life easy.

Now, let us run it and see the results:

```
root@ip-172-31-33-97:/etc/ansible# ansible-playbook  devsec.yaml -u ashutmch -k -K
SSH password:
BECOME password[defaults to SSH password]:

PLAY [Dev-Sec work] ***************************************************************

TASK [Gathering Facts] **** *******************************************************
[WARNING]: Platform linux o  host 172.31.5.52 is using the discovered Python interprete
meaning of that path. See h tps://docs.ansible.com/ansible-core/2.14/reference_appendic
ok: [172.31.5.52]

TASK [kuberpackage : Start  he services of Docker] ********************************
changed: [172.31.5.52]

TASK [kuberpackage : Install the latest version of kubelet] **********************
ok: [172.31.5.52] => (item= ubelet)
ok: [172.31.5.52] => (item= ocker)
changed: [172.31.5.52] => (item=kubeadm)
ok: [172.31.5.52] => (item= ubernetes-cni)

TASK [kuberpackage : start k belet services] *************************************
ok: [172.31.5.52] => (item=k belet)
ok: [172.31.5.52] => (item=d cker)
```

Figure 13.14: Play recap shows the execution performed one item at a time

In the result, we can see the packages being iterated one by one. Now, **kubelet** and **docker** were installed already, and therefore, it was showing **ok**, which means that this is already present in the target host. **kubeadm**, is the new package we recently added to the list, and that is installed while this execution and that is why we are seeing **changed item=kubeadm**. In the end, Kubernetes **Container Network Interface (CNI)** services were already installed with the other packages and that is why that shows as **ok** too.

Finally, we need to enable the stateful firewall bridge. The way to do that is simple. It is shown as follows:

```
- name: IPTABLES Configuration
  ansible.builtin.shell: |
    cat << EOF | sudo tee /etc/sysctl.d/k8s.conf
    net.bridge.bridge-nf-call-ip6tables = 1
    net.bridge.bridge-nf-call-iptables = 1
    EOF
    sudo sysctl --system
```

Figure 13.15: Enabling the stateful firewall bridge

Now, we have used a simple shell command module here to set the value to 1. The other option in Ansible is to use the **sysctl** module of ansible. We will see the same thing by using both of these Ansible modules:

```
- name: start kubelet services
  service:
    name: "{{item}}"
    enabled: yes
    state: started
  with_items:
    - kubelet
    - docker

- name: IPTABLES Configuration
  ansible.builtin.shell: |
    cat << EOF | sudo tee /etc/sysctl.d/k8s.conf
    net.bridge.bridge-nf-call-ip6tables = 1
    net.bridge.bridge-nf-call-iptables = 1
    EOF
    sudo sysctl --system

root@ip-172-31-33-97:/etc/ansible#
root@ip-172-31-33-97:/etc/ansible# ansible-playbook  devsec.yaml -u ashutmch
SSH password:
BECOME password[defaults to SSH password]:

PLAY [Dev-Sec work] ********************************************************

TASK [Gathering Facts] *****************************************************
[WARNING]: Platform linux on host 172.31.5.52 is using the discovered Python
meaning of that path. See https://docs.ansible.com/ansible-core/2.14/reference
ok: [172.31.5.52]

TASK [kuberpackage : Start the services of Docker] *************************
changed: [172.31.5.52]

TASK [kuberpackage : Install the latest version of kubelet] ****************
ok: [172.31.5.52] => (item=kubelet)
ok: [172.31.5.52] => (item=docker)
ok: [172.31.5.52] => (item=kubeadm)
ok: [172.31.5.52] => (item=kubernetes-cni)

TASK [kuberpackage : start kubelet services] ******************************
ok: [172.31.5.52] => (item=kubelet)
ok: [172.31.5.52] => (item=docker)

TASK [kuberpackage : IPTABLES Configuration] ******************************
changed: [172.31.5.52]

PLAY RECAP ****************************************************************
172.31.5.52                : ok=5    changed=2    unreachable=0    failed=0
```

Figure 13.16: *Successful playbook execution shows IPTABLES changes performed on the target host*

We can see that our execution is successful and we can verify the same by logging into the target host. So, let us do it now and see the result:

```
root@ip-172-31-33-97:/etc/ansible# ssh ashutmch@172.31.5.52
ashutmch@172.31.5.52's password:
Last login: Sun Jul 23 11:21:09 2023 from ip-172-31-33-97.ap-s

    _|  _|_  )
   _|  (    /    Amazon Linux 2 AMI
   _|\___|___|

https://aws.amazon.com/amazon-linux-2/
21 package(s) needed for security, out of 23 available
Run "sudo yum update" to apply all updates.
[ashutmch@ip-172-31-5-52 ~]$ cat /etc/sysctl.d/k8s.conf
net.bridge.bridge-nf-call-ip6tables = 1
net.bridge.bridge-nf-call-iptables = 1
```

Figure 13.17: Output clearly show the iptable rule is present in the target host

As expected, the **iptable** rules are present on the target host.

Let us go ahead and try using the **sysctl** module of Ansible:

```
- name: start kubelet services
  service:
    name: "{{item}}"
    enabled: yes
    state: started
  with_items:
    - kubelet
    - docker

- name: enable IPTABLES STATEFUL FW Bridge
  sysctl:
    name: "{{item}}"
    value: 1
    state: present
    reload: false
  with_items:
    - net.bridge.bridge-nf-call-ip6tables
    - net.bridge.bridge-nf-call-iptables
root@ip-172-31-33-97:/etc/ansible#
```

Figure 13.18: Role to push the iptable rules using sytctl module

This is how we can do it by using the **sysctl** module of Ansible. Since we had to set the value for IPv4 and IPv6, we have used the loop. There is no sense in putting same module configuration twice for two commands:

```
TASK [kuberpackage : Install the latest version of kubelet] ******
ok: [172.31.5.52] => (item=kubelet)
ok: [172.31.5.52] => (item=docker)
ok: [172.31.5.52] => (item=kubeadm)
ok: [172.31.5.52] => (item=kubernetes-cni)

TASK [kuberpackage : start kubelet services] ********************
ok: [172.31.5.52] => (item=kubelet)
ok: [172.31.5.52] => (item=docker)

TASK [kuberpackage : enable IPTABLES STATEFUL FW Bridge] *********
ok: [172.31.5.52] => (item=net.bridge.bridge-nf-call-ip6tables)
ok: [172.31.5.52] => (item=net.bridge.bridge-nf-call-iptables)

PLAY RECAP ******************************************************
172.31.5.52                  : ok=5    changed=1    unreachable=0
```

Figure 13.19: Successful playbook execution

This is how our final execution looks like. As expected, things are good. Now that we are done with the configuration of the master node, let us launch the child node and do the required configuration.

Refer to the following figure:

```
root@ip-172-31-33-97:/etc/ansible# ansible-playbook  devsec.yaml -u ashutmch -k -K
SSH password:
BECOME password[defaults to SSH password]:

PLAY [Dev-Sec work] *********************************************************

TASK [Gathering Facts] *****************************************************
[WARNING]: Platform linux on host 172.31.15.85 is using the discovered Python interprete
meaning of that path. See https://docs.ansible.com/ansible-core/2.14/reference_appendice
ok: [172.31.15.85]

TASK [kuberpackage : Start the services of Docker] *************************
changed: [172.31.15.85]

TASK [kuberpackage : Install the latest version of kubelet] ***************
changed: [172.31.15.85] => (item=kubelet)
changed: [172.31.15.85] => (item=docker)
changed: [172.31.15.85] => (item=kubeadm)
ok: [172.31.15.85] => (item=kubernetes-cni)

TASK [kuberpackage : start kubelet services] ******************************
changed: [172.31.15.85] => (item=kubelet)
changed: [172.31.15.85] => (item=docker)

TASK [kuberpackage : enable IPTABLES STATEFUL FW Bridge] ******************
changed: [172.31.15.85] => (item=net.bridge.bridge-nf-call-ip6tables)
changed: [172.31.15.85] => (item=net.bridge.bridge-nf-call-iptables)

PLAY RECAP ***************************************************************
172.31.15.85              : ok=5    changed=4    unreachable=0    failed=0    skipped=0
```

Figure 13.20: Successful playbook execution on the child node

Now, we have run the same playbook on the child node. kubectl was not needed on the child node but we still ran it, however, we will remove it manually later if that creates the issue in our cluster creation. Let us go ahead with the further configurations.

Playbook creating the Kubernetes objects

The master node, which we created, was t2.micro, and that is not enough for creating a master node, since it requires at least 2vCPU and enough RAM, which was not present in our host. So, we had to terminate our old instance and create a new one from the scratch. We could have increased the resources, but wanted a new one, so here we are with the new master node.

Figure 13.21 shows us how we can create the Kubernetes objects using Ansible:

```
root@ip-172-31-33-97:/etc/ansible# cat roles/masternode/tasks/main.yml
---
- name: Start the services of Docker
  ansible.builtin.shell: |
    kubeadm config images pull
- name: initiate the master node
  ansible.builtin.shell: kubeadm init --apiserver-advertise-address=172.31.1.216 --pod-network-cidr 10.1(
  register: output
- debug:
    msg: "{{output}}"
- name: start kubelet services
  service:
    name: "{{item}}"
    enabled: yes
    state: restarted
  with_items:
    - kubelet
    - docker
- name: directory
  file:
    path: $HOME/.kube
    state: directory
    mode: 0766
- name: kube configuration copy
  copy:
    src: /etc/kubernetes/admin.conf
    dest: /root/.kube/config
    remote_src: yes
- name: Flannel configuration
  command: kubectl apply -f https://github.com/coreos/flannel/raw/master/Documentation/kube-flannel.yml
```

Figure 13.21: Role to create the master node

The entire command is not visible in the preceding figure, so the same is as follows:

```
kubeadm    init    --apiserver-advertise-address=x.x.x.x    --pod-network-cidr
10.10.0.0/16 --ignore-preflight-errors=all
```

Let us go ahead and execute it:

```
root@ip-172-31-33-97:/etc/ansible# ansible-playbook  devsec.yaml -u ashutmch -k -K
SSH password:
BECOME password[defaults to SSH password]:

PLAY [Dev-Sec work] ************************************************************

TASK [Gathering Facts] ********************************************************
[WARNING]: Platform linux on host 172.31.1.216 is using the discovered Python interpret
meaning of that path. See https://docs.ansible.com/ansible-core/2.14/reference_appendi
ok: [172.31.1.216]

TASK [masternode : Start the services of Docker] *****************************
changed: [172.31.1.216]

TASK [masternode : initiate the master node] ********************************
changed: [172.31.1.216]

TASK [masternode : debug] ****************************************************
ok: [172.31.1.216] => {
    "msg": {
        "changed": true,
        "cmd": "kubeadm init --apiserver-advertise-address=172.31.1.216 --pod-network-
        "delta": "0:00:06.630343",
        "end": "2023-07-23 14:51:00.224320",
        "failed": false,
        "msg": "",
        "rc": 0,
```

Figure 13.22: Successful playbook execution

Output suppressed:

```
        "",
        "Then you can join any number of worker nodes by running the following on each as root:",
        "",
        "kubeadm join 172.31.1.216:6443 --token p2muqk.y2hk89d59q6af2vp \\",
        "\t--discovery-token-ca-cert-hash sha256:216dac72d186c2e6e8731ca71a1b9a4b3913ab2a32d5875b31b3fe43df830b77 "
    ]
  }
}
TASK [masternode : start kubelet services] *********************************************************
changed: [172.31.1.216] => (item=kubelet)
changed: [172.31.1.216] => (item=docker)

TASK [masternode : directory] *********************************************************
ok: [172.31.1.216]

TASK [masternode : kube configuration copy] *********************************************************
ok: [172.31.1.216]

TASK [masternode : Flannel configuration] *********************************************************
changed: [172.31.1.216]

PLAY RECAP *********************************************************
172.31.1.216              : ok=8    changed=4    unreachable=0    failed=0    skipped=0    rescued=0    ignored=0
```

Figure 13.23: Play recap summary shows the 4 changes performed on the target host

The reason we ran a debug in the command is that we have the commands for the child nodes to join us. So let us highlight that here:

```
""
"kubeadm join 172.31.1.216:6443 --token p2muqk.y2hk89d59q6af2vp \\",
"\t--discovery-token-ca-cert-hash sha256:216dac72d186c2e6e8731ca71a1b9a4b3913ab2a32d5875b31b3fe43df830b77 "
```

Figure 13.24: Execution output provide us the syntax to add child node

This is the command we need to use for our child nodes to join us. Now, let us go ahead to the master host and verify if the services are up:

```
[root@ip-172-31-1-216 ~]# kubectl get nodes
NAME                                          STATUS    ROLES           AGE    VERSION
ip-172-31-1-216.ap-south-1.compute.internal   Ready     control-plane   14m    v1.27.4
[root@ip-172-31-1-216 ~]#
[root@ip-172-31-1-216 ~]#
```

Figure 13.25: Node status

We can see the master node is ready and up from last 14 mins, and has the role assigned as control plane. Let us go ahead and create the child nodes too, as shown:

**kubeadm join 172.31.1.216:6443 --token 0anscz.ntm22tfr113znno0 **

--discovery-token-ca-cert-hash sha256:216dac72d186c2e6e8731ca71a1b9a4b3913ab2a32d5875b31b3fe43df830b77

The **kubeadm join** command, which we see on the terminal shown in *Figure 13.24*, contains an escape character. So, we should remove the escape character before we run the code. After removing all the special characters from the output, the syntax used to look like *Figure 13.26*. Now, let us go ahead and execute the commands in the child host:

```
[root@ip-172-31-15-85 ~]# kubeadm join 172.31.1.216:6443 --token 0anscz.ntm22tfr113znno0 \
>          --discovery-token-ca-cert-hash sha256:216dac72d186c2e6e8731ca71a1b9a4b3913ab2a32d5875b31b3fe43df830b77
[preflight] Running pre-flight checks
        [WARNING FileExisting-tc]: tc not found in system path


[preflight] Reading configuration from the cluster...
[preflight] FYI: You can look at this config file with 'kubectl -n kube-system get cm kubeadm-config -o yaml'
[kubelet-start] Writing kubelet configuration to file "/var/lib/kubelet/config.yaml"
[kubelet-start] Writing kubelet environment file with flags to file "/var/lib/kubelet/kubeadm-flags.env"
[kubelet-start] Starting the kubelet
[kubelet-start] Waiting for the kubelet to perform the TLS Bootstrap...

This node has joined the cluster:
* Certificate signing request was sent to apiserver and a response was received.
* The Kubelet was informed of the new secure connection details.

Run 'kubectl get nodes' on the control-plane to see this node join the cluster.

[root@ip-172-31-15-85 ~]#
```

Figure 13.26: kubeadm join command execution on the child node

We can see that the execution was successful. Let us go ahead and verify the things now.

On the control node, we run the command **kubectl** get nodes' again to see the status of the new node and verify if this node has joined there:

```
[root@ip-172-31-1-216 ~]# kubectl get nodes
NAME                                        STATUS   ROLES          AGE     VERSION
ip-172-31-1-216.ap-south-1.compute.internal Ready    control-plane  28m     v1.27.4
ip-172-31-15-85.ap-south-1.compute.internal Ready    <none>         8m29s   v1.27.4
[root@ip-172-31-1-216 ~]#
[root@ip-172-31-1-216 ~]#
```

Figure 13.27: Nodes status after running kubeadm join command

We can see that the device is ready and active since the last 8 minutes.

Now, we have shown you the manual way of adding the child node and you need to use all the learning and automate the child node part.

Cluster should be up

Using the preceding roles, we have created our cluster, and when we see the cluster output, we should find the list of nodes in the output. We should get a master node created and ensure that both nodes are in the ready status. If your system is stuck with a not-ready status, then we need to use the following configuration to make it work:

```
kubectl apply -f https://github.com/weaveworks/weave/releases/download/
v2.8.1/weave-daemonset-k8s.yaml
```

This will fix the errors of the network level, which you might have been seeing during debugging or troubleshooting.

Once this is done, you should be able to see your cluster in the ready status.

Now, let us go back to the Pod creation.

Running K8 Pod for NGINX

Once our cluster is ready and we have fixed all the errors, we are going to perform application deployment, and we will run the Pods and deploy the application. We are using the official documentation of Kubernetes deployment. For your reference, visit the following link:

https://kubernetes.io/docs/tasks/run-application/run-stateless-application-deployment/

We are going to run the NGINX deployment in this demo. If your organization uses something else, feel free to use the appropriate templates. For our Pod deployment, we simply need to use the following command to deploy our Pod. NGINX Pods should be up, but let us see the content of the code here:

```
Kubectl apply -f https://k8s.io/examples/application/deployment.yaml
```

YAML file output:

```
apiVersion: apps/v1
kind: Deployment
metadata:
  name: nginx-deployment
spec:
  selector:
    matchLabels:
      app: nginx
  replicas: 2 # tells deployment to run 2 pods
  template:
    metadata:
      labels:
        app: nginx
    spec:
      containers:
      - name: nginx
        image: nginx:1.14.2
        ports:
        - containerPort: 80
```

Figure 13.28: Example of Kubernetes Pod

We can see that the YAML code contains the NGINX deployment. This uses the containers of NGINX, and the image and port numbers will be well-defined in the container's configuration. The replica simply means how many Pods we want to run. If you want 4, adjust the value accordingly.

Let us go ahead and use the shell command module to deploy the NGINX, as shown in the following *Figure 13.29:*

```
root@ip-172-31-38-76:/etc/ansible#
root@ip-172-31-38-76:/etc/ansible# cat roles/kubernetes/tasks/main.yml
---
- name: Demo of Nginx Deployment
  shell:  kubectl apply -f https://k8s.io/examples/application/deployment.yaml

root@ip-172-31-38-76:/etc/ansible#
root@ip-172-31-38-76:/etc/ansible#
root@ip-172-31-38-76:/etc/ansible# ansible-playbook firstplayb.yaml -u ashutmch -k  -v
Using /etc/ansible/ansible.cfg as config file
SSH password:

PLAY [Demo] ********************************************************************

TASK [Gathering Facts] ********************************************************
ok: [172.31.38.201]

TASK [kubernetes : Demo of Nginx Deployment] **********************************
changed: [172.31.38.201] => {"changed": true, "cmd": "kubectl apply -f https://k8s.io/examples/applic
"msg": "", "rc": 0, "start": "2023-09-07 04:54:40.294661", "stderr": "", "stderr_lines": [], "stdout"
ployment created"]}

PLAY RECAP ********************************************************************
172.31.38.201              : ok=2    changed=1    unreachable=0    failed=0    skipped=0    rescued=0
```

Figure 13.29: Successful playbook execution

The command is very simple to deploy in the nginx on the target host which is **kubectl**. For this, apply **-f** URL. The next thing we need to do is run the code, and that is what we have done in our next line. We have executed our playbook, and the execution was successful. One change was performed on the target host.

Let us go back to the target host and see the result:

```
[ashutmch@ip-172-31-38-201 ~]$ kubectl get pods -l app=nginx
NAME                                    READY    STATUS     RESTARTS    AGE
nginx-deployment-756d9fd5f9-6tmp8       0/1      Pending    0           9s
nginx-deployment-756d9fd5f9-fhqnr       0/1      Pending    0           9s
[ashutmch@ip-172-31-38-201 ~]$
```

Figure 13.30: NGINX Pod status after playbook execution

We can see the **nginx-deployment** was successful on the target host. Now, we need to wait for a few minutes for the status to change from pending, and then all the things will be sorted. From there, we will be good to proceed further.

If you want to view the entire process of Pod coming up, then please run the same command (shown in *Figure 13.30*) for the next few seconds, and you will see the status getting changed and at the running status. So, let us run the command again and see the result:

```
NAME                                  READY    STATUS              RESTARTS
nginx-deployment-756d9fd5f9-6tmp8     0/1      ContainerCreating   0
nginx-deployment-756d9fd5f9-fhqnr     0/1      ContainerCreating   0
[ashutmch@ip-172-31-38-201 ~]$ kubectl get pods -l app=nginx
NAME                                  READY    STATUS              RESTARTS
nginx-deployment-756d9fd5f9-6tmp8     0/1      ContainerCreating   0
nginx-deployment-756d9fd5f9-fhqnr     0/1      ContainerCreating   0
[ashutmch@ip-172-31-38-201 ~]$
[ashutmch@ip-172-31-38-201 ~]$ kubectl get pods -l app=nginx
NAME                                  READY    STATUS              RESTARTS
nginx-deployment-756d9fd5f9-6tmp8     0/1      ContainerCreating   0
nginx-deployment-756d9fd5f9-fhqnr     1/1      Running             0
```

Figure 13.31: Pod coming up

After few minutes, we can see all the things in a running status as the following:

```
[ashutmch@ip-172-31-38-201 ~]$
[ashutmch@ip-172-31-38-201 ~]$ kubectl get pods -l app=nginx
NAME                                  READY    STATUS     RESTARTS    AGE
nginx-deployment-756d9fd5f9-6tmp8     1/1      Running    0           18m
nginx-deployment-756d9fd5f9-fhqnr     1/1      Running    0           18m
[ashutmch@ip-172-31-38-201 ~]$
```

Figure 13.32: Pod is finally up and running

We will skip the output of the describe deployment command here, as it will make this chapter lengthy. The list is not just limited to Pod deployment, but there are a lot of things that we can do with Ansible that we cannot cover here.

Note: **There are dedicated modules of Ansible designed for Kubernetes, like the K8 module and so on.**

It is now recommended that you prepare the control machine for those Ansible modules and start using them. We have already seen the process of all the previous Ansible modules, and now we are in that phase where we should start doing things on our own.

We will discuss more about this in the chapter on Kubernetes.

Installing Docker APK

Just like any other IT technology and infrastructure, Ansible has a wide range of modules for Docker too. Ansible works great with Docker compose, Docker container, Docker image and image info. These are some of the most widely used Docker modules of Ansible. We will explore a few of them in this section.

Docker is even capable of building the dynamic inventory of all available containers inside the Docker host. Just like any cloud module of Ansible, we need to install a few Python SDK in our control machine for Docker to work efficiently.

The command to simply install the Python SDK is **pip install docker** is as follows:

```
root@ip-172-31-38-76:~# pip install docker
Collecting docker
  Downloading docker-6.1.3-py3-none-any.whl (148 kB)
                                          148.1/148.1 KB 2.5 MB/s eta 0:0
Requirement already satisfied: websocket-client>=0.32.0 in /usr/local/lib/pyt
Requirement already satisfied: urllib3>=1.26.0 in /usr/lib/python3/dist-packa
Collecting requests>=2.26.0
  Downloading requests-2.31.0-py3-none-any.whl (62 kB)
                                          62.6/62.6 KB 8.4 MB/s eta 0:00:
Requirement already satisfied: packaging>=14.0 in /usr/lib/python3/dist-packa
Requirement already satisfied: certifi>=2017.4.17 in /usr/lib/python3/dist-pa
Requirement already satisfied: idna<4,>=2.5 in /usr/lib/python3/dist-packages
Collecting charset-normalizer<4,>=2
  Downloading charset_normalizer-3.2.0-cp310-cp310-manylinux_2_17_x86_64.many
                                          201.8/201.8 KB 15.8 MB/s eta 0:
Installing collected packages: charset-normalizer, requests, docker
  Attempting uninstall: requests
    Found existing installation: requests 2.25.1
    Not uninstalling requests at /usr/lib/python3/dist-packages, outside envi
    Can't uninstall 'requests'. No files were found to uninstall.
Successfully installed charset-normalizer-3.2.0 docker-6.1.3 requests-2.31.0
```

Figure 13.33: Installation of docker

Once the installation is successful, our control machine is prepared for the Docker modules. Of course, some additional configuration will be required, which we will do step by step as this chapter progresses.

For now, let us go ahead and install the Docker on a Linux host using Ansible.

Installing Docker on the target host

Installation of Docker packages on the target host is a very easy process and you might have mastered it by this point but let us still see a few steps which we have followed so far in our journey. You might need to perform a few tricks in the following code, and we will see how that can be achieved.

Let us go ahead and create the role for the Docker package installation, as shown in the following figure:

```
root@ip-172-31-38-76:/etc/ansible# cat roles/kubernetes/tasks/main.yml
---
- name: Add repository
  ansible.builtin.yum_repository:
    name: epel
    description: Docker repo
    baseurl:  https://download.docker.com/linux/centos/docker-ce.repo
- name:
  ansible.builtin.yum:
    name:
      - docker-ce
      - docker-ce-cli
      - containerd.io
      - docker-buildx-plugin
      - docker-compose-plugin
    state: present
- name: start the services
  shell: sudo systemctl start docker
```

Figure 13.34: Playbook to install docker on the target host

As you can see in the preceding figure, the package will install the repo and then start the installation process of Docker.

Note: We have used the name of the repo as EPEL since we already had it created in our test environment. This is not going to cause any harm in the lab environment, but be cautious when you are in production. Use the unique name and create a new repo name as this Ansible module will remove all the old configuration from the repo and replace it with the new one. That might result in failure in the future. So, for production, create a new unique name. In lab, you can use the existing repo.

```
root@ip-172-31-38-76:/etc/ansible# ansible-playbook firstplayb.yaml
SSH password:
BECOME password[defaults to SSH password]:

PLAY [Demo] **********************************************************

TASK [Gathering Facts] **********************************************
ok: [172.31.35.81]

TASK [kubernetes : Add repository] *********************************
ok: [172.31.35.81]

TASK [kubernetes : ansible.builtin.yum] ***************************
changed: [172.31.35.81]

TASK [kubernetes : start the services] ****************************
changed: [172.31.35.81]

PLAY RECAP *********************************************************
172.31.35.81                 : ok=4      changed=2    unreachable=0     f
```

Figure 13.35: Successful playbook execution

We can see that the execution of the code is successful and this has installed the Docker in the target host. Let us go ahead and verify the few things manually:

```
[root@ip-172-31-35-81 ~]# service docker status
Redirecting to /bin/systemctl status docker.service
● docker.service - Docker Application Container Engine
   Loaded: loaded (/usr/lib/systemd/system/docker.service; disabled; vendor preset: disabled)
   Active: active (running) since Fri 2023-09-08 10:50:50 UTC; 3min 6s ago
     Docs: https://docs.docker.com
 Main PID: 14374 (dockerd)
    Tasks: 7
   Memory: 28.8M
   CGroup: /system.slice/docker.service
           └─14374 /usr/bin/dockerd -H fd:// --containerd=/run/containerd/containerd.sock

Sep 08 10:50:49 ip-172-31-35-81.ap-south-1.compute.internal systemd[1]: Starting Docker Application Co
Sep 08 10:50:49 ip-172-31-35-81.ap-south-1.compute.internal dockerd[14374]: time="2023-09-08T10:50:49.
Sep 08 10:50:50 ip-172-31-35-81.ap-south-1.compute.internal dockerd[14374]: time="2023-09-08T10:50:50.
Sep 08 10:50:50 ip-172-31-35-81 ap-south-1 compute internal dockerd[14374]: time="2023-09-08T10:50:50
```

Figure 13.36: Docker service is finally active

We can see that the services are up as expected.

Now, let us go ahead and run **hello world** and see the results:

```
[root@ip-172-31-35-81 ~]# sudo docker run hello-world
Unable to find image 'hello-world:latest' locally
latest: Pulling from library/hello-world
719385e32844: Pull complete
Digest: sha256:dcba6daec718f547568c562956fa47e1b03673dd010fe6ee58ca806767031d1c
Status: Downloaded newer image for hello-world:latest

Hello from Docker!
This message shows that your installation appears to be working correctly.
```

Figure 13.37: Docker testing

We can see that we are getting a hello message from Docker. This means the installation is performed correctly:

```
[root@ip-172-31-35-81 ~]# sudo docker run hello-world
Unable to find image 'hello-world:latest' locally
latest: Pulling from library/hello-world
719385e32844: Pull complete
Digest: sha256:dcba6daec718f547568c562956fa47e1b03673dd010fe
Status: Downloaded newer image for hello-world:latest

Hello from Docker!
This message shows that your installation appears to be work
```

Figure 13.38: Testing gave us the desired result

Playbooks for gathering information about the image

Let us go ahead and start our journey by gathering the information about the Docker image we ran just now. We will try to gather the information about it using the Ansible module **docker_image_info**.

docker_image_info

Let us go ahead and use it in our lab environment. There is no harm in running this module so let us try it. As the name suggests, this will give us information about the Docker image:

```
root@ip-172-31-38-76:/etc/ansible# cat roles/infoimage/tasks/main.yml
---
- name:  Image details
  docker_image_info:
    name: hello-world
root@ip-172-31-38-76:/etc/ansible#
root@ip-172-31-38-76:/etc/ansible#
```

Figure 13.39: Role to gather information about the docker image

The module is very easy to use. We need to call the module and provide the parameters. In this case, the parameter is name of repository. Have a look at the list of images installed in the Docker container. Let us go to the target host and verify the images installed in the target host:

```
[root@ip-172-31-35-81 ~]# docker image ls
REPOSITORY      TAG       IMAGE ID       CREATED        SIZE
nginx           latest    f5a6b296b8a2   26 hours ago   187MB
ubuntu          latest    c6b84b685f35   3 weeks ago    77.8MB
hello-world     latest    9c7a54a9a43c   4 months ago   13.3kB
[root@ip-172-31-35-81 ~]#
```

Figure 13.40: List of docker image to gather repository name

We can see that we have three images installed. We can provide any one of them or all of them in our playbook, and we will get all the information about them.

Let us run our code for **hello world**, as shown in the following figure:

```
root@ip-172-31-38-76:/etc/ansible# ansible-playbook -u ashutmch -k second.yaml -K
SSH password:
BECOME password[defaults to SSH password]:

PLAY [Demo] ****************************************************************

TASK [Gathering Facts] ****************************************************
ok: [172.31.35.81]

TASK [infoimage : Image details] *****************************************
ok: [172.31.35.81]

TASK [infoimage : debug] *************************************************
ok: [172.31.35.81] => {
    "msg": {
        "changed": false,
        "failed": false,
        "images": [
            {
                "Architecture": "amd64",
                "Author": "",
                "Comment": "",
                "Config": {
                    "AttachStderr": false,
                    "AttachStdin": false,
                    "AttachStdout": false,
                    "Cmd": [
```

Figure 13.41: Debug output of docker image info

We have now added the register and debug module in the role to make the output better and visible. The following figure shows how the image information will now look like:

```
    "Hostname": "",
    "Image": "sha256:62a15619037f3c4fb4e6ba9bd224cba3540e393a55dc52f6bebe212ca7b5e1a7",
    "Labels": null,
    "OnBuild": null,
    "OpenStdin": false,
    "StdinOnce": false,
    "Tty": false,
    "User": "",
    "Volumes": null,
    "WorkingDir": ""
},
"Container": "347ca68872ee924c4f9394b195dcadaf591d387a45d624225251efc6cb7a348e",
"ContainerConfig": {
    "AttachStderr": false,
```

Figure 13.42: Debug output of docker image info continued

Here, we can find the information about the image and Docker container.

Playbook for container management

In this section, we will begin our journey with a very basic use case and that is pulling an image for our containers. In the preceding example, we had pulled the hello world image from the repository, which was done locally from the Docker server. Now, we will be doing the same using the Ansible.

Let us prepare our playbook and run it, as shown in the following figure:

```
root@ip-172-31-38-76:/etc/ansible#
root@ip-172-31-38-76:/etc/ansible# cat roles/docker/tasks/main.yml
---
- name: Create default containers
  community.docker.docker_image:
    name: pacur/centos-7:56
    source: pull
root@ip-172-31-38-76:/etc/ansible#
```

Figure 13.43: Role to pull the docker image centos-7 using Ansible

This time we will pull the **centos-7** image and that will be installed in our Docker container:

```
root@ip-172-31-38-76:/etc/ansible# ansible-playbook -u ashutmch -k firstplayb.yaml -K
SSH password:
BECOME password[defaults to SSH password]:

PLAY [Demo] *********************************************************************

TASK [Gathering Facts] *********************************************************
ok: [172.31.35.81]

TASK [docker : Create default containers] **************************************
fatal: [172.31.35.81]: FAILED! => {"changed": false, "msg": "Error pulling image pacur/centos-7:56
/create?tag=56&fromImage=pacur%2Fcentos-7: Not Found (\"manifest for pacur/centos-7:56 not found:
```

Figure 13.44: Playbook execution failed with error of image not found

The execution failed as the image **centos-7:56** is no longer available on the repo. So, we will change the code to **centos-7**, as shown in the following figure:

```
root@ip-172-31-38-76:/etc/ansible# cat roles/docker/tasks/main.yml
---
- name: Create default containers
  community.docker.docker_image:
    name: pacur/centos-7
    source: pull
root@ip-172-31-38-76:/etc/ansible#
```

Figure 13.45: Fixed the error and provided the new image name

Let us run the code and see the results:

```
root@ip-172-31-38-76:/etc/ansible# ansible-playbook -u ashutmch -k first
SSH password:
BECOME password[defaults to SSH password]:

PLAY [Demo] ***************************************************************

TASK [Gathering Facts] ***************************************************
ok: [172.31.35.81]

TASK [docker : Create default containers] *******************************
changed: [172.31.35.81]

PLAY RECAP ***************************************************************
172.31.35.81              : ok=2    changed=1    unreachable=0    faile
```

Figure 13.46: Successful playbook execution after changing the image name

This time, the execution was successful. Now, let us go ahead and verify the same from the target host. We should see the four images this time, as shown in the following figure:

```
[root@ip-172-31-35-81 ~]# docker image ls
REPOSITORY        TAG        IMAGE ID        CREATED          SIZE
nginx             latest     f5a6b296b8a2    27 hours ago     187MB
ubuntu            latest     c6b84b685f35    3 weeks ago      77.8MB
hello-world       latest     9c7a54a9a43c    4 months ago     13.3kB
pacur/centos-7    latest     bd6dee3523dc    4 years ago      1.42GB
[root@ip-172-31-35-81 ~]#
```

Figure 13.47: We can find the newly pulled image in the image list

We can see that the **cento-7** is now visible to us. This means the installation was successful.

The Docker image is not only limited to one feature or parameter, and has many features like image push, building an image and tagging them.

Let us go ahead and create our data container. *Figure 13.48* shows us how we can create the data container using Ansible:

```
root@ip-172-31-38-76:/etc/ansible# cat roles/infoimage/tasks/main.yml
---
- name: Our first container using ansible
  community.docker.docker_container:
    name: mydata
    image: busybox
    volumes:
      - /data
root@ip-172-31-38-76:/etc/ansible#
```

Figure 13.48: Role to create a data container

Now, our role is ready. So, we are good to create our playbook:

```
root@ip-172-31-38-76:/etc/ansible#
root@ip-172-31-38-76:/etc/ansible# cat second.yaml
---
- name: Demo
  hosts: all
  become: yes
  roles:
    - infoimage
root@ip-172-31-38-76:/etc/ansible#
```

Figure 13.49: Playbook for the data container creation

Let us run our code and see the following results:

```
root@ip-172-31-38-76:/etc/ansible# ansible-playbook -u ashutmch -k second.yaml
SSH password:
BECOME password[defaults to SSH password]:

PLAY [Demo] ******************************************************************

TASK [Gathering Facts] ******************************************************
ok: [172.31.35.81]

TASK [infoimage : Our first container using ansible] ************************
changed: [172.31.35.81]

PLAY RECAP ******************************************************************
172.31.35.81               : ok=2    changed=1    unreachable=0    failed=0
```

Figure 13.50: Successful playbook execution

We can see that our execution is successful this time. You can go back to the target host and verify how things are. This code execution has created a new container and installed images in them and this is how we can create the container and install the images in it. In this case, the data container is created.

Kindly use the command **docker container inspect mydata** to verify the current status of the container.

In the end, let us go ahead and clean up the recently created Docker container. The state needs to be changed to absent and this will remove the container from the host:

```
root@ip-172-31-38-76:/etc/ansible# cat roles/infoimage/tasks/m
---
- name: Our first container using ansible
  community.docker.docker_container:
    name: mydata
    image: busybox
    volumes:
      - /data
    state: absent
root@ip-172-31-38-76:/etc/ansible#
```

Figure 13.51: Removing the data container

Let us verify and see if our cleanup role worked or not:

```
[root@ip-172-31-35-81 ~]# docker container inspect mydata
[]
Error response from daemon: No such container: mydata
[root@ip-172-31-35-81 ~]#
[root@ip-172-31-35-81 ~]#
```

Figure 13.52: Successfully verified the container is removed from the target host

We can see that **mydata** container is totally removed from the target host.

This is how you can perform as many as task you want on the docker containers. The module has many features like restarting the container, defining the port information and sending the sleep command on the container. We can define the environment variables and we can also restrict the network of containers. Now, it is recommended that all readers should go through the documentation and explore more options about what Ansible offers us and try sending the commands directly to the containers.

Playbooks to execute commands in a Docker container

Now, this is an easy task for the one who has already read the documents as per our suggestion, but for the others, they need to start digging into the module a bit more and perform this task.

Tip: **The container module has the command parameters which can be used to send the commands to the container. For now, perform sleep 2day task.**

Command: **sleep 2d**

Go ahead and spend some time creating this role and executing it.

Conclusion

There are wide range of tasks which we can perform using Ansible in the Docker and Kubernetes. So, let us go ahead and start exploring more options. Create a lab, run the code and destroy the lab again. Recreate it until you find perfection, as there is no better way of learning Ansible than practicing it.

In the next chapter, we will focus on the ansible tower. How we can create the role and playbook in Ansible Tower.

Join our Discord space

Join our Discord workspace for latest updates, offers, tech happenings around the world, new releases, and sessions with the authors:

https://discord.bpbonline.com

## CHAPTER 14

Migration to Ansible Tower

Introduction

As we have seen so far, Ansible is a powerful tool, and there is a wide range of things we can do with it. Red Hat has not limited itself to simply being an open-source project, and if you are a big fan of paid stuff, then Ansible Tower is for you. In case you are not comfortable with command line interface, then Red Hat offers you Ansible Tower. Now, there are a few things that are very useful in Ansible Tower. The first and the most important is a great looking GUI, good dashboard, easy templates, and the list continues. These things will attract you towards the Ansible Tower, but a suggestion is to learn Ansible from the command line first and then turn to Ansible Tower.

Structure

The chapter contains the following topics:

- Downloading and installing Ansible Tower
- Creating an Ansible Tower project
- Git as the second method

Objectives

In this chapter, we will learn about Ansible Tower. We will start with organization, inventory, and then, move to templates. At the end of the chapter, you will be able to perform all the tasks using Ansible Tower, which we performed using CLI. Ansible Tower is much more easy and convenient to use, so let us learn it.

Downloading and installing Ansible Tower

We have already installed Ansible Tower in *Chapter 2, Introducing Ansible and Ansible Tower*. For this chapter, we have created a new demo environment. You can refer to the following figure for the same:

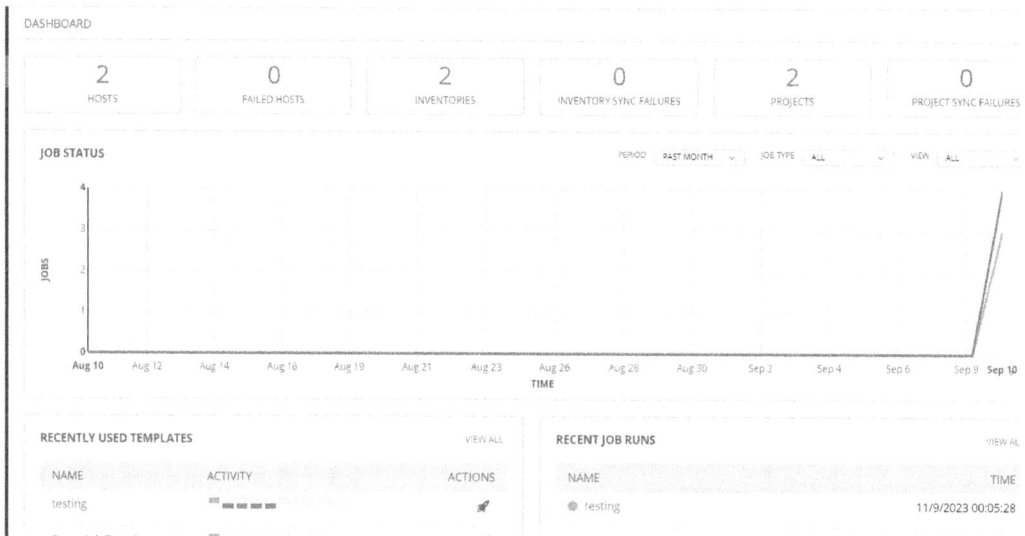

Figure 14.1: Ansible Tower dashboard

Now, the dashboard might appear a little green and red since We were testing few things on Ansible Tower, but this gave us the opportunity to have a look at different options on the dashboard:

- **Hosts**: As expected, it contains the information about the hosts/target hosts. In the preceding example, one host was already created by the auto build, and the second one was configured by the author, which is why you are seeing two hosts.

- **Failed host**: As its name explains, it contains the information of the failed host. Now, the reason might be different for the failure, but they will be maintained in this section.

- **Inventories**: This is the same inventories what we have learned in the Ansible. We can create the custom inventory where we can define our target host information and variables.

- **Inventory sync failure**: This value will increase if the dynamic inventory fails. Now, dynamic inventory might be like a shock for a few of you, but yes this is also possible.

- **Projects**: This will give us the information about the current project we have created. Now, since we are talking about the projects for the first time here, let us put more light on this topic. A project is basically a collection of playbooks, and this playbook can be placed on the Ansible Tower server or Git.

- **Project sync failure**: As we have discussed, our projects can be placed on the Git. If the sync with those Git Repos fails, then our counter increases in this place.

Creating an Ansible Tower project

Before we create any of the tower projects and templates, we need to do some preparatory work. We will start our journey from the organization.

If we will draw the hierarchy of Ansible, then the organization will be placed at the top of hierarchy. Now, one might think if it is on the top, then why have we not heard of it so far? Well, this is not really an important part of CLI. However, in Ansible Tower it plays huge role. Let us consider a real use case.

Organization

Assume you own a company that the offers IT services to its clients. Let us assume that company is named *ABCD Solution*. Now, ABCD Solution has 100 small customers. All those small customers own five to six hosts. So, they have nearly 500 hosts to manage for 100 different customers. In the case of Ansible, it was easy to create a new control machine for each of the customers, however, that will not be the case. If you keep on buying the license for all 100 customers separately, then you will end up buying 100 licenses.

So, what can be a cost-effective solution? Well, the cost-effective solution will be buying a single license for 1000 uses and creating multiple organizations for each customer. You can create an organization in the name of *ABC Tech* and *XYZ Solution* the inventory and credentials of ABC Tech will not be shared with XYZ Solution.

In simple words, a tower organization is a set of Users, projects, and inventories. Ansible Tower creates a default organization. So, even if you do not create any organization, everything will be placed in the default organization, and the users will be assigned on the organization levels. The user who has been assigned to the ABC Tech will not be able to see the content (which includes the users, inventories, roles, playbooks, and templates) of XYZ Solution.

Let us go ahead and create an organization from scratch. Refer to the following steps for the same:

1. Navigate to the Ansible Tower menu, and under **Access,** you will find the **ORGANIZATIONS**. Click on it.

2. On the right-hand side corner, we can see the add option as shown in the following *Figure 14.2*. Click on it:

ORGANIZATIONS

ORGANIZATIONS **1**

| SEARCH | Q | KEY |

Default   ✏ 🗑

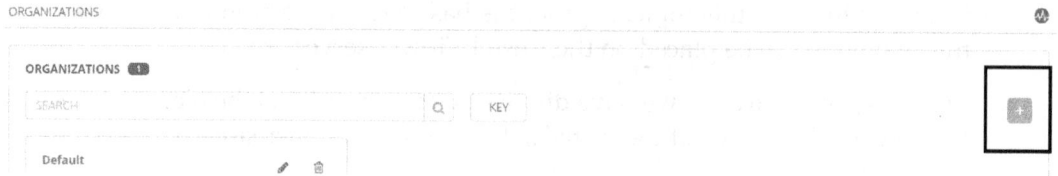

Figure 14.2: Navigating and adding a new organization

3.   This will open the option of new organization registration. Here we need to provide the name and other parameters. Only name is the mandatory field. Once it is filled, we can click on save option and organization will be registered, as shown in the following figure:

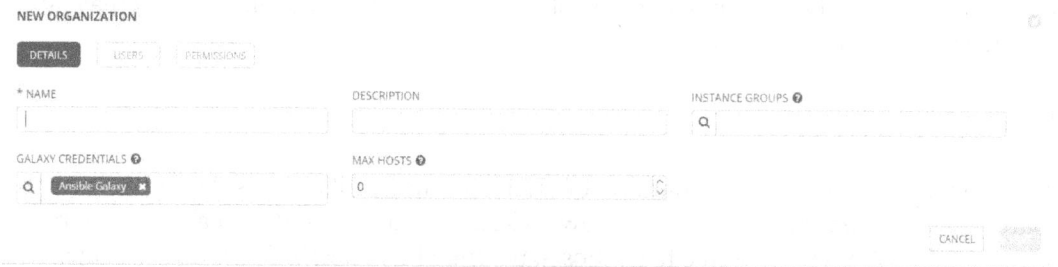

NEW ORGANIZATION

| DETAILS | USERS | PERMISSIONS |

* NAME   DESCRIPTION   INSTANCE GROUPS ❷

GALAXY CREDENTIALS ❷   MAX HOSTS ❷

Q Ansible Galaxy ✖   0

CANCEL

Figure 14.3: Provide the name and required details to the new organization

4.   As we clicked on save, the new organization is registered. We can clearly see two organizations over there, as shown in the following figure:

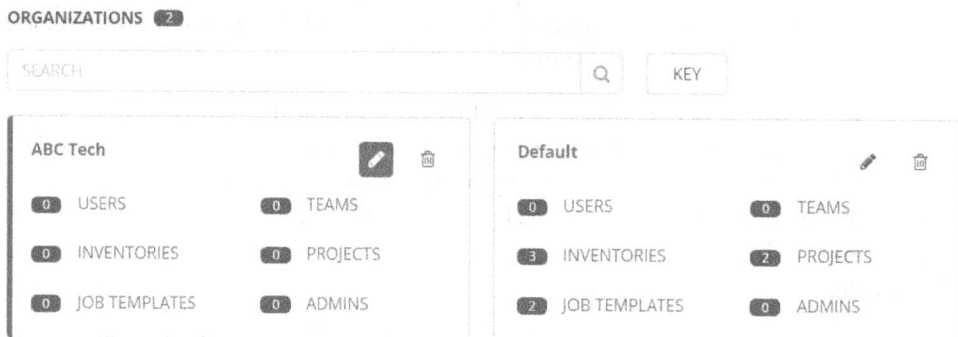

ORGANIZATIONS **2**

| SEARCH | Q | KEY |

ABC Tech   ✏ 🗑

0 USERS	**0** TEAMS
0 INVENTORIES	**0** PROJECTS
0 JOB TEMPLATES	**0** ADMINS

Default   ✏ 🗑

0 USERS	**0** TEAMS
3 INVENTORIES	**2** PROJECTS
2 JOB TEMPLATES	**0** ADMINS

Figure 14.4: Newly created organizations with default organization

Now, we are done with the creation of the organization. Let us go ahead and create an inventory now. The host IP address or FQDN will be added here.

Inventory

In order to create an inventory, we need to navigate to the inventory and click on the add button. That will give us a dropdown with two options—inventory and smart inventory. We need to click on the inventory and provide the details, as shown in the following figure:

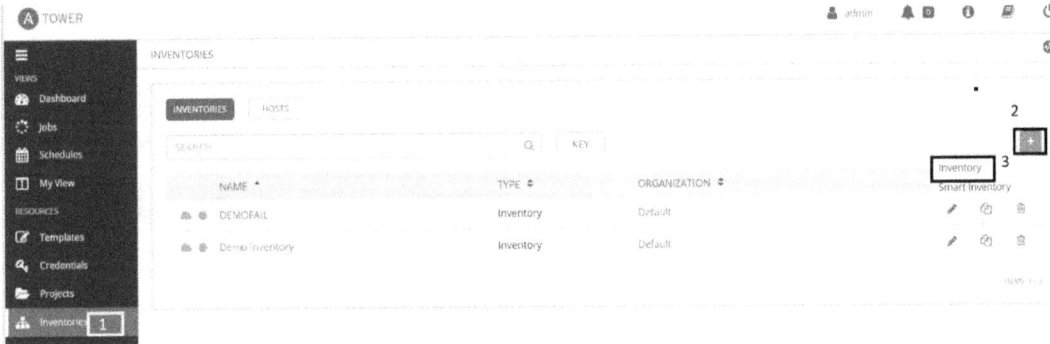

Figure 14.5: List of inventories

First of all, we need to name the inventory. In this case, the inventory will be known as **TARGETHOST**, as shown in the following *Figure 14.6*. Once that is done, we need to click on the organization and select the organization ABC Tech which we created right now:

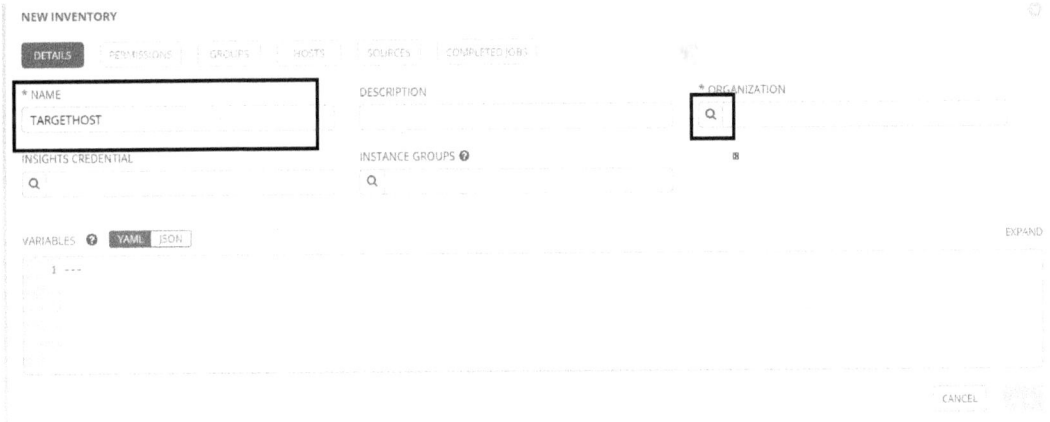

Figure 14.6: Creation of new inventory from scratch

The organization window will look as shown in *Figure 14.7*. We need to click on the organization **ABC Tech** and click on select. Once that is done, we are good to proceed further:

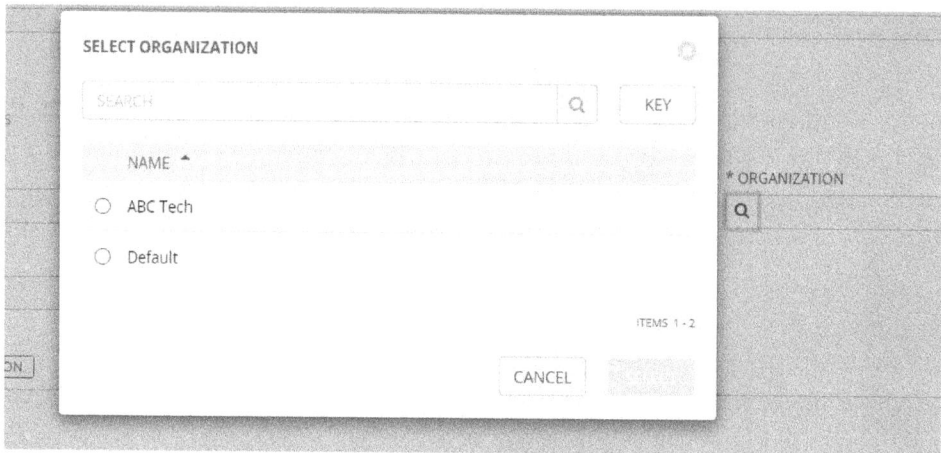

Figure 14.7: Select right organization from list

Once these details are entered the graded out, save option is available to us. We need to click on save, as shown in *Figure 14.8*:

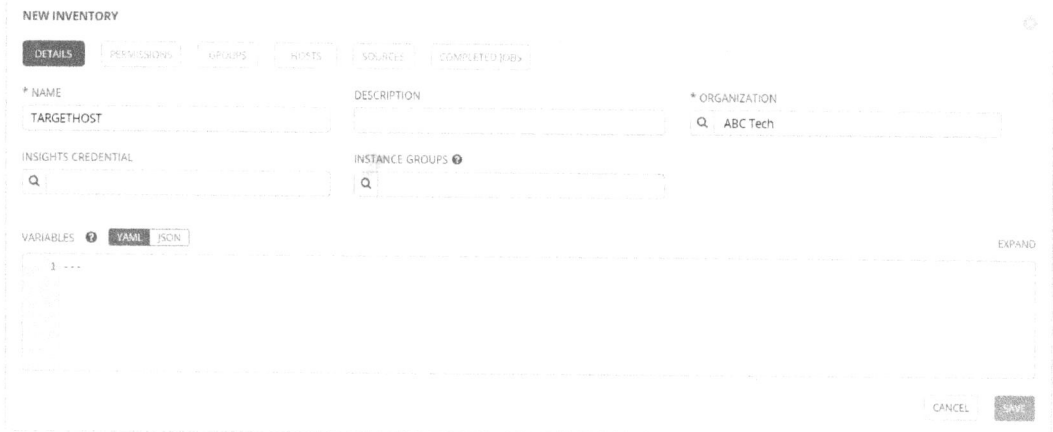

Figure 14.8: Once organization is selected this is how it will look like

The next thing we need to do is add the IP address of target hosts in **HOSTS**. For this, click on the **HOSTS** and a new option window will appear, as shown in the following figure:

Figure 14.9: Navigate to the hosts

Once again, we need to click on the add option:

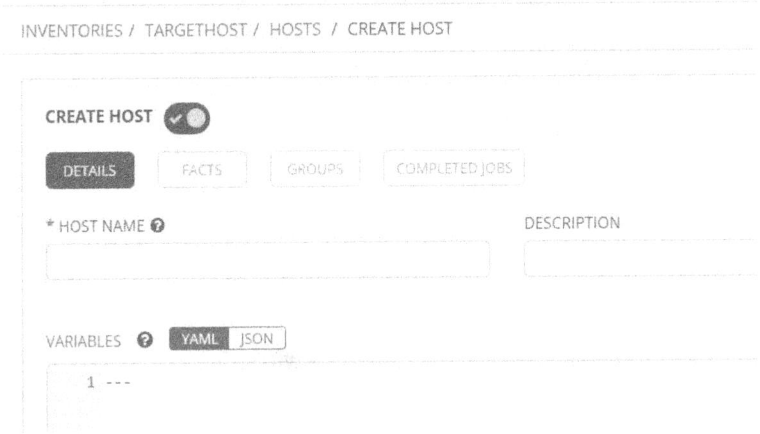

Figure 14.10: Create a host

In the hostname field, we need to enter the FQDN or IP address of the target host. In our case, we have both IP address and FQDN, but we will use the IP address for now, as shown in the following figure:

Figure 14.11: Added the IP address in host name and save the hosts file

Once we click on save and the IP address details are added in the inventory, it will look as shown in the following figure:

Figure 14.12: This is how the host file will look like

We can navigate back to the Inventories, and this will show us the information about all the inventories we have added.

If you see the details of **TARGETHOST** inventory, it shows the organization as **ABC Tech**. Now, the user who is assigned to the **ABC Tech** will be able to see just the **TARGETHOST** inventory **DEMOFAIL**, and the **Demo Inventory** will not be visible to them. Refer to *Figure 14.13:*

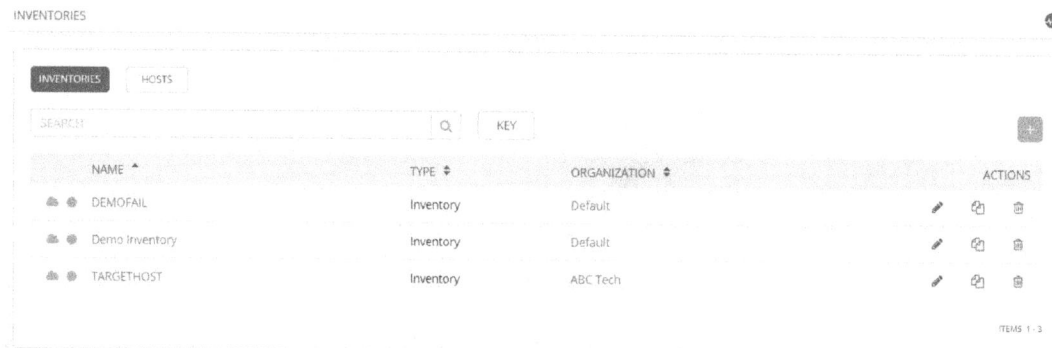

Figure 14.13: Inventory is ready

Credentials

The next very important thing we need to provide are credentials. Now, Ansible Tower supports the wide range of authentication method. You can connect any of the vaults like Cyber Ark or cloud based vault and authenticate your target hosts. Tower also supports the password and key based authentications. So, whatever method you have in your organization for authentication, it will be supported in Ansible Tower.

Let us go ahead and try to add our credentials as shown in the following figure:

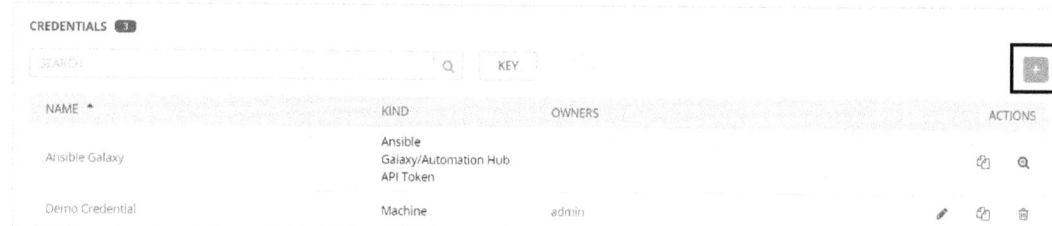

Figure 14.14: List of credentials and add new button

Click on add and then mention the details like username, password, and organization, as shown in the following figure:

demouser

DETAILS PERMISSIONS

* NAME ❓

demouser

DESCRIPTION ❓

ORGANIZATION

🔍 ABC Tech

* CREDENTIAL TYPE ❓

🔍 Machine

TYPE DETAILS

USERNAME

🔍 ashutmch

PASSWORD

🔍 ▮▮▮▮▮▮▮▮▮▮

☐ Prompt on launch

Figure 14.15: Define username and password with organization name

Finally, let us start working on the project.

The project is the location where we let the Ansible Tower know where our playbooks are located. Now, one might think, wait so far, we have just seen that playbooks are located in control machines. That is not the only case with the Ansible Tower. It offers us wide range of options. We can place our playbooks on places like Git, Ansible Tower server, Red Hat Insights, and so on. In our case, we will explore both manual and Git options. In the first example, we have chosen the manual method. The method is defined in the **Source Code Management** (**SCM**) type, and we all know the biggest vendor in this SCM is GitHub. However, in this case, we are doing manual SCM. Our project base path (on the new project page) contains the location of the playbook directory.

In our case, we need to navigate to the Tower server and create a directory named as playbook in the location **/var/lib/awx/projects**. Inside that directory we will create our playbooks.

On the Ansible Tower server:

```
[root@ip-172-31-46-6 projects]# cd /var/lib/awx/projects
[root@ip-172-31-46-6 projects]# mkdir playbook
[root@ip-172-31-46-6 projects]# cd playbook/
[root@ip-172-31-46-6 playbook]# vi first.yaml
[root@ip-172-31-46-6 playbook]#
```

Once this directory is created, we are good to create the project. Click on a new project and configure the parameters. Then, select the name and organization. In the playbook directory, from the dropdown, we need to select the playbook, as shown in the following figure:

Figure 14.16: Creation of new project

Once this is done, click on save, and we should be able to see multiple projects right below it. Refer to *Figure 14.17*:

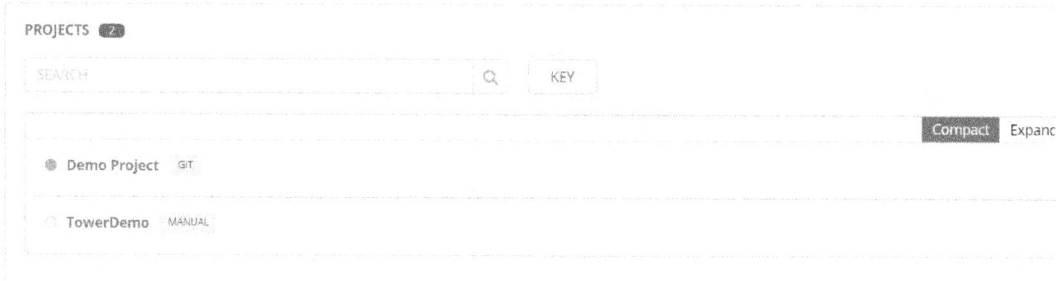

Figure 14.17: List of projects where old successful shown with green sign

As we can see, the default demo project is there. If you see a small graded out box next to it, which says **GIT**, then it means the SCM used here is Git. Similarly, the second project which we created right now contains **MANUAL** next to it and the reason for manual is quite clear to us (we chose the manual while creating it).

For reference, look at the following *Figure 14.18*:

Figure 14.18: Highlighted box shows how it was created

So, we are now done with the creation of the manual project. Let us go ahead and have a look at the template.

Working with job template

This is the place where we define the set of parameters for the Ansible jobs. In simple language, the template will do the following things:

- Create a set of parameters where we will define which playbook will be executed on which target host (using inventory).

- Define what credentials will be used to execute the preceding playbook.

- Provide the location of that playbook (whether that is manual or on Git).

Now, let us go ahead and create a new template from scratch. We need to navigate to the templates and click on the add button. That will open a new window, as shown in the following figure:

Figure 14.19: Adding a new template from add button

Let us create our first ever job template, by following the given steps:

1. We need to start with the name of the job template.

2. Write a description as that is the best way to do the code.

3. The third option is Job type, since we want to run the playbook, we will choose the run option.

4. The forth option is the place where we will call our host/inventory.

5. The fifth option is a project. The newly created project Towerdemo has to be called here.

6. Next option is our playbook. Remember we have created the **first.yaml** in our Tower server on the location defined in the project. Just for your visibility please have a look on code and location:

```
[root@ip-172-31-46-6 ec2-user]#  cd /var/lib/awx/projects
[root@ip-172-31-46-6 projects]#
[root@ip-172-31-46-6 projects]#
[root@ip-172-31-46-6 projects]# cd playbook/
[root@ip-172-31-46-6 playbook]# ll
total 8
-rw-r--r--. 1 root root 82 Sep 10 18:30 first.yaml
-rw-r--r--. 1 root root 14 Sep 10 18:30 hosts
[root@ip-172-31-46-6 playbook]# pwd
/var/lib/awx/projects/playbook
[root@ip-172-31-46-6 playbook]#
[root@ip-172-31-46-6 playbook]#
[root@ip-172-31-46-6 playbook]# cat first.yaml
---
- name: testing
  hosts: all
  tasks:
    - name: testing
      shell: uptime
[root@ip-172-31-46-6 playbook]#
[root@ip-172-31-46-6 playbook]# cat hosts
172.31.45.163
[root@ip-172-31-46-6 playbook]# 
```

Figure 14.20: Content of playbook

7. The next option is credentials. Here, we will call the username and password of the target hosts.

8. Forks is the next option. If you do not remember, this is the feature of Ansible which allows us to define the number of target hosts on which parallel execution will be done at a time before the next batch starts. It is chosen as five, then Ansible will execute a task on the first five target hosts and wait for the results. Once it is done, Ansible will go for the next batch.

9. Limit feature can be used to select one or more than one target hosts out of inventory. If your inventory has ten servers, but right now you want to execute code on just one of the target hosts then you can use this feature.

Verbosity is well known to every Linux engineer, but if you are still not aware then it is the debug level we want to enable:

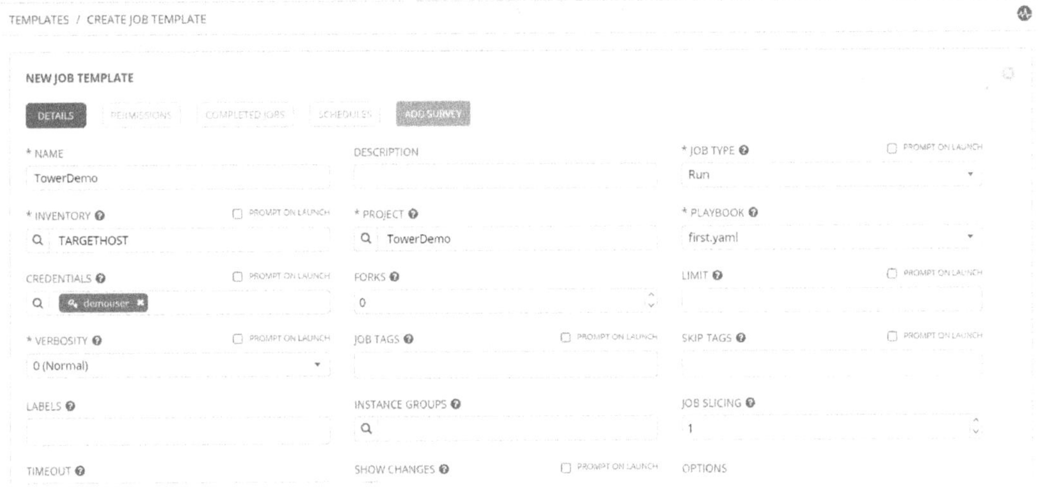

Figure 14.21: Providing the inventory, project, credentials and playbook information in template

There are a few other options too, which we can define in the job. The most important one is privilege escalation, which is used widely. Refer to the following *Figure 14.22:*

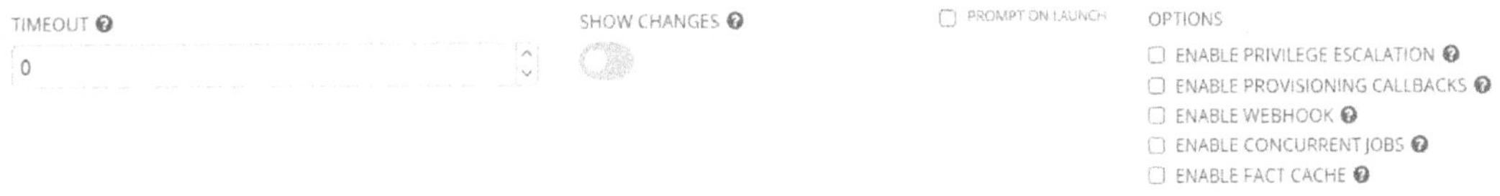

Figure 14.22: Extra options like privilege escalation

Let us go ahead and start the execution. To start the execution, we need to save the template and click on launch, once it is saved.

Launching Ansible Tower jobs template

Let us go ahead and launch our first Ansible Tower template. Simply click on the save and launch to start the execution. We also see the options of the extra variable. So, this is another place where we can define the variables. We can define the variables as **json** and **yaml**. We can also enable the prompt at launch from this place:

Figure 14.23: Places where we can define the extra variable and launch instance

Once the execution begins, the following window will open. Now, either the job will fail or succeed. In our case, the job was successful. Let us have a look at the same, in the following *Figure 14.24:*

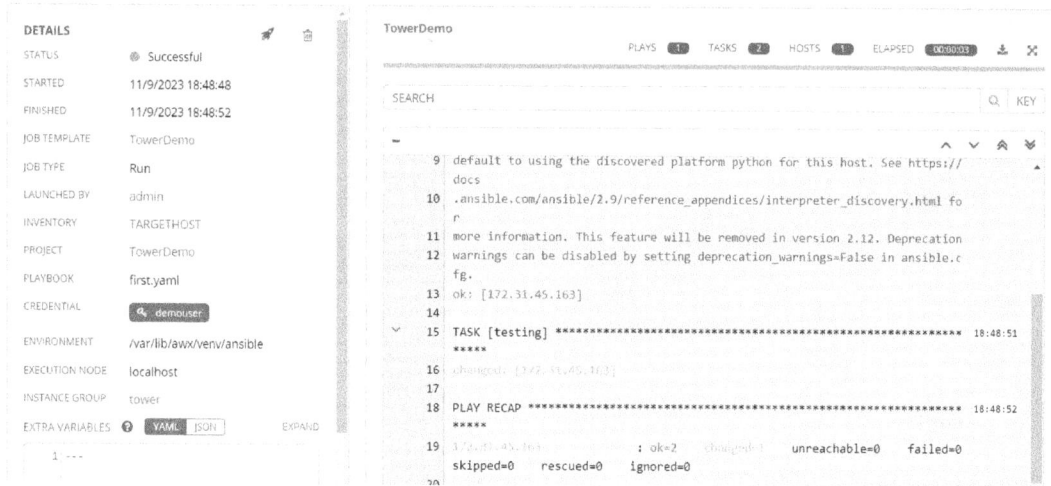

Figure 14.24: *Successful playbook execution from the template*

There is another place where we can see the status of all the jobs we ran which can be found in Jobs, right under the **Dashboard**:

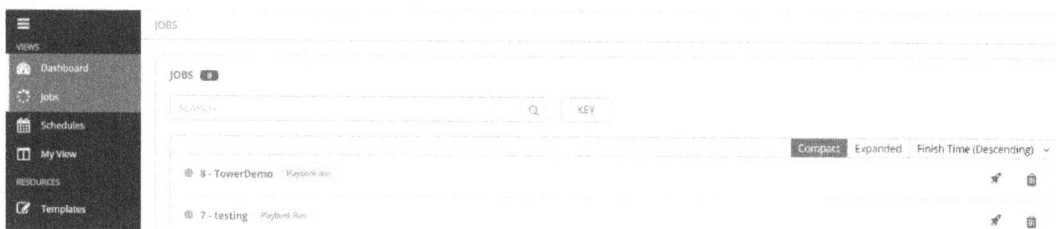

Figure 14.25: *Both jobs looks green after successful execution*

As we can see, the job number 8 was successful. We can click on it and this will open the same window we saw after execution. If we want to re-launch the code, then the rocket symbol is there. We can click on that and re-launch the job.

As promised, we will use both methods in project. The first one was manual where we stored the playbook locally on the Ansible Tower server. In the second method, we will use Git to store our playbook.

Git as the second method

In the second method, we have chosen the option of GitHub. You can also chose GitLab, but if it is GitHub and the repo is private, then you will need the Git credentials. In that case, we will create a GitHub personal access token in credentials.

Let us see how to do it.

Note: In my case, my repo is public, so this will not be required.

However, you should be aware how to do it. Let us have a look at it, as shown in the following figure:

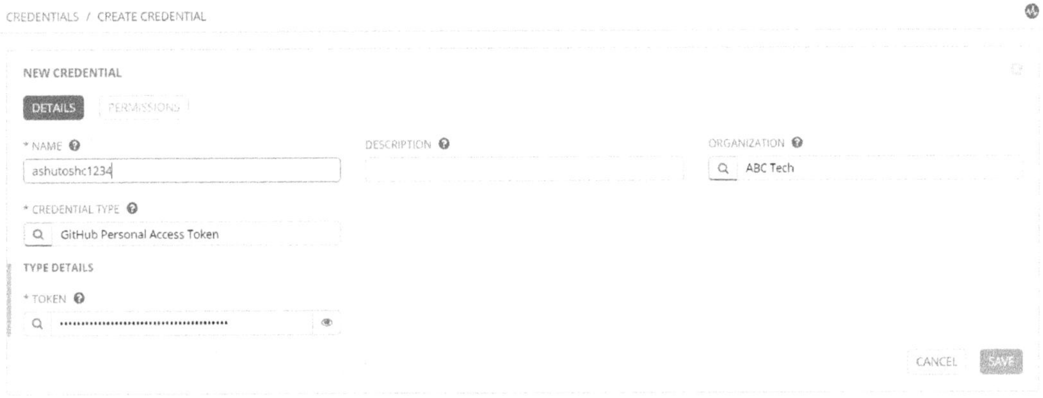

Figure 14.26: Credentials for our Git Repo

As you can see, we have chosen the option GitHub PAT as credential type here. We can save it and proceed further.

The next step is the creation of the project. Let us navigate to the project and have a look on same. We need to enter the required parameters here. Start from the name, which can be anything you like. The organization will be ABC Tech as we want to keep it isolated from XYZ Solution.

Selecting Git as the SCM tool:

- **SCM type**: In this step, we are opting for Git as our SCM system to manage and synchronize our codebase. This choice enables us to store the code on a Git Repo and pull updates directly from it. Upon selecting Git, additional configuration options appear, such as providing the SCM URL—typically a GitHub link in our case. For other platforms like GitLab or Bitbucket, make sure to enter the respective repository URL.

- **SCM branch**: Here, we define the branch as a master/child or anything else.

- **SCM credential**: This is the credentials that we created previously for Git Hub. We can choose that if your repo is private. Since our is public, we will keep it like blank only.

At the end, we have marked the Update revision on launch as we want the revision. Refer to the following figure for the same:

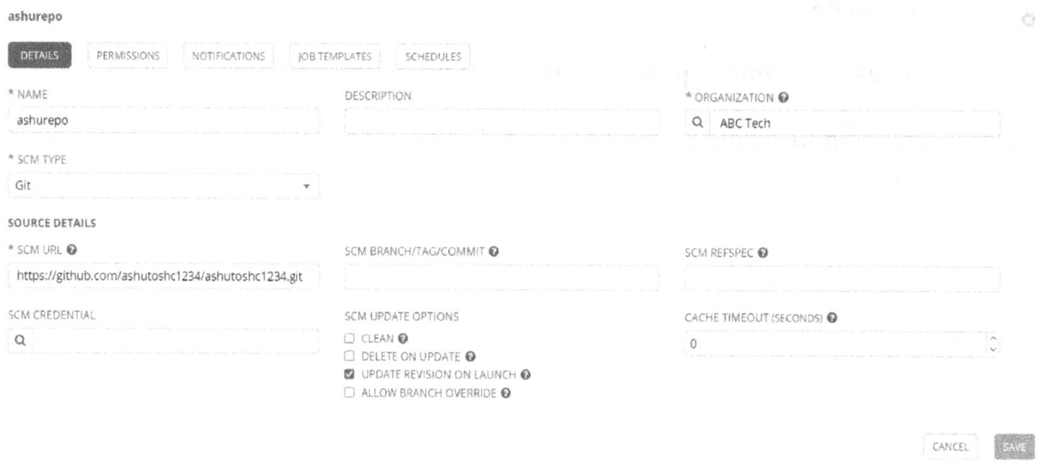

Figure 14.27: Defining all the details in the project

At last, we can click on save. Now, as soon as we save the project one job triggers in the backend.

The job tries to sync the Git Repo to the Ansible Tower. Let us go ahead and have a look on the triggered job. Navigate to the **Jobs** and view it, as shown in the following figure:

Figure 14.28: Successful execution

This job was successful. If your job fails, then you will see the error. The successful execution results in full sync with the branches on the repo.

Let us go ahead and create a template and see if we can see the playbooks of Git Repo on the Ansible Tower. Refer to the following steps:

1. Add a new template and provide it with a name.

2. Use a description if you want.

3. Job type will run like last time.

4. Inventory is also the same.

5. The project will be chosen as ashurepo this time and is synced to the GitHub Repo.

6. Playbook dropdown will give us all playbooks which are available in that Git Repo, as shown in the following figure:

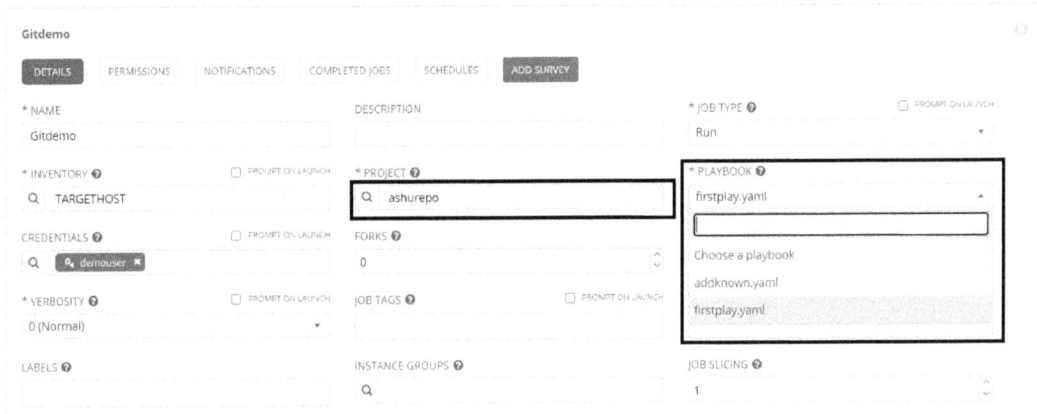

Figure 14.29: Choosing our playbook from the drop down

We can see that **addknown.yaml** and **firstplay.yaml** are the two playbooks available for selection in the **Playbook** tab.

Let us go back to the Git Repo and see if these are the two playbooks available. Refer to the following figure:

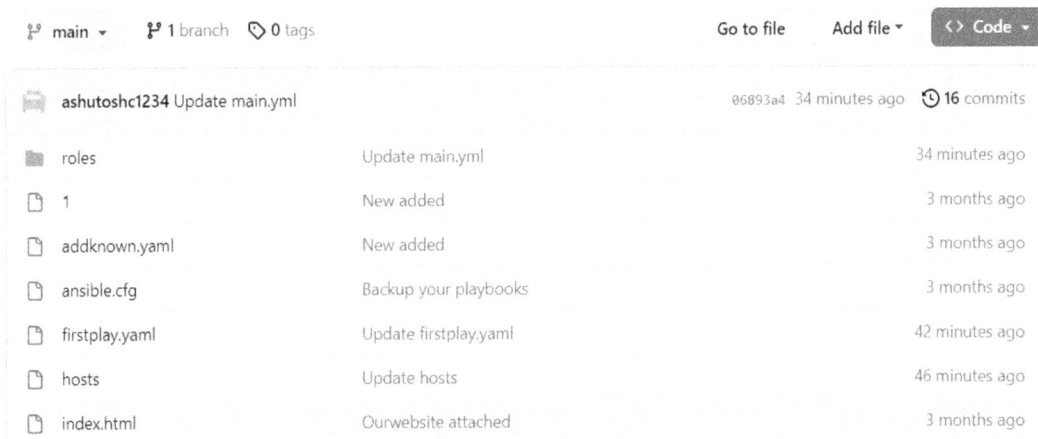

Figure 14.30: List of playbooks from our Git Repo

If we see it properly, we just have two YAML playbooks here and both of them are well visible to us. We can call any of them in our templates, and they should work as expected.

The playbook is shown in the following figure:

ashutoshc1234 / **firstplay.yaml**

ashutoshc1234 Update firstplay.yaml

| Code | Blame | 5 lines (5 loc) · 62 Bytes | Code 55% faster witl |

```
1    ---
2    - name: First playbook
3      hosts: all
4      roles:
5        - whenint
```

Figure 14.31: Content of playbook from Git which will be used in our template

The playbook is calling a role named as **whenint**. We have attached the content of the same as follows:

ashutoshc1234 / roles / whenint / tasks / **main.yml**

ashutoshc1234 Update main.yml

| Code | Blame | 4 lines (3 loc) · 74 Bytes | Code 55% faster with GitHub Copilot |

```
1    ---
2    - name: Gather the information about the target host
3      shell: uptime
```

Figure 14.32: Role used in our playbook

Basically, we are just running uptime command on the target host.

Let us go back to the template that we were creating and save the same.

7. Credentials are the next thing we need to define in our template. We had already created the **demouser** credentials we have called the same here:

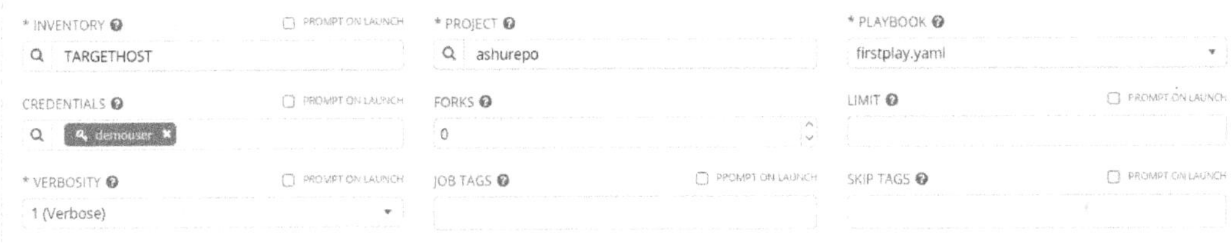

Figure 14.33: Defining the credentials

8. Verbosity is another parameter we have modified this time, as we want to see the uptime in the terminal. Alternatively, we all know the register and debug module of Ansible.

At the last, we can click on save. In the following figure, we can see the launch is graded out. Once we save the template, then only the launch will be visible. Let us save the template and click on the **Launch**, as shown in the following figure:

Figure 14.34: Save and launch once all parameters are set

As we launch the template, we will see that the execution is successful. Since we increased the verbosity of playbook this time, the output contains the uptime information of the target host, as shown in the following figure:

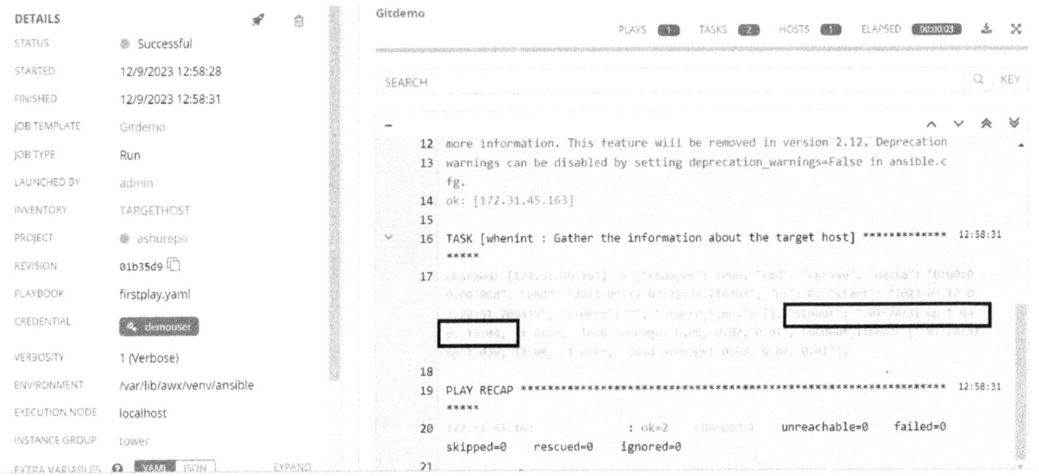

Figure 14.35: Successful execution

We can view all the information used and the execution of template and the parameters defined, like the playbook name, credentials used, and the template names. So, this is how we can perform the configuration changes on the target host using Ansible Tower.

One more thing which we will focus on in this chapter is **schedules**. There is nothing like this in case of Ansible. If we had to schedule some job, like configuration backup, then we had to use the cronjob in Ansible, but in case of Ansible Tower we have very good option. Let us explore it a bit more.

Now, this is not configured directly from the schedule. So, you will not find the add button there, as shown in the following figure:

Figure 14.36: List of scheduled jobs

We can see that there is no new add option in the schedule. We need to go to the template and edit that template. From there, we will create a schedule, as shown in the following figure:

Figure 14.37: Creating a schedule from templates

We have highlighted the schedule in the preceding figure, click on it. Once we click on it, it will open a window where we will see the option to add a new schedule. Click on that, as shown in the following figure:

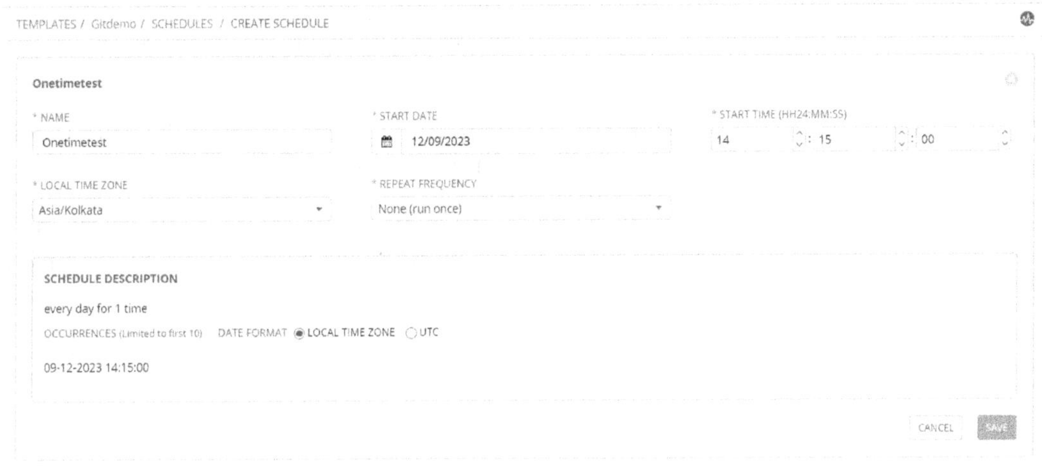

Figure 14.38: Defining the time and saving the schedule

The schedule will look like the preceding figure. We have chosen the one-time execution, but you can do it multiple times based on your use case.

Once saved, the result will be as follows:

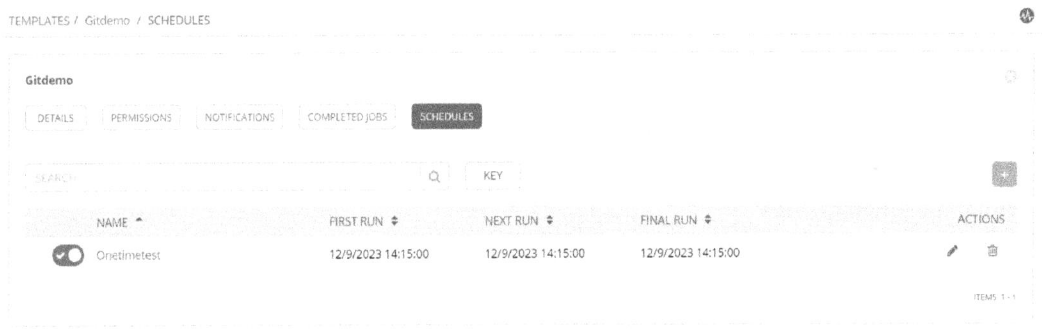

Figure 14.39: List of schedules

We had to wait for a few minutes before the automatic execution started. Let us go back to the jobs and see if the job ran there. Refer to the following figure for the same:

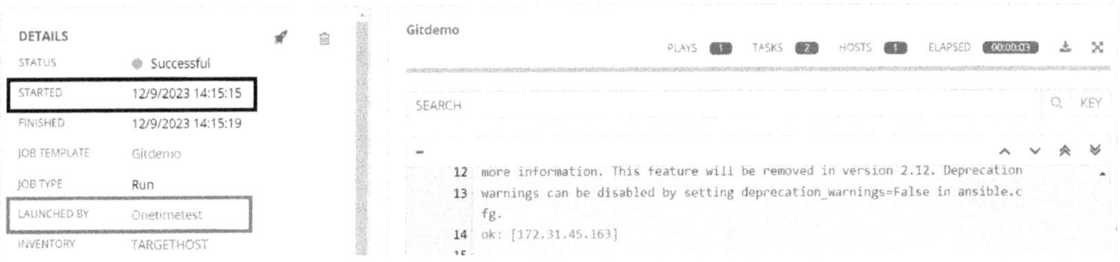

Figure 14.40: Execution triggered at the correct time

The job was finally started at 14:15, now if we want to see how it was started, then focus on launched by. It says the name of our recently created schedule named as **Onetimetest**. This is how we can create the schedules too.

Now, schedules are very important if you want to run the daily configuration backup or database backup. You can easily create the schedule and there no hassle of cronjob.

Now, we need to focus on the practice and create as many labs as possible. Practicing is very important in learning anything, and that is no different with Ansible. Whether it is Ansible or Ansible Tower, the more you explore better you will become.

10 hours spent in the lab environment will save your four hours outage time. So, practice and explore more modules, features and read the latest documents always.

Conclusion

Ansible Tower is a powerful web-based solution for managing Ansible automation at scale. It provides a user-friendly interface, role-based access control, job scheduling, visual workflows, and centralized logging — all of which simplify and secure automation across large environments. We have learned how we can use the Ansible Tower efficiently and perform a few of the tasks using Ansible Tower. In the next chapter, we will understand how to use our knowledge efficiently to get a job in this highly competitive market.

Join our Discord space

Join our Discord workspace for latest updates, offers, tech happenings around the world, new releases, and sessions with the authors:

https://discord.bpbonline.com

CHAPTER 15
Finding and Landing a Job

Introduction

Finally, we are at the stage where we have built a few servers and infrastructure. We also know the concept of Ansible and are now ready to work in the real production environment. Now, our priority should be finding a job and gaining some production exposure. As people say, there is no better instructor than the production environment. Every day, you get a new challenge and a few ways of fixing it. In this chapter, we will learn how we can find a job and start our day one journey.

Structure

The chapter contains the following topics:

- Employment opportunities
- Job search strategies
- Compensation and getting noticed
- Planning for interviews
- Answering questions during the interview
- Salary negotiation

Objectives

In this chapter, we will prepare you for the job search and help you choose your first job if you have multiple offers in hand. We will learn how we can get noticed and shortlisted in the interview.

Employment opportunities

There are a few rumors in the market about recession and layoffs, but one should not be afraid of them. Big organizations are firing old resources, but they are hiring new ones. This helps them streamline the cost. If you are a fresher or have one to three years of experience, then you will be a potential target employee for IT giants. If you are a good engineer, then there are always 5+ jobs for you in your chosen field. If you have read the book and practiced the practical labs enough, then it is not difficult to get a few good jobs in the market.

Yes, recession is there but that will not impact engineers like us. We are getting new job postings every single day, and that is great for us. It simply means the requirement of an engineer is increasing in the market.

Job search strategies

If you are someone who enjoys spending time on *Twitter* or social media, then consider *LinkedIn* as another social media platform. You should start your day by sending connection requests to the concerned people. For those who do not know about LinkedIn, connection requests are just like friend requests on any social media platform. You should connect with hiring managers, hiring consultants, and the senior resources in the field you want to work.

Compensation and getting noticed

The second thing that you should do in a day is create a technical post. For example, an Ansible command line cheat sheet. This will be useful for others, and at the same time, it will increase your visibility on LinkedIn. More people and tech leads will watch your post, which will create a good impression on them.

At last, you should start applying for jobs on job posting websites. Keep in mind to always be available to take calls and reply to emails as soon as possible. A delay in responding to emails might result in rejection, as there are tons of people applying for the same jobs, and you might not get noticed in the flood of job applications. Applying for the job first and responding to emails with priority will help you a lot.

If you are in the initial phase of your career, then it is recommended that you do not focus excessively on the compensation part. You can earn money later in your career if you have good skills. For now, you should focus on the job profile. Once you have 3+ years of experience, you can focus on your salary. In the initial phase, you should try to learn as much as possible.

Planning for interviews

Confidence is the key factor for any interview, which you will gain through knowledge. The best way to get knowledge is by reading a book and practicing in the lab. You can brush up your skills by creating multiple independent projects and revising key concepts before an interview. You should also read about the organization and try to gather as much information about the employer as possible.

It is also recommended that you go through the job description a few times and learn about the expected skills for that job. Once you get their skills requirements, you should focus on and acquire them as soon as possible. You should also practice a small introduction five times before you go for the interview.

Answering questions during the interview

The first thing you should do in an interview is to calm yourself, get comfortable with the interviewer, and ask for a glass of water to distract the interviewer if you need more time.

Asking **how are you sir** is not a bad thing. It might sound like a formality, but you should still do it. It is a good thing to do and might send a positive vibe to your communication.

If you know the answers to the questions, then do not rush to finish the answer. Rather, you should take more time and explain it in depth. This will create a good impression on the interviewer and will reflect how in-depth knowledge you have.

If you find that the information is not enough to answer the question, then do not hesitate to ask the interviewer a follow up question.

Some interviewers will become aggressive in the interview but that is normal. They are just checking your ability to handle the pressure.

For example, an interviewer can ask you the same question five times. You can answer four times, but if you get annoyed on the fifth time, you might get rejected for temperament issues. Behavior analyst generally does this kind of trick to annoy you, but you should always keep calm.

Do not try to bluff the interviewer, as they have been conducting the interview for years and will catch you easily.

Salary negotiation

You should rather focus on the job profile rather than getting a huge salary. It is imperative to get a job in your core field. If you have no further interest in your core field, than it is better to choose another field and prepare for that. Once you have prepared enough, try to get a job in the same field, even if the pay is a little less than the other job profiles. Once you have spent 3+ years in your core field, start focusing on the pay. Always focus on cracking more than a single job interview, and keep attempting more jobs at the same time. This will give you an advantage in salary negotiation. You can show the offer letter from your last employer and get a good hike.

Note: **There were many times in the author's career where he had recevied five offer letters and the hike was more than 100%, so this is a tested way of earning good and negotiating well.**

Conclusion

You should start your preparation with a good CV. Take advice from a professional, if needed. Once you are shortlisted, start focusing on the **job description (JD)**, and start preparing for the job accordingly. Cover all the required skills for the job, and prefer a good job profile over a big cheque. If you stay focused and learn the skills, then finding a new job is not a big challenge.

Join our Discord space

Join our Discord workspace for latest updates, offers, tech happenings around the world, new releases, and sessions with the authors:

https://discord.bpbonline.com

Index